AF559782

METHODS IN FORENSIC SCIENCE

ENCYCLOPAEDIA OF FORENSIC SCIENCE - 2

METHODS IN FORENSIC SCIENCE

By

Ashok Kumar

Dept. of Zoology
Bundelkhand University
Campus Department
Jhansi

D P H

DISCOVERY PUBLISHING HOUSE PVT. LTD.
NEW DELHI-110 002

First Published - 2010

Reprinted - 2015

ISBN: 978-81-8356-422-9 (Set)

ISBN: 978-81-8356-565-3

© Author

Methods in Forensic Science

Published by:

DISCOVERY PUBLISHING HOUSE PVT. LTD.

4383/4B, Ansari Road, Darya Ganj

New Delhi-110 002 (India)

Phone: +91-11-23279245, 43596064-65

Fax: +91-11-23253475

E-mail: discoverypublishinghouse@gmail.com

sales@discoverypublishinggroup.com

web: www.discoverypublishinggroup.com

Printed at:

Infinity Imaging Systems

Delhi

Preface

The present title *"Encyclopaedia of Forensic Science"* has been written for undergraduate, post-graduate students and those engaged in pharmaceutical, pathological, and clinical research. Actually the explosion of new technologies with their vast potential has brought with it the need for forensic scientists to equip themselves and their laboratories with a whole array of new expertise. With the high discriminating power of the DNA systems has come high potential in evidentiary terms, high profile status for many investigations, and not least, a high degree of professional scruting of evidence produced by such technology. The present book provides protocols for the major methods of DNA analysis that have been introduced for identity testing in forensic laboratories. It also deals with the developments intersecting with the neighbouring fields of law inforcement and the justice system. This book will prove a useful guide for public awareness, health authorities, professional and industrial organizations. The aim of writing this book has .been to show how it is possible to enjoy the benefits of technology in detecting the criminals. The language used in it is simple and lucid, and illustrations are clear and labelled.

To make the work more comprehensive and informative, the author has consulted many authoritative books, research journals, abstracts, monographs etc., so there can be no claim to originality except in the .manner of treatment.

The author expresses his thanks to his friends and colleagues whose continue inspirations have initiated him to bring out this book.

The author expresses his gratitude to Mr. Wasan and staff of M/s Discovery Publishing House Pvt. Ltd. for their whole hearted co-operation in the publication of this book.

In the mean time, the author will remain sincerely responsible for any shortcomings of the book and be grateful to the readers for their suggestions and constructive criticism for the continuous betterment of the book. He takes this opportunity to appeal to the readers to send their suggestions straightaway to his Publisher.

Author

CONTENTS

1

INTRODUCTION

Over the last 20 years the development and application of genetics has revolutionized forensic science. In 1984, the analysis of polymorphic regions of DNA produced what was termed 'a *DNA fingerprint*'. The following year, at the request of the United Kingdom Home Office, DNA profiling was successfully applied to a real ease, when it was used to resolve an immigration dispute. Following on from this, in 1986, DNA evidence was used for the first time in a criminal case and identified Colin Pitchfork as the killer of two school girls in Leicestershire, UK. He was convicted in January 1988. The use of genetics was rapidly adopted by the forensic community and plays an important role worldwide in the investigation of crime. Both the scope and scale of DNA analysis in forensic science is set to continue expanding for the foreseeable future.

FORENSIC GENETICS

The work of the forensic geneticist will vary widely depending on the laboratory and country that they work in, and can involve the analysis of material recovered from a scene of crime, paternity testing and the identification of human remains. In some cases, it can even be used for the analysis of DNA from plants, animals and micro-organisms. The focus of this book is the analysis of biological material that is recovered from the scene of crime – this is central to the work of most forensic laboratories.

Forensic laboratories will receive material that has been recovered from scenes of crime, and reference samples from both suspects and victims. The role of forensic genetics within the investigative process is to compare samples recovered from crime scenes with suspects,

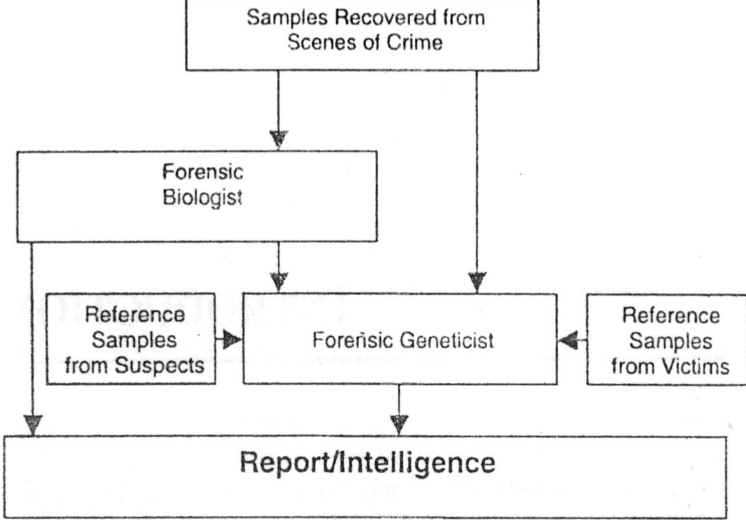

Fig. 1.1. The role of the forensic geneticist is to assess whether samples recovered from a crime scene match to a suspect.

resulting in a report that can be presented in court or intelligence that may inform an enquiry.

In some organizations one person will be responsible for collecting the evidence, the biological and genetic analysis of samples, and ultimately presenting the results to a court of law. However, the trend in many larger organizations is for individuals to be responsible for only a very specific task within the process, such as the extraction of DNA from the evidential material or the analysis and interpretation of DNA profiles that have been generated by other scientists.

Brief History of Forensic Genetics

In 1900 Karl Landsteiner described the ABO blood grouping system and observed that individuals could be placed into different groups based on their blood type. This was the first step in the development of forensic haemogenetics. In 1915 Leone Lattes published a book describing the use of ABO typing to resolve a paternity case and by 1931 the absorption-inhibition ABO typing technique that became standard in forensic laboratories had been developed. Following on from this, numerous blood group markers and soluble blood serum protein markers were characterized and could be analysed in combination to produce highly discriminatory profiles. The serological techniques were a powerful tool but were limited in many forensic

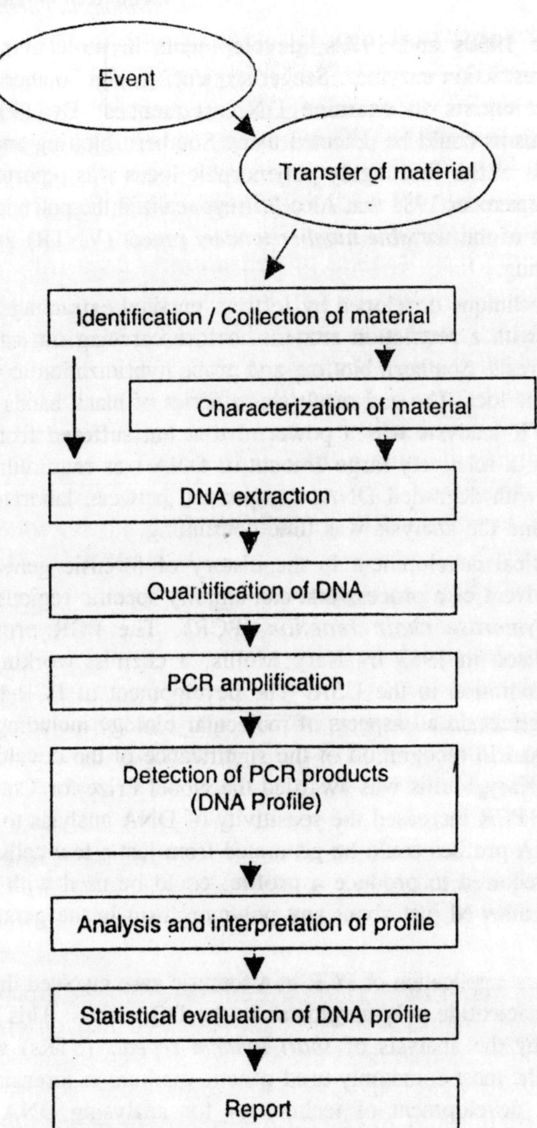

Fig. 1.2. Processes involved in generating a DNA profile following a crime. Some types of material, in particular blood and serum, are often characterized before DNA is extracted.

cases by the amount of biological material that was required to provide highly discriminating results. Proteins are also prone to degradation on exposure to the environment.

In the 1960s and 1970s, developments in molecular biology, including restriction enzymes, Sanger sequencing, and Southern blotting, enabled scientists to examine DNA sequences. By 1978, DNA polymorphisms could be detected using Southern blotting and in 1980 the analysis of the first highly polymorphic locus was reported. It was not until September 1984 that Alec Jeffreys realized the potential forensic application of the *variable number tandem repeat* (VNTR) loci he had been studying.

The technique developed by Jeffreys entailed extracting DNA and cutting it with a restriction enzyme, before carrying out agarose gel electrophoresis, Southern blotting and probe hybridization to detect the polymorphic loci. The end result was a series of black bands on X-ray film. VNTR analysis was a powerful tool but suffered from several limitations: a relatively large amount of DNA was required; it would not work with degraded DNA; comparison between laboratories was difficult; and the analysis was time consuming.

A critical development in the history of forensic genetics came with the advent of a process that can amplify specific regions of DNA – the *polymerase chain reaction* (PCR). The PCR process was conceptualised in 1983 by Kary Mullis, a chemist working for the Cetus Corporation in the USA. The development of PCR has had a profound effect on all aspects of molecular biology including forensic genetics, and in recognition of the significance of the development of the PCR, Kary Mullis was awarded the Nobel Prize for Chemistry in 1993. The PCR increased the sensitivity of DNA analysis to the point where DNA profiles could be generated from just a few cells, reduced the time required to produce a profile, could be used with degraded DNA and allowed just about any polymorphism in the genome to be analysed.

The first application of PCR in a forensic case involved the analysis of single nucleotide polymorphisms in the DQα locus. This was soon followed by the analysis of *short tandem repeats* (STRs) which are currently the most commonly used genetic markers in forensic science. The rapid development of technology for analysing DNA includes advances in DNA extraction and quantification methodology, the development of commercial PCR based typing kits and equipment for detecting DNA polymorphisms.

In addition to technical advances, another important part of the development of DNA profiling that has had an impact on the whole field of forensic science is quality control. The admissibility of DNA evidence was seriously challenged in the USA in 1987 – '*People* v. *Castro*'; this case and subsequent cases have resulted in increased levels of standardization and quality control in forensic genetics and other areas of forensic science. As a result, the accreditation of both laboratories and individuals is an increasingly important issue in forensic science. The combination of technical advances, high levels of standardization and quality control have led to forensic DNA analysis being recognized as a robust and reliable forensic tool worldwide.

2

Tools and Techniques

The purpose of this chapter is to provide a perspective on basic molecular biology techniques that are of special relevance to forensic genetics. Genetic polymorphisms are the most valuable tools for human identification and for determining genetic relationships and have consequently become a mainstay for forensic science. Throughout the history of forensic genetics, genetic polymorphisms have been studied at various levels from the cellular and serological, such as the determination of blood groups and HLA types, gene product analysis, such as the red cell isozyme and serum protein polymorphisms, to the direct examination of nuclear and mitochondrial DNA. The last has afforded a variety of polymorphic systems, notably fragment length polymorphisms, due to *variable number tandem repeats* (VNTRs) and *single nucleotide polymorphisms* (SNPs).

DNA analysis offers exquisite resolution compared with the former cellular and gene product analysis approaches to characterizing genetic variation; for the first time it has enabled a direct view of the entire genome. It is the techniques and procedures for working with and analysing segments of DNA.

Isolation and Separation of Nucleic Acids Isolation of DNA

The use of DNA for forensic analysis or manipulation usually requires that it is isolated and purified to a certain extent. It should be noted that the level of purity of template DNA to be amplified by the polymerase chain reaction is frequently far less critical than the knowledge that the sample to be analysed is uncontaminated and exclusively contains only material from the stated source.

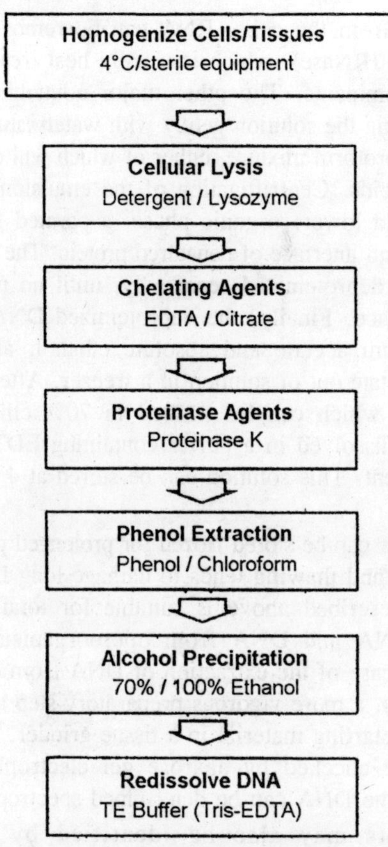

Fig. 2.1. General steps involved in extracting DNA from cells or tissues.

DNA is recovered from cells by the gentlest possible method of cell rupture to prevent the DNA from fragmenting by mechanical shearing. This is usually in the presence of EDTA, which chelates the Mg^{2+} ions needed for enzymes that degrade DNA, termed DNases. Ideally the cell membrane should be solubilized using detergent, and cell walls, if present, should be digested enzymatically (e.g. lysozyme treatment of bacteria). If physical disruption is necessary, it should be kept to a minimum, and should involve cutting or squashing of cells rather than the use of shear forces. Cell disruption should be performed at 4°C, using disposable plastics where possible; all glassware and solutions are autoclaved to destroy DNase activity. Techniques such as laser microdissection are being investigated as exciting new tools for the recovery of genetic material from crime scenes. After release of nucleic acids from the cells, RNA can be removed by treatment with ribonuclease (RNase), which is usually heat treated to inactivate any DNase contaminants. The other major contaminant, protein, is removed by shaking the solution gently with water-saturated phenol, or with a phenol/chloroform mixture, either of which will denature proteins but not nucleic acids. Centrifugation of the emulsion formed by this mixing produces a lower, organic phase, separated from the upper, aqueous phase by an interface of denatured protein. The aqueous solution is recovered and deproteinized repeatedly, until no more material is seen at the interface. Finally, the deproteinized DNA preparation is mixed with sodium acetate and absolute ethanol, and the DNA is allowed to precipitate out of solution in a freezer. After centrifugation, the DNA pellet, which can be washed in 70% ethanol to remove excess salt, is redissolved in a buffer containing EDTA to inactivate any DNases present. This solution can be stored at 4°C for at least a month.

DNA solutions can be stored frozen for prolonged periods, although repeated freezing and thawing tends to damage long DNA molecules. The procedure described above is suitable for total cellular DNA, mitochondrial DNA and DNA from microorganisms and viruses. However, in the case of the extraction of DNA from difficult sources such as hair shafts, a more vigorous preparatory step is required, such as disrupting the starting material in a tissue grinder. The integrity of the DNA can be checked by agarose gel electrophoresis and the concentration of the DNA can be determined spectrophotometrically.

Contaminants may also be identified by scanning UV spectrophotometry from 200 nm to 300 nm. A ratio of 260 : 280 nm of approximately 1.8 indicates that the sample is free of protein contamination, which absorbs strongly at 280 nm.

Automated and Kit-based Extraction of Nucleic Acids

Automation and kit-based manipulations in molecular biology are steadily increasing, and the extraction of nucleic acids by these means for forensic analysis is no exception. There are many commercially available kits for nucleic acid extraction. Although many rely on the methods described here, their advantage lies in the fact that the reagents are standardized and quality-control-tested, providing a high degree of reliability. Essentially the same reagents for nucleic acid extraction may be used in a format that allows reliable and automated extraction. This is of particular use where a large number of DNA extractions are required.

Automated Analysis of Nucleic Acid Fragments

Gel electrophoresis remains the established method for the separation and analysis of nucleic acids. Indeed a number of automated systems using precast gels are available that are gaining popularity. This is especially useful in situations where a large number of samples or high-throughput analysis is required. In addition, new technologies such as Agilents' Lab-on-a-chip have been developed that obviate the need to prepare electrophoretic gels. These systems employ microfluidic circuits where a small cassette unit that contains interconnected micro-reservoirs is used. The sample is applied in one area and driven through microchannels under computer-controlled electrophoresis. The channels lead to reservoirs allowing, for example, incubation with other reagents such as dyes for a specified time. Electrophoretic separation is thus carried out in a micro-scale format. The small sample size minimizes sample and reagent consumption, and as such is useful for DNA and RNA sample analysis. In addition the units, being computer controlled, allow data to be captured within a very short time-scale. Alternative methods of analysis, including denaturing high-performance liquid chromatography-based approaches, have gained in popularity, especially for mutation analysis. Mass spectrometry is also becoming increasingly used for nucleic acid analysis.

Molecular Biology and Bioinformatics

Databases and Basic Bioinformatics

Bioinformatics has become a vital resource for applied forensic molecular biology and is a key component of the routine detection and identification of *short tandem repeat* (STR) profiles in forensic casework. The *National DNA Database* (NDNAD) established in 1995 was the first forensic science database. It contains STR profiles from subjects in the UK. Samples are normally taken from mouth swabs, though less frequently blood samples are taken. The NDNAD also contains information on samples from volunteers and crime scenes. Many countries now maintain their own forensic DNA databases. For example, in the USA the FBI has developed the *Combined DNA Index System* (CODIS).

The emergence of nucleic acid and the accompanying bioinformatics tools has been driven principally by the Human Genome Project with its need to store, analyse and manipulate vast numbers of DNA sequences. There are now a huge number of sequences stored in genetic databases from a variety of other organisms. The largest of the sequence databases include GenBank at the *National Institutes of Health* (NIH) in the USA, EMBL at the *European Bioinformatics Institute* (EBI) at Cambridge, UK and the DNA database of Japan (DDBJ) at Mishima in Japan. All the genome databases are accessible to the public via the Internet.

Polymerase Chain Reaction (PCR)

Basic Concept of the PCR

The polymerase chain reaction or PCR is currently the mainstay of forensic molecular biology. One of the reasons for the wide adoption of the PCR globally is the elegant simplicity of the reaction and relative ease of the practical manipulation steps. Indeed, combined with the relevant bioinformatics resources for its design and for determination of the required experimental conditions, it provides a rapid means for DNA identification and analysis. It has opened up the investigation of cellular and molecular processes to those outside the field of molecular biology.

The PCR is used to amplify a precise fragment of DNA from a complex mixture of starting material, usually termed the template DNA, and in many cases requires little DNA purification. It does require the knowledge of some DNA sequence information, which flanks the fragment of DNA to be amplified (target DNA). From this information two oligonucleotide primers may be chemically synthesized, each complementary to a stretch of DNA to the 3' side of the target DNA, one oligonucleotide for each of the two DNA strands. It may be thought of as a technique analogous to the DNA replication process that takes place in cells since the outcome is the same: the generation of new complementary DNA stretches based upon the existing ones. It is also a technique that has replaced, in many cases, the traditional DNA cloning methods since it fulfils the same function - the production of large amounts of DNA from limited starting material - however this is achieved in a fraction of the time needed to clone a DNA fragment. Although not without its drawbacks, the PCR is a remarkable development that is changing the approach of many scientists to the analysis of nucleic acids and continues to have a profound impact on core biosciences and biotechnology.

Stages in the PCR

The PCR consists of three defined sets of times and temperatures, termed steps: (i) denaturation, (ii) annealing and (iii) extension. Each of these steps is repeated 30–40 times, termed cycles. In the first

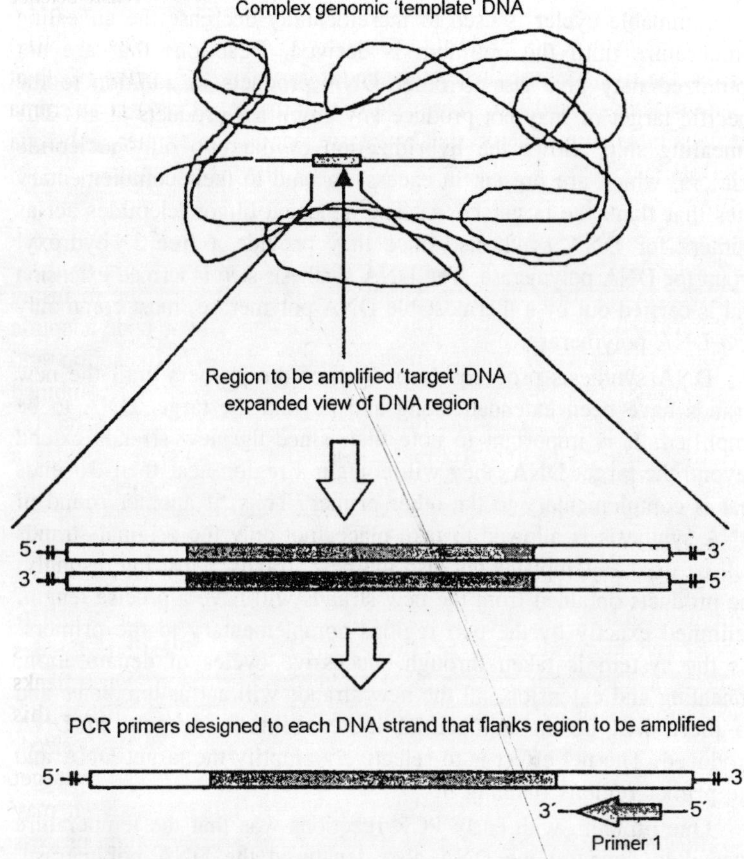

Fig. 2.2. The location of PCR primer.

cycle the double-stranded template DNA is (i) denatured by heating the reaction to above 90°C. Within the complex DNA the region to be specifically amplified (target) is made accessible. The temperature is then cooled to between 40 and 60°C. The precise temperature is critical and each PCR system has to be defined and optimized. One useful technique for optimization is Touchdown PCR where a programmable cycler is used to incrementally decrease the annealing temperature until the optimum is derived. Reactions that are not optimized may give rise to other DNA products in addition to the specific target or may not produce any amplified products at all. The annealing step allows the hybridization of the two oligonucleotide primers, which are present in excess, to bind to their complementary sites that flank the target DNA. The annealed oligonucleotides act as primers for DNA synthesis, since they provide a free 3' hydroxyl group for DNA polymerase. The DNA synthesis step is termed extension and is carried out by a thermostable DNA polymerase, most commonly *Taq* DNA polymerase.

DNA synthesis proceeds from both of the primers until the new strands have been extended along and beyond the target DNA to be amplified. It is important to note that, since the new strands extend beyond the target DNA, they will contain a region near their 3' ends that is complementary to the other primer. Thus, if another round of DNA synthesis is allowed to take place, not only the original strands will be used as templates but also the new strands. Most interestingly, the products obtained from the new strands will have a precise length, delimited exactly by the two regions complementary to the primers. As the system is taken through successive cycles of denaturation, annealing and extension, all the new strands will act as templates and so there will be an exponential increase in the amount of DNA produced. The net effect is to selectively amplify the target DNA and the primer regions flanking it.

One problem with early PCR reactions was that the temperature needed to denature the DNA also denatured the DNA polymerase. However, the availability of a thermostable DNA polymerase enzyme isolated from the thermophilic bacterium *Thermus aquaticus* found in hot springs provided the means to automate the reaction. *Taq* DNA polymerase has a temperature optimum of 72°C and survives prolonged exposure to temperatures as high as 96°C, so it is still active after each of the denaturation steps. The widespread utility of the technique is also due to the ability to automate the reaction and, as such, many thermal cyclers have been produced in which it is possible to program in the temperatures and times for a particular PCR reaction.

Polymerase Chain Reaction Primer Design and Bioinformatics

The specificity of the PCR lies in the design of the two oligonucleotide primers. These have to be complementary to sequences flanking the target DNA but must not be self-complementary or bind each other to form dimers since both prevent DNA amplification. They also have to be matched in their GC content and have similar annealing temperatures. The increasing use of bioinformatics resources such as Oligo, Generunner and Primer Design Assistant in the design of primers makes the design and selection of reaction conditions much more straightforward. These resources allow the sequences to be amplified, the primer length, product size, GC content, etc. to be input and, following analysis, provide a choice of matched primer sequences. Indeed the initial selection and design of primers without the aid of bioinformatics would now be unnecessarily time-consuming.

Polymerase Chain Reaction Amplification Templates

DNA from a variety of sources may be used as the initial source of amplification templates. It is also a highly sensitive technique and requires only one or two molecules for successful amplification, thus enabling the genetic material of a single cell to be analysed. This property of the PCR has been exploited by forensic scientists through the use of *low copy number* (LCN) DNA profiling. The sensitivity of the LCN profiling process depends on an increased number of PCR cycles, typically 34. Unlike many manipulation methods used in current molecular biology, the PCR technique is sensitive enough to require very little template preparation. The PCR may also be used to amplify RNA, a process termed *reverse transcriptase PCR* (RT-PCR).

Sensitivity of the PCR

The enormous sensitivity of the PCR system is also one of its main drawbacks since the very large degree of amplification makes the system vulnerable to contamination. Even a trace of contaminating DNA, such as that contained in dust particles, may be amplified to significant levels and may give misleading results. Hence a rigorous sample-handling protocol is essential for casework when carrying out the PCR and dedicated equipment and even laboratories are preferable. All precautions must be taken to prevent previously amplified products (*amplicons*) from contaminating the PCR.

Applications of the PCR

Many traditional methods in molecular biology have now been superseded by the PCR and the applications for the technique appear to be unlimited. The success of the PCR process has given impetus to the development of other amplification techniques, which are based on either thermal cycling or non-thermal cycling (*isothermal*) methods. The most popular alternative to the PCR is termed the *ligase chain reaction* (LCR). This operates in a similar fashion to the PCR but a thermostable DNA ligase joins sets of primers together that are complementary to the target DNA. Following this a similar exponential amplification reaction takes place, producing amounts of DNA that are similar to the PCR.

Quantitative and Real-time PCR

One of the most useful PCR applications is *quantitative PCR* (Q-PCR). Quantitative PCR is gaining popularity in forensic science mainly because of the rapidity of the method compared to conventional PCR amplification whilst simultaneously providing a lower limit of detection and greater dynamic range. Another advantage is that Q-PCR enables a rigorous analysis of PCR problems as they arise. Early quantitative PCR methods involved the comparison of a standard or control DNA template amplified with separate primers at the same time as the specific target DNA. These types of quantitation rely on the reaction being exponential and so any factors affecting this may also affect the result. Other methods involve the incorporation of a radiolabel through the primers or nucleotides and their subsequent detection following purification of the amplicon.

An alternative automated real-time PCR method is the 5' fluorogenic exonuclease detection system or TaqMan assay. In its simplest form a DNA binding dye such as SYBR Green is included in the reaction. As amplicons accumulate, SYBR Green binds the double-stranded DNA proportionally. Fluorescence emission of the dye is detected following excitation. The binding of SYBR Green is non-specific, therefore in order to detect specific amplicons an oligo-nucleotide probe labelled with a fluorescent reporter and quencher molecule at either end is included in the reaction in the place of SYBR Green. When the oligonucleotide probe binds to the target sequence the 5' exonuclease activity of *Taq* polymerase degrades and releases the reporter from the quencher. A signal is thus generated that increases in direct proportion to the number of starting molecules. Thus a detection system is able to induce and detect fluorescence in real-time as the PCR proceeds. In addition to quantitation, real-time PCR systems may also be used for genotyping and for accurate determination of amplicon melting temperature using curve analysis. This allows accurate amplicon identification and also offers the potential to detect mutations and SNPs. Further developments in probe-based PCR systems have also been used and include scorpion probe systems, amplifluor and real-time LUX probes.

Nucleotide Sequencing of DNA

Concepts of Nucleic Acid Sequencing

The determination of the order or sequence of bases along a length of DNA is one of the central techniques in molecular biology and has a key role to play in the development of polymorphic systems and analysis of the mitochondrial genome in forensic science. The precise usage of codons, information regarding mutations and polymorphisms and the identification of gene regulatory control sequences are also only possible by analysing DNA sequences.

Two techniques have been developed for this, one based on an enzymatic method, frequently termed *Sanger sequencing* after its developer, and a chemical method called Maxam and Gilbert, named for the same reason. At present Sanger sequencing is by far the most popular method and many commercial kits are available for its use. However, there are certain occasions, such as the sequencing of short oligonucleotides, where the Maxam and Gilbert method is more appropriate.

One absolute requirement for Sanger sequencing is that the DNA to be sequenced is in a single-stranded form. Traditionally this demanded that the DNA fragment of interest be inserted and cloned into a specialized bacteriophage vector termed M13, which is naturally single-stranded. Although M13 is still universally used the advent of the PCR has provided the means to not only amplify a region of any genome or complementary DNA but also very quickly to generate the corresponding nucleotide sequence. This has led to an explosion in the accumulation of DNA sequence information and has provided much impetus for gene discovery and genome mapping.

The Sanger method is simple and elegant and mimics in many ways the natural ability of DNA polymerase to extend a growing nucleotide chain based on an existing template. Initially the DNA to be sequenced is allowed to hybridize with an oligonucleotide primer, which is complementary to a sequence adjacent to the 3' side of DNA within a vector such as M13 or in an amplicon. The oligonucleotide will then act as a primer for the synthesis of a second strand of DNA, catalysed by DNA polymerase. Since the new strand is synthesized from its 5' end, virtually the first DNA to be made will be complementary to the DNA to be sequenced. One of the deoxyribonucleoside triphosphates (dNTPs) that must be provided for DNA synthesis is radioactively labelled with ^{32}P or ^{35}S, and so the newly synthesized strand will be labelled.

Dideoxynucleotide Chain Terminators

The reaction mixture is then divided into four aliquots, representing the four dNTPs A, C, G and T. In addition to all of the dNTPs being present in the A tube, an analogue of dATP is added (2',3'-dideoxyadenosine triphosphate, ddATP) that is similar to A but has no 3' hydroxyl group and so will terminate the growing chain because a 5' to 3' phosphodiester linkage cannot be formed without a 3'- hydroxyl group. The situation for tube C is identical except that ddCTP is added; similarly the G and T tubes contain ddGTP and ddTTP, respectively.

Since the incorporation of ddNTP rather than dNTP is a random event, the reaction will produce new molecules varying widely in length, but all terminating at the same type of base. Thus four sets of DNA sequence are generated, each terminating at a different type of base, but all having a common 5' end (the primer). The four labelled and chain-terminated samples are then denatured by heating and loaded next to each other on a polyacrylamide gel for electrophoresis. Electrophoresis is performed at approximately 70°C in the presence of urea, to prevent renaturation of the DNA, since even partial renaturation alters the rates of migration of DNA fragments. Very thin, long gels are used for maximum resolution over a wide range of fragment lengths. After electrophoresis, the positions of radioactive DNA bands on the gel are determined by autoradiography. Since every band in the track from the ddATP sample must contain molecules that terminate at adenine, and those in the ddCTP that terminate at cytosine, etc., it is possible to read the sequence of the newly synthesized strand from the autoradiogram, provided that the gel can resolve differences in length equal to a single nucleotide, hence the ability to detect and characterize point mutations. Under ideal conditions, sequences up to about 300 bases in length can be read from one gel.

Direct PCR Pyrosequencing

Rapid PCR sequencing has also been made possible by the use of pyrosequencing. This is a sequencing by synthesis whereby a PCR template is hybridized to an oligonucleotide and incubated with DNA polymerase, ATP sulphurylase, luciferase and apyrase. During the reaction the first of the four dNTPs is added and, if incorporated, it releases pyrophosphate (PPi). The ATP sulphurylase converts the PPi to ATP, which drives the luciferase-mediated conversion of luciferin to oxyluciferin in order to generate light. Apyrase degrades the resulting component dNTPs and ATP. This is followed by another round of dNTP addition. A resulting pyrogram provides an output of the sequence. The method provides short reads very quickly and is especially useful for the determination of mutations or SNPs.

It is also possible to undertake nucleotide sequencing from double-stranded molecules such as plasmid cloning vectors and PCR amplicons directly. The double-stranded DNA must be denatured prior to annealing with primer. In the case of plasmid an alkaline denaturation step is sufficient, however for amplicons this is more problematic and a focus of much research. Unlike plasmids, amplicons are short and re-anneal rapidly, thereby preventing the reannealing process or biasing the amplification towards one strand by using a primer ratio of 100 : 1 to overcome this problem to a certain extent. Denaturants such as formamide or dimethylsulphoxide (DMSO) have also been used with some success in preventing the re-annealing of PCR strands following their separation.

It is possible to physically separate and retain one PCR strand by incorporating a molecule such as biotin into one of the primers. Following PCR one strand with an affinity molecule may be removed by affinity chromatography with strepavidin, leaving the complementary PCR strand. This affinity purification provides single-stranded DNA derived from the PCR amplicon and although it is somewhat time-consuming it does provide high-quality single-stranded DNA for sequencing.

Polymerase Chain Reaction Cycle Sequencing

One of the most useful methods of sequencing PCR amplicons is termed PCR cycle sequencing. This is not strictly a PCR since it involves linear amplification with a single primer. Approximately 20 cycles of denaturation, annealing and extension take place. Radiolabelled or fluorescent-labelled dideoxynucleotides are then introduced in the final stages of the reaction to generate the chain- terminated extension products. Automated direct PCR sequencing is increasingly being refined, allowing greater lengths of DNA to be analysed in one sequencing run, and provides a very rapid means of analysing DNA sequences.

Automated DNA Sequencing

Advances in fluorescent dye terminator and labelling chemistry have led to the development of high-throughput automated sequencing techniques. Essentially most systems involve the use of dideoxynucleotides labelled with different fluorochromes. The advantage of this modification is that since a different label is incorporated with each ddNTP it is unnecessary to perform four separate reactions. Therefore the four chain-terminated products are run on the same track of a denaturing electrophoresis gel. Each product with their base-specific dye is excited by a laser and the dye then emits light at its characteristic wavelength. A diffraction grating separates the emissions, which are detected by a *charge-coupled device* (CCD), and the sequence is interpreted by a computer. The advantages of these techniques include real-time detection of the sequence. In addition, the lengths of sequence that may be analysed are in excess of 500 bp. Capillary electrophoresis is increasingly being used for the detection of sequencing products. This is where liquid polymers in thin capillary tubes are used, obviating the need to pour sequencing gels and requiring little manual operation. This substantially reduces the electrophoresis run times and allows high throughput to be achieved. A number of large-scale sequence facilities are now fully automated using 96-well microtitre-based formats. The derived sequences can be downloaded automatically to databases and manipulated using a variety of bioinformatics resources. Developments in the technology of DNA sequencing have made whole genome sequencing projects a realistic proposition within achievable time-scales, and a number of these have been or are nearing completion.

Maxam and Gilbert Sequencing

Sanger sequencing is by far the most popular technique for DNA sequencing, however an alternative technique developed at the same time may also be used. The chemical cleavage method of DNA sequencing developed by Maxam and Gilbert is often used for sequencing small fragments of DNA such as oligonucleotides, where Sanger sequencing is problematic. A radioactive label is added to either the 3' or the 5' ends of a double-stranded DNA. The strands are then separated by electrophoresis under denaturing conditions, and analysed separately. DNA labelled at one end is divided into four aliquots and each is treated with chemicals that act on specific bases by methylation or removal of the base. Conditions are chosen so that, on average, each molecule is modified at only one position along its length; every base in the DNA strand has an equal chance of being modified. Following the modification reactions, the separate samples are cleaved by piperidine, which breaks phosphodiester bonds exclusively at the 5' side of nucleotides whose base has been modified. The result is similar to that produced by the Sanger method, since each sample now contains radioactively labelled molecules of various lengths, all with one end in common (the labelled end) and with the other end cut at the same type of base. Analysis of the reaction products by electrophoresis is as described for the Sanger method.

The impact of molecular biology on forensic science has been massive and far-reaching. The combined information content of molecular polymorphisms has literally revolutionized the aim of the scientists to the extent that exclusion probabilities have given way to positive identification of individuals matched with evidential material. Bioinformatics and greater emphasis on mapping complex trait genes could lead to the identification of DNA markers for many common characteristics, enabling crime detection at the levels of the genotype and phenotype simultaneously. The future is also likely to witness the widespread introduction of genotyping microchips for both nucleic acids and proteins. Proteomics offers the significant potential of utilizing gene products for the advancement of forensic analysis.

3

Biometric Applications

This chapter evaluates the usability of known protein markers for quantitative protein profiling assays applicable to forensic and biometric applications. We will discuss the use of competitive displacement assays and peptidomics technology in the design of multiplex protein assays for laboratory-based and potentially *scene-of-crime* applications. Competitive displacement assays embody the most accurate multiplex protein affinity assay system to date, applicable to a wide range of protein profiling applications. The peptidomics technology is the most generic and multiplatform-compatible affinity assay system to date, applicable for protein identification, quantification and expression profiling. It relies on proteolytic protein digestion, requires only the availability of small peptide fragment(s) and is therefore capable of a reliable analysis of denatured, partially degraded proteins and protein fragments. Protein microarrays and peptidomics are combined in a single system capable of simple yet quantitative protein analysis from real samples (i.e. imperfectly stored, partially degraded samples, *scene-of-crime* applications, etc.).

Protein Assays in Molecular Forensics

Biometric technologies aim to identify individuals using biological traits, the major one being based on fingerprint recognition (~50% of current biometrics market share), followed by face, hand and iris recognition (12%, 11% and 9%, respectively), and voice and signature recognition (6% and 2%, respectively). Biologically-based technologies in forensic sciences are mostly limited to *polymerase chain reaction* (PCR)-based DNA '*fingerprinting*'. Whilst DNA can be matched against databases relatively easily, in the absence of a match, tissue samples, body fluids or stains may still reveal vital intelligence information useful for fitting the person's biometric or behavioural profiles or for gathering additional forensic information. DNA assays are most suitable for matching and identification of individuals, whilst protein and metabolite profiles are more representative of the state of health, lifestyle,. behavioural patterns, sample origin (tissue/organ/time), the severity and type of trauma or the cause of death. DNA profiling is incapable of monitoring these. mRNA profiling may be, but mRNAs are restricted to their respective tissues and cells (and are very unstable molecules), whilst proteins and metabolites are often secreted and can be detected/measured in body fluids, e.g. blood/serum/urine/saliva. Single protein assays have been proposed for forensic analysis before, but so far the research has been fragmented and until very recently no technical capabilities existed for highly parallel and quantitative analysis of proteins and scene-of-crime assays.

Affinity immunoassays have been widely used for achieving specific and sensitive detection of analytes of interest. A wide range of existing assay types includes colorimetric, radiometric, fluorescence and chemiluminescence detection methods, each incorporating their own form of labels, such as radioisotopes for radiometric tests or organic dyes for fluorescence-based assays. The performance of these tests is usually restricted to central laboratories because of the need for long assay times, complex and expensive equipment and highly trained individuals, but there is an ever-increasing market for new, faster, more accurate and cost-effective diagnostics that can be supplied in kit format for use in the field. The ability to multiplex such assays is also highly desirable, allowing for the simultaneous detection of more than one analyte in a given assay.

Liquid Chromatography Assays

Size exclusion chromatography permits the separation of molecules by physical size and thus can be harnessed for use in a potentially very attractive immunoassay format. The assay can be in the form of a large-scale gel filtration set-up utilizing a column packed with gel media of chosen fractionation range, or a small – scale set-up by way of MicroSpin columns. Gel filtration media separate molecules according to size, with larger molecules being eluted first, followed by smaller molecules in order of their size. This can be harnessed in an immunoassay format by exploiting the size differences between antigen–antibody complexes and unbound antibody and antigen. Antibody molecules are ~150 kDa; other proteins are of variable size but far larger than peptides, which are ~ 1–3 kDa, and small-molecule drugs (< 1 kDa). Therefore a column containing gel with a fractionation range capable of resolving molecules of ~ 150 kDa (antibody) from molecules of larger size (antigen–antibody complexes) would be suitable for use in such an assay format. The assay is compatible with both competitive and non-competitive formats, both of which can be designed a number of different ways:

Competitive

(a) Fluorescently labelled reference competes for antibodies with sample antigen. Fluorescence intensity is inversely proportional to sample antigen concentration.

(b) Fluorescently labelled sample competes for antibodies with unlabelled reference. Fluorescence intensity is proportional to sample antigen concentration.

Non-competitive

(a) Fluorescently labelled antibodies are mixed with sample to form labelled antibody–antigen complexes. Fluorescence intensity is proportional to sample antigen concentration.

(b) Fluorescently labelled sample is mixed with antibodies to form labelled antibody–antigen complexes. Fluorescence intensity is proportional to sample antigen concentration.

Given the small size of peptides and small drug molecules, labelling antibodies may pose problems in that the column may not be capable of resolving the relatively small differences in size between unbound antibody and antibody–antigen complexes. In this instance labelled antibody would provide a potentially misleading result as to the amount of sample antigen concentration and an overall low level of detection. A better choice would be to label antigen, which will be dramatically different in size to antibody within the system, and thus if the column was to elute some free antibody with antibody–antigen complexes then this would not provide such a misleading result.

Eluted buffer should be collected from the column up until the point where only antibody–antigen complexes have had a chance to elute. This collection can then be scanned with a spectrofluorimeter. Standard curves should be made for a range of known sample antigen concentrations by using single antigen–antibody pairs. Following successful completion of this, a multiplex assay may be attempted, which can be achieved though using a range of fluorescent tags for different analytes. For multiplexing, competitive assays with fluorescently labelled reference are the only suitable option because they provide the simplest way to assign different fluorescent tags to specific analytes. Miniaturizing the assay results in a format more applicable to the field-based studies. A microspin format or small cartridge-like gravity-flow format with columns containing the same gel capable of quantitative separation of antigen–antibody complexes from unbound antibody presents such a solution. A portable spectrofluorimeter could then be used to check for fluorescence intensity as described above, making the format applicable for *scene-of-crime* applications.

Immunochromatography Assay Format

Otherwise known as lateral flow or strip tests, immunochromatographic assays exhibit a number of highly desirable benefits, including a user-friendly format, rapid sample turnaround, as well as being relatively inexpensive to produce. Such features make them ideal for affordable field-based or point-of-care testing. Pregnancy tests are an example of an immunochromatographic assay designed for qualitative determination of *human chorionic gonadotrophin* (hCG) in urine for early detection of pregnancy. Lateral flow devices have been applied successfully to a wide range of detection applications, including aflatoxin B_1 in pig feed, botulism neurotoxins in foods and drugs of abuse. In their simplest form, lateral flow tests consist of a porous membrane strip such as nitrocellulose that has a band of capture antibodies immobilized at a discrete point across its width. This mixture diffuses through the membrane towards the capture line where hybridization occurs, detectable by standard fluorescence detection methods. A control line is added to the membrane after the capture line, consisting of immobilized antibodies that bind to the reporter but not to the analyte of interest. Lateral flow assays are compatible with competitive and non-competitive immunoassay formats, outlined below:

Competitive

(a) Fluorescently labelled reference competes with sample antigen for antibodies discretely spotted on a membrane strip. Fluorescence intensity is inversely proportional to sample antigen concentration.

(b) Fluorescently labelled sample competes with unlabelled reference for antibodies discretely spotted on a membrane strip. Fluorescence intensity is directly proportional to sample antigen concentration.

(c) Fluorescently labelled antibody is added to sample and then run on membrane strip with reference antigen discretely spotted at a certain point. Fluorescence intensity is directly proportional to sample antigen concentration.

Non-competitive

(a) Fluorescently labelled sample antigen binds to antibodies at a discrete capture line on membrane strip. Fluorescence intensity is directly proportional to sample antigen concentration.

(b) Fluorescently labelled antibody binds to sample antigen spotted at a discrete capture line on a membrane strip. Fluorescence intensity is proportional to sample antigen concentration.

In practice neither of the non-competitive forms of the assay are ideal because they require the sample to be either fluorescently labelled or spotted onto the membrane strip prior to testing. Minimum sample preparation should be the focus and for this reason the first and third competitive formats are the most appealing. Competitive forms of lateral flow tests can also be used for small-molecule analytes with single antigenic determinants that are incompatible with sandwich forms of the assay. Predictive tools have been developed by computer modelling, allowing simulation and optimization of a device and reducing the number of laboratory experiments needed in the development of lateral flow devices.

The membrane strip can be scanned, with intensity of fluorescence at the capture line quantitatively indicating the presence or absence of sample antigen. The assay may first be assessed using single antigen–antibody pairs for which standard curves can be plotted for a range of known sample concentrations, followed by a multiplexed approach once conditions for each analyte have been optimized. Multiplexing may be achieved by spatially separating the capture lines for each analyte or by using a single capture line and assigning a fluorescent tag of different colour to each analyte of interest.

Immunochromatographic assays are highly suited to incorporation into kit format that would usually consist of a mould essentially enabling the user to plug-and-play by simply adding a sample to a defined region of the membrane. Such kits offer standardization of use each time for position/sample application/detection, and can be achieved with minimal effort.

Other Formats

Quartz crystal microbalance

The *quartz crystal microbalance* (QCM) is a simple and convenient method of quantitatively measuring very small masses in real time. It is a form of acoustic wave technology, so called because an *acoustic* wave is the mechanism of detection. The velocity or amplitude of the wave can be changed as it passes through the surface of the material, and such changes can be detected by measuring the frequency or phase characteristics of the sensor. Any changes can be correlated to physical interactions occurring on the surface of the sensor, such as binding of sample analyte to surface-immobilized antibody, which would result in a frequency decrease due to a mass increase from the biological interactions. Such devices are classified by the mode of wave that propagates through or on the substrate, and, of the many wave modes available, *shear-horizontal surface acoustic wave* (SH-SAW) sensors are best as biosensors due to their superior ability to operate with liquids. A special class of these is the Love wave sensor, which consists of a series of coatings on the surface of the device, including a final coating with biorecognition capability. The Love wave sensor has demonstrated excellent sensitivity and the ability to detect anti-goat IgG in solution in the concentration range of $3 \times 10^{-8} - 10^{-6}$ m. The QCM technology has been applied to a number of other fields, such as detection of a class A drug and mutations in DNA, and is commercially available from a number of providers, e.g. Attana Sensor Technologies Ltd or Akubio Ltd.

Rupture event scanning

The QCM technology is used in another form of biosensor known as *rupture event scanning* (REVS). However, rather than being used to measure mass increase, as is the case with other QCM-based detection systems such as the Love wave sensor, a piezoelectric substrate is used to detect the binding and estimate the affinity of analyte binding to antibodies covalently attached to the surface by detecting *acoustic* noise produced from the rupturing of bonds between antigens and antibodies. By applying an alternating voltage to gold electrodes on the upper and lower surfaces of a disc of crystalline quartz, and monotonously increasing the voltage and thus the amplitude of the transverse oscillation of the QCM, Cooper et al. (2001) demonstrated a novel way of directly, sensitively and quantitatively detecting virus particles bound to specific antibodies immobilized on the QCM surface. Both the Love wave sensor and REVS are suitable for forensic applications and have the additional advantage of providing label-free detection of molecules, allowing interactions to be monitored between unmodified reactants.

Surface plasmon resonance and BIAcore

Another label-free approach to assaying an analyte of interest in a sample is by way of the BIAcore system. The BIAcore system is based on *surface plasmon resonance* (SPR), an optical phenomenon occurring when polarized light is reflected off a thin metal film under conditions of total internal reflection. In the BIAcore system, this thin metal film composed of gold forms the floor of a small flow cell, and can be modified so that antibodies are immobilized on its surface. Running buffer is passed continuously through the flow cell and a sample containing the analyte of interest can be injected into this mobile phase. Any interactions that occur between sample antigen and immobilized antibody results in a change in the local refractive index that subsequently changes the SPR angle. The change in intensity of reflected light is plotted against time, producing a sensorgram. BIAcore systems have been used for a range of detection applications, including detection of cancer biomarkers in human saliva.

Amperometric, potentiometric, capacitance and ion-selective field-effect transistor-based sensors

Electrochemical sensors are capable of detecting changes in a solution's electrochemical properties that result from binding or biocatalytical events. Electrochemical biosensors are the most common form used for clinical analysis and amperometry is the technique usually applied. *Amperometric* devices exploit electroreactive substances and were demonstrated first in 1962 for the detection of glucose in blood, which spawned continual progression in their application to this field. *Potentiometric* sensors monitor the electrical potential difference between a reference electrode and an indicator electrode that is placed in the sample solution. The potential difference is related to the concentration of analyte in solution in a logarithmic manner. The indicator electrode, although immersed in the sample solution, is surrounded by a semi-permeable membrane coated with an entrapped biocatalyst. Changes in capacitance were used in the recent development of a novel formaldehyde-sensitive biosensor, further expanding the range of electrochemical-based detection techniques. Finally, *ion-selective field-effect transistor* (ISFET)-based biosensors were recently separated as a distinct class of electrochemical sensors, and have a promising scope for application.

Novel Technologies and the Remaining Challenges

Microarray- and Macroarray-based Protein Assays

Nucleic acid amplification using PCR has revolutionized forensic science by providing a powerful tool for mitochondrial and chromosomal DNA typing and other nucleic acid-based analyses. Hundreds of publications available so far report the use of PCR amplification in forensics and related disciplines. DNA microarrays are another relatively new technology that allows a much higher multiplexity of nucleic acid analysis (by hybridizing a probe simultaneously to many thousands of spots of various cDNAs or oligonucleotides in a single array). Today DNA microarrays have become a routine tool in transcriptomics, but have not so far been used widely in forensic science, where PCR remains the preferred tool (due to its sensitivity).

One of the difficulties is that DNA analysis using microarrays requires orders of magnitude larger amounts of initial material to be used compared to PCR-based analysis, therefore if only little material is available, which is often the case in forensic applications, microarrays may be unsuitable for the job. For example, PCR sensitivity is ultimately one DNA molecule, whilst microarrays (i.e. hybridization analysis) would typically require several hundred nanograms of mRNA. Protein microarrays would seem to be an obvious successor to DNA arrays and many formats have already been attempted.

Unlike nucleic acids, however, protein targets are typically nonhomogeneous and affinity capture agents are often poorly characterized, making the experiments difficult to perfect and reproduce. Moreover, running multiple affinity assays in parallel (multiplexing) is not possible due to the heterogeneity of antibody affinities to their protein targets.

Unlike genomic DNA, which is present at one of two copies per cell, proteins are often present in millions of copies per single cell. This could make a protein affinity assay (which is analogous to DNA hybridization) possible in cases where DNA microarrays may fail. There is very little, if any, research published so far on the use of protein microarrays in forensics, and this is not surprising taking into account the technical difficulties of working with immobilizing proteins in their affinity-active conformational states.

Protein array-based proteomics has many advantages over traditional proteomic techniques based on two-dimensional gels and chromatography. Highly multiplexed assays can be achieved by spatially separating antibodies on the membrane when spotting, and standard curves can be plotted for a range of known sample antigen concentrations, from which unknown sample concentrations can be derived. An experiment with a single protein chip can supply information on thousands of proteins simultaneously and this provides a considerable increase in throughput. A micro- or macroarray is compatible with both competitive and non-competitive immunoassay formats:

Competitive

(a) Fluorescently labelled reference competes with sample antigen for antibodies discretely spotted on solid support. Fluorescence intensity is inversely proportional to sample antigen concentration.

(b) Fluorescently labelled antibody is added to sample and then hybridized with reference antigen discretely spotted on solid support. Fluorescence intensity is directly proportional to sample antigen concentration.

Non-competitive

(a) Fluorescently labelled sample binds to antibody discretely spotted on solid support. Fluorescence intensity is directly proportional to sample antigen concentration.

(b) Fluorescently labelled antibody (primary or secondary) binds to sample antigen discretely spotted on solid support. Fluorescence intensity is proportional to sample antigen concentration.

A novel modification of the competitive displacement strategy has been reported recently and is a technique that can utilize almost any antibody or indeed other types of affinity reagents or their mixtures (affinity heterogeneity is not an issue) and allows a high degree of multiplexing (the number of proteins assayed being limited only by antibody availability). It is tolerant towards high levels of non-specific binding and does not require any potentially interaction-disrupting labelling of the experimental samples. It is capable of quantitative comparison of unlabelled experimental samples over a wide concentration range. Other advantages of the method include its relative simplicity and low cost (only a single labelled reference sample per series and a single array per sample are required), and intrinsic signal normalization and compatibility with known signal amplification techniques (e.g. ELISA, electrochemical luminescence, RCAT, DNA fusions, etc.).

Affinity and Combinatorial Peptidomics Approaches

Affinity peptidomics is the most generic affinity assay system reported to date, which is applicable for protein identification and quantification for forensic and biometric applications. It is multiplatform compatible (liquid chromatography, microarrays, microfluidics and mass spectrometry). In the peptidomic approach the assayed mixture of proteins (typically a mixture of heterogeneous proteins) is enzymatically digested (e.g. with trypsin) prior to affinity capture to form a homogeneous mixture of short peptides. These peptides can also be predicted by *in silico* digestion of individual proteins or protein databases. Capture agents can therefore be specifically designed for all or a subset of suitable peptides from each of the proteins. Such peptides are fully predictable on the basis of protein sequence alone (or even predicted sequence). The use of mass spectrometry (e.g. MALDI-ToF-MS) for a direct confirmation of the identity of the species captured provides an additional advantage compared to the more usual method of detection in which fluorescently labelled captured species are scanned to give a spatially resolved image of the array.

In peptidomics, each protein is broken down into many smaller components, resulting in the availability of a large range of peptides with less heterogenic physical and chemical properties (which are also more predictable). Large numbers of proteolytic peptides allow multiple independent assays for the same protein target to be performed, thus also increasing the reliability of the assay. Peptidomics enables a high-throughput screening of proteins (e.g. in a microarray format) and has several advantages over the affinity capture of intact proteins:

1. As peptides are much more stable and robust than proteins, protein denaturation and degradation is not an issue since only one or a few intact peptides would be required for the analysis. Affinity peptidomics does not have to struggle with unstable or degraded proteins, it uses proteolytically digested samples and relies on anti-peptide affinity reagents e.g. antibodies, but these can also be antibody mimics, molecularly imprinted reagents, etc.
2. Peptides are also particularly suited for detection by mass spectrometric techniques, such as MALDI-ToF-MS, for direct analysis of samples on a solid substrate such as microarrays. The peptide mass range is such that isotopic resolution is easily achieved and hence fully quantitative analysis is possible (e.g. using isotopically labelled standards as in AQUA, MCAT or ICAT).
3. Digestion of cellular fractions or even intact tissues results in the release of peptides, which in most cases will contain more than one hydrophilic peptide per protein, thus improving the assay.
4. Antibody can be against linear unfolded fragments, not native folded proteins, and therefore peptide '*antigens*' can be more easily generated, such as by chemical synthesis of in silico predicted peptides (as opposed to traditionally used fully folded proteins or their fragments).
5. Such affinity reagents can be obtained at lower costs and in a truly high-throughput manner and against most antigenic peptides, and their specificities and affinities can be more easily controlled.

6. The affinity peptidomics approach is suitable for both microarray-based assays (for quick/routine applications, whether field or laboratory-based) and analytical mass spectrometry-based analysis (e.g. quantitative mass spectrometry using AQUA / ICAT / MCAT approaches), suitable for resolving difficult cases or independent confirmation of the array data if required.

Another approach suitable in principle for use in forensic applications is the combinatorial approach to peptidomics analysis. It utilizes the original peptidomics approach where protein samples are proteolytically digested using one or a combination of proteases, but in place of affinity purification the peptide pool is depleted through selective chemical binding of a subset of peptides to a solid support. This combinatorial approach utilizes the selective chemical reactivities of the side chains of individual amino acids, and thus is the nearest to a sequence-dependent analysis (e.g. DNA-based analyses). Together, the affinity peptidomics (fast and high throughput) and the combinatorial approaches (more sequence-dependent analysis) provide a viable alternative to traditional protein analysis techniques (protein preservation–separation pathway). Peptidomics approaches provide the most generic protein assay system to date, applicable for protein identification, quantification and expression profiling. These are multiplatform compatible and are capable of the analysis of partially degraded proteins, which makes them especially suitable for forensic applications. Combining the peptidomics approach with a protein microarray platform will eventually yield a new miniature tool for on-site analysis and scene-of-crime applications.

Protein Markers for Use in Forensic and Biometric Applications

A survey of over 15 years' worth of relevant forensic and biomedical literature reveals a shortlist of candidate protein markers for use in protein-based forensic analysis. For clarity we have divided these into five main categories: Biometrics, Blood Origin, Lifestyle, Time of Death, Trauma and Death. We have also included a few 'small molecule' metabolites (e.g. *testosterone*, etc.) as these are also relevant to molecular forensics and antibodies are commercially available and the same assay format can be used. We have recently obtained 40 antisera against 20 of the ~100 targets. Prediction of antigenic peptide sequences is a crucial part of any antibody generation programme. The choice of the peptides was made on the basis of their predicted immunogenicity using in-house software.

Another parameter requiring special attention is the choice of the solid support for the microarrays. Extensive data on protein array production parameters have been published in recent years by us and others. Protein arrays have been produced on plastic or glass slides (most similar to DNA microarrays), hydrogels, filters or nitrocellulose (CAST and FAST), in microtitre plate wells or on beads. We have tested a number of surfaces to ensure maximum compatibility with crude rabbit antisera, the printing robot and the assay (in which the binding of labelled peptides, typically at saturated concentrations, competed with unlabelled samples). Based on these results, positively charged nylon appears to be the best substrate for most of the experiments, with the main advantages being high binding capacity and the absence of fluorescence quenching. The disadvantage of having a three-dimensional solid support is the increased washing time, but taking into account that the analyte would be small peptides, this would not have any adverse effect on the assay.

An example of the affinity peptidomics analysis of blood samples is as follows. In order to simulate a forensic scenario, whole blood samples provided by volunteers were transferred onto filter paper discs, dried and stored under different environmental conditions. Following a 9-month storage period, paper discs were incubated with trypsin/Tween-20 for 24 hours at 37°C to achieve solubilization and digestion of the samples. Inactivation of trypsin by heating was followed by the addition of protease inhibitors. The samples were used in the competitive displacement assay in which either labelled synthetic peptides or labelled pooled human tryptically digested plasma were used. It was possible to match some of the five samples in most cases tested, except for the samples from two batches, most probably due to complete loss of the proteinaceous matter. The sensitivity of detection can be improved by reducing the reaction volume (in the above experiment, 5 μl of whole blood was used per 1-ml assay). Pearson's correlation coefficient was calculated for each pair of arrays (identically made arrays, assayed with differently stored samples) and was used as an indicator of matching (or mismatching) samples. Note that fewer antibodies could have been used to achieve a correct match.

The effect of sample collection and storage conditions on the sample stability has been discussed in the literature for many years, mostly in relation to clinical chemistry applications. Affinity peptidomics is the most generic affinity assay system to date, applicable for protein identification, quantification and expression profiling. In its concept it is the opposite of the '*sample preservation*' strategies employed or attempted in traditional biomolecular diagnostics. It requires complete proteolytic digestion of the proteinaceous samples as the first step of any analysis. It is therefore suitable for the analysis of inconsistently stored or partially degraded samples, hence is suitable for a wide range of application, ranging from routine biomedical diagnostics to biometrics and forensics analyses. Protein microarrays and peptidomics are the two enabling technologies that allow fast and accurate protein profiling and would yield a new alternative methodology that is likely to supersede traditional protein analysis techniques. There appears to exist a sufficient number of protein markers highly relevant to the forensics and biometrics fields. We have listed ~ 100 such markers and for many of these some quantitative data already exist regarding their up/down-regulation (lifestyle, trauma, disease, etc.). A serious meta-analysis of the literature is necessary for transforming the outcome of each study into a '*common currency*', a measure of the effect size, which reflects the magnitude of the effect and could be compared across studies. Otherwise, existing literature data cannot be used reliably. However, even with a conservative estimate of a twofold expression difference for each marker (there are examples of ×4000-fold differences) and 25% error in quantification, 100 different protein markers may yield very approximately up to 4 100 different combinations (or expression states) of these markers. This simple estimate shows the huge potential of protein-based diagnostics and especially its application to forensics and biometrics.

4

AMPLIFIED FRAGMENT-LENGTH POLYMORPHISMS

Highly polymorphic *variable number tandem repeat* (VNTR) loci have proven very useful for human DNA testing purposes. Initially, these variants were characterized by *restriction fragment-length polymorphism* (RFLP) analysis. Subsequently, the *polymerase chain reaction* (PCR) provided significant methodological improvements, particularly enhanced sensitivity and specificity. The PCR-based technology for detection of VNTR alleles has been termed *amplified fragment-length polymorphism* (AMP-FLP) analysis. AMP-FLP analysis already has proven useful for the detection of multiallelic profiles, D17S5, the 3' hypervariable region of the apolipoprotein B gene, and particularly D1S80.

A subgroup of VNTR loci is the *short tandem repeats* (STR) loci. These loci are highly polymorphic and abundant in the human genome. The STR loci are composed of tandemly arrayed repeat sequences, each 2 base pairs in length. Because the allele size is generally <350 base pairs, STRs are amenable to amplification by the PCR. The alleles at a locus also are less likely to be subject to preferential amplification due to their small size. STR alleles are electrophoretically separated with high resolution on native or denatured polyacrylamide gels. Alleles differing in size by as little as 1 bp can be discriminated.

The typing of STR loci for human identity testing has been facilitated by the ability to amplify two or more STR loci simultaneously in one amplification reaction by a procedure known as *multiplex PCR*. The advantages of a multiplex system are that less sample DNA is required than when each locus is amplified independently, fewer reagents are consumed, and the time needed to perform validation studies, particularly population studies, on several loci, is greatly reduced. Multiple STR loci can be separated simultaneously by polyacrylamide-gel electrophoresis, and the amplicons are detected by silver staining or by a fluorescence detection system. The latter method includes a fluor attached to the 5' end of one primer in the amplification reaction and subsequent detection in real time or by using a decoupled detection system after gel electrophoresis. Both detection schemes manual silver staining and automated fluor detection can be used to obtain reliable data for STR typing. The silver-staining approach is simple and does not require expensive equipment. However, in order to obtain unequivocal typing of the various loci in the multiplex, their sizes cannot overlap. In contrast, the loci in the fluor-labeled multiplex can be labeled with different colored fluors and thereby not necessarily be of different size.

The locus D1S80 is an AMP-FLP containing repeat sequences that generally are 16 bps in length; it has been well-defined in the human-identity typing literature. The loci CSF1PO, TPOX, and HUMTHO1 are STRs containing tetranucleotide repeat sequences. These STR loci can be coamplified and generally exhibit less stutter (or shadow) bands than STR loci containing smaller repeat units (i.e., tri- and dinucleotide repeat units). Also, the size of the largest allele in the triplex (allele 15 in the CSF1PO locus allelic ladder) is <330 bp in size. Thus, forensic biospecimens that contain substantially degraded DNA may be successfully typed. This chapter describes several approaches for typing the AMP-FLPs D1S80, CSF1PO, TPOX, and HUMTHO1 and can serve as a guideline for analyzing these, as well as other, VNTR/STR loci.

Materials

1. The primer sequences for amplifying the D1S80 locus are:

   D1S80 5'GAA ACT GGC CTC CAA ACA CTG CCC GCC G3' (forward)

   D1S80 5'GTC TTG TTG GAG ATG CAC GTG CCC CTT GC3' (reverse)

2. The primer sequences for amplifying the three STR loci in a multiplex fashion are:

   HUMTHO1 5'GTG GGC TGA AAA GCT CCC GAT TAT3' (forward)

   HUMTHO1 5'ATT CAA AGG GTA TCT GGG CTC TGG3' (revaerse)

   TPOX 5'ACT GGC ACA GAA CAG GCA CTT AGG3' (forward)

   TPOX 5'GGA GGA ACT GGG AAC CAC ACA GGT3' (reverse)

   CSFIPO 5'AAC CTG AGT CTG CCA AGG ACT AGC3' (forward)

   CSFIPO 5'TTC CAC ACA CCA CTG GCC ATC TTC3' (reverse)

3. PCR buffers, dNTPs, and/or TAQ polymerase can be obtained commercially.
4. Bovine serum albumin (BSA).
5. Tris-sulfate buffer, pH 9.0, is used to provide the leading sulfate ion. A stock solution of 0.09 M Tris-sulfate is prepared using 130 mL of 1 NH_2SO_4 and 89 g Tris diluted to 1 L.
6. Tris-formate buffer, pH 9.0, also can be used to provide a leading ion. A stock solution of 0.09 M Tris-formate is prepared using 3.51 mL. concentrated formic acid and 67 g Tris diluted to 1 L.
7. Tris-borate, pH 9.0, is used to provide the trailing and counter ions. A stock solution of 0.42 M Tris-borate is prepared using 33.2 g boric acid and 183 g Tris diluted to 1 L.
8. Tris-serine, pH 9.0, also can be used to provide the trailing ion. A stock solution of 0.29 M Tris-serine is prepared by using 30.2 g serine and 74.4 g Tris diluted to 1 L.
9. Allelic ladders for the D1S80 locus and the STR triplex loci can be obtained commercially from Promega Corp.
10. Rehydratable polyacrylamide gels (cross-linker N,N-methlenebis-acrylamide [BIS]).
11. Acrylamide stock solution: acrylamide, 29.4g; piperazine diacrylamide, 0.6 g. Dissolve in 50 mL of distilled water, filter, and make up to a final volume of 100 mL with distilled water.
12. 20% glycerol.
13. Ammonium persulfate.
14. Tetrathylmethylene diamine (TEMED).
15. Whatmann paper strips.
16. Sponge strips.
17. 10% ethanol.
18. 1% nitric acid.
19. 0.012 M silver nitrate solution.
20. 0.28 M sodium carbonate (anhydrous), 0.019% formalin.
21. 10% glacial acetic acid.
22. Sample loading solution: 25 μg xylene cyanol, 25 μg bromophenol blue, and 4 g sucrose per 10 mL of 120 mM trisformate, pH 9.0.
23. EC Electrophoresis Apparatus 1001.
24. SA 32 electrophoretic apparatus.
25. FluroImager SI.

METHODS

Extraction

Take aliquots of whole blood from EDTA vacutainer tubes (from venipuncture) or by fingerprick, place on cotton cloth, and air dry. The DNA is extracted by the phenol-chloroform method and washed using microcon 100 filters according to the method of Comey et al.

DNA Quantitation

The quantity of extracted DNA was estimated using the slot-blot procedure described by Waye et al. using D17Z1, a human-specific alphoid probe, and chemiluminescent detection.

PCR Amplification of the D1S80 Locus

1. The PCR is carried out in 50 μL reaction volumes containing 0.4 ng template DNA, 10 mM Tris-HC1, pH 8.3, 50 mM KC1, 1.5 mM $MgCl_2$, 0.001% gelatin, 1 nmole of each of the four deoxyribonucleoside trihosphates, 12.5 pmol of each primer, and 2.5 units of Taq DNA polymerase.
2. Place the reaction tubes into a Perkinelmer 9600 thermal cycler and subject to 27 cycles of denaturation at 95°C for 10 s, primer annealing at 67°C for 10 s, and primer extension at 70°C for 30s.

Electrophoretic Separation of Amplified D1S80 Products in Vertical, Native, Discontinuous Polyacrylamide Gels

1. Prepare an acrylamide solution (7.5%T, 2.0%C; crosslinker was piperazine diacrylamide) and pour between two glass plates separated by 0.4 mm thick spacers. Affix Gel bond to one plate, such that the hydrophilic side was in contact with the gel. The gel dimensions are 17 × 33.5 cm. The gel buffer is trisformate, pH 9.0, which was 60 mM with respect to the formate ion. Use an 18-tooth comb.
2. Allow the gel in an SA 32 apparatus and add 250 mL of 28 mM Tris-borate, pH 9.0, (28 mM with respect to the borate ion) to the bottom reservoir. To the top buffer reservoir, and 300 mL of 60 mM trisformate.
3. Mix 4 μL of amplified DNA sample with 2.5 μL of sample loading solution. Apply the entire sample volume to a gel well at the cathodal end of the gel submersed in the Trisformate buffer. After all samples are loaded onto the gel, remove the upper reserviour buffer by draining and replace with 300 mL of 28 mM Tris-borate.

4. Electrophoresis is performed at ambient temperature with settings of 995 V, 200 mA, and 50 W. Allow to continue until the xylene cyanol tracking dye has migrated to the top of the lower reservoir buffer.

PCR Amplification of the STR Loci CSF1PO, TPOX, and HUMTHO1

The coamplification of HUMTHO1, TPOX, and CSFIPO is performed using the GenePrint kit according to the following conditions.

1. PCR is carried out in 25 or 50 μL reaction volumes containing 0.1 ng template DNA, 10 mM Tris-HC1, pH 9.0, 50 mM $MgC1_2$, 0.1% Triton X-100, 200 μM of each of the four deoxyribonucleoside triphosphates. 12.5 pmol of each primer, and 2.5 U of Taq DNA polymerase per 50 μL reaction.
2. Place the reaction tubes into a Perkin-Elmer 9600 thermal cycler and subject to denaturation at 95°C for 30 s, primer annealing at 67°C for 30 s, and primer extension at 70°C for 30 s, for a total of 28 or 30 cycles, depending on the initial quantity of template DNA.

Electrophoretic Separation of Amplified STR Products in Vertical, Denaturing, Discontinuous Polyacrylamide Gels

1. Prepare a polyacrylamide gel (6%T, 2%C; crosslinker, piperazine diacrylamide; 31 cm long and 0.4 mm thick) containing 7 M urea and 60 mM tris-formate, pH 9.0 (with respect to the formate ion). Allow the gel to polymerize for a minimum of 1 h at ambient temperature. Place the gel in a SA 32 apparatus. The electrode buffer is 90 mM Tris-borate, pH 8.3 (90 mM with respect to the borate ion).
2. Mix 3 μL of sample loading dye with 3 μL PCR product. Denature the samples for 2 min in a Perkin-Elmer Model 480 DNA thermal cycler and load 5 μL onto the cathodal end of the gel.
3. Electrophoresis is performed initially at 80 W for approx 5 min, and then continued with settings of 25 W at ambient temperature. Allow the run to continue until the xylene cyanol tracking dye migrates to the top of the lower reservoir buffer.

Rehydratable Gels

Alternatively, PCR-generated DNA fragments can be separated electrophoretically in precast rehydratable gels.

1. The empty (i.e., devoid of polymerization byproducts and buffer), dried polyacrylamide gels, which are cast on a mylar support, are

submerged, gel-side down, in a leading ion buffer of choice. Rehydration is accomplished in 1 h. After rehydration, the excess surface liquid is removed by using a piece of polyester film as a squeegee.

2. Gels of the appropriate pore size, e.g., 7%T, 3%C may be rehydrated in a variety of buffers containing the leading ions, such as chloride, formate, or sulfate ranging from 30 to 60 mM. Mobility modifiers, such as glycerol or ribose, may be added when the trailing ion is borate. Alternatively, continuous buffer systems may also be employed.
3. Samples may be loaded directly onto the surface of the horizontal rehydrated gel by either of the following techniques:
   (a) Schleicher and Schuell nylon DNA loading tabs (dimensions depend on the sample volume) are placed on the gel surface 1.0 cm anodal to the cathode wick edge. Between 0.25 and 10 μL of sample is applied to the tabs with a micropipet.
   (b) Samples may be loaded directly on the gel surface using a micropipet.
4. Gels are then run open-faced in a horizontal position. In this electrophoretic system, the temperature is controlled with Peltier cooling devices under the platen on which the rehydrated gel is placed. Separations of 20 cm are carried out for 2.5 h at 20°C at a constant current of 7 mA. Water-dampened sponge strips can be placed along the edges of the gel to prevent a "smile" effect from extended separation times, particularly when using high-ionic-strength buffers or 7 M urea in the gel.

Silver Staining

After electrophoresis, gels can be stained with silver according to the method of Budowle et al.

1. Oxidize the gel in 1% nitric acid solution for 3 min.
2. Briefly rinse the gel in distilled water.
3. Briefly rinse the gel in a 0.012 M silver-nitrate solution for 100 min.
4. Decant silver solution, rinse briefly in water, and reduce the gel in a 0.28 M sodium carbonate (anhydrous) and 0.019% formalin solution. Change solution when it turns brown. Continue to change every few minutes until the DNA bands show up well.
5. Stop reduction (and thus image development) by placing gel in 10% glacial acetic acid for 5 min.

6. Wash gel in distilled water for 10 min.
7. Place gel in 3% glycerol solution for 5 min.
8. Air dry or photograph the gel.

Fluor Detection

If one of the primer pairs was labeled at the 5' end with a fluorescent tag, the fluor-labeled amplicons can be detected using the FluorImager SI with the PMT set at 1000 or the FMBIO 100.

Notes

1. Stutter bands: The tetranucleotide STR loci were selected for analysis because the alleles can be resolved by polyacrylamide gel electrophoresis, and these loci generally exhibit less stutter (or shadow) bands than STR loci containing smaller repeat-size sequences. The stutter bands are due to strand slippage and are much less intense than the true allelic product. In general, these stutter bands do not complicate interpretation of STR profiles, but should be evaluated carefully when there are mixed samples (when, for example, the two contributions in a mixed sample are not at equal concentration). The major component generally can be interpreted easily, but complications may arise when the minor component has bands of similar intensity as the stutter bands of the major component.
2. Inhibition of PCR may be overcome by the addition to the reaction of BSA at a concentration of 160 μg/mL. The BSA may bind (a) soluble inhibitory factor(s) that copurify with DNA, and/or BSA may stabilize the Taq polymerase. The source and quality of BSA can impact on effectivity.
3. The D1S80, as well as the STR, typing systems display a high sensitivity of detection. PCR samples containing from 4 ng to as little as 125 pg of template DNA can be typed readily. However, the slot-blot technique is a semiquantitative method for determining the quantity of DNA in a sample, and there is a need to avoid stochastic effects during PCR. Therefore, it is recommended that, for most forensic purposes, a minimum of approx 400 pg template DNA be used for the PCR.
4. The PCR conditions for amplifying the STR loci used in this study differ from those recommended by the manufacturer. A higher annealing temperature of 67°C (i.e., a higher stringency) instead of 64°C during amplification did not compromise typing efficiency. A fluorescently tagged quadplex kit also can be used. The quadplex

contains the same three loci as the triplex, with the addition of the locus VWF.

In order to obtain amplification of all four STR loci, the annealing temperature in the PCR is reduced to 60°C. Thus, an annealing temperature of 60°C is recommended when attempting to multiplex VWA with the other three STR loci.

5. With the vertical gel format, D1S80 variants tend to migrate to the nearest step in the allelic ladder. However, Budowle et al. described the presence of anodal and cathodal D1S80 variants detected using a horizontal gel-electrophoresis system. The AMP-FLPs separated in vertical gels are in a warmer environment (45°C) compared with those separated in horizontal gels (15°C). Conformational differences in the DNA fragments resulting from sequence polymorphisms are less likely to manifest themselves during electrophoresis in a warmer gel because secondary structures are denatured. This observation suggests that most of the anodal and cathodal variants are caused by sequence polymorphisms.
6. Data obtained by typing the D1S80 locus can be useful for human-identity testing purposes. However, the method described here only enables typing D1S80 singly. The advantages of a multiplex system are that less template DNA is consumed than when analyzing each locus independently, less reagents are consumed, and labor is reduced. As an example, Budowle et al. demonstrated that the D1S80 locus can be analyzed simultaneously with the amelogenin gene. Typing the amelogenin gene enables determination of the sex of the contributor of a biological sample. The only differences in the protocols for typing the D1S80 locus individually as compared with the multiplex fashion with the amelogenin locus are the addition of amelogenin primers to the D1S80 PCR, and the acrylamide concentration in the analytical gel is increased from 7.5%T to 8.5%T.
7. Horizontal rehydratable polyacrylamide gel electrophoresis systems for the separation of PCR-amplified products have been developed specifically to take advantage of the high resolution, discontinuous buffer techniques, and to provide flexibility of use that is not possible with conventionally cast gel systems. To provide the best possible electrophoretic conditions and reproducibility, these gels are washed free of all polymerization byproducts following casting and then dried for storage at room temperature. These gels afford a number of significant advantages over conventionally cast gel

systems. First, with commercially available rehydratable gels, the scientist is not exposed to potentially toxic acrylamide monomer. Second, a greater degree of reproducibility is possible; many gels can be made at one time from a single batch of reagents, and potentially deleterious polymerization by-products are removed prior to initial dehydration. If not removed, these unwanted contaminants, most notably sulfate ion, derived from the breakdown of the common polymerization catalyst persulfate, can produce an unintentional multizonal electrophoresis system. This observation, in fact, led in part to the original "Disc" system described by Ornstein and Davis. Perhaps the most important advantage is that the pre-prepared, empty, dried gels may be rehydrated in a variety of reagents that otherwise could interfere with the polymerization process.

Although the E-C Apparatus 1001 system is used here, any horizontal system designed for isoelectric focusing may be used, as long as the temperature is held constant during the electrophoretic run. Care must be taken not to use a platen temperature so low that moisture condenses on the surface of the gel. This can decrease resolution and result in surface smearing and band distortion.

9. With silver staining, both fragments of the denatured STR products may be observed, depending on the conditions of the separation method. In the denaturing electrophoretic approach described in this chapter, the HUMTHO1-denatured, single-strand products are resolved, whereas the single strands for the CSF1PO and TPOX products are not separated. When one of the two primers for amplification of a locus is fluor-labeled, silver staining is not recommended as a detection method. The addition of a fluor molecule to the 5' end of one of the strands in the duplex (when denatured), will result in an altered migration of that strand, compared with the unlabeled complementary strand.

5

MOLECULAR BIOLOGY IN FORENSIC SCIENCE

QUANTITATION OF VIRAL LOAD

Viruses, the world's smallest organisms, are a large group of single cell organisms comprised of nucleic acid surrounded by a protein coat. Pathogenic viruses play an important role in many human diseases, including hepatitis, cancer, and AIDS, as well as the common cold. These viruses are of particular concern for patients who are immune compromised, those undergoing transplant procedures with donor organs, and/or those receiving blood from human sources.

Because of the intracellular nature of viral diseases, it was very difficult to diagnose and monitor disease progress. With modern immunological techniques, which rely on detection of the host response to the virus, by production of specific antibodies, it is now possible to detect viral infection. With the advent of molecular biology, it is now possible to detect viral particles (also called viral load) present in the host. Measurement of viral loads is an emerging technique for the diagnosis and monitoring of viral disease. Although treatment options currently are limited for many virally mediated diseases, improved diagnostic and monitoring techniques may lead to improved treatment options in the near future.

Current methods for assessing viral loads generally rely on an amplification step followed by detection of a fluorescent, chemiluminescent, or radioactive label. *Capillary electrophoresis* (CE) with *laser induced fluorescence* (LIF) is a method that allows for sensitive, reliable, rapid and automated quantitation of nucleic acids. Although not currently used for routine analysis of viral loads, further research may reveal it to be an important advance in the diagnosis and monitoring of viral disease.

Clinical Virology

DNA and RNA viruses and human disease

Viruses are infectious particles generally composed only of nucleic acid surrounded by a protein coat. Viruses survive by infecting a host cell, where viral proteins take over host cellular machinery to produce viral progeny. The host cell may be killed in the process, as in the case of most adenoviral infections, or harbor a latent viral infection, such as *herpes simplex virus* (HSV), for many years. The type of nucleic acid and the presence or absence of an envelope categorizes viruses. The nucleic acids may be DNA or RNA and double-stranded, single-stranded, sense, or antisense.

Table 5.1. Classification of viruses associated with human disease

Virus family	*Nucleic acid*	*Sense*	*Envelope*	*Example of human disease*
Picornaviridae	RNA	+	–	Polio
Calciviridae	RNA	+	–	Gastroenteritis
Togaviridae	RNA	+	+	Rubella
Flaviviridae	RNA	+	+	Hepatitis C
Coronaviridae	RNA	+	+	Avian infectious bronchitis
Rhabdoviridae	RNA	–	+	Rabies
Paramyoxoviridae	RNA	–	+	Mumps, measles, pneumonia
Orthomyxoviridae	RNA	–	+	Influenza
Filoviridae	RNA	–	+	Ebola
Bunyaviridae	RNA	–	+	Hantaan
Arenaviridae	RNA	–	+	Lassa fever
Reoviridae	RNA	ds	+	Diarrhea, encephalitis
Retroviridae	RNA	–	+	AIDS (HIV)
Hepadnaviridae	DNA	–	+	Hepatitis B
Papovaviridae	DNA	ds	–	Genital warts
Adenovirus	DNA	ds	–	Colds
Herpesviridae	DNA	ds	+	Cold sores (HSV1), shingles, Chicken pox (HSV3), Genital ulceration (HSV2)
Poxviridae	DNA	ds	+	Smallpox

Analysis of viral loads, which estimates the virus particles present in the host serum at a given time, may be very important in diagnosing, treating, and monitoring viral illness. In particular, viral loads may

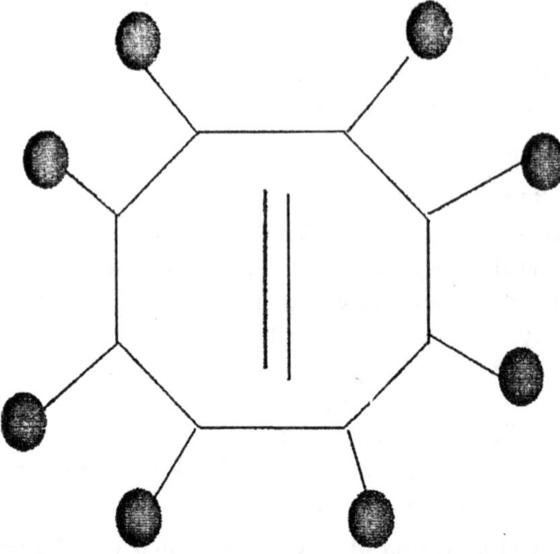

Fig. 5.1. Schematic representation of a adenovirus made up of a icosohedral proteins surrounding a dsDNA genome.

be very useful in detecting the presence of latent infections, when low copy numbers of virus are present (as in early viral illness) and to determine response to antiviral therapy.

Clinical utility of viral loads

DNA viruses: CMV

Human cytomegalovirus (CMV) is a DNA virus associated with significant human disease. CMV is a pathogen in immunocompromised individuals, especially those with end-stage AIDS, solid organ, and allogeneic bone marrow transplant recipients. Risk factors associated with serious CMV infection include; (1) degree of immunosuppression, and (2) the presence of CMV viremia.

Quantitative nucleic acid detection methods, including *polymerase chain reaction* (PCR), branched-DNA assay, and the DNA hybrid capture assay for CMV, have been developed in recent years. The DNA hybrid assay is able to detect viral particles present in the pg/mL range, corresponding to 675 copies for the lower limit of detection and 1446 copies for the lower limit of quantitation.

Due to their high sensitivity, these assays can detect CMV early, and quantitation may be able to predict disease risk and monitor the effect of antiviral therapy. Generally, a high systemic viral load is correlated with CMV disease. This correlation is strong in the HIV-infected population and in solid-organ transplant recipients but less clear in allogeneic marrow transplant recipients.

Alternatively, viral loads may be measured at specific anatomic sites. This may be a more accurate method to assess disease activity in clinical situations where the systemic viral load does not correlate with disease activity. A reduction of the systemic CMV load also correlates with a response to antiviral treatment. Quantitative CMV detection techniques are used widely to direct and monitor antiviral treatment, however, reproducibility and standardization of the various assays needs further analysis. In addition, the FDA has not approved to date a viral load assay for CMV.

DNA viruses: hepatitis B

Hepatitis B is a blood-borne disease representing a serious, worldwide public health problem. More than 1 million individuals in the United States alone are infected the virus. Hepatitis B is endemic in China, Southeast Asia, and the Middle East as well as parts of Africa and South America. In addition to the acute manifestations of hepatitis, individuals infected with hepatitis B may develop chronic hepatitis and are at increased risk of liver cancer. The risk of liver cancer appears to be higher for patients with higher viral loads, indicating actively replicating virus, whereas viral titers (indication of the host immune response to the virus) are not predictive of progression to liver cancer.

In the United States, the primary routes of transmission are through direct contact with infected blood and body secretions and the clinical use of infected blood products. Routine screening of the blood supply for the hepatitis B surface antigen (HbsAg) has virtually eliminated post-transfusion hepatitis B infection. However, other blood products, such as clotting factors produced from blood concentrates, can still transmit infection. Currently, viral loads are not used routinely to screen blood, blood products, or donated organs. Analysis of viral loads may, however, be useful in decreasing transmission of infection. Viral loads are also often quantified to assess response to therapy with *interferon* (IFN) or lamivudine. Lower viral loads are associated with an increased rate of seroconversion for patients, which lowers the risk for clinical disease progression. Lower viral titers are also associated with a decreased frequency of mutations associated with resistance.

RNA viruses: hepatitis C

Hepatitis C is an RNA virus and like hepatitis B is transmitted via contact with infected blood or other body fluids. Infection with hepatitis C results in chronic hepatitis in up to 70% of individuals and cirrhosis in approx 50% of those developing chronic hepatitis. Currently, the only treatment of patients with hepatitis C is with IFN and more recently IFN in combination with ribavirin. In chronic hepatitis C infection, a high viral load per liver cell predicts long-term response to therapy. Loss of viremia at the second week of therapy is the strongest predictor for a long-term IFN response, followed by the initial viral load and loss of viremia at the fourth week of therapy. It may be possible to predict a long-term response as early as at the second and fourth weeks after the start of therapy by screening for HCV-RNA. Patients unlikely to respond to therapy could be discontinued after 2 wk, decreasing the adverse effects and associated cost of prolonged therapy.

RNA viruses: HIV

Primarily infection with the human immunodeficiency virus type 1 (HIV- 1) and less frequently by HIV-2 cause *acquired immune deficiency syndrome* (AIDS). AIDS, first identified as a clinical syndrome in 1981, is currently a worldwide epidemic. The CDC estimates that 1.2 million individuals are infected in the United States and the WHO reports 2.5 million cases of AIDS worldwide.

Viral loads are routinely assessed in AIDS patients and are the single best predictor of disease progression. A major advance in monitoring has been development of plasma HIV RNA assays of increased sensitivity, which have a detection range of approx 20–50 to approx 50,000 copies/mL of plasma. These assays are suitable for monitoring the majority of patients on anti-retroviral treatment. Assay precision at lower limits is usually poor with CVs approaching 90% making quantitation at these levels questionable. Current methodology, however, can be viewed as a detection tool at the 50-copies/mL lower limit. Assays will likely improve even further regarding lower limits of sensitivity, reliability, and quantitation as described in the following sections on *capillary electrophoresis* (CE).

The International AIDS Society-USA panel recommends anti-retroviral therapy for any patient with established HIV infection and a confirmed plasma HIV-1 RNA level greater than 5000–10,000 copies/mL and willingness to undergo the complex, long-term therapy. Viral load is a strong, independent predictor of clinical outcome. Degree and durability of viral response correlates directly with plasma HIV-RNA level and CD4+ cell count at diagnosis. For asymptomatic patients with low (e.g., <5000–10,000 copies/mL) plasma HIV-RNA level and high CD4 counts, deferral of therapy with close follow-up may be recommended. These individuals may be categorized as potential long-term nonprogressors. For those with low HIV RNA level and low CD4+ cell count, initiation of therapy is recommended, since the CD4 count gives independent prognostic information and data from clinical trials document the benefit of initiating therapy when the CD4 count is low.

The goal of antiretroviral therapy is to reduce plasma HIV-RNA below the detection limit of the most sensitive assays. Even modest reductions in viral load (e.g., 0.5–1 log reductions) provide clinical benefit, therefore regimens that provide maximal suppression of HIV replication are expected to improve survival and decrease morbidity via continuous suppression of HIV replication. A combination of three drugs, including a *nucleoside reverse transcriptase inhibitor* (nRTI) (zidovudine, didanosine, zalcitabine, lamivudine, and stavudine), a nonnucleoside reverse transcriptase inhibitor (nnRTI) (nevirapine and delavirdine), and *protease inhibitor* (PI) (ritonavir, indinavir, nelfinavir, and saquinavir) is commonly used as initial therapy. These regimens result in virologic success rates of 60–90% in anti-retroviral naive patients, as determined by plasma HIV-1 RNA level <500 copies/mL at 24 wk or beyond. Currently, the combination of a potent PI and 2 nRTIs should remain the primary consideration, based on clinical trials documenting the efficacy and durability of responses.

Since clinical outcome clearly correlates with disease activity and antiretroviral treatment is made based on viral-load determinations, the most sensitive assays available are recommended with viral-load monitoring every 2 mo for patients treated with antiviral therapy. Ongoing viral replication is reported for patients with a consistent viral load between 50 and 500 copies/mL. For patients with levels <50 copies/mL, development of resistance is decreased, although low levels of viral replication may persist. The strictest definition of treatment failure is that of confirmed detectable plasma HIV RNA (i.e., >50 copies/mL) in an compliant patient who had achieved a viral-load level below the detection limit and has not experienced a recent acute infectious illness. Clearly, viral diseases play a significant role in the health of individuals worldwide. Currently, viral loads are used to monitor disease progression and response to therapy for patients with HIV. Viral loads may also play an emerging role in assessing the response to therapy for patients with hepatitis B, hepatitis C, and CMV. Other potential applications include instances where early and very low-level detection is required. Examples of these include screening of donor blood, organs for transplant, and very early infection after exposure to an infected individual.

Methods of Viral-load Assessment

Current methods for assessing viral loads generally rely on amplification reactions of either the viral nucleic acid (PCR) and reverse-transcription (RT-PCR) or the signal (bDNA) and are labeled with fluorescence or chemiluminescence probes for analysis in plate readers or by slab gel electrophoresis. Quantification by current assays is relative and quantitative results obtained by different methods are not interchangeable.

Immunoassays

Many viral diseases are routinely diagnosed by immunological testing. These tests screen for an antibody generated by the infected host against the viral pathogen. As such, immunological-based tests are evaluating a host response to an infection, rather than the infectious organism itself. This type of testing was initially developed because isolation and culture of the infecting virus was very difficult. Antibody tests have the advantages of being relatively inexpensive, rapid and accurate with specificities often in excess of 99%. For the HIV-*enzyme-linked immunosorbent assay* (ELISA) reported sensitivities range from 93 to 97%. The limitations of antibody testing are:

1. Inability to detect early infection when the virus is present while the immune response is still being generated. Patients have a viral load but will test negative by antibody testing. Since most diseases are more curable at an early stage, diagnosis at this stage would be advantageous.
2. When there are low levels of infection or immunological response indicating that the level of infection may be inadequate to stimulate a host immunological response, or if a patient is immunosuppressed, they may not be able to mount an immunological response. In both these situations, the patient may test negative by antibody testing, while still having an active disease process.
3. When quantitative results are required. Since an antibody test measures a host response to an infection, it does not give a quantitative measure of virus present.

Nucleic acid-based assays

PCR and RT-PCR

The primary limitation to genetic analysis prior to the conception of PCR was the small quantity of nucleic acid available for analysis.

PCR is in essence a nucleic acid xerox machine, making many genetic analyses routine. Initially, primers flanking the region of interest are designed and synthesized. The PCR reaction is set-up in a micro-centrifuge tube with the reaction components consisting of the template DNA, primers, nucleotide bases, TAQ polymerase, and the appropriate buffer and salt concentration. The tube is heated to approx 95°C, allowing denaturation of the target DNA and attachment of the primers. TAQ polymerase then uses the nucleotide building blocks to fill in the space between the primers, creating an exact replica of the target DNA and doubling the amount of target DNA strands. This process is repeated again and again, making a large number of fragments, all which contain the DNA region of interest.

PCR requires DNA for a template, however, RNA can also be used. RNA isolated by standard methods is reverse-transcribed into cDNA by the enzyme reverse transcriptase. The cDNA can then be amplified by PCR as described earlier. PCR and RT-PCR can also be used to increase the quantity of nucleic acid present to amounts that are easily detectable. PCR products are then run on a gel matrix, which separates by molecular size and are visualized by *ultraviolet* (UV), radiolabeled, or fluorescence detection.

Other nucleic acid-based detection techniques relying on amplification

Branched DNA (bDNA) is a technique that relies on the amplification of the signal rather than the amplification of the target nucleic acid. Target nucleic acid is hybridized to a probe that is attached to a platform. Bound probe is then hybridized to additional probes, with a fluorescent or chemiluminescent label, which amplifies the signal. This approach is commercially available as the Quantiplex

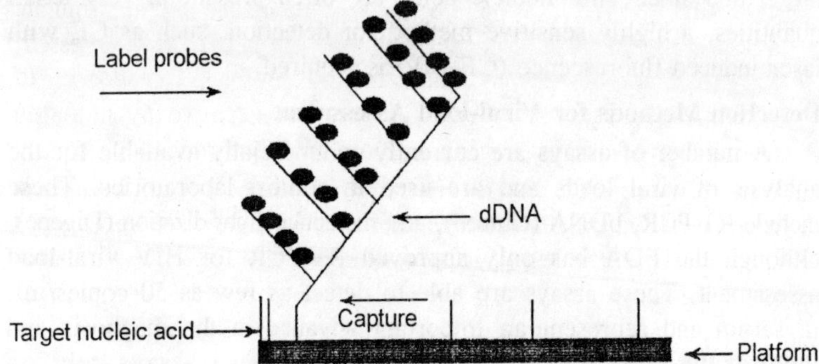

Fig. 5.2. bDNA assay. Target nucleic acid is hybridized to the capture probe attached tothe platform, which is then hybridized to the label.

assay. This technique relies on amplification to detect very low levels (50 copies/mL plasma) of HIV virus. The DNA hybrid capture assay is an alternative approach using an RNA probe directed towards a DNA virus. An antibody with a chemiluminescent label then recognizes the resulting DNA/RNA hybrid. Since a large portion of the genome is probed, there are multiple sites for antibody attachment. The long probe, which increases the number of antibody binding sites serves as the signal amplification step in this technique.

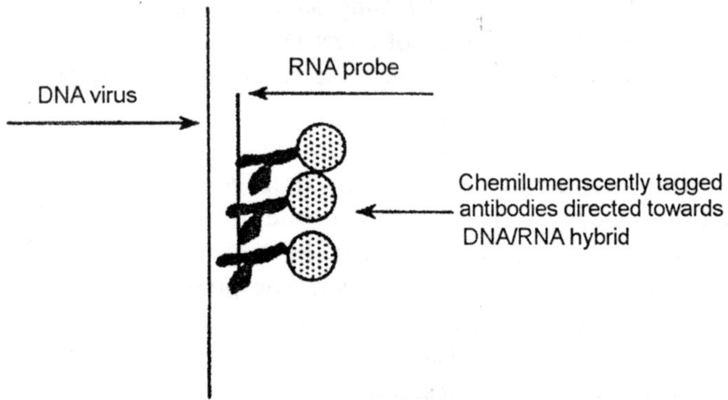

Fig. 5.3. Molecular hybridization assay.

Direct detection

In direct detection, target viral DNA or RNA is hybridized with a specific fluorescent-labeled probe. Excess single stranded RNA or DNA is then digested away. Because this method does not rely on amplification of target or signal, variability resulting from amplification is eliminated. The method does require separation of the hybridized target and since viral nucleic acids are often present in very small quantities, a highly sensitive method for detection, such as CE with laser induced fluorescence (CE-LIF) is required.

Detection Methods for Viral-load Assessment

A number of assays are currently commercially available for the analysis of viral loads and are used in clinical laboratories. These include RT-PCR, bDNA (Chiron), and molecular hybridization (Digene), although the FDA has only approved RT-PCR for HIV viral-load assessment, These assays are able to detect as few as 50 copies/mL in serum and represent an important advance in the diagnosis and monitoring viral disease. Since most of these assays rely on amplification, variability is introduced and CVs are often high. As such, advances in technology, i.e., CE-LIF, that improve reliability, quantitation, and detection are needed. CE-LIF detection that is able to detect attomolar concentrations is highly reproducible and fully automatable has the potential for improving viral-load analysis.

Slab gel electrophoresis

PCR products are commonly analyzed by *slab gel electrophoresis* (SGE), where an agarose gel containing ethidium bromide acts as the separation medium and products are visualized directly with UV light. Visualization by SGE is a rapid and inexpensive method for the analysis of PCR products. The major limitation of SGE is a relatively high detection limit, usually on the order of nanograms. Slab gel electrophoresis with radiolabeled probes is able to detect 1–5 pg of target DNA with an overnight exposure. Radioactive-detection methods, however, have significant disadvantages with respect to safety, stability of the labeled nucleic acids, and automation.

Capillary electrophoresis with laser-induced fluorescence

High pressure liquid chromatography (HPLC) was initially studied as a replacement for slab gel electrophoresis, although restricted intraparticle diffusion of biopolymers resulted in only limited improvement of resolution and speed. Alternatively, electrophoretic separations (CE) can be performed in narrow-bore tubes or capillaries and may be viewed simply as another mode of electrophoresis. Originally, CE utilizing hydroxyethylcellulose and ethidium bromide was shown to have increased resolving power when compared to HPLC for dsDNA, however, the detection level still remained in the nanogram range. CE has since been used successfully in the research setting to separate and quantitate PCR products of HIV-1, HBV, CMV, and HCV. The introduction of CE with LIF and intercalating dyes improved detectability to the attomole level with sample volumes as little as a few picoliters. CE represents a safe and automatable assay system for quantitative analysis and routine laboratory analysis may soon be the norm.

Capillary gel electrophoresis (CGE) initially used either a fixed or immobilized polymerized matrix which acts as a "*molecular sieve*" within the capillary to separate DNA based on size and charge. Since the mass to charge ratio of DNA remains constant with increasing mass, separations are made based on differences in molecular weight. As charged solutes migrate through the polymer network, they are retarded with larger molecules being retarded, more than smaller ones, allowing for separation based on molecular weight. Initially, CE used crosslinked agarose and polyacrylamide for the separation of DNA.

However, polymerization of gels within the capillary is difficult and time-consuming. Polymerization that occurs too rapidly, use of impure chemicals and solutions that are not degassed can lead to bubble formation and unstable gels. Additionally, these capillaries are very rigid, making hydrodynamic injections impossible and the capillary susceptible to breakage. Linear polymer solutions are more flexible and pressure can be used to refill the capillary. Additionally, they are much less susceptible to bubble formation and breakage. Although the polymer structure of the cross-linked gel is much different than the linear polymer solution, the mechanism of separation is identical and the ease of use with the replaceable polymer networks have made these the capillary system of choice for most laboratories. CGE is used most frequently for the analysis of nucleic acids and will be the focus of this discussion.

CE-LIF analysis of RT-PCR products

To quantitate viral load, the measured concentration must be a reliable gauge of the amount of nucleic acid present in the original sample. This is usually a two-part process; amplification followed by detection. RNA samples are usually amplified by RT-PCR. In this process an internal standard that will amplify under the same conditions as the target sequence is introduced prior to amplification. The internal standard is used to control for variability within the PCR reaction as well as to provide a reference to calculate the initial concentration of unknown.

To ensure peak areas reported by CE-LIF are an accurate measure of the amount of RT-PCR product present in the sample, a calibration curve is generated by injecting known concentrations DNA. The same solution of standard DNA fragments can also be used to calibrate the capillary and determine the molecular weight of fragments based on retention times. In addition to being an additional step towards the accurate quantitation of gene expression, this technique offers several advantages. Sample volumes are small (1–5 μL), sensitivity is high (attomolar), and the hazards associated with isotopic storage, use and disposal are eliminated. This technique can also be automated, used for fraction collection, and validated. There are, however, drawbacks to CE-LIF, including expense. Initially, there is an investment in equipment, CE, laser, computer and application software that must be made. In addition, consumable supplies, primarily intercalating dyes and capillaries can also be expensive and in the case of capillaries, fragile.

With current CE-LIF technology, samples are analyzed individually. Each sample usually has a 15–45 min run time, whereas multiple samples can be analyzed simultaneously by SGE. For analysis of a single sample, CE-LIF may be faster, but when multiple analyses are required, SGE may be more time efficient. With the multicapillary instruments currently under development, analysis of multiple samples simultaneously by CE-LIF will be possible. In addition to requiring a longer time, individual sample processing also means that each sample is analyzed separately increasing risk of bias. Of the steps involved in analyzing PCR products, injection bias is the most frequent source of error, although this can be minimized by using hydrodynamic injections. Interassay variation can also be minimized by the addition of a reference of known concentration into each of the samples after PCR amplification. DNA fragments of similar, but not identical molecular weight to the unknown sample are best used as a reference. Although not currently used for commercial analysis of viral loads, CE-LIF represents an important avenue for exploration. CE-LIF has been used to analyze HIV, HBV, HCV, and CMV, in addition to many other PCR-generated fragments.

RNA purification. Total cellular RNA and RNA obtained from human tissue samples including tumor biopsies and whole blood can be obtained by standard procedures. Alternatively, commercially available system such as Ultraspec II RNA isolation system may be used. This system isolates total RNA by disruption and homogenization of samples with 14 *M* guanidine salts and urea followed by chloroform extraction. The sample is centrifuged and the upper aqueous phase containing the RNA is isolated followed by isopropanol precipitation. A proprietary RNATack resin that specifically binds RNA and then eluted with TE (Tris-EDTA, pH 7.4) buffer purifies the RNA. The RNA concentration is quantitated spectrophotometrically. The entire isolation can be completed in approx 1 h, which is a significant advantage over standard methods. RNA can also be extracted directly from lymphocytes obtained from whole blood. Concentrations of 10–15 ng of RNA are routinely obtained from 10 mL of whole blood comparing favorably to standard methods.

Design of internal standard. An internal standard may be designed by purifying, using SGE, the desired PCR product and identifying restriction sites 30–70 base pairs apart that will generate compatible ends. Digestion with the appropriate enzymes and re-ligation generates a DNA fragment that is identical to the target DNA, but 30–70 base pairs smaller. The primer recognition sites and the sequence are identical and the internal standard should amplify under identical conditions. After gel purification and elution in TE, the internal standard is quantified spectrophotometrically and stored at –20°C. The internal standard concentration is then titrated to determine what concentration is optimal for amplification, usually 10^{-6} ng/PCR reaction.

Using a DNA standard has the benefit of ease of preparation and storage, amplification under identical conditions, and low expense. It does not, however, control for variability present within the RT step. Thus, RNA standards are usually introduced prior to reverse transcription to control for variability throughout the RT-PCR process.

RT-PCR. To improve reproducibility, all RT and PCR steps are done with master mixes that contain all components except the target nucleotides and Taq polymerase. Since PCR is by nature prone to contamination and false-positive results, precautions must be taken to ensure the validity of results. All reagents should be aliquotted into single use portions and separate pipets should be set aside to be used only for PCR. Reactions can be set-up in a biological hood and all surfaces exposed to UV light between reactions. Adequate controls (both positive and negative) should be used for all reactions.

Instrument parameters. Separations are performed on a CE-LIF system, with the temperature held constant at 20°C. PCR products are detected by LIF in the reversed polarity mode (anode at the detector site) with excitation at 488 nm and emission at 520 nm. Samples are introduced hydrodynamically using 10-s injections at 0.5 psi into a 100 mm i.d. × 65 cm coated (neutral) capillary filled with TBE containing replaceable linear polyacrylamide. No sample preparation of PCR products is required. The capillary is conditioned with buffer containing 60 μg thiazole orange (an intercalator) per 20 mL and rinsed at high pressure for 3 min. Separations are performed under constant voltage at 7.0– 9.0 kV for 15–50 min. The capillary is rinsed with gel buffer for 3 min prior to each injection.

Direct detection of nucleic acids

Reliance on an amplification step is the major problem associated with PCR based methodology. Despite the incorporation of internal standards, quantitation is still problematic, particularly when the target template is small. To decrease the variability associated with PCR-based assays and to take advantage of the exquisite sensitivity of CE-LIF, the direct detection of nucleic acids has been developed.

A report has attempted to quantify HIV-1 RNA directly from the plasma by assuming that all plasma RNA is due to HIV-1. However, without specific HIV-1 probes, plasma samples may contain non-HIV-1 viral RNA including HTLV-1 (human T-cell leukemia virus Type-1), and hepatitis A, C, D, and E, which reduces the specificity for HIV-1. Additionally, contamination of plasma with leukocytes or other cells would result in the presence of nonspecific human RNA.

In an alternative approach, cellular RNA is hybridized with a HIV-1 specific probe that has been labeled with fluorescene. A complex is formed if HIV-1 RNA is present and unbound RNA is digested with RNAase I. Samples are then analyzed by CE-LIF with thiazole orange or other intercalators present in the buffer system. Two peaks elute if HIV-1 RNA is present; the first is the DNA/DNA unbound probe complex, followed by the DNA/RNA hybrid. Although the complexes are the same lengths, the DNA/RNA complex has a different secondary structure and slightly higher molecular weight and a subsequently longer retention time.

Thiazole orange present in the buffer intercalates into 1 out of 2 bp for DNA and 1 out of 10 bp for RNA. Although the intercalation parameters of thiazole orange into a DNA/RNA complex is unknown, it is assumed to be between 10 and 50%, providing a 10–50% enhancement in sensitivity over the RNA/RNA complex. The addition of a fluorescein label to the probe provides a double-detection system over the intercalator alone, also enhancing sensitivity.

The double-detection system is linear from 0.072–21.46 pg, the migration time precision is <1% and the peak-area precision ranges from 1–11%. The minimal detectable level is 36 atg, which corresponds to 4 equivalents (4 copies/mL) of HIV. As little as 19 fg (1710 copies per 1 mL of starting plasma) of HIV-RNA can be reliably and quantitatively detected. Although still a research tool, direct detection of nucleic acids may be an important improvement in assay reliability.

Validation and Quantitation Issues

Standardization and validation methodology

Determination of the injection volume

The injection volume is an important parameter in quantitating samples by CE-LIF. Based on literature values, the calculated injection volume is 7. 1 nL when a sample is injected onto a 100 μm i.d. capillary at 0.34 Pa for 10 s. The injection volume can be verified for each system by measuring the mass difference after injection by placing

20 mcL of hybridization sample in a microcuvet and weighing on a Sartorius BP 210D balance. After weighing, the microcuvette containing the sample is transferred to the auto-sampler tray and injected hydrodynamically at 0.34 Pa for 990 s (99 s × 10 injections, 99 s maximum injection time). The microcuvet is then re-weighed with a mean decrease in weight after injection of 707 ng (n = 3). Since the hybridization solution was very dilute, it was assumed to have the specific gravity of water (1.00 g/L), corresponding to a mean volume of 706.86 nL/990 s injection or 7.14 nL/10 s injection (n = 3).

Calibration of CE-LIF: Preparation of DNA solution for standard curve

A commercially available DNA ladder, ranging from 36 to 2645 bases at a concentration of 1.0 mg/mL, can be used to calibrate the CE-LIF. The DNA standard is aliquotted in 10 μL portions and stored at -20°C. The solution contains a 222 bp fragment present in a concentration of 129 μg/mL initially. This solution is diluted 1:10 with DEPC-treated water and injected for 5–20 s. To generate a standard curve, 10 μL of diluted DNA standard solution is placed in a microcuvet and six pressure injections at 0.5 psi are made from the vial for 5, 10, 12.5, 15, 17.5, and 20 s. Separations are performed based on the parameters detailed under instrument parameters.

To determine the linear range, the peak area reported on the electropherogram vs the concentration of the 222 bp fragment injected is plotted. With this assay, a linear relationship between the peak area and concentration exists for the 222 bp fragment over the range 0.5–183 pg. The concentration of unknown samples can be determined in this range by comparison of the peak areas obtained to the standard curve.

The same solution of standard DNA fragments can also be used to determine the molecular weight of fragments based on retention times. Plot the migration time for each peak vs the known molecular weights and determine the linear range. The linear range will not be over the entire range of molecular weights since intercalating dyes such as thiazole orange can affect migration times at higher (>1000 bp) molecular weights. With this assay, a linear relationship exists between retention time and molecular weights of the standard fragments between 126 bp and 460 bp (r^2 = 0.996). This standard can then be used to determine the molecular weights of unknown samples.

Validation of RT-PCR CE-LIF assay

To validate the assay, cDNA from two different sources is amplified in triplicate and analyzed on three separate days generating

18 data points. The ratio of the peak area of the internal standard to the peak area of the gene of interest is calculated. The linear range is then determined by plotting the ratio vs the starting amount of cDNA. We have found a linear relationship ($r^2 = 0.991$) over the range of 0–312.5 ng of starting cDNA, (the RNA is quantitated spectrophotometrically and the RT process is assumed to be 100%). The PCR is no longer linear when more than 400 ng of cDNA is amplified. This is consistent with data reported by Rossomondo and colleagues, who also showed a linear relationship between peak area and starting amount of RNA at low concentrations and a nonlinear relationship when higher concentrations were amplified.

The mean retention time for the reference peak is determined (we commonly analyze the internal standard fragment as well as the target sequence) and used to calculate interday precision and the intraday precision, a measure of the method reproducibility. With this assay, we have interday and intraday migration-time precision of <1.0%. The same samples can also be used to determine the peak-area precision, a measure that represents the reproducibility of both the CE and PCR aspects of this assay. The ratio of the peak area of the gene of interest to internal standard is calculated and compared. Because PCR with an internal standard is competitive, the peak area of one or the other product is not representative. This assay has a peak area intraday precision of 12–15% and interday precision of 10–16%. Strategies to improve assay precision should target the RT-PCR portion and could include automation and use of RNA standards.

The major limitations to accurate quantitation in the assay are: (1) the inability of spectophotometric analysis to predict accurately RNA concentration, (2) the assumption that the reverse transcription step was 100% efficient, and (3) the need for accurate calibration of the RNA internal standard. To overcome these limitations a calibrated RNA internal standard could be added prior to reverse transcription.

Viral diseases play a significant role in the health status of individuals worldwide. Viral loads are used routinely to monitor disease progression and response to therapy of patients with HIV. Viral-load analysis also plays an emerging role in assessing the response to therapy of patients with hepatitis B, hepatitis C, and CMV. Other potential applications include instances where early and very low-level detection is required.

A variety of assays are currently commercially available for the analysis of viral loads and are used in clinical laboratories including

RT-PCR, bDNA, and molecular hybridization. Able to detect as few as 50 copies/mL of serum, these assays represent an important advance in the diagnosing and monitoring viral disease. However, since most assays rely on amplification, variability is introduced and CVs are often high. As such, advances in technology, such as CE-LIF, that improve reliability, quantitation, and detection are needed.

Capillary electrophoresis may be an important step in improving viral- load analysis. CE-LIF offers several advantages over current detection techniques. Required sample volumes are small (1–5 μL), sensitivity is high (attomolar) and the hazards associated with isotopic storage, use, and disposal are eliminated. Additionally, CE-LIF can be readily automated, used for fraction collection, and the assay can be validated. Combining CE-LIF with existing assays for viral-load analysis may improve the reliability, speed, and sensitivity of viral-load analysis. In addition, CE-LIF can be applied to the analysis of gene expression, gene therapy, single-stranded oligonucleotide, and point mutations.

Application of Capillary Electrophoresis

The development of methods for the amplification and detection of specific regions of the DNA molecule using the *polymerase chain reaction* (PCR) has resulted in rapid and dramatic advances in biochemical analysis. With the advent of the PCR it is now possible to easily produce analytically significant amounts of a specified DNA product. A typical PCR reaction can produce microgram quantities of target DNA, allowing rapid and efficient screening of genetic defects, cancer susceptibility, and low level bacterial contamination. The sensitivity of the technique has freed biochemists from the many laborious processes necessary to isolate and examine small quantities of DNA. In the forensic arena, PCR methods have permitted rapid and specific tests of evidence produced in a crime.

The impact of PCR has also resulted in a need for efficient and automated procedures to analyze the reaction products. For many years it has been recognized that *capillary electrophoresis* (CE) has had the potential to fill this requirement. The capillary system can produce rapid and efficient separations of DNA, as a result of the efficient heat dissipation of the capillary when compared to standard slab gel methods. Additionally, the capillary can be easily manipulated for efficient and automated injections. Despite these advantages, it has been only recently that dedicated commercial systems for PCR product analysis have begun to appear.

The slow development of CE systems for PCR analysis has been because of the scarcity of efficient methods for injection, separation, and detection of DNA fragments. For example, the high ionic strength of the PCR reaction mixture is incompatible with CE injection methods. Gel-based separations are difficult to implement in the capillary format, and commonly utilized *ultraviolet* (UV) detection techniques have poor sensitivity. These problems have been overcome as a result of better understanding of the nature of the CE procedure.

This section will focus on the development of capillary systems for the analysis of PCR products. Advancements in separation, sample preparation, and detection will be emphasized, and the chapter will conclude with a discussion of forensic applications.

Polymerase Chain Reaction

In the PCR process, a thermostable DNA polymerase (Taq) is used to copy small amounts of DNA template by means of a temperature dependent reaction. The PCR reaction mixture is prepared by combining the target DNA, oligonucleotide primers, the polymerase and a mixture of four deoxyribonucleotide triphosphates (dNTPs) in a Tris-HCl buffer containing approx 50 m*M* KCl and 1.5 m*M* MgCl. The primers consist of two short 20–30 oligomer (mer) segments that are selected to bracket a specific location of interest on the target DNA. The reaction is initiated using a three-step temperature program in which the two strands of DNA template are separated (melted) by heating at 95°C. The primers are then annealed to the template at approx 60°C. The enzyme then extends the primer sequence at approx 72°C by incorporating the individual deoxyribonucleotide using the target DNA as a template.

By cycling through these temperatures using an oven that rapidly and precisely alters the reaction temperature, it is possible to double the amount of target DNA with each cycle. Theoretically, 30 cycles of heating and cooling the mixture can produce up to a billion copies of the target DNA from one copy of template. In situations where the quantity of sample is limited, it is also possible to perform amplifications of multiple loci by simultaneously targeting different regions of the genome in a single reaction. Such multiplexed reactions are carefully balanced by optimizing the reaction conditions and primer sequences in order that one locus with its respective set of primers does not preferentially amplify over the others. The result of a multiplex amplification is the production of a series of DNA fragments that must be optimally separated over a specific size range.

Separation Techniques

Polymer matrix

One of the earliest efforts to use CE to separate DNA fragments was carried out by Kasper et al., who concluded that effective separation of large, linear DNA must either be carried out using affinity or gel electrophoresis. DNA fragments have proved difficult to separate because all DNA fragments have virtually the same charge-to-mass ratio. The logical solution was to perform sieving experiments by filling the capillary with an agarose or polyacrylamide gel similar to those used in slab gel electrophoresis. However, it was clear from the beginning that at the high field strengths and temperatures used in CE, the stability of these "*chemical gels*" would be a problem. One solution was to attach chemically (cross-link) the gel to the capillary wall. Separations using this procedure with polyacrylamide gels produced exceptional separations of PCR products with analysis times typically <30 min. These capillaries can still be purchased from a number of commercial manufacturers. The problem with the chemical gels is that even when manufactured under well-controlled conditions, they are still susceptible to such problems as bubble formation and contamination from the sample matrix. In addition, sample injections were only possible using the electrokinetic mode. For the CE technique to be truly automated, a replaceable sieving matrix was required.

The development of replaceable "*physical gels*" was initiated by Zhu and coworkers. Experiments carried out using hydroxy propylmethyl cellulose, methyl cellulose, and *polyethylene glycol* (PEG) showed that it was not necessary to use crosslinked gels in the capillary format. Additionally, with these physical gels, a variety of injection techniques could be utilized, and capillaries could be flushed and chemically etched between each analysis. The disadvantage of these gels was that early experimental systems could not achieve the separation efficiency of cross-linked polyacrylamide. Since then a large amount of research has been carried out in order to understand the theory of electrophoresis in physical gels. As a result of this research it has been shown that at least three different mechanisms have been found to be responsible for the separation of DNA in these physical gels, transient entanglement coupling, Ogston sieving, and reptation. At low polymer concentrations, separation takes place through a frictional interaction between the DNA and the polymer strands known as *transient entanglement coupling*. As the polymer concentration increases, the strands of different polymer molecules begin to interact producing a solution of entangled polymers.

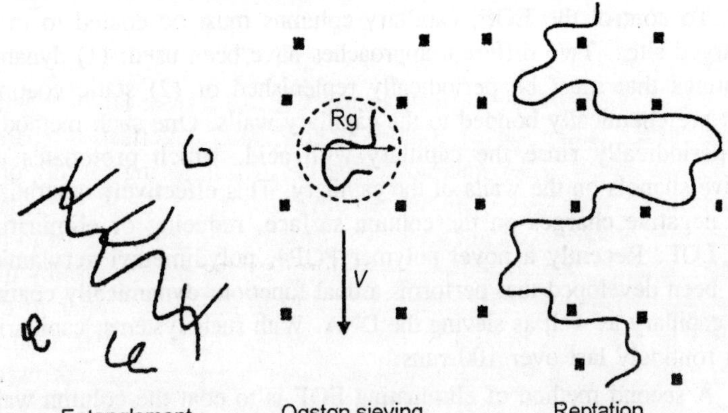

Fig. 5.4. Three different mechanisms for the separation of DNA.

The polymer concentration at which this occurs is known as the entanglement threshold. Above the entanglement threshold, DNA fragments separate by sieving through transient pores created in the polymer mesh. Fragments that are larger than the average pore size reptate or move in a snakelike manner through the mesh. The key to producing an acceptable separation is to determine a polymer concentration at which the size of these virtual pores approximates the radius of the DNA in solution. Additionally, the polymer length must not be too great or the solution will become too viscous.

Other characteristics that have been found to be of importance include the relative stiffness and polydispersity of the polymer. With these characteristics in mind, a number of water-soluble polymers have been found to be particularly useful for DNA separations including linear polyacrylamide, Methyl cellulose hydroxyethylcellulose, hydroxy propyl methyl cellulose polyethylene oxide, and poly (*N*-acryloylamino-ethoxyethanol). In addition, a commercial polymer known as POP4 has also been described. Thus, the key to producing an acceptable separation is to optimize the polymer molecular weight and concentration relative to the DNA fragment size and desired resolution.

Capillary

In uncoated capillary columns, residual charges on the silica surface induce a flow of the bulk solution toward the negative electrode. This is known as *electroosmotic flow* (EOF). The magnitude and direction of the EOF is dependent of the number and type of active sites on the capillary surface and the pH of buffer. EOF is generally considered a detriment to stable DNA separations because its velocity can change from run to run, making peak migration times irreproducible.

To control the EOF, capillary columns must be coated to mask charged sites. Two different approaches have been used: (1) dynamic coatings that must be periodically replenished or (2) static coatings that are chemically bonded to the capillary walls. One such method is to periodically rinse the capillary with acid, which protonates the active silanols on the walls of the capillary. This effectively neutralizes the negative charges on the column surface, reducing or eliminating the EOF. Recently a novel polymer POP4, polydimethyl acrylamide has been developed that performs a dual function, dynamically coating the capillary as well as sieving the DNA. With such systems, capillaries can routinely last over 100 runs.

A second method of eliminating EOF is to coat the column walls with an inert substance that masks the charged sites on the capillary walls. Such coatings must be stable at the pH of analysis and free from contamination. These coatings include hydrophilic substances such as polyacrylamide and polyvinyl alcohol, as well as more hydrophobic coatings such as the phenyl methyl and C18 coatings adapted from *gas chromatography* (GC) and *high-performance liquid chromatography* (HPLC). The key factor in selecting a coating is its stability and its ability to last under the conditions used in the separation. With periodic rinsing, coated capillaries can last for months before needing to be replaced. Continued development in this area is necessary as periodic replacement of capillaries limits the ability of large multicapillary systems to run unattended.

Buffer

Buffers commonly used in DNA analysis by CE include Tris-borate, Trisacetate, and TAPS in a pH range of 7.0–9.0. These buffers have the advantage of low conductivity, minimizing Joule heating and allowing higher buffer concentrations to be used. High buffer concentrations also can help minimize interactions between the DNA and the capillary wall and stabilize DNA conformation. Other buffers have also been examined. For example, residual primers and dNTPs are separated better at low pH, presumably due to differences in charge between the four bases under these conditions.

The choice of buffer additives for PCR analysis is dependent on whether single-stranded (ssDNA) or double-stranded DNA (dsDNA) is to be analyzed. In general, ssDNA separations yield higher resolution and are less complicated by PCR artifacts such as heteroduplex formation and variations in sequence. Detection of ssDNA requires labeling the DNA through the use of fluorescent primers or other means. The DNA solution is denatured prior to analysis by dilution in a formamide solution and heating to 95°C prior to analysis. To prevent reannealing, urea or formamide is added to the buffer, and the temperature of the separation is increased to greater than 50°C. Problems with the use of these additives include the limited shelf-life of urea solutions, the tendency of urea solutions to sublimate, and the toxic nature of formamide.

Double-stranded DNA requires less treatment prior to analysis. For both UV and fluorescence detection, intercalating dyes can be added to the buffer to enhance resolution. These dyes have also been shown to minimize the effects of sequence variations on migration time. In addition, EDTA can be added to the buffer to chelate excess magnesium from the PCR reaction, and alkaline salts can be used to alter the ionic strength of the buffer and minimize osmotic flow. The use of such salts may also aid in preventing the formation of secondary structures, as the formation of ion pairs will help to stabilize the DNA molecule in solution.

Injection and sample preparation

One of the major advantages of a CE system is its capability to perform automated injections. In general, there are two modes of injection: hydrodynamic and electrokinetic. Hydrodynamic injections are performed using pressure to force the sample solution into the capillary. This injection technique can only be carried out using soluble polymer buffers, as pressure injections into crosslinked gels would disrupt the interior of the capillary. Hydrodynamic injections are particularly well suited for quantitative analyses. When properly initiated, reproducible quantities of sample may be introduced onto the capillary. *Standard deviations* (SD) of injection volume have been shown to be approx 3%. However, the broad injection bands produced in this technique tend to limit resolution.

Electrokinetic injections are performed using an applied voltage to induce the sample to migrate into the capillary. Unlike hydrodynamic injections, this process is a function of the injection voltage, injection time, and sample matrix. Sample ions with a higher charge-to-mass ratio than DNA will tend to be injected selectively into the capillary. Thus, the ionic strength of the sample may alter the applied field.

The injection of PCR products into a capillary is particularly difficult because the products are contained in a salt matrix (>50 m*M* Cl^-), which inhibits the injection. To overcome these problems, PCR samples are purified by means of dialysis, spin columns, or ethanol

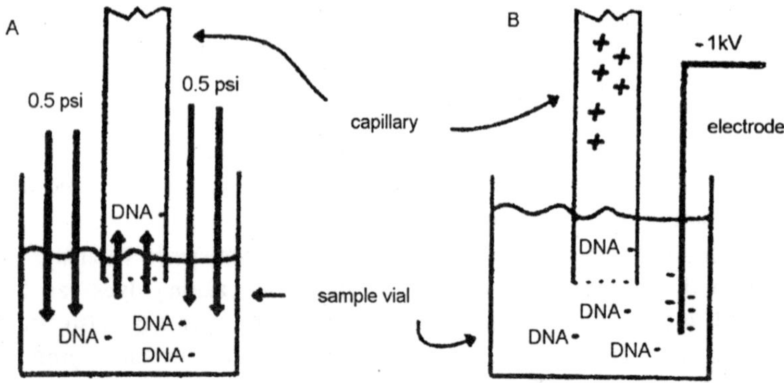

Fig. 5.5. The two injection modes of CE. A–In hydrodynamic injection; B–In electrokinetic injection.

precipitation. The dialysis step appears to be the most effective for removing excess salt, whereas the spin columns are more effective at removing primer peaks, enzyme, and dNTPs. Dilution of the sample in water or deionized formamide is another technique for eliminating injection interferences.

These steps greatly improve the injection by removing interferences, and by enhancement of a process known as *stacking*. Stacking, also called *field amplified injection*, occurs when the ionic strength of the sample zone is lower than that of the buffer. Because the current through the system is constant, the lack of charged carriers in the sample zone produces a strong electric field that ends abruptly at the

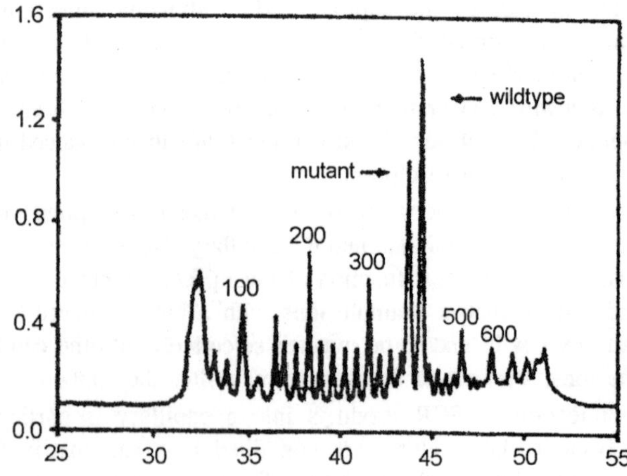

Fig. 5.6. An illustration of the 45-s separation of two PCR products coinjected with a 20 basepair sizing ladder.

interface between the sample zone and the buffer inside the capillary. DNA molecules mobilized by this field move rapidly towards the capillary as the injection voltage is applied and "*stack*" in a narrow zone at the interface. Stacking allows a large sample zone to be loaded onto the capillary with a minimum of band broadening. Stacking also aids in producing efficient separations. The sharper the injection zone, the less gel media is required to effect a separation. Extremely short columns and microchips have exploited this fact to produce rapid and efficient separations of PCR products. The effective length of the capillary was 2 cm.

Detection and Data Analysis

In early separations of PCR products by CE, UV absorbance was the method of detection. PCR products analyzed by this procedure required extensive deionization and concentration prior to analysis. The relatively short path length and the dispersion produced by the capillary walls limited sensitivity. *Laser-induced fluorescence* (LIF) solved the problem of sensitivity by focusing the light beam directly onto the capillary window. Detection enhancements of 400-fold or more have been achieved using LIF as compared to UV detection.

Fluorescence detection of dsDNA is primarily achieved through the use of intercalating dyes. These dyes bind to the DNA molecule by inserting themselves into the DNA helix, affecting the configuration of the aromatic rings of the dye and enhancing the fluorescence signal. Additionally, intercalating dyes help to minimize effects of DNA structure on migration rate, resulting in better estimates of fragment lengths. The low background fluorescence of the uncomplexed dyes allows them to be added directly to the CE buffer. Monomeric intercalating dyes such as ethidium bromide, thiazole orange, and oxazole yellow have proven to be the most useful, providing precise and reproducible estimates of DNA size and quantity.

Fluorescent dye molecules may also be covalently bound to the DNA fragments. Labeling one or both of the primers prior to the amplification step can perform this most efficiently. After completion of the PCR, all of the target DNA molecules are labeled with a fluorophore. By labeling a series of different primers with a number of different dyes, several loci may be targeted, amplified, and labeled in a single multiplexed reaction. These dyes absorb at similar wavelengths but emit at different wavelengths. A multichannel analyzer can then identify the specific PCR product by detecting the various emission wavelengths of the bound dye.

The development of methods for data analysis by CE is of particular importance in the examination of PCR products. Precise and reliable methods must be developed for product analysis. Slab gel methods permit the analysis of multiple samples run concurrently. At present, CE is a serial technique and samples can only be run one at a time. Thus, comparison of multiple samples requires the addition of internal standards to correct for the inevitable variations in injection, temperature, and current. This observation is particularly relevant in quantitative methods where variations in sample injection can limit the usefulness of the technique.

When adding internal standards for quantitation, it is important that they do not interfere with the detection of the PCR product. When intercalating dyes are used in the analysis, peak intensity is a function of the length of the PCR product, and corrections for product length may be necessary. A further concern in PCR analysis using these dyes is the effect of buffer depletion on the sample fluorescence intensity and migration time. For this reason, buffer vials must be periodically replenished to avoid depletion of the intercalating dye and pH variations.

Size estimates of PCR products can be performed by interpolation of size based on the migration of one or more internal standards. For products in the size range from 100–400 bp, a linear relationship exists between size and migration time. The size of larger products may

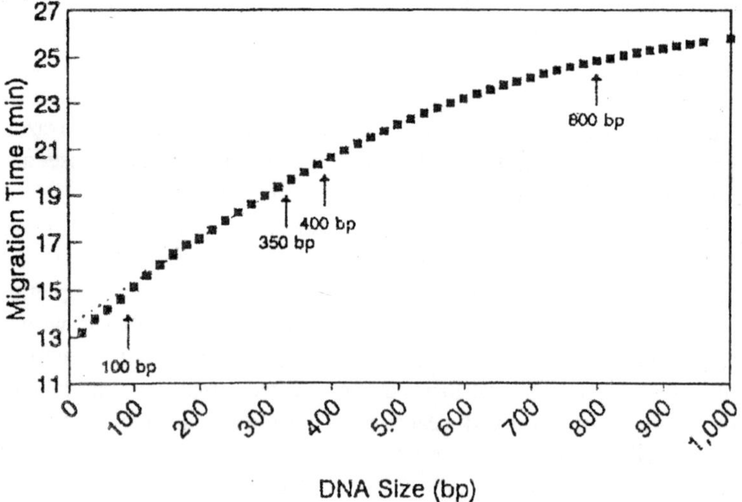

Fig. 5.7. The relationship between DNA size and migration time for native DNA.

also be estimated using nonlinear, curve-fitting algorithms. Specialized instrumentation has been developed specifically for DNA analysis utilizing internal standards that have been labeled with a fluorescence dye different than that of the product. For such systems, interferences between sample and standard are much less of a problem, and specific algorithms have been developed to deconvolute the fluorescence signals and perform size estimates.

Applications

Most applications of CE for the analysis of PCR products have been adapted from slab gel assays. A number of current reviews have discussed many of these applications. Recently, studies have begun to appear in which the advantages of CE, such as high speed, low sample requirement, and automation, have been exploited. These advantages, which aid in tracking of large databases and permit easy setup and operation of the equipment, match the needs of the forensic community. They are also responsible for the increasing acceptance of the technique.

In the next section, the two main applications of the technique, DNA sizing and quantitation, will be covered. The section will conclude with a discussion of future applications including DNA sequencing, in-line PCR, and microchip based separations.

DNA sizing/genetic analysis

DNA fragments above a certain minimum length have roughly the same charge to mass ratio, making them migrate at approximately the same rate in free solution. As mentioned earlier, the addition of a sieving agent permits a separation of the DNA as a function of its size. By correlating migration time with the molecular weight of the fragments, an estimate of the DNA size is produced. Conformational differences can create some variations in this result, especially for dsDNA. However, the analysis of DNA used in forensic analysis has shown precise correlations between DNA size and migration time.

Most applications of CE involving DNA sizing utilize PCR to amplify specific regions in the genome in which changes in length or sequence can occur. Highly variable, polymorphic sites are located that contain repetitive DNA in which a particular sequence of bases is repeated multiple times. This type of polymorphism is known as a *variable number tandem repeat* (VNTR). The different alleles, which are produced by the VNTRs used in forensic testing, are distributed randomly through a population. The frequency of occurrence of a particular allele in a population potentially can be used to identify the perpetrator of a crime. A useful subset of VNTRs known as *short tandem repeats* (STRs)contains repeat motifs that are typically four bases in length. An example of an STR might be the sequence ATTGC $(AATG)_n$ AAGTG. STRs are typically produced with sizes ranging from 100–400 base pairs in length depending on the primers used.

Recently, CE has been used to detect STR fragments resulting from reactions in which several sets of primers are combined. These multiplexed amplifications allow a series of genetic markers to be probed simultaneously. In situations where the amount of available DNA is limited, multiplexed amplifications also allow a larger amount of information to be gathered from a single sample.

The development of commercial CE with multichannel fluorescence detection has extended such applications by enabling the user to track the positions of different amplified products individually labeled with specific fluorescent dyes. The dyes that are used are excited by one or more laser lines and contain emission maxima that are sufficiently separated to allow deconvolution of overlapped peaks. Kits have been developed that allow amplification of 10 or more STR systems simultaneously, which allow identification of a unique person with probabilities of 1 in 10^{11} or greater. For these reasons, multiplexed amplification of STRs using multiwavelength fluorescence is currently

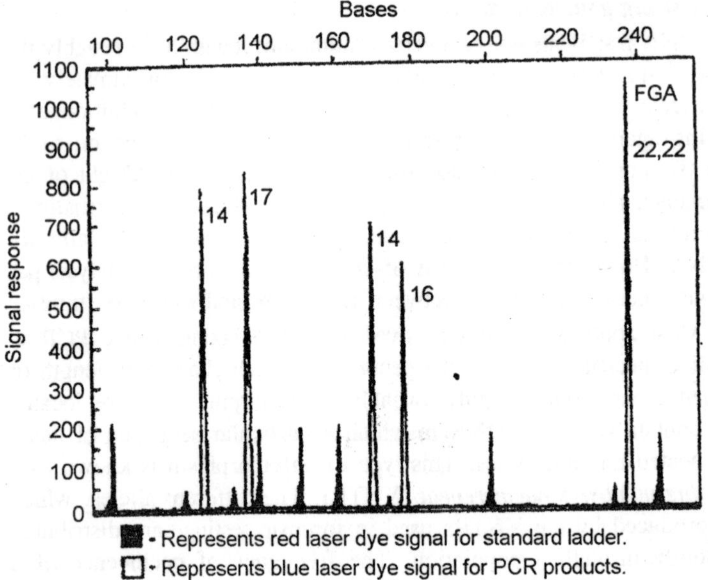

Fig. 5.8. Dual wavelength detection of a multiplex amplified PCR product consisting of three genetic loci, D351358, vWA, and FGA.

being implemented in many forensic laboratories worldwide. The sample is diluted in purified formamide and denatured. An internal standard labeled with a red-emitting dye is added to each sample to estimate fragment size. The samples are then analyzed using a viscous buffer containing a soluble polymer in addition to 7 *M* urea to keep the sample DNA denatured. The analysis temperature is kept at 60°C to melt out (eliminate) secondary structures that can cause problems with reproducibility.

Analytical aspects in developing a CE separation

Among the instrumental factors that are important in developing a CE assay for genetic typing, precision and resolution are perhaps the most important. These two issues, however, are not dependent on each other. Precision is determined by the run to run reproducibility of the migration time of the peak apex, whereas resolution is a function of band broadening and column efficiency.

The precision of the assay is important because it defines the minimum difference in allele size that can be determined. For example, if the size of a particular allele is 200 bases with a standard deviation of 0.17 bases, then 99.3% of the time that allele will be given a size of 200 bases, assuming a normal distribution of the data. Such precision is important given the existence of variant alleles that can differ from the normal 4 base repeat motif by 1–3 bases. In addition, many forensic samples are mixtures of more than one donor.

The mixture problem also can be a factor when resolution is considered. In the aforementioned example, the precision of 0.17 bases permits us to distinguish between a peak at 200 and 201 bases. However if the resolution,

$$R = \frac{(t_2 - t_1)}{0.5(w_2 - w_1)},$$

between the two peaks is 0.67 or less, it will be difficult to resolve these two peaks. If the area of peak 1 is more than three times that of peak 2, the two peaks will appear to co-elute, as the system will not have the capacity to separate the two peaks.

Thus, when developing a protocol for the analysis of mixtures by CE, it is important to consider both precision and resolution. As mentioned earlier, the precision is determined by factors that affect the stability of the measurement; temperature, injection, and sample conformation. The resolution is primarily affected by the polymer concentration and by the effects of sample stacking on injection. Both factors must be characterized to achieve optimum results.

A third issue that can be of importance is the determination of peak area. In situations where mixtures are present, the peak area can help define which samples are related. With proper control of the PCR conditions, the areas of related sample alleles will be consistent from one locus to the next, allowing the user to determine major and minor contributors to the electrophoretic profile. There are, however, important exceptions to this rule, which arise from the nature of the PCR reaction and from the injection process. Issues in the PCR process include artifacts such as stutter, in which a minor product band is produced one repeat unit shorter than the main allele. Values of stutter of 4–9% were reported for the vWA locus. The presence of stutter can affect the areas of peaks by decreasing the efficiency of amplification of the main peak, and by interfering with the areas of nearby peaks. PCR efficiency can also be affected by low quantities of template and improper reaction conditions. Another factor to consider is matrix effects on sample injection. The sample matrix can influence the overall peak area from one run to the next, however, this effect can be corrected through proper reference to the internal standard.

At present there have been a number of reports in the literature regarding the analytical capability of capillary systems for typing STRs. At least three different polymer systems have been reported for multiplex PCR analysis: hydroxyethyl cellulose, polydimethyl acrylamide, and linear polyacrylamide. Resolution varies between 1 and 2 bases depending on the size of the allele and the concentration and type of the polymer. Reported precision of the estimated allele size as measured by standard deviation ranges from 0.16–0.23 bases. These results clearly show that 2 base differences will be easily distinguished by these systems and depending on the allele size and polymer type, single-base differences may also be distinguished. In an extensive forensic validation study, Wallin and coworkers demonstrated and compared the results on the validation of the AmpliSTR Blue locus using both slab gels and CE. In this work, population samples from different racial groups were examined as well as studies on the effect of environment, sample matrix, and sample mixtures. The results portray an exclusion of the suspect in the first case: however, in the second case suspect 2 is a potential contributor of the sample DNA.

Other applications for CE in forensic DNA analysis

In certain situations, such as the analysis of hair or highly degraded DNA, there is insufficient nuclear DNA to yield an amplified product of sufficient quantity to type. In this situation, there may still be enough mitochondrial DNA to provide genetic information. The DNA present in mitochondria is approx 16,000 bases long and contains a section known as the *control region* that contains a number of polymorphic sites, which are usually point mutations. Amplifying the region of interest and sequencing the product DNA can identify these polymorhic sites. CE is used in this process to determine if the amplified product is present in sufficient quantity and purity to be sequenced. CE has also been used to identify these mutations by subjecting the amplified mitochondrial fragments to restriction enzymes. Point mutations present in these products will affect the fragment patterns produced by the digestion. Finally, as CE sequencers become more widespread, both the product quantitation and the sequence analysis will be performed via CE.

Future Trends for CE and DNA Analysis

Capillary array electrophoresis

Because CE is by nature a serial operation, a single capillary system cannot match the sample throughput available in a multi-lane slab gel experiment. Higher throughput, however, is available with *capillary array electrophoresis* (CAE), where multiple capillaries are run in parallel. Separation times are on the order of 15–50 min, but up to 96 samples can be analyzed simultaneously. Each DNA sample is analyzed in an individual capillary and migration times are adjusted using an internal lane standard. A recent demonstration of the throughput capabilities of CAE included the generation of over 8000 genotypes on a 48-capillary instrument in a matter of days. This type of CAE instrument will probably find application in laboratories which genotype a large number of samples.

Automation and CE

Automation of the entire process from extracted DNA to analyzed PCR product is an important issue for large laboratories. The potential of coupling CE analysis to the previous sample preparation steps of DNA extraction, PCR amplification, or restriction digestion has already been demonstrated with robotics and microchip fluidics. The rapid speed of CE separations cannot be translated into sustainable high-throughput operations until the entire process, including sample preparation and data analysis, is fully automated.

Microchip CE assays

The advent of photolithography has permitted micromachining of capillary channels in glass. Because of the small dimensions of the

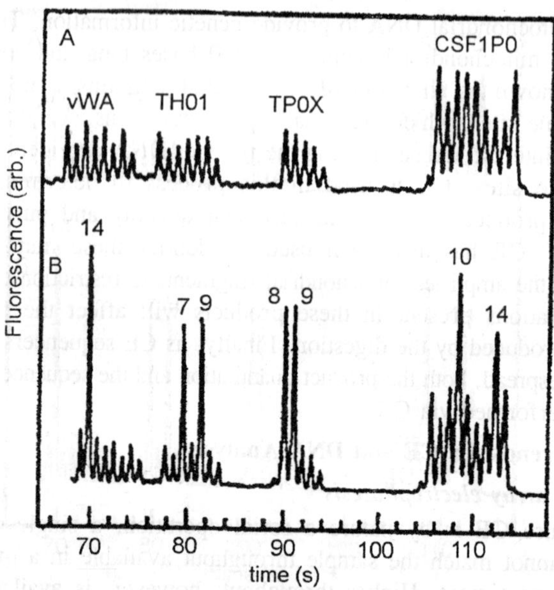

Fig. 5.9. Microchip separation of a multiplex of 4 STRs: (A) allelic ladder (B) allelic ladder spiked with amplified sample.

separation channels, separations may be performed even more rapidly than with conventional CE equipment. DNA restriction fragments have been separated in a matter of seconds using channels that are only a few centimeters in length. One of the major challenges in microchip CE analysis is sample preparation on a scale that is compatible with the small device. Integration of sample preparation steps with the separation portion is one solution to this dilemma. The recent integration of PCR and CE on a microchip illustrates that such devices may soon be available.

The advantages of CE, including single-sample analysis speed and automation, have resulted in its increasing visibility in molecular biology and forensic DNA laboratories. Multichannel fluorescence CE systems have become the instrument of choice for STR analysis in many DNA typing laboratories, primarily because of the appealing aspect of unattended operation, a fact that frees busy forensic scientists to work on other tasks. Recently developed commercial 96-capillary array instruments promise to improve dramatically sample throughput capabilities. CE is reliable and reproducible when performed carefully, and as the number and variety of applications increase, a greater role for CE in the future of DNA separations can be anticipated.

Combining Capillary Electrophoresis with Electrospray Ionization Mass Spectrometry

Since its first introduction in 1981 by Lucaks and Jorgenson, *capillary electrophoresis* (CE) has become a rapidly expanding analytical technique that has been successfully employed in a wide range of analytical areas, including pharmaceutical, agrochemical, and environmental fields and in clinical, pharmacological, and drug metabolism studies. The reasons for this fast breakthrough are the high efficiency, short analysis time, rapid method development, and simple instrumentation. Other advantages include the very small sample quantities (e.g., femtomoles) that can be analyzed. This is particularly important for studies in which sample size is limited. In addition, exotic and/or expensive *background electrolyte* (BGE) solutions can be used with minimal cost and disposal problems because of the low usage associated with CE compared to liquid chromatography. Because of the numerous publications in peer-reviewed journals, CE has been established as a method that is complementary to the more conventional separation techniques, such as *high-performance liquid chromatography* (HPLC) and *gas chromatography* (GC).

Ultraviolet-visible (UV-VIS) spectrophotometry has been found to be one of the better methods for the on-line detection of compounds after separation by CE. (However, the CE-UV bottleneck is a relatively low sensitivity due to the short optical path-length afforded by the small internal diameters of capillaries.) Several approaches, such as extended path-lengths in Z-shaped detection cells, bubble cells, or rectangular capillaries, have been used to enhance sensitivity, but usually at the expense of efficiency. In addition, many important biological substances do not possess a chromophore, thus requiring derivatization to detect them. In an effort to over-come this problem, indirect UV detection was developed. This technique, however, has serious sensitivity limitations. Electrochemical detection (EC) has also been investigated but has found only limited applications since it depends on the electrochemical characteristics of the specific analyte. In addition, interfacing EC with CE presents two unique problems: electrical decoupling of CE and EC electronics, and physical alignment of the electrode with the end of the capillary. In order to enhance sensitivity efforts have recently focused on the use of fluorescence, especially laser-induced fluorescence, however, this detection mode is limited to compounds that are fluorescent. As with some of the other detection methods most of the compounds of interest have to be tagged, e.g., with a fluorophore. Such procedures require additional expertise, are tedious and generally compromise the advantages of CE. Another problem with spectroscopic detectors is that peak identity is generally confirmed using migration times. This information, however, is often insufficient to unequivocally identify compounds of interest since real world samples often contain unknown interferences and the parameters influencing migration time are not easily controlled in CE.

Mass spectrometry, on the other hand, is rapidly becoming one of the detectors of choice in micro-separation techniques, including μ-LC and CE. This selective and highly sensitive detector opens up additional possibilities in analytical techniques by allowing high analysis speed in addition to providing information about the mass and, potentially, the structure of the separated compounds. This information is highly desirable to unequivocally identify components in complex mixtures. However, as a result of the small loading capacity and high separation efficiency, coupling of CE to MS is not without problems.

This section will not attempt to review the numerous methods that researchers have used to overcome the problem in interfacing (hyphenation) CE to MS since excellent reviews (on the interfacing of CE to MS) have been published during the last few years. Instead, this section will focus on practical considerations for successful CE-MS coupling using electrospray ionization interface with special emphasis on the sheath flow or coaxial design which is currently applied in most CE-MS combinations. Practical aspects including background electrolyte composition for effecient and selective CE preparation as well as optimal ESI-MS detection are developed. Additionally, representative CE modes, such as capillary zone electrophoresis, nonaqueous CE, chiral CE and *micellar electrokinetic chromatography* (MEKC) illustrating the potential of CE-ESI-MS in drug analysis are discussed. Further, collision-induced dissociation to differentiate positional isomers which cannot be separated by CZE is also presented. Finally, a survey of CE-MS analytical applications dealing with small molecules, such as drugs and metabolites, is included.

Combining CE with ESI-MS

Electrospray ionization

Since the first report developed by Olivares and coworkers, several ionization methods have been applied for CE-MS coupling. *Matrix-assisted laser desorption ionization* (MALDI), *inductively coupled plasma* (ICP) ionization, as well as soft ionization techniques, such as continuous flow *fast atom bombardment* (FAB) and *electrospray ionization* (ESI), have been described for the coupling of CE to MS. However, as indicated by literature, electrospray ionization is still the most widely used ionization technique. It has been applied to a large variety of compounds interfacing with many types of MS, including quadrupoles, magnetic sector, fourier transform ion cyclotron resonance, time-of-flight, and trapping devices.

Electrospray (ES), first introduced by Yamashita and Fenn, is a method by which ions present in a solution can be transferred to the gas phase. Today, it is generally agreed that the ES process involves three steps prior to mass analysis:

1. Generation and charging of the electrospray droplets at the ESI capillary tip;
2. Shrinkage of the charged droplets by solvent evaporation and repeated droplet disintegration, ultimately leading to very small highly charged droplets capable of producing gas-phase ions; and
3. The actual mechanism by which gas-phase ions are produced from the very small and highly charged droplets.

The benefits of ESI include the ability to produce extensively multiply charged ions and direct mass information on virtually all types of mass spectrometers, small sample requirement, and compatibility with high resolution techniques, such as CE. The ESI technique is especially suited for the analysis of moderately polar and thermo labile compounds possessing a mass range from 10^2 to 10^5 Daltons.

CE-MS interface

The interface between CE and ESI-MS is one of the keys to the success of CE-ESI-MS technique. Unlike UV-VIS or fluorescence detection, which can be performed on-column, the effluent from CE must be physically transported to the mass spectrometer without sacrificing separation efficiency. Three main interfaces have been described, including liquid–liquid junction interfaces, sheath–liquid interfaces, and sheathless interfaces. However, because of its instrumental simplicity and versatility, along with the possibility of enhancing the ionization process by chemical reaction, the coaxial sheath-flow interface is by far the most popular interface for CE-ESI-MS. A concise description of the interfaces used and their working principle are described in considerably more detail elsewhere.

However, to successfully interface CE to ESI-MS, a number of points have to be considered and specific problems overcome, as outline below:

1. In conventional CE the capillary ends (at the anode and cathode) are placed in separation buffer reservoirs and an electric field is applied to achieve electrophoretic separation. Thus, the first purpose of the CE-MS interface is to establish an electrical connection at the capillary terminus, which serves to define the electric field along the CE capillary. The electrical connection at the capillary terminus also serves to establish an electrospray source voltage difference (3–5 kV) between the terminus and sample aperture of the mass spectrometer.
2. The electrospray process is optimal for an effluent flow rate on the order of 1–10 μL/min. In order for the interface to function properly it is necessary to closely match the CE flow rate, typically between 0 and 100 nL/min, with the flow rates generally required by ESI techniques. To overcome this difference in flow rate, an additional fluid (make-up flow) is added coaxially to the CE capillary outlet supplementing the CE flow to that required for ESI. The addition of an external sheath liquid may, however, induce dilution of the separated analytes. In this context, the use of micro- or nanospray sources are interesting alternatives to produce a stable electrospray at the very low flow rates typical of CE while still providing a highly sensitive and efficient interface.
3. CE-ESI-MS coupling induces some limitations concerning the type and concentration of the background electrolyte solution. As such, nonvolatile buffers commonly used in *capillary zone electrophoresis* (CZE), such as phosphate, borate, and citrate, are not compatible with CE-MS. The use of a makeup flow containing 50–80% organic solvent, however, may overcome this problem. Nonvolatile buffers also adversely affect the performance of the MS by enhancing the risk of contamination of the ionization chamber and suppressing the analyte signal. In addition, other additives, such as surfactants, cyclodextrins, as well as ion-pairing agents, commonly used to improve selectivity in CZE, are not suitable for ESI-MS. Because of these problems, volatile buffers, such as formic acid, acetic acid, ammonium acetate, ammonium formate, and ammonium carbonate, are often recommended for CE-ESI-MS. The use of capillary electrochromatography, partial-filling technique, or nonaqueous media are interesting alternatives to extend the application range of CE-MS and will be discussed in more detail in the following section. It is also well documented that efficiency of CZE is best in the presence of high ionic strength buffers, the opposite required for optimum ESI-MS to produce gas phase ions.

4. The scan rate of MS may not be adequate to reflect the high separation efficiency (peak width of a few seconds) and resolution of CE. However, by using *selected ion monitoring* mode (SIM) on single quadrupole instruments, significant enhancement of detection limits compared to those obtained with scanning MS operation is possible. This is because of the greater dwell time for signal acquisition at each selected m/z value. Thus, if the MW is known prior to separation, SIM can be used to further improve separation resolution and reduce detection limits. Another alternative in dealing with the speed of CE is to use ion trap and time-of-flight analyzers, which can record a full-scan spectra over a large mass range within 100–200 ms. In addition, using a reduced flow rate method, Goodlett and coworkers were able to both improve sensitivity and alleviate scan speed limitations for CE-MS. In this technique just prior to elution of the first analyte of interest into the ESI source, the electrophoretic voltage is decreased, slowing solute elution, and thus allowing more scans to be recorded without significant loss in ion intensity. This has been found to be particularly useful for polypeptides and proteins where broad m/z range spectra can be important in determination of the molecular weight.

Once each of these issues has been identified and resolved CE can then be interfaced to MS. The fused silica capillary is located in the center of the sprayer and performs the electrophoretic separation. The middle capillary (usually stainless steel) provides a coaxial sheath liquid make-up flow to ensure stable electrospray as well as electrical contact at the capillary outlet. The outer capillary, also in stainless steel, supplies a nebulizing gas flow to assist in droplet generation and shrinkage during the electrospray. In contrast to the API sources described so far, the sprayer is positioned orthogonally to the sampling orifice.

The addition of a nebulizing gas, in combination with a high voltage, is generally used to assist solvent evaporation, a prerequisite for successful electrospray ionization. This co-flow reduces the likelihood of ions penetrating from the sheath liquid into the CE capillary. However, the aspirating (siphoning) effect of a high flow rate of the coaxial sheath gas has been reported to affect separation quality resulting from a pressure-induced flow. Moreover, to avoid siphoning effects, CE and MS instruments must be positioned close together and the outlet end of the CE capillary maintained at the same height as the inlet end.

Several investigations directed toward optimization of CE-MS performance have demonstrated that small inner diameter capillaries (5–10 μm) provided a 25–50-fold gain in sensitivity as compared to 50–100 μm id capillaries. This sensitivity enhancement was attributed to an increase in ionization efficiency resulting from a decreased mass flow rate of the background electrolyte for smaller id capillaries. In addition to reducing the size of the capillaries, Tomlinson et al. described methods for conditioning the CE capillary as well as configuring the CE-ESI-MS interface to further optimize CE-MS performance. Dimensions of the capillaries used to construct a typical coaxial CE-ESI-MS interface have also been shown to affect the sensitivity and stability. These studies demonstrated that thick-walled capillaries can further enhance the system performance. Additionally, appropriate selection of the sheath liquid may improve significantly electrospray characteristics and ionization efficiency. Finally, the positioning of the CE capillary with regard to the spray needle tip was found to significantly affect CE separation efficiency and resolution. To achieve the best performance, the CE capillary must barely protrude from the ESI needle. If the capillary protrudes too much, stability of the Taylor cone is compromised and electrical contact with the CE capillary may be lost. If the CE capillary is withdrawn inside the ESI needle, separation efficiency can be dramatically affected, to an extent that the signal may be lost. Because of this problem commercial CE-ESI-MS interfaces have been designed to adjust capillary protrusion using a screw.

Applications

Since CE-MS applications have already been presented and reviewed for analysis of large macromolecules like peptides, proteins, nucleotides, and oligosaccharides, the present application review will be restricted to small molecules like drugs, byproducts, and metabolites.

This section will concentrate on four major modes:

1. Capillary zone electrophoresis (CZE);
2. Nonaqueous CE (NACE);
3. Micellar electrokinetic chromatography (MEKC); and
4. Chiral CE.

Capillary zone electrophoresis

CZE, which is strictly based on the electrophoretic properties of the analyte and buffer solution, is powerful and frequently used for CE-MS coupling. Two specific applications, amphetamines and carnitines, will be used to highlight the potential of CZE-MS coupling as well as the quantitative performance of the technique.

Because of their increasing illicit popularity, amphetamines and related derivatives are receiving more attention in clinical, pharmacological, and toxicological science, and monitoring their levels in biological fluids is of paramount importance. In our laboratory, a validated CZE method was reported for the determination of amphetamines and related derivatives sold on the black market in the form of tablets of various compositions. However, because of the relatively low sensitivity afforded by the short optical path-length of the capillary, UV detection (UV) of these drugs in biological matrices (e.g., urine or serum) was a challenge. To overcome the limitation of sensitivity, CZE was interfaced with ESI-MS for the analysis of ecstasy and its derivatives. Considering the large number of parameters involved in CE-ESI-MS coupling, a chemometric approach was carried out to optimize such factors as nebulization pressure, drying gas temperature and flow rate, electrospray voltage, skimmer voltage, sheath liquid composition, and its flow rate. After optimization of the CE-ESI-MS parameters and using a liquid–liquid extraction procedure, SIM was used to monitor only $(M+H)^+$ signals, which allowed a sensitive and unambiguous determination of these drugs in urine samples.

The other CE-MS application was used to separate free carnitine and acylcarnitines (carnitine esters), which play an important role in the metabolism of fatty acids. Many genetic disorders are also characterized by abnormal production of these compounds in biological

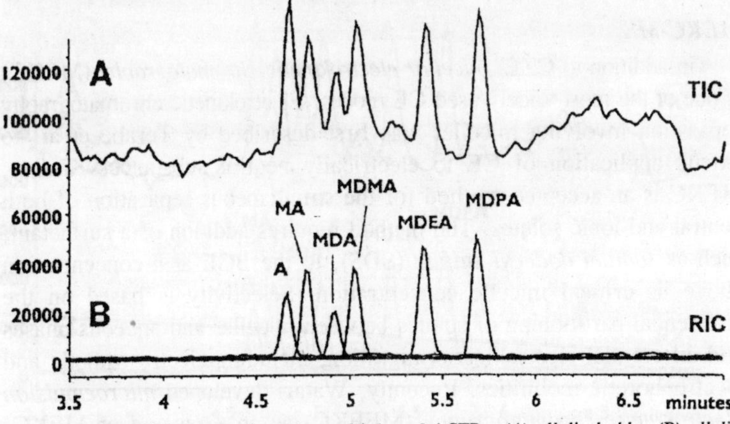

Fig. 5.10. Microchip separation of a multiplex of 4 STRs: (A) allelic ladder (B) allelic ladder spiked with amplified sample.

fluids. Henion et al. reported a CE-MS method for the determination of carnitine and several of its esters in human blood, plasma, and urine using preconcentration via sample preparation techniques. They tested a variety of MS detection modes, including scan, SIM, and *selected-reaction monitoring* (SRM) modes. For their application the latter (SRM) was preferred because of better selectivity and sensitivity. They also developed an abbreviated validation method to demonstrate the robustness of the SRM CE-MS method. Good quantitative data were achieved in terms of linearity, precision (0.8–14%), accuracy (85–111%), and limit of quantitation (0.1–1 nmol/mL). This application clearly indicates that CE-MS can meet the acceptance criteria for bioanalytical determinations and makes it an alternative for acylcarnitine determination in clinical samples.

The detection of several other classes of substances, e.g., designer drugs, nonopiod analgesics, nonsteroidal anti-inflammatory drugs (NSAIDs), benzodiazepines, β-adrenergic agents, plant metabolites, pesticides, and so forth have also been investigated. Depending on the nature of the compounds, both positive and negative ionization modes have been applied. Most applications are performed in the presence of volatile buffers to preserve ESI-MS sensitivity and minimize ion source fouling problems. In addition, organic solvents are often used in the BGE to increase analyte solubility, improve resolution, and lower surface tension, thus enhancing the electrospray process. Low concentration nonvolatile buffers can be used, although at the expense of some loss of ionization efficiency resulting from competition with analytes in ESI.

MEKC-MS

In addition to CZE, *micellar electrokinetic chromatography* (MEKC) is one of the most widely used CE modes. Electrokinetic chromatography separation involving micelles was first described by Terabe et al. to extend application of CE to electrically neutral substances. Today, MEKC is an accepted method for the simultaneous separation of both neutral and ionic solutes. The method requires addition of a surfactant, such as *sodium dodecyl sulfate* (SDS), to the BGE at a concentration above its critical micelle concentration. Selectivity is based on the differential partitioning of solutes between micellar and aqueous phases and differential electrokinetic migration, including electro-osmotic and electrophoretic mobilities. Recently, Watari developed *microemulsion electrokinetic chromatography* (MEEKC) as an extension of MEKC. However, hyphenation of MEKC with MS is severely hampered by the presence of nonvolatile ionic surfactants, which often leads to a significant loss of electrospray efficiency and ion source contamination. The signal suppression mechanism can best be explained by two factors: the reduction in the amount of solution that can be sprayed by ESI interface at elevated SDS concentrations, and interference of the transfer of cationic analytes from the droplet to the gas phase, because of coulombic interactions between analytes and negatively charged surfactant (SDS) ions. Various approaches have been reported for the on-line coupling of MEKC with MS and a recent review was given by Yang and Lee. MEKC-ESI-MS using high-molecular-mass surfactants (e.g., 40,000) to reduce the level of background ions in the low m/z region has been described. This method was applied to the separation and detection of a standard mixture of sulfamides. MEKC-MS hyphenation using a chemical ionization interface was also described for the analysis of aromatic amines. These authors pointed out that although ion intensity was not appreciably affected by the high concentration of nonvolatile salts and surfactants, the signal was completely quenched in the ESI mode.

In analogy to the phase-switching approach in liquid chromatography, a coupled capillary set-up allowing the possibility of voltage switching and buffer renewal has also been described. This system allows the transfer of zones of interest in the MEKC capillary to a second capillary and then to the MS. Foley and Masucci have also demonstrated that a semipermeable membrane can selectively allow small analyte molecules to pass through to a MS while retaining large buffer additives, such as surfactants. Anodically migrating micelles moving away from the ESI-MS have also been used to prevent micelles from entering the MS interface. This was done by adjusting the buffer pH and was applied to the analysis of chlortriazine herbicides and barbiturates. Alternatively, the *partial-filling* (PF) technique was found to be very useful for MEKC-MS applications. This technique involves filling the capillary with a BGE minus SDS, followed by a short period of introduction of enough solution containing SDS to achieve separation, and finally by a sample injection. Mechanistic studies of PF-MEKC have been discussed by Nelson and Lee. On-line PF-MEKC-MS applying an APCI interface was demonstrated for some pharmaceuticals as well as for industrial surfactants.

NACE-ESI-MS

Recently, the use of nonaqueous NA buffers in CE has been an area of increasing interest. When compared to water, the different chemical and physical properties of organic solvents (viscosity, dielectric constant, polarity, auto-protolysis-constant, electrical conductivity, and so forth) can improve selectivity considerably (a challenging task in the separation science) and reduce Joule heating. Moreover, organic solvents have proved to be useful in analyzing hydrophobic compounds as well as drugs and metabolites, which are difficult to separate in aqueous buffers. Very high efficiency and resolution, short analysis times, and the ability to selectively increase analyte solubility are the main reasons for this success. The selectivity differences observed between aqueous and nonaqueous media have been attributed to changes in solvation of the analytes, dissociation of both analytes and silanol groups from the capillary surface, as well as possible ion-pairing effects. Finally, using an organic solvent with a volatile electrolyte affords MS compatibility because it improves the evaporation of the electrospray droplets.

When we were investigating the potential of electrophoretic techniques for the analysis of amphetamines, NACE was interfaced with ESI-MS and UV detection at 200 nm. This method was optimized and applied to the analysis of amphetamine derivatives in urine samples. The quantitative performances of the method were also evaluated and showed high sensitivity as well as good reproducibility in terms of migration time and peak area ratio. In comparison to aqueous CE-ESI-MS methods previously described, NACE had different selectivities

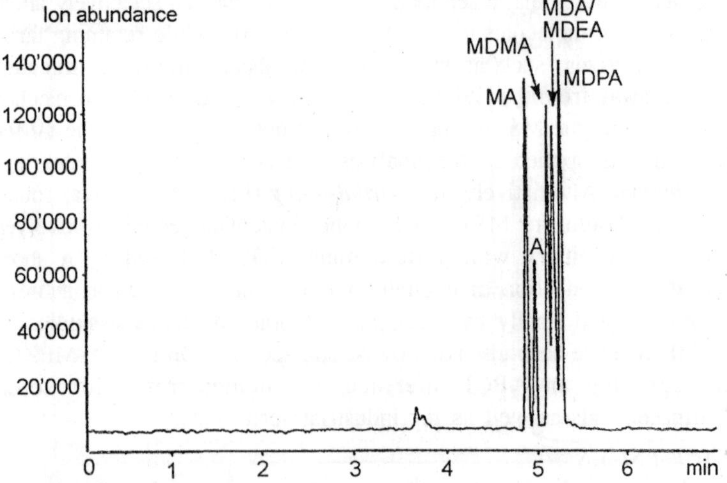

Fig. 5.11. NACE-ESI-MS of RIC of a urine sample spiked with a standard amphetamine mixture.

and resulted in an efficiency improvement. In addition, the electric current was very low in presence of the methanol-acetonitrile mixture and allowed good CE-MS compatibility.

A NACE-ESI-MS method was also developed and successfully applied to the analysis of several NSAIDs. UV detection was performed at 200 nm, 20 cm from the inlet end, whereas ESI-MS detection occurred at the capillary outlet, which accounts for the apparently greater migration times for the ESI-MS separation. Both MS and UV signals from the DAD were acquired in the same run, allowing peak assignment with a very high confidence. Moreover, with volatile organic solvents a lower electrospray voltage can be applied, considerably reducing the electric discharge that can be observed in the negative polarity mode. NACE has been successfully applied to a large number of clinically relevant compounds, including phospholipids, organic acids, venlafaxine and metabolites, tamoxifen, and tricyclic antidepressants. NACE-ESI-MS was also useful in determining the mechanism of the in vitro microsomal metabolism of pyrazoloacridine, an antitumor drug, as well as the in vitro metabolism of H2-antagonist mifentidine.

Chiral CE-MS

Enantiomeric separation of chiral molecules is an area of utmost importance in separation science since enantiomer may have different pharmacological and toxicological properties. Thus, rapid, efficient, and sensitive analytical methods must be developed for the chiral purity control of drugs as well as pharmacokinetic and/or clinical studies. Recently, CE has become an interesting alternative to classical chromatographic techniques, such as GC and HPLC, for the stereoselective analysis of chiral drugs. Enantioseparations are generally performed by adding a chiral selector to the running buffer. Various additives acting as chiral selectors, such as *cyclodextrins* (CDs), crown ethers, proteins, antibiotics, bile salts, and chiral micelles, have been reported in the literature. Nevertheless, CDs are by far the most widely used selectors in chiral CE. Neutral CD derivatives, presenting various functional groups, have been developed to induce different stereoselective interactions and enhance enantiomeric resolution. Recently, anionic substituted CDs, such as sulfated, sulfobutylether, phosphated, and carboxymethylated CDs, as well as cationic CDs, such as quaternary ammonium β-CD, have become commercially available and have been applied as chiral selectors. Just like MEKC-MS, coupling chiral CE with ESI-MS can be difficult because of the negative effect of nonvolatile chiral selectors on MS performance.

Using MEKC-MS as a guide, Lamoree et al. described the on-line coupling of CE with MS for the enantioseparation of ropivacaine. Chiral purity determination by CE-MS was also demonstrated for pharmaceuticals, including terbutaline, ephedrine, ketamine, and propranolol. Under these conditions, the suppression effect of CD on the analyte signal was reported. However, by using the partial filling technique introduction of chiral selector into the MS was avoided. Similar to PF-MEKC, this involves filling a discrete portion of the capillary with a background electrolyte containing a chiral selector to achieve enantiomeric separation. Generally, a coated capillary is recommended to avoid any electroosmotic flow. In the case of basic compounds, negatively charged CDs are chosen since the application of the electric field results in a countercurrent process in which the chiral selector and the enantiomers migrate in opposite directions. This approach was applied in our laboratory for the enantioseparation of various pharmaceutical drugs and metabolites, including methadone, venlafaxine, and tramadol. In addition, negatively charged CDs add to the already high selectivity of MS to distinguish between metabolites with the same molecular mass, such as M1 and M2 as well as M3 and M5. CE-ESI-MS employing partial-filling technique was also reported in the literature for the separation of acidic and basic drugs in the presence of CDs, vancomycin, or avidin.

Collision-induced dissociation

Although electrospray is a soft ionization source, ions can be fragmented and structural information about a particular ion is sometimes available. Fragmentation can also be performed by means of tandem mass spectrometry (MS-MS), which requires a triple quadrupole or ion trap schemes for *collision-induced dissociation* (CID) of specified parent ions. It is, however, possible to perform fragmentation with a single quadrupole instrument by increasing the potential between the entrance capillary and the first skimmer (referred to as fragmentation voltage) within the ion-focusing region. (Insource CID is often used to provide information for structural elucidation of unknown compounds and confirmation of target analytes by using the abundance ratios of several diagnostic fragment ions.) CID with a single quadrupole system was successfully applied in our laboratory to separate and identify structural isomers, 3 ,4-methylenedioxyethyl-amphetamine (MDEA), and *N*-methyl-1 -(3,4-methylenedioxyphenyl)-2-butamine (MBDB), as well as plant secondary metabolites, hyocsyamine, and its positional isomer littorine. In addition to the protonated molecular ion m/z 290, both MS spectra showed a peak at m/z 124, which corresponds to the loss of tropic acid and phenyllactic acid for hyoscyamine and littorine, respectively. However, at high fragmenting voltage, the intermediate complex of littorine is less stable and results in the formation of tropine with a mass of 142. Therefore, at 200 V, this additional mass at m/z 142 indicates, without ambiguity, the presence of littorine in a plant extract. These results were assessed by tandem mass spectrometry (ESI/MS/MS) instrumentation. Thus, up-front CID can either afford structural information or generate confirmation ions in quantitative analysis with single MS, which increases result reliability.

Concluding Remark

The coupling of CE (with its high separation efficiency) and electrospray ionization MS (with its high selectivity and low concentration detection limits) can provide rapid, sensitive, and unequivocal quantification and identification of drugs and metabolites in body fluids and complex mixtures. Various laboratories are awaiting this potential for purity testing, quantitation, elucidation, and confirmation of drug metabolism as well as pharmacological and toxicological studies.

Combining CE with MS allows efficient separation and identification of important biological compounds, such as pharmaceuticals, carbohydrates, peptides, proteins, and glycoforms. As more instruments interfacing CE with MS become more available, the number of applications will continue to grow. However, since most of the published applications have used model compounds, future work should focus on real-life samples. Moreover, additional studies will be necessary to evaluate whether this technique fulfills the validation criteria recommended by official guidelines required for the quantification of drugs and metabolites. Widespread acceptance of CE-MS within the electrophoretic and chromatographic community, as well as clinical and forensic laboratories, can only be realized by achieving such objectives.

Future CE-MS development will depend on increased sensitivity improvements. To overcome the insufficient concentration detection limit of CE caused by low injection volumes (approx 1–10 nL), several approaches are under investigation. These include sample stacking, isotachophoresis, and other sample concentration techniques commonly used in liquid chromatography, such as liquid–liquid and solid phase extraction, and more recently nanoelectrospray sources operating at low nanoliter per minute flow rates. With the advent of nonconventional MS instrumentation, such as ion-trap and TOF-MS, further sensitivity enhancements can be expected. Finally, considerable effort is directed toward the miniaturization of these techniques. Along these lines, direct coupling of compact and versatile micromachined chip devices to nanoelectrospray mass spectrometry systems is under development in different laboratories to achieve fast, selective, and sensitive analyses.

6

Sequencing of Mitochondrial DNA

Mitochondrial DNA (mtDNA) typing is increasingly used for the forensic identification of human remains. This is especially true when only limited quantities of sample are present, such as when the sample has undergone extensive degradation and nuclear-typing methods are ineffectual. One characteristic of mtDNA responsible for the increasing reliance is the high copy number of mtDNA per cell, with mtDNA existing in hundreds if not thousands of copies per cell. The discriminatory power of mtDNA testing arises from the polymorphic nature (between unrelated individuals) of the two hypervariable regions (HV1 and HV2) located within the D-loop of the mtDNA genome. The haploid, maternal inheritance patterns of mtDNA transmission between generations, allow an inclusion or exclusion to be made when the sample sequence is compared to that of a maternal reference. Related individuals will share similar polymorphisms relative to a consensus standard.

The initial DNA extraction and PCR amplification steps are crucial to obtaining mtDNA-sequence information from biological samples. A number of procedures for extraction of DNA from bone have been published, including the standard organic extraction (SDS/proteinase K and phenol-chloroform) procedure, a silica-based extraction method, and chelation. PCR amplification of degraded samples is generally more successful if smaller sequences are amplified. In our laboratory, each hypervariable region is amplified completely when amplified from fresh, or well-preserved templates, or in four separate reactions when amplified from degraded samples. Primer sets one (PS1) and two (PS2) are designed to amplify the HV1 region, while primer sets three (PS3) and four (PS4) amplify the HV2 region. Each primer-set pair contains overlapping regions, providing an additional quality-control check of the data. Both strands of the PCR product are then cycle-sequenced, using both forwardand reverse-sequencing primers.

DNA Sequence Analysis of PCR Products

Cycle sequencing combined with automated sequence analysis is a highthroughput strategy for DNA typing of the mtDNA. In our laboratory, PCR products of the mtDNA control region are cycle-sequenced using dye-terminator chemistry and then analyzed on a 373A DNA Sequencer. Dye-primer chemistry results in more normalized peak heights than that obtained with dye terminators; however, the technique also requires four separate sequencing reactions as well as increased quantities of template. The newest generation of cycle-sequencing polymerases, AmpliTaq, FS and Thermo Sequenase, greatly improve the disparity in peak heights found with the dye-terminator chemistry. Since each technique has additional advantages and disadvantages, an evaluation regarding which strategy to pursue should be made based on the application.

Analysis of the sequence electrophoretograms generated in cycle sequencing can require considerable manual editing. Typical problems include the incomplete removal of dye-terminators post-cycle sequencing, multiple PCR products in the template preparations, and mtDNA heteroplasmy (either lengthor sequence-based). Additionally, some inherent limitations in the methodology include the 5' sequence-dependent pattern for insertion of dye-terminators resulting in uneven peak heights and the differential migration of the distinct dye-terminators potentially disrupting the spacing of the ladder.

Materials

PCR Amplification of the Mitochondrial DNA Hypervariable Regions

1. The optimum amount of DNA template is between 10 and 1000 pg; however, amplification can be performed on <10 pg.
2. Taq DNA polymerase.
3. 2.5 mM deoxynucleoside triphosphates (dNTP) mixture (working concentration of 0.2 mM).
4. DNA-grade bovine serum albumin (BSA) at a working concentration of 4 μg.

5. Amplification primers at a working concentration of 10 μM.
6. 10X PCR buffer (1X): 10 mM Tris-HCl, pH 8.3, 50 mL KCl, and 1.5 mM $MgCL_2$.
7. Sterile deionized water.
8. Agarose (electrophoresis grade).
9. Agarose gel-loading buffer (6X): 50% glycerol, 1.5 mM bromophenol blue, 100 mM EDTA.
10. 10X TBE (1X): 89 mM Tris-HCl, pH 8.3, 89 mM boric acid, and 2 mM Na_2 EDTA.
11. 5 mg/mL ethidium bromide (working concentration 0.5 mg/mL).
12. DNA sizing ladder (123 base pair or other suitably sized control ladder).
13. 10% commercial bleach (7 mM sodium hypochlorite solution).
14. 667 Polaroid film.
15. 95% ethanol.
16. Centricon 100 Spin Dialysis Columns.
17. 9600 Perkin Thermal Cycler or suitable equivalent from another manufacturer.

DNA Sequence Analysis of PCR Products

1. The optimal amount of PCR template is 10-200 ng.
2. Urea, ultrapure.
3. PRISM Ready Reaction DyeDeoxy Terminator Cycle Sequencing Kit.
4. Sequencing primers diluted to a working concentration of 10 μM.
5. Quick Spin G-50 Spin Dialysis Columns.
6. Nalgene Disposable Filter Units, 0.2 μm.
7. 40% bis-acrylamide premix 19:1 5%C (electrophoresis purity).
8. Deionized formamide.
9. EDTA, 50 mM
10. 10% ammonium persulfate (made fresh weekly and stored at 25°C).
11. TEMED (*N*, *N*, *N*, *N*-tetramethylethylenediamine).
12. 373A DNA sequencer.
13. Heto vac (vacuum evacuator).
14. Heatblock.
15. DNA sequencing loading buffer (prepared fresh every day): 40 μg of 50 mM EDTA, 200 μg of deionized formamide (60 sequencing reactions).

METHODS

PCR Amplification of the Mitochondrial Hypervariable Regions

1. Due to the high sensitivity of the PCR-amplification technique, rigorous care must be taken to eliminate all potential contaminating practices or procedures prior to amplification. Wipe all pipeters, PCR tube racks, and the outside of gloves with 10% bleach. Allow bleach to dry before proceeding.
2. To prepare the PCR master-mix, add a volume of reagent equal to N + 1 times the volume added to a single reaction tube (where N is the total number of amplification reactions to be performed). Reaction components added to the master-mix include dH_2O, PCR buffer, dNTPs, the primers, and Taq polymerase (added last).
3. Thirty-two PCR cycles are run when amplifying good-quality template and 38 cycles for poor-quality templates. Each PCR cycle is composed of a 94°C denaturation step (20 s), followed by a 56°C annealing step (10 s), and a 72°C extension step (30 s). To increase the specificity of the primer set I reaction, replace the 56°C annealing temperature with 62°C.
4. Analyze PCR products on 1% agarose gels. Analysis should focus on the specificity and robustness of the reaction.
5. Unincorporated nucleotides and primers are removed from the PCR reactions by centrifugation through Centricon 100 spin dialysis columns. PCR products are added to 2 mL of sterile deionized water in a Centricon 100 spin dialysis column and centrifuged at a maximum of 1000 g for 15-20 min. An additional 2 mL of sterile deionized water is added and the columns are recentrifuged. The samples are collected into the supplied retentate cups by inverting the columns and centrifuging for 1 min. Transfer the recovered PCR product to a microtube, estimate the volume, and store at 4°C.
6. The recommended quantity of DNA template to use for sequencing depends on the size of the template, but 10-100 ng (25 ng optimal) for the AmpliTaq polymerase sequencing kits and 10 ng for the AmpliTaq FS polymerase kit work well with the PCR products described in this procedure.

DNA Sequence Analysis of PCR Products

1. At least two sequencing reactions are run per PCR product with forward and reverse primers. The sequence obtained from the reverse primer will complement that obtained from the forward

primer, providing additional confirmation of the data. The sequencing primers may be the same primers used in the PCR amplification reaction; however, certain advantages exist in using sequencing primers distinct from those used in the PCR reactions. Before sequencing, analyze product gels and determine which samples to sequence based on success of the amplification. Prepare each sequencing reaction as follows in a 0.2 mL thin-walled PCR microamp tube. A pGEM-3Zf(+) DNA control reaction (provided with both terminator kits) is set up (according to the manufacturer's instructions provided with the kit) as are the appropriate quality controls.

(a) 1 μg of 10 μM sequencing primer (either a forward or reverse primer).
(b) 1000 ng purified PCR product (10 ng if using the AmpliTaq FS kit).
(c) 9.5 μg of DNA Prism Ready Reaction mix.
(d) Q.S. to 20 μg with sterile deionized water.

2. The cycle-sequencing conditions are 96°C for 15 s (DNA denaturation), 50°C for 5 s (annealing), and 60°C for 2 min (extension). Twenty-five cycles are run followed by a rapid ramp to a 4°C holding temperature.
3. Quick spin columns are used to remove the unincorporated dye-terminators from sequenced products according to manufacturer's instructions.
4. Speed-desiccate the samples to dryness at room temperature. Desiccated samples may be stored for at least 1 mo at –20°C.
5. Prepare a 4.75% polyacrylamide-gel solution in 1X TBE. Allow the gel to polymerize for at least 1 h at room temperature. Ensure that plates are on a level surface during polymerization.
6. After polymerization, prerun the gel for at least 10 min at constant power of 28 W for ABI 373A stretch model or 30 W for regular 373A model. Ranges should be 980 600 V, 16 1 mA, and temperature at 40°C (although 40°C may not be reached during the prerun).
7. Resuspend the samples in 4 μg of loading buffer.
8. Heat the products at 96 μg for 2 min in a heat block and immediately place on ice before loading.
9. Gel run times are 8 h for the primer sets or 12 h for the entire HV1 or HV2 regions. Use the same run parameters as those used during the prerun.

Notes

1. In order to prevent contamination, all steps in this procedure should be performed in a laminar flow or dead-space hood, in a PCR-product-free environment. This is especially critical when poor-quality template is being amplified. Individuals performing the reactions should avoid exposure to previously amplified DNA on the day of the experiment. No specimens or materials used for the extraction of DNA from biological specimens should be allowed in a postamplification PCR product room. Gloves, disposable lab coats and/or disposable sleeves must be changed after working with each individual specimen. Use specially designated PCR set-up pipetters and aerosol-resistant pipet tips to minimize contamination. Change pipet tips between each transfer or addition.
2. An extraction reagent blank control (prepared during sample extraction) should also be processed. This control will regulate for the presence of contaminants during the sample extraction. Provided enough evidentiary sample remains, a second extraction of the sample, completely independent from the first extraction, should be performed. The sequence obtained from the second extraction will provide additional confirmation that the sequence obtained is authentic.
3. Include two negative controls with every set of amplification reactions. The first negative control (set up first) should test the reagents used in the PCR master mix. The second negative control should be set up last, in order to test the cleanliness of the master mix following additions to all other reaction tubes. A known human positive-control sequence should also be included with each amplification reaction. The positive control should be set up as the second-to-last tube. All other tubes should be set up and closed prior to adding the positive control (with the exception of the last negative control).
4. Preparing a PCR master mix containing all common reagents saves considerable time and helps normalize the reactions. The standard 50 μg PCR reaction contains 10 mM Tris-HCl, pH 8.3, 50 mM KCl, 1.5 mM $MgCl_2$, BSA at 4 μg, a primer concentration of 0.4 μM, 0.2 mM dNTPs, and 2.5 U of Taq polymerase.
5. Amplification may not be successful due to PCR inhibition, which in some cases may be seen by the absence of primer-dimer on the product gel. If primer-dimer is expected, but not observed, inhibition of the reaction is suspected. Taq DNA polymerase can

be elevated (not greater than a total of 12.5 U) or the volume of extract added to the reaction decreased.

6. In cases where low concentrations of template or badly degraded samples result in no product, it may be beneficial to run a second round of PCR, using an aliquot of the first reaction for the template. A seminested or nested primer strategy, where one or both of the second set of primers are internal to the first set, will help control for the contamination problems inherent with running a large number of PCR cycles. If nested reactions are run, the products from two completely independent series of nested reactions with the same sample should be compared to assure that the sequences are identical.
7. Centricon 100s are more effective in removing nucleotides than primers in some cases. The presence of PCR primers in the sequencing reactions may result in secondary-sequencing initiation sites at positions autonomous to the desired start position. The resulting data may contain higher background or display multiple overlapping peaks. This is especially critical when using dye-terminator chemistry, since all sequenced products are labeled. If this appears to be a problem, the use of lower concentrations of primers in the PCR reaction, multiple washings of the Centricon 100s, or gel purification of the PCR products may alleviate the problem.
8. In addition to the strategy presented here, a number of different amplification and sequencing schemes for the mitochondrial D-loop region have been published, each of which focuses on obtaining the sequence of the two hypervariable regions. The technical working group for DNA analysis methods (TWGDAM) has established the recommended region for HV-1 sequence from base pairs 16024 6365 and 7340 for the HV-2 region. The most straightforward procedures involve amplification of both HV-1 and HV-2 in two separate PCR reactions using primers "*tailed*" with a universal sequencing primer site. The PCR products are then analyzed with dye-labeled primers. Another procedure employs a nested PCR strategy after first amplifying the entire D-loop region in a single reaction. The hypervariable regions are then amplified in the nested PCR reactions. Although nested PCR may generate a cleaner product, it may also be more susceptible to contamination problems due to the large number of total amplification cycles performed. Furthermore, in highly degraded samples, it may be difficult to amplify the entire D-loop region in a single amplification reaction.

9. Primer-dimer formation during PCR reactions may affect the resulting data generated during cycle sequencing. Primer dimers formed during PCR may not be eliminated by centrifugation through the Centricon 100s. Subsequent annealing of the sequencing primer to primer dimer instead of the sequence of interest will result in sequencing of the dimer. This may result in obscured data toward the beginning of a sequence (within the first 250 base pairs). Designing sequencing primers to avoid complementarity with PCR primers will reduce the problem.
10. In addition to the pGem control, a positive sequencing control should be sequenced to provide known sequence information for the region being analyzed. If the sequence obtained from the extraction reagent blank is different from the sample sequence(s), and the sample sequence(s) are consistent from one specimen to the next over multiple extractions and/or amplifications, the sequence information from the sample can be considered authentic.
11. If using Boehringer-Mannheim G-50 gel-filtration columns, a single dH_2O wash prior to purification has been found to be superior to multiple washings. Multiple washings with dH_2O diminishes the columns' retentive capacity. Failure of the columns may be seen by yellow "*smearing*" on the gel image (red on the electrophoretograms) caused by labeled thymine terminators eluting through the column. Manifestations of incomplete terminator-dye removal include increased background throughout the entire lane, obscured sequence data at the beginning of the sequence, and/or formation of a particularly broad "*thymine-smear*" that migrates at a position equivalent to approx 200-40 base pairs on the gel.
12. Clean sequencing plates are essential. Do not air dry the plates after washing. If ethanol is not completely removed, a blue or green fluorescence may result when plates are scanned on the 373A sequencer. Some brands of urea and old formamide also result in a higher fluorescent background.
13. Sequencing with kits containing the Amplitaq, FS polymerase results in more normalized peak heights and easier sequence-editing than data generated with kits containing the Amplitaq polymerase. The concentration of dye-terminators is diminished due to the increased efficiency of the AmpliTaq, FS polymerase to incorporate dye-terminators in the cycle-sequencing reaction, ultimately simplifying sample cleanup (ethanol precipitation may replace gel filtration for removing dye-terminators postcycle sequencing). Our laboratory

is in the process of converting to the Amplitaq, FS kit for all of our cycle-sequencing reactions.

14. The concentration of terminator mix used in the mtDNA sequencing reactions may be halved with the volume difference made up with dH_2O. Peak heights obtained with 0.5X terminator mix are approx 95% of the heights obtained with 1X terminator mix. No difference in the length of read of the small templates mentioned in this procedure was seen. This observation was obtained with the AmpliTaq cycle-sequencing kit; it is not known if similar results would be obtained with the AmpliTaq FS cycle-sequencing kit. Independent verification should be performed if longer cycles are sequenced.
15. Sequence information at each base position should be confirmed by data from both DNA strands when possible. A specific exception is when a polycytosine stretch prohibits confirmation in both directions. In these instances, confirming sequence information from a single DNA strand will be acceptable. In general, data should be obtained from at least two independent amplifications when sequence information from only one strand is being reported.
16. Patterns for the sequence-dependent insertion of terminators have been published and are reflected by uneven peak heights. The patterns for the AmpliTaq FS kit have not been characterized as extensively as those for the AmpliTaq kits, therefore only a few rudimentary observations are presented. For AmpliTaq FS, the rules include Gs after Cs are small; Gs after As are small; Gs, As, and Ts after Gs are large; and Cs after Ts are "often" larger. The information may be used to justify editing a base call, however, this should not be the sole criterion for base editing.
17. Sequence data at the poly-cytosine stretches are often difficult to confirm. In particular, the range between 16182 and 16193 in HV1 may be hard to interpret if there is a 16189 T-C polymorphism or length-based heteroplasmy present in the sample. Length-based heteroplasmy through this region is common and results in poor sequencing data due to the multiple overlapping peaks in the electrophoretogram at all positions distal to the insertion. Sequence data in positions leading up to the poly-cytosine stretch will be normal. If there is no confirming data from reverse strand, then length-based heteroplasmy is suspected.

7

Profiling of Genetic Material

Several countries have developed national DNA databases that contain large numbers of DNA profiles - the UK and the USA national DNA databases now both contain the DNA profiles of over 3 million individuals. DNA databases that store STR profiles have emerged as a powerful tool in the investigation of crime. The effective use of the DNA database, in particular in the UK, has acted as a catalyst for the establishment and expansion of DNA databases in other countries, including the USA and many European countries that now have databases with hundreds of thousands of profiles stored in them. This chapter will examine the development and application of the UK national DNA database, which is the first and most extensive database of its kind. It will briefly examine the development of databases worldwide.

National DNA database (NDNAD)

The UK NDNAD was established in 1995, shortly after STR profiling using six STR loci was introduced into criminal casework.

Rationale for Criminal Databases

There are several justifications for the time, effort and money that a criminal DNA database consumes:

1. Criminals tend to re-offend - 90% of rapists have had a previous conviction; 50% of armed robbers have a previous conviction.
2. The severity of crimes often increases — in many instances criminal activity starts at a young age with many criminals committing their first offence between 16–19 years of age.

3. A small number of criminals can be responsible for a large number of crimes – linking these crimes together can aid police investigations. This is particularly the case for burglaries, auto crimes, and serious cases such as sexual assaults.

Legislation

The UK DNA database did not require specific statutes for its establishment although the police service launched the national DNA database at the same time that the provisions of the Criminal Justice and Public Order Act 1994 came into force on 10th April 1995. Subsequent legislation has increased the scope of samples that may be collected and retained on the NDNAD.

Criteria for Entry onto NDNAD

The original criterion for addition of a sample from an individual to the National DNA Database was that the person had been arrested for an offence punishable by imprisonment. If the person was found not guilty at a subsequent trial, or the case was discontinued, then their profile would be removed. In 2001 the Criminal Evidence Act allowed samples to be retained on the NDNAD, even if the individual was not found guilty. The regulations were further relaxed in 2003 with the Extension to the Criminal Justice Act. Calls have been made in the UK by police chiefs and politicians for everybody to be entered onto the NDNAD – this prospect is still some way in the future.

Technology Underlying the NDNAD

The development of STR profiling was essential for the successful implementation of a large-scale DNA database. Attempts had been made to construct databases of VNTR profiles, and these did produce some successes. However, the difficulty of comparing VNTR profiles was a major limitation. STR profiles can be digitized very easily and this has allowed for the effective computerization of DNA profiles.

The UK NDNAD was established using the SGM multiplex, which analysed six STR loci and the amelogenin locus. The match probability of SGM was 1 in 10^8 of the population, which for a population of 58 million within the UK was deemed acceptable. However, when six loci were used there were a number of coincidental matches.

In 1999, the six-locus SGM test was changed to the ten locus AmpF*l*STR SGM Plus test. The chance that two DNA profiles from unrelated people will match at all ten loci is less than 1 in 1 billion. To date no two people have been found to match at all ten loci; matches to two or more people can occur if a partial DNA profile is searched against the NDNAD.

Operation of the NDNAD

The NDNAD has two main sets of data: profiles generated from evidence that has been collected from crime scenes (263000 at the end of 2005) and profiles generated from individuals.

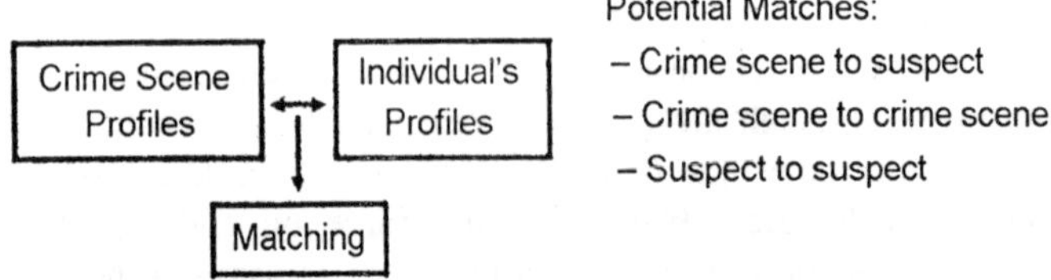

Fig. 7.1. Following entry onto the database the new samples are searched against all other samples on the NDNAD.

A biological sample from a scene will be collected by the scene-of-crime officers and submitted for DNA analysis. The resulting DNA profile will be compared to those currently held on the NDNAD and if there is a match then this will be reported back to the police force that collected the sample. A fresh sample from the individual to which there was a match will be collected and the DNA analysis will be repeated.

While the intention had been to use the NDNAD to match samples from serious crimes such as sexual assaults and murders, the addition of samples from high volume crime such as burglary resulted in an increase of DNA profiles on the NDNAD. In an average year the NDNAD produces around 40000 crime scene to individual matches: the majority of these are high volume crime but there are invariably matches to more serious crimes such as murder, rape and assaults. With such a large number of DNA profiles held on the NDNAD there is currently a 45% chance that a DNA profile obtained from an incident will match a DNA profile on the NDNAD.

In the UK, approximately 1 in 20 people are on the NDNAD; this includes 8% of the male population. Ethical concerns have been raised that the NDNAD discriminated against vulnerable sections of society –75% of young black males between the ages of 15 to 34 are on the database whereas only 22% of white males in the same age bracket are found on the NDNAD.

Familial Searching

Familial searching was devised by the Forensic Science Service of the UK and is used when there is not a full DNA profile match between the crime scene and the NDNAD samples but a match is achieved at 15 or more alleles and the perpetrator most likely lived in the vicinity of the incident. While the person on the NDNAD can not be the donor of the sample obtained from the incident, it is highly likely that the originator of the sample is a relative of this person.

Cold Cases

Since the advent of PCR-based techniques it is now possible to obtain DNA profiles from old case samples. The application of *low copy number* (LCN) PCR has further increased the chance of obtaining DNA profiles from highly degraded material. Cases, such as those of murder, that have remained open from dates prior to the introduction of DNA typing can now be re-examined using either standard DNA testing or LCN in combination with the NDNAD. The current technology has allowed numerous cases to result in a conviction and therefore closure.

Caution must be excercised when examining samples collected by crime scene operators prior to the advent of PCR-based techniques as it is unlikely that those handling the items will have taken the standard precautions to minimize contamination that are now standard practice.

International Situation

Following the success of the operation in the UK, other countries developed their own DNA databases. For many countries there was a need to enact special legislation leading to delays in the implementation of DNA databases.

New Zealand implemented a DNA database in 1996 along similar lines to that of the UK. The population is significantly smaller but as a percentage of the population New Zealand is second only to the UK in terms of the number of DNA profiles held on its database. Australia and South Africa were also rapid in developing DNA databases.

In mainland Europe, almost all countries have established DNA databases although all are limited in comparison to the UK version. The Netherlands and Austria established their version of a DNA database in 1997, with Germany following one year later and Finland and Norway in 1999.

Two countries in the Middle East, Kuwait and the United Arab Emirates, are both currently developing plans that would see the entire population analysed and placed on a DNA database.

US DNA Database

The US Army established a database of their own in 1992 to identify missing persons in operation Desert Storm and this experience helped to pave the way for a national database within the US. In 1994 the US congress passed the DNA Identification Act which enabled the establishment of the *Combined DNA Index System* (CODIS). The CODIS, which is the federally held DNA database, has expanded very quickly and comprises the *National DNA Index System* (NDIS), the *State DNA Index System* (SDIS) and the *Local DNA Index System* (LDIS). The information about each sample that is loaded onto the CODIS database includes a laboratory identifier, a specimen identifier, information to classify and review the integrity of the DNA record, and the DNA profile itself. CODIS links local, state and federal crime laboratories. The FBI selected 13 STR loci (CODIS loci) for developing the database. Like the UK NDNAD there are two main segments called '*indices*' of CODIS:

1. The Forensic Index contains DNA profiles from crime scene samples.
2. The Offender Index contains DNA profiles of individuals convicted of certain categories of violent crime, though now many states are expanding their databases and are profiling persons arrested for all felonies.

Other CODIS indices are:

1. Unidentified human remains;
2. Relatives of missing persons.

All 50 US states now have databases of which only 13 obtain DNA samples for databasing for all felonies. At the moment there are about 180 DNA laboratories around the USA that are designated and accredited as CODIS laboratories. These laboratories are validated according to the standards of FBI and are authorized to submit the DNA profile information into CODIS.

The situation in the US as of late 2006 is:

total number of profiles: 3676971

total forensic profiles: 148 068

total convicted offender profiles: 3528903

When compared with the UK, the USA is a much larger jurisdiction but due to lack of funding, coherent structure and variable legal approaches, there are lengthy delays in DNA profiling of casework samples that has led to massive backlogs. The President of the USA announced the 'President's DNA Initiative' in 2003 in order to enhance and streamline the use of DNA as a forensic tool and also signed an act to enhance the facilities for DNA databasing. The main aims of this initiative are to clear the backlogs quickly and also to improve the capacity of the forensic laboratories for databasing the samples besides promoting research and development in the field.

Cross-border Databases

Criminals tend to operate in their own country but there are circumstances when crimes will be committed in more that one country. In order for criminal databases to be effective in these circumstances there is a need to share data. Interpol has been instrumental in facilitating cross-border comparisons of DNA profiles. The STR loci commonly used in the forensic community were combined to make the Interpol Standard Set of Loci (ISSOL); these have since been expanded from seven loci to ten loci. Other organizations, such as the *European DNA Profiling Group* (EDNAP), are working towards the standardization of DNA profiling such that an organization in one country will be able to access DNA data in the database of another country. The biggest obstacle to cross-border data sharing is now political rather than technical.

8

SNP AND ITS APPLICATIONS

Ever since the first human '*DNA fingerprint*' was made by hybridization of multi-locus probes to *variable number tandem repeats* (VNTRs) and the first DNA evidence was presented at court, tandem repeat sequences have been the favoured targets for forensic DNA analyses. Today, *short tandem repeats* (STRs) with four nucleotide repeat units are preferred, mainly because they are easily amplified in *polymerase chain reactions* (PCRs) and because they are shorter than VNTRs and more likely to be intact in low-quality samples often recovered from crime scenes. Thirteen STRs located on different chromosomes were selected for the *Combined DNA Indexing System* (CODIS) database, and today there are several commercial products available that allow amplification of all CODIS loci in one multiplex PCR. These kits are validated and used by forensic laboratories all over the world, and they have facilitated the development of standardized databases, which have proved to be highly valuable tools for national and international law enforcement. Each CODIS locus has many different alleles because mutations happen frequently in tandem repeat sequences (on average 1 mutation per 300 generations), and therefore it is highly likely that different alleles are found in different individuals, which makes tandem repeat sequences very suitable for identification purposes.

Traditionally, the main purpose of forensic genetic investigations has been the identification of human remains found at crime scenes and mass disasters, or the determination of family relations where the available information is disputed or uncertain (e.g. in paternity or immigration cases). However, with the increase in the number of DNA profiles in national and international databases of criminal offenders,

DNA profiling has become more and more important as an investigative tool for the police. This trend will most likely continue as more knowledge of the human genome is disclosed and new forensic genetic tools are developed. In this chapter, the present and potential applications of *single nucleotide polymorphisms* (SNPs) are discussed.

Single Nucleotide Polymorphisms

An SNP is formed by a point mutation, where one base pair is substituted by another base pair. Per definition, a genetic variation at a single base pair locus is not considered to be an SNP unless at least two alleles have frequencies of more than 1 % in a large, random population. Thus, 'private alleles' identified in small selected populations (e.g. families) are considered to be mutations and not SNPs.

The vast majority of SNPs have only two alleles because the mutation rate at a particular base pair position in the genome is extremely low (on average 1 mutation per 100 million generations) and it is highly unlikely that two point mutations happen at the same position. For this reason, SNPs can be used to distinquish between populations and the geographical history of a given population can be mapped by identifying the distribution of a particular SNP allele among existing populations. Recently, the National Geographic Society, IBM and the Waitt family foundation initiated a worldwide survey of human populations with the purpose of mapping all major human migrations since modern humans left Africa approximately 60 000 years ago. The markers used in this study are Y chromosome SNPs and *mitochondrial DNA* (mtDNA) SNPs, which are particularly useful for mapping large human migrations, because the Y chromosome is inherited from father to son and the mtDNA genome is inherited from mother to any offspring without recombination. Thus, a point mutation in the Y chromosome or the mtDNA creates a new male or female lineage, respectively, and the lineage remains distinct from all other lineages in future generations.

The human genome consists of approximately 3000 million base pairs (bp) and the most recent estimate of SNPs is 10 million, which gives an average of one SNP per 300 base pairs. The density of SNPs across the genome varies up to ten-fold, because of variations in selection pressure, and local recombination and mutation rates,. and the majority of SNPs are located in repeat regions, which are notoriously difficult to analyse. Nevertheless, SNPs are the best choice for construction of a dense set of polymorphic markers that cover the whole genome. The marker set can be used for studying association between the markers and a particular human trait or disease. Once an association has been found, a more detailed analysis of the region surrounding the relevant marker(s) can be performed and the polymorphism(s) responsible for the human trait(s) or disease(s) may be identified.

The human genome consists of 30,000–35,000 genes, but the coding regions of these genes only comprise 1.1–1.5% of the genome. The SNPs located outside coding regions can influence gene expression if they are located in regulatory DNA sequences, but the majority of SNPs probably have very little or no functional consequences for the organism.

An SNP located in a gene may have diverse effects on the cellular function of the protein encoded by the gene. If the SNP is located in the coding region of the gene, the different alleles may encode different proteins, because the trinucleotide sequence (the codon) that codes for one amino acid differs. For example, the codon TGC can be changed to TGT, TGG or TGA by a point mutation in the third position of the codon. The original C allele will code for the amino acid cysteine. The T allele will also code for the amino acid cysteine (known as a silent mutation), whereas the G allele will code for the amino acid tryptophan (known as a missence mutation) and the A allele will code for termination of protein synthesis (known as a nonsense mutation). Obviously, the nonsense mutation is the most severe form of mutation and will almost always result in a non-functional protein. A missence mutation can have all kinds of consequences on the protein, including mis-folding, mis-placement and decreased or increased activity, which again may affect the organism in various ways. Even a silent mutation may not be neutral for the cell, because a silent mutation may affect the efficiency of protein synthesis and thus alter the cellular concentration of the protein.

DNA sequence	TTC	GAC	TGC	AAA
Protein sequence	Phe	Asp	Cys	Lys
DNA sequence	TTC	GAC	TGT	AAA
Protein sequence	Phe	Asp	Cys	Lys
DNA sequence	TTC	GAC	TGG	AAA
Protein sequence	Phe	Asp	Trp	Lys
DNA sequence	TTC	GAC	TGA	AAA
Protein sequence	Phe	Asp	Stop	

Fig. 8.1. Examples of how an SNP may change the amino acid sequence of a protein

SINGLE NUCLEOTIDE POLYMORPHISM TYPING TECHNOLOGY

Numerous methods have been developed for SNP genotyping. The methods all employ one of four common technologies: hybridization, primer extension, ligation or invasive cleavage. For forensic applications, *single base extension* (SBE) is currently the preferred method, because it is highly accurate and can be performed with the same instruments used for STR analyses (polymerase chain reaction machines and electrophoresis instruments). The SBE reaction is performed as consecutive cycles of denaturation of double-stranded DNA, annealing of the SBE primers to the *polymerase chain reaction* (PCR) products and single base extension. The SBE primer anneals to the single-stranded PCR product immediately upstream of the SNP position, and the DNA polymerase adds a fluorescently labelled dideoxyribonucleotide, complementary to the nucleotide in the SNP position, to the SBE primer. Single base extension reactions can be multiplexed and many SBE products can be analysed simultaneously

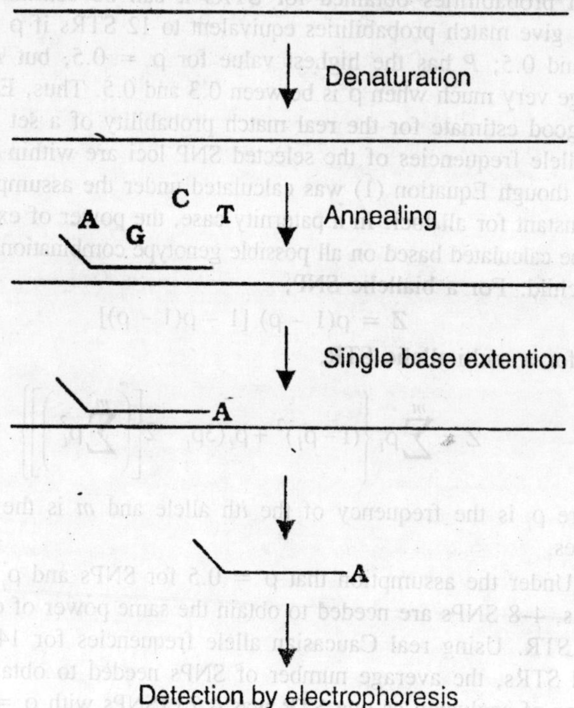

Fig. 8.2. Schematic diagram of the SBE reaction.

by electrophoresis. In the electropherogram, the length of the SBE primer identifies the SNP locus and the colour of the fluorescent label identifies the SNP allele.

Single Nucleotide Polymorphisms for Human Identification

For human identification purposes, one SNP locus is obviously less informative than one STR locus, because the SNP locus has only two possible alleles and the STR locus typically has 8–15 different alleles. The match probability *P* for *n* SNP loci (between the SNP profiles from two randomly selected individuals) can be approximated by assuming that all SNPs are in Hardy–Weinberg equilibrium and that the frequency of the least common allele ρ is constant for all loci:

$$P = (\rho^2)^n + [2\rho(1 - \rho)]^n + [(1 - \rho)^2]^n \quad ...(1)$$

This is a simple function of ρ and *n*, and by comparing *P* to the match probabilities obtained for STRs it can be estimated that 50 SNPs give match probabilities equivalent to 12 STRs if ρ is between 0.2 and 0.5; *P* has the highest value for ρ = 0.5, but *P* does not change very much when ρ is between 0.3 and 0.5. Thus, Equation (1) is a good estimate for the real match probability of a set of SNPs if the allele frequencies of the selected SNP loci are within this range, even though Equation (1) was calculated under the assumption that ρ is constant for all loci. In a paternity case, the power of exclusion, *Z*, can be calculated based on all possible genotype combinations of mother and child. For a biallelic SNP,

$$Z = \rho(1 - \rho)\,[1 - \rho(1 - \rho)] \quad ...(2)$$

and for a multi-allelic STR,

$$Z = \sum^{m} \rho_i \left\{ (1-\rho_i)^2 + \rho_i (3\rho_i - 2\left[\left(\sum^{m} \rho_i^2\right)\right]\right\} \quad ...(3)$$

where ρ_i is the frequency of the *i*th allele and *m* is the number of alleles.

Under the assumption that ρ = 0.5 for SNPs and $\rho_i = 1/m$ for STRs, 4–8 SNPs are needed to obtain the same power of exclusion as one STR. Using real Caucasian allele frequencies for 14 commonly used STRs, the average number of SNPs needed to obtain the same power of exclusion as one STR was 4.23 (SNPs with ρ = 0.5), 4.41 (SNPs with ρ = 0.4) or 5.04 (SNPs with ρ = 0.3), respectively. This indicates that 50–60 SNPs with ρ = 0.3–0.5 have the same discriminatory power for analysis of stains (match probability) and disputed family relations (power of exclusion) as the 13 CODIS loci currently in use by most forensic laboratories.

There are two important reasons why it is preferred to analyse 50–60 SNP loci instead of 13 STR loci. First of all, the length of the PCR product containing an SNP locus need only be the length of the PCR primers plus one base pair (the SNP position). In theory, a DNA sequence is unique if it is 16 bp long (4^{16} = 4295 million combinations, which is more than the number of base pairs in the human genome). Thus a PCR product containing an SNP locus need only be $(2 \times 16) + 1 = 33$ bp long. In reality, the PCR primer design restrains the positioning of the PCR primer, and the PCR product must be longer. Nevertheless, most SNPs can be amplified on PCR products less than 100 bp in length. In contrast, some CODIS STR alleles have up to 40 tandem repeat units, each with a size of 4 bp, and consequently the PCR products containing the STR locus need to be 200 bp or longer. In the commercial kits used in most forensic laboratories to amplify the 13 CODIS STRs, the loci are amplified in the same tube (multiplex PCR) and the lengths of the PCR products (i.e. the alleles) are determined by electrophoresis. In order to separate and identify the many PCR products, the longest PCR products have been designed to be 400–450 bp, but in highly degraded DNA samples the average length of DNA fragments is shorter than 150 bp, and therefore many of the STR loci are not amplified when the sample has been exposed to high temperatures or high humidity that degrades the DNA. So-called *mini-STR* kits have been developed, where the PCR products have been reduced in length, but these kits only target 4–6 STRs and the discriminatory power is significantly smaller. Furthermore, unfinished extension products will be formed in higher numbers when PCR is performed on highly degraded DNA, because PCR primers may anneal to a strand where the target sequence is interrupted. The unfinished extension products from mini-STR kits consist almost exclusively of tandem repeat sequences and can anneal to many different positions in the STR target locus during subsequent PCR cycles. This will increase the risk of amplifying fragments with a different number of tandem repeats than was originally present in the sample. If such products are made during the first critical cycles of the PCR, false alleles may be detected and assigned to the sample. In contrast, unfinished extension products from amplification of SNP loci cannot create false SNP alleles, because they can only anneal to one unique position.

The second reason why SNPs are preferred over STRs is the low mutation rate of SNPs. If the investigated man and a child in a typical paternity case do not share any alleles for a given locus (genetic inconsistency), it indicates that the man is not the father, but one genetic inconsistency between the father and the child is observed in approximately $100(13 \times 0.003) = 3.9\%$ of the cases, where the 13 CODIS loci have been investigated. This is a highly unfortunate, but unavoidable, consequence of the relatively high mutation rate of tandem repeats. In rare cases where relatives (e.g. two brothers, or father and son) are investigated, it may even be impossible to draw a conclusion, because relatives share a high number of genetic markers and few genetic inconsistencies are expected between an investigated relative (e.g. uncle or grandfather), who is not the father, and a child. For comparison, one genetic inconsistency between the father and the child will be observed in approximately $100(60 \times 0.0000001) = 0.0006\%$ of the cases if 60 SNPs were investigated.

There are three reasons why STRs are preferred over SNPs. First, the national and international databases contain STR profiles from known criminal offenders, victims and samples collected from crime scenes during the past two decades. It is an overwhelming task to type all these samples again for SNP markers, and in some cases it is impossible, because the samples may have been used up and cannot be replaced. Secondly, samples collected from crime scenes often contain DNA from more than one person, and mixtures are difficult to detect when analysing DNA markers with only two alleles. In contrast, STRs are very useful for detection of mixtures, because two individuals are likely to have three or four different alleles in some STR systems. Sometimes, it is even possible to estimate the STR profiles of the two individuals based on the amplification strength of the alleles, and it is always possible to calculate a match probability between a reference sample from an individual and the mixture. If the mixture contains DNA from more than two people, SNPs will be almost useless, whereas STRs may still be used for calculation of match probabilities. Thirdly, very little DNA is often recovered from crime scenes (e.g. from fingerprints or hair), and since all such samples are unique and cannot be replaced it is essential to obtain as much information as possible from every investigation performed on the sample. This is one of the reasons why amplification of multiple fragments (multiplex PCR) is important for forensic genetic analyses. In addition, multiplexing also simplifies analysis, reduces cost and decreases the number of times a sample is handled in the laboratory, which reduces the risk of contamination and mix-ups. However, it is difficult to develop PCR multiplexes with 5–10 fragments, and construction of a robust multiplex with 50–60 fragments is a very serious undertaking.

Nevertheless, several large SNP panels have been suggested for human identification purposes, and recently a 52-SNP-plex assay was described by a group of five forensic laboratories, where 52 fragments are amplified in one multiplex PCR and the SNPs are detected by two multiplex SBE reactions. Each of the SNPs in the 52-SNP-plex assay maps to unique locations on the autosomal chromosomes and has a minimum distance of 100 kb from known genes. The SNPs are polymorphic in the three major population groups with $\rho = 0.3$–0.5, and all SNPs can be amplified and detected from as little as 200 pg of genomic DNA (approximately the amount of genomic DNA in 30 human cells). Currently, this is the most promising SNP multiplex for human identification, and the European DNA Profiling Group (EDNAP), a working group under the International Society for Forensic Haemogenetics (ISFH), and commercial companies have expressed strong interest in the 52-SNP-plex.

Single Nucleotide Polymorphisms in Mitochondrial DNA

Analysis of mitochondrial DNA (mtDNA) has been used successfully for a number of years in anthropology and forensic genetics. The high copy number of mitochondrial genomes (typically more than 3000) in a somatic cell makes it more likely to amplify mtDNA markers than nuclear DNA markers from old and highly degraded sample materials. In addition, mtDNA can also be collected from hair shafts, which do not contain any nuclear DNA, and hair shafts are one of the frequent samples recovered from scenes of violent crimes. Mitochondrial DNA is maternally inherited, and there is no recombination between mitochondrial genomes, because there is only one chromosome per mitochondria. Therefore, the variation of mtDNA genomes among humans is relatively small and the power of discrimination is limited compared to the analysis of autosomal chromosomes. The mtDNA genome is approximately 16,569 bp long and it was sequenced already in 1981. It encodes 13 genes, two rRNAs and 22 tRNAs and has a 1100 bp non-coding sequence, known as the mtDNA control region, where the mutation rate is unusually high. Within the control region there are at least three hypervariable (HV) regions with a high number of SNPs and these regions can be amplified by PCR and sequenced. In 1999, EDNAP's mitochondrial DNA population database project (EMPOP) was initiated with the purpose of creating a common forensic standard for mtDNA sequencing and an on-line mtDNA database with high-quality mtDNA population data. The initiative was a reaction to the significant number of errors in public mtDNA databases and only forensic laboratories qualified by successful participation in EMPOP collaborative exercises have permission to submit mtDNA sequences. Today, the typical targets for forensic and anthropological investigations are HV-I (position 16 024–16 400) and HV-II (position 44–340). However, there is a growing interest for SNPs in the mtDNA coding region, because certain sequences in HV-I and HV-II are very common (e.g. 7% of all Caucasians have the same HV1/HV2 haplotype). Several SNP panels have been proposed and a selection of coding region SNPs for forensic caseworks are likely to be recommended in the near future.

Forensic DNA Phenotyping

When the police initiate a search for a person based on a witness report, they usually put out a description of the person based on just a few facts, such as sex, age, height, weight, distinct features and the colours of hair, eyes and skin. Some of these traits (phenotypes) are genetically determined and can, in theory, be predicted by typing the person's DNA, if the genetic markers causing the phenotype are known. In the reverse situation, where the police have no witnesses and no suspect, but only a biological sample left at the crime scene, information on phenotypes can be pivotal for the police inquiry.

Special attention has been addressed to genetic markers determining the colours of hair, eyes and skin, mainly because animal models have been studied for decades and many genes involved in the regulation of melanin synthesis have been identified. Melanin is a complex polymer synthesized from the amino acid tyrosine via a number of toxic intermediates. The synthesis is performed in specialized compartments (organelles known as *melanosomes*) in the melanocytes to protect the cell from the destructive intermediates. The mature melanosomes filled with melanin are transported from the melanocytes to keratinocytes in the skin and hair, where melanin shields the body from damaging UV light. The regulatory mechanisms involved in melanocyte differentiation, melanin synthesis and melanosome transport are very complicated and not fully understood, and since genetic variations in any of the dozens of regulatory and functional proteins involved in these processes may influence melanin synthesis, there are many candidate genes to investigate and many possible combinations of alleles that eventually make up the haplotype responsible for a certain colour. The melanocortin 1 receptor (*MC1 R*) is one of the key regulators of melanogenesis in humans and several SNPs in *MC1 R* are associated with red hair colour, number of freckles, nevus count and increased risk of skin cancer (melanoma). In one model, various combinations of seven SNPs in *MC1 R* were shown to account for 67% of the red-haired individuals in an Australian population and a similar model was proposed for north Europeans. Four SNPs in two of the genes commonly deleted in albinos, *OCA2* and *MATP* (two membrane proteins without any known function), are associated with dark colours of hair, skin and eyes in Caucasians, and recently an SNP in the *SLC24A5* gene (encoding a putative Na^+/Ca^+ exchanger) was estimated to account for 30% of the difference in skin melanin between Caucasians and Africans. Many of these SNPs have large differences in allele frequencies in different populations and some of them were originally categorized as *ancestry informative markers* (AIMs), which can be used to divide the entire human population into groups of ethnical origin. This is not particularly surprising, since one of the most prominent traits distinguishing major population groups is the colour of the skin, and it has been suggested to use AIMs for the prediction of traits related to ethnic origin instead of identifying and typing the causative markers. However, for forensic purposes, it will be more prudent to report on genetic markers with known effects on specific phenotypes. Today, there is insufficient knowledge about such markers, but after the completion of the human genome (sequencing) project, genetic markers for complex human traits are rapidly being identified and it is expected that tools for the prediction of human phenotypes can become sufficiently accurate to be used in forensic investigations.

Ethical Considerations of SNP Genotyping

The information deduced from a DNA profile has been an important issue of discussion in the last two decades, and the fact that the CODIS STR loci do not reveal anything about race, intelligence, physical characteristics or possible genetic disorders of an individual has been important for the appliance to ethical criteria imposed on forensic DNA investigations in some countries. With the introduction of SNP typing in forensic genetics, these criteria may be challenged, because SNPs can reveal information that may be considered to be sensitive or private. For example, the ethnic origin of a person can be determined with a high degree of certainty by analysing AIMs or Y chromosome SNPs. This information could be very important for the police investigation, but for some people it may be problematic if the DNA profile reveals that a person has different ancestors than the person presumed, and the public may express concern that 'ethnic SNPs' are used to criticize a certain population in the community. On the other hand, if the typing of AIMs is prohibited by law, it will not be possible to type for certain human phenotypes (e.g. skin colour), because such traits are used to distinguish between populations and an important tool for law enforcement may be lost.

The advantages of using SNP markers for routine caseworks are so large that there is no doubt that SNP typing will be employed by forensic laboratories in the future. Whether typing of SNPs in coding regions and forensic DNA phenotyping should be permitted is an issue that needs to be addressed by the public and the forensic genetic community, and most likely it has to be discussed continuously in the years to come as more and more genetic markers are discovered and associated with distinct phenotypes.

9

Polymerase Chain Reaction

The specific quantification of human DNA from forensic evidentiary materials is a recommended procedure for a reliable *short tandem repeat* (STR) analysis, which is the current gold standard for DNA profiling in forensic casework. An estimation of the DNA quantity is made to adjust the DNA input of subsequent end-point *polymerase chain reaction* (PCR)-based DNA profiling methods, preventing PCR failures that are due to the absence of DNA, and avoiding PCR artefacts such as random allele dropout produced by stochastic amplification effects from *low copy number* (LCN) DNA samples (under 100 pg of DNA), and also preventing off-scale over-amplification artefacts (including $n + 1$ peaks, increased stutter bands and pullout) associated with an excess of DNA input in the PCR. In addition, an accurate DNA quantification helps to prevent the unnecessary waste of DNA, which is especially important when analysing LCN DNA samples.

In the past, forensic laboratories have used the slot-blot hybridization approach to target the D17Z1 locus – a highly repetitive alphoid primate-specific sequence – for DNA quantification in forensic casework. However, this methodology, with a detection limit above the limit of the STR profiling approaches, was often not sensitive enough to detect LCN forensic DNA samples. In addition, the method is labour-intensive, time-consuming and poorly suited to high-throughput sample flow.

Several studies have demonstrated the usefulness of real-time PCR for a sensitive, specific and high-throughput quantification of both human nuclear DNA (nuDNA) and mitochondrial DNA (mtDNA) in forensics and ancient DNA studies.

The recent development of a commercially available real-time PCR human DNA quantification kit has also contributed to a worldwide use of real-time PCR in forensic genetics.

In this chapter we will review all the different real-time PCR assays that have been applied in forensic genetics for the specific quantification of human autosomal, X and Y chromosome and mitochondrial DNA targets. We also review some real-time PCR assays for rapid quantification of non-human species of interest in forensic and ancient DNA studies, including the identification of pathogens in microbial forensics. Other applications of real-time PCR assays, such as allele discrimination and single nucleotide polymorphism genotyping, are outside of the scope of this review.

Current Real-time PCR Chemistries

There are two general fluorogenic methods to monitor the real-time progress of the PCR: by measuring *Taq* polymerase activity using double-stranded DNA binding dye chemistry (SYBR Green or ethidium bromide) or by measuring the 5'-nuclease activity of the *Taq* DNA polymerase to cleave a target-specific fluorogenic probe (a TaqMan probe: an oligonucleotide complementary to a segment of the template DNA, with both a reporter and a quencher dye attached, that only emits its characteristic fluorescence after cleavage). Although TaqMan assays are the most popular probe-based assays in forensic laboratories, alternative probe-based chemistry, such as molecular beacons or scorpion primers and probes, could also be employed for specific target detection.

Real-time analysis of the fluorescence levels at each cycle of the PCR (amplification plot) allows a complete picture to be obtained of the whole amplification process for each sample. In the initial cycles of the PCR a baseline is observed without any significant change in fluorescence signal. An increase in fluorescence above the baseline indicates the detection of accumulated PCR product. The higher the initial input of the target genomic DNA, the sooner a significant increase in fluorescence is observed. The cycle at which fluorescence reaches an arbitrary threshold level during the exponential phase of the PCR is named *Ct* (threshold cycle). A standard curve can be generated by plotting the log of the starting DNA template amount of a set of previously quantified DNA standards against their *Ct* values. Therefore, an accurate estimation of the starting DNA amount from unknown samples is accomplished by comparison of the measured *Ct* values with the *Ct* values of the standard curve. Compared to end-point PCR quantification methods, the use of *Ct* values is a more reliable quantification assay. This is mainly due to the fact that *Ct* determination is performed during the high-precision exponential phase of the PCR when none of the reaction components are limiting, contrary to PCR end-point measurements.

Although SYBR Green assay provides the simplest and most economical format for detecting and quantifying PCR products in real-time reactions, the main limitation is that non-specific amplifications (primer-dimer, non-human products, etc.) cannot be distinguished from specific amplifications. On the other hand, the amplicon/dye ratio varies with amplicon length. In addition, SYBR Green can only be used in single PCR reactions, therefore the use of this assay should be restricted to optimized PCR reactions producing single PCR products free from non-specific PCR artefacts.

The probe-based real-time PCR assay has been the method of choice to quantify human nuDNA and mtDNA in forensic genetics because of its superior specificity and quantitation accuracy in comparison with SYBR Green assays. Another advantage of probe-based methods is the feasibility to perform multiplex PCR of different targets. Probe-based assays also provide the possibility to perform, in a single PCR reaction, not only specific human DNA quantification but also different qualitative analyses, such as gender determination, DNA degradation and *Taq* inhibition rate.

Human Nuclear DNA Quantifcation

Single-copy Autosomal Targets

The use of probe-based real-time PCR to quantify human nuclear DNA in forensic analysis was firstly described by Andreasson *et al.* (2002). A 78 bp region of the human retinoblastoma susceptibility gene (RB1), a nuclear-encoded single-copy gene located on chromosome 13, was the target in a multiplex PCR quantification assay that was also designed to amplify an mtDNA target. The system has been shown to detect down to nuDNA single copies in the dilution series of the standard curve and has been applied to quantify nuDNA from different forensic specimens such as skin debris, saliva stains, hair and bloodstains. This assay has been used recently to quantify nuDNA in the roots and distal sections of plucked and shed head hairs and also from fingerprints and accessories. However, the choice of RB1 as a real-time quantitative PCR target may not be ideal because the RB1 sequence is relatively conserved among different species and perhaps it is not sufficiently primate-specific to be of general forensic utility.

A TaqMan-MGB (minus groove binder) real-time PCR design has been developed to target a small region of 62 bp located 31 bp downstream from the polymorphic repeat region of the HumTH01 locus. The assay has been applied to the quantification of human nuDNA from a variety of body fluid stains.

A human DNA quantification kit was developed for the quantification of human nuDNA by targeting a 62 bp portion of the *human telomerase reverse transcriptase* (hTERT) locus using a TaqMan-MGB assay that includes an internal PCR control (IPC) for the assessment of PCR efficiency against *Taq* inhibitors. The kit has been validated for use in forensic casework according to the Scientific Working Group on DNA Analysis Methods (SWGDAM) guidelines and now is the most used assay in forensic casework for nuDNA quantitation.

More recently, a multiplex quantitative PCR assay has been described to amplify simultaneously two target sequences of different length, the TH01 STR locus (170–190 bp) and the upstream flanking region of the CSF1PO STR locus (67 bp), which allows for the assessment of DNA degradation in samples of forensic interest. The assay also includes an internal PCR control target sequence to allow for an assessment of PCR inhibition.

Alu Repetitive Elements

Several real-time PCR assays have also been developed to target different *Alu* repetitive sequences for highly sensitive nuDNA quantification. Nicklas and Buel (2003) have described a SYBR Green real-time PCR assay using specific primers to target a 124 bp *Alu* sequence with primate specificity and 1 pg sensitivity. Walker *et al.* (2003) presented two alternative SYBR Green real-time PCR designs to target inter-*Alu* (including a complex pool of sequences of different sizes) and intra-*Alu* (200–226 bp) sequences, respectively. Inter-*Alu* assay was found to be not completely human-specific while intra-*Alu* PCR was demonstrated to be a specific and sensitive method for human nuDNA quantification in the range of 10 ng to 1 pg.

The main advantages of SYBR Green real-time PCR designs to target *Alu* assays are simplicity and high sensitivity. The disadvantages are the necessity of optimization to avoid the possibility of unspecific PCR artefacts and the possible inaccuracy in the DNA quantification as a consequence of a hypothetical individual variation in the copy number of *Alu* sequences. Walker *et al.* (2005) have described a TaqMan-MGB triplex real-time PCR assay for simultaneous quantitation of human nuDNA (based on an intra-*Alu* sequence design), mtDNA and Y chromosome DNA.

X and Y Chromosome Targets

Alonso *et al*. described a method for nuDNA quantification based on TaqMan-MGB real-time PCR amplification of a segment of the X–Y homologous amelogenin (AMG) gene that allowed the simultaneous estimation of a Y-specific fragment (AMGY: 112 bp) and an X-specific fragment (AMGX: 106 bp), making possible not only DNA quantitation but also sex determination. Detection of the specific AMGX fragment (106 bp) and AMGY fragment (112 bp) was achieved using the primer pair sequences previously described and two fluorogenic MGB probes that specifically detect the AMGX fragment (FAM-labelled) or the AMGY fragment (VIC-labelled). The MGB probes were designed to target the 6 bp X- deletion/Y-insertion segment within the AMG second intron fragment. The method has been applied to the analysis of LCN DNA samples in forensic and ancient DNA studies.

A SYBR-green real-time PCR assay of the human amelogenin gene using specific primers to produce a Y-specific fragment of 73 bp and a 3-bp-deleted X-specific fragment of 70 bp was described. The assay allows quantification of the nuDNA copy number, but sex determination, which is based on a dissociation curve analysis that displays the different melting temperatures of X- and Y-specific products, has certain limitations for forensic applications and especially for the analysis of mixed male–female forensic samples.

A specific real-time PCR quantification kit based on the TaqMan-MGB detection of a region (61–64 bp) of the SRY locus is also commercially available. The assay, which detects only male DNA, is intended particularly for use in samples with mixed male–female DNA, such as sexual assault evidence, where it may be useful for specific male DNA detection. The kit has also been validated for use in forensic casework according to SWGDAM guidelines.

A sex chromosome TaqMan-MGB assay was designed around a 90 bp deletion on the X chromosome in an X–Y homologous region to target a 77 bp fragment on the human X chromosome and a 167 bp fragment on the human Y chromosome.

Human Mitochondrial DNA Quantifcation

The use of a TaqMan real-time PCR assay for quantification of mitochondrial human DNA from forensic specimens was first described by Andréasson *et al*. (2003) by targeting a 142 bp region spanning over the genes for tRNA lysine and ATP Synthase 8 that can be amplified in a single PCR reaction or in combination with an nuDNA target. The assay was tested on 236 forensic specimens (hair, bloodstains, fingerprints, skin debris, saliva stains and others) containing from zero to >100 000 mtDNA copies and more recently on different LCN DNA samples such as fingerprints.

Alonso *et al*. (2003, 2004) reported the specific quantification of human mtDNA by monitoring the real-time progress of the PCR amplification of two different fragment sizes (113 bp and 287 bp) within the hypervariable region 1 (HV1) of the mtDNA control region, using two fluorogenic probes to specifically determine the mtDNA copy of each fragment size category. This additional information – number of copies in each size category – has been demonstrated to be very helpful to evaluate the mtDNA preservation state from ancient bone samples.

A 69 bp fragment of the mtDNA NADH dehydrogenase subunit 1(ND1) locus has also been used as a target for mtDNA quantitation in forensic specimens using a TaqMan duplex real-time PCR assay that allows simultaneous quantification of human nuDNA. Another mtDNA target used in forensics by TaqMan-MGB assays is a 79 bp fragment of a conserved region of the human mtDNA, which is co-amplified with an autosomal and a Y chromosome target.

Recently a novel forensic use of quantitative *real-time PCR* (rtPCR) using TaqMan-MGB probes has been described, targeting the highly variable mitochondrial single nucleotide polymorphism 165 19T/C to investigate heteroplasmic mixtures with an accurate quantification of the minor allele down to 9%.

Detection and Quantification of Non-human Species

Forensic analysis of non-human evidence is gaining importance and becoming widely used in forensic laboratories for the identification of animal material recovered from the crime scene (usually pet hairs). A SYBR Green quantitative real-time PCR assay has been developed for the quantification of genomic DNA extracted from domestic cat samples. Investigation of the illegal trade in endangered species is another field of application of real-time quantitative PCR. A highly sensitive tiger-specific real- time PCR assay has been described using primers specific to the tiger mitochondrial cytochrome *b* gene. Successful amplification has been demonstrated from blood, hair and bone as well as from a range of traditional Chinese medicines spiked with 0.5% tiger bone.

Real-time quantitative PCR is also an emerging technique in ancient DNA studies of non-human species. Poinar *et al*. (2003)

quantitated the number of mitochondrial 16S rDNA copies for fragments of three different lengths (114/252/522 bp) by using a TaqMan real-time PCR assay from ancient coprolite remains, demonstrating that there was roughly a 100-fold drop in the number of amplifiable mtDNA molecules for every doubling in amplification length.

Quantitative PCR analysis of DNA from non-invasive samples with low DNA content is also a useful tool for molecular characterization of wild animal populations in molecular ecology, including nuDNA quantification and sex determination.

Real-time quantitative PCR is also a rapid and highly sensitive methodological tool for detection, identification and individualization of microbial agents that could be used in bioterrorist acts. For instance, real-time PCR assays are routinely used to detect the presence of DNA from *Bacillus anthracis* in environmental samples by using both unique plasmid-borne and chromosomal genes. Other highly sensitive real-time PCR assays for the detection of potential bioterrorism agents such as *Yersinia Pestis*, *Francisella tularensis*, *Brucella* spp. and *Burkholderia* spp. have also been developed.

PERSPECTIVES

Real-time quantitative PCR has become a widely used technique for sensitive and specific quantification of both human nuDNA and mtDNA in forensics and ancient DNA studies, offering several advantages with respect to other current methodologies (hybridization or end-point PCR methods), including: higher sensitivity and dynamic range of quantitation, unnecessary post-PCR processing, automation feasibility and high throughput, and the possibility to simultaneously perform different qualitative analyses (gender determination, mtDNA degradation, *Taq* inhibition rate, etc.).

However, the data obtained by comparing different real-time PCR methods across different laboratories show differences with regard to precision and bias. These results emphasize the need to develop a standard reference material for DNA quantification in the forensic field.

Real-time PCR methods will continue to take advantage of technical developments to improve the multiplexing capability, the automation feasibility and the detection limit.

The use of real-time quantitative PCR methods for body fluid (saliva, semen and blood) identification by targeting messenger RNA markers is a novel molecular approach within the forensic field that will probably increase in use and importance. The forensic application of real-time quantitative PCR assays to target other markers of gene expression remains to be explored.

Recovery of DNA for PCR Amplification

A wide range of biological samples are encountered in the field of forensic science, including blood, soft tissue, semen, urine, saliva, teeth, and bone. Forensic samples are routinely found as stains on various substrates, including cotton, denim, carpet, wallboard, wood, envelopes, and cigaret butts. Prior to collection, these samples have often been exposed to severe environmental conditions, such as varying degrees of temperature and humidity, microbial and chemical contaminants, and exposure to soils and other natural substances, such as salt water.

Not only do the precollection conditions effect the quality and quantity of DNA recovered from a specimen, but the postcollection storage conditions may also have a deleterious effect on the DNA. The short- and long-term storage conditions of both evidence specimens and isolated DNA have been evaluated. Although DNA is among the most stable biomolecules, it has been found that storage of various biological samples at different temperatures for varying amounts of time can have a marked effect on the ability to isolate high-mol-wt DNA. Consequently, this poses a problem for *restriction-fragment-length polymorphism* (RFLP) analysis of many forensic samples. RFLP analysis which is commonly used in forensic casework, generally requires between 20 and 100 ng of high-mol-wt DNA. Polymerase chain reaction PCR-based typing methods, however, do not require high quantities of DNA and therefore have a higher success rate with degraded samples. The selected method for isolating DNA from forensic samples, therefore, often influences the ability to successfully perform DNA analysis.

As a result, several DNA extraction methods have been developed and evaluated by the forensic community. The organic extraction method (e.g., SDS/proteinase K, phenol/chloroform, ethanol precipitation) is very successful and is routinely used for forensic samples analyzed by RFLP. When applied to PCR-based typing methods, however, this method was found to have limitations. Although sufficient DNA was recovered for analysis, it did not always amplify. This failure of amplification was thought to have been caused by the inability to remove inhibitors, such as heme, during the extraction process. Greater amplification success was obtained by following organic extraction with a dialysis and concentration step using a Centricon 100 device rather than ethanol precipitation. In addition to organic methods of DNA extraction, several inorganic methods have also been developed, including the use of high salt concentrations, glass powders, and silica-gel suspensions to recover high-mol-wt DNA. Unfortunately, all of the above extraction methods are time-consuming and require several steps, washing/desalting procedures, and multiple tube transfers. An alternative DNA extraction method has been developed that involves the addition of a chelating-resin suspension directly to the sample.

The chelating-resin-based procedure is a simple, one-tube, minimal step extraction process that requires very little time. The risk of operator-induced error, such as contamination or sample mixup, is also reduced, since the procedure requires fewer manipulations. Most importantly, the use of a chelating resin to extract DNA eliminates the use of hazardous chemicals, such as phenol-chloroform.

The simplicity of chelating-resin-extraction methods has made this extraction method very desirable in the forensic community. DNA has successfully been extracted using Chelex 100, a chelating resin, from a variety of forensic samples, including whole blood, bloodstains, tissue, and bone. Chelex 100 scavenges metal contaminants to an extremely high degree of purity without altering the concentration of nonmetallic ions. The resin is composed of styrene divinylbenzene copolymers containing paired iminodiacetate ions that act as chelating groups in binding polyvalent metal ions. Chelex 100 has a particularly high selectivity for divalent ions and differs from ordinary ion exchangers because of its high selectivity for metal ions and its higher bond strength.

Using this method, the basic procedure for recovering DNA from forensic samples, such as whole blood and bloodstains, consists of an initial wash step to remove possible contaminants and inhibitors, such as heme and other proteins. For other forensic samples, such as tissue and bone, the wash step is not necessary. The samples are then boiled in a 5% suspension of Chelex 100. After a quick spin, an aliquot of the supernatant can be added directly to the amplification reaction. The alkalinity of Chelex 100 suspensions and the exposure to 100~ temperatures result in the disruption of the cell membranes and denaturation of the DNA. The exact role of Chelex 100 during the boiling process is still unclear; however, Walsh et al. has shown that purified DNA that has been subjected to temperatures of 100°C in distilled water alone is inactive in PCR. Therefore, the presence of the chelating resin during the boiling step may have a protective role and prevent the degradation of DNA by chelating metal ions. These ions may act as catalysts in the breakdown of DNA in low ionic strength solutions at high temperatures.

The effectiveness of a particular DNA extraction method may be evaluated on the DNA yield itself; however, the more important measurements of the effectiveness are the suitability of the extracted DNA for amplification and the quality of the obtained results. A variety of DNA extraction methods have been evaluated based on their ability to yield DNA from bloodstains that had been deposited on several different substrates. Included in the following study were two common extraction methods utilized in the field of forensic science: Chelex 100 and the organic method. Additional studies were also performed to compare PCR-typing results obtained from samples extracted by each method. The results revealed that there was no difference between the human leukocyte antigen DQα locus (HLA DQα) genotypes obtained by PCR amplification of DNA extracted by the Chelex 100-based procedure or from those extracted via the organic method.

Our laboratory has been able to successfully extract DNA from blood and tissue samples that have been exposed to extreme environmental conditions by using the Chelex 100 method. Additionally, these samples have been successfully amplified and analyzed using several PCR-based methods. The DNA-typing systems applied include the following: HLA-DQα, PolyMarker (PM-LDLR, GYPA, HBGG, D7S8, GC), D1S80, a *short-tandem-repeat* (STR) quadruplex (HUMVWFA31, HUMTH01, HUMF13A01, and HUMFESFPS) and mitochondrial DNA sequencing. The AmpliType HLA DQα and AmpliType systems are both reverse-dot blot, colorimetric assays, based on DNA-sequence polymorphisms. The D1S80 and STR quadruplex systems detect length polymorphisms of repeated DNA sequences. Mitochondrial DNA sequencing detects sequence polymorphisms within two hypervariable regions.

To conclude, although Chelex 100 is an excellent extraction method, the forensic community is continuing to investigate new automatable methods of extraction. Methods have been developed that involve the use of chemically impregnated filter papers amenable to automation. One such procedure involves the immobilization of DNA onto filter paper while cell and body-fluid contaminants are selectively removed. The filter paper containing DNA is then dehydrated by rinsing with alcohol followed by a drying step. This allows the sample to be amplified directly from the filter paper by adding amplification reagents.

Another example of a new method is one in which the chemicals impregnated on the filter paper disrupt and release DNA from nucleated cells while simultaneously discouraging the release of inhibitory substances. The inhibitory substances are trapped on the filter paper and the DNA is captured in solution. Finally, the choice of an extraction method is an important decision and one that must be carefully considered. When processing forensic samples, selecting the appropriate method can have significant impact on the end result.

Materials

1. Chelex 100.
2. Sterile deionized H_2O.

Methods

Chelex extraction of whole blood and bloodstains

1. Pipet 1 mL of sterile deionized water into a 1.7-mL microcentrifuge tube.
2. Add approx 3 ml of whole blood or a piece of bloodstained material (approx 1/8 in. diameter hole punch or a 3 mm^2 piece of material).
3. To wash the sample, mix and incubate at room temperature for 15 min.
4. Prepare a 5% Chelex solution in sterile deionized H_2O.
5. Centrifuge samples for 3 min at 10,000*g* in a microcentrifuge to pellet the red blood cells.
6. Carefully remove all but approx 20 ml of the supernatant and discard. Leave the substrate and pelleted material in the tube.
7. Resuspend the pellet in 5% Chelex 100 to a final volume of 200 ml.
8. Incubate at 56°C for 30 min.
9. Vortex at high speed for 5 s.
10. Incubate in a boiling water bath for 8 min.
11. Vortex at high speed for 5 s.
12. Centrifuge samples for 3 min at 10,000*g* to pellet the Chelex 100 resin, substrate, and remaining tissue/bone.
13. Extracts are now ready for quantitation and the PCR amplification process.
14. For short-term storage (up to 1 mo), store extracts at 2°C on the Chelex 100 resin. To use the extracts after storage, repeat steps 11 and 12. For long-term storage (>1 mo), the extracts should be centrifuged and the supernatant removed from the Chelex 100 resin and stored in a new tube at -20°C.

Chelex extraction of tissue and fresh bone

1. Prepare a 5% Chelex 100 suspension in sterile deionized H_2O.
2. Add 200 ml of 5% Chelex 100 suspension to a 1.7 mL microcentrifuge tube.
3. Cut an approx 2 mm^2 piece of tissue or, if present, scrape the marrow from inside of a fresh bone and place directly into Chelex 100 suspension.
4. Incubate at 56°C for 30 min.
5. Continue with protocol for whole blood and bloodstains.

Notes

1. Protocols for extracting DNA using the Chelex 100 method are available for other forensic specimens, such as postcoital samples and oral swabs containing sperm, hair, semen, semen stains, and paraffin-embedded tissue.
2. If DNA is boiled in a solution of 0.01 *M* Tris-HCl, pH 8.0 with 0.1 *M* EDTA (TE buffer), it is protected for PCR. EDTA is a chelating agent that can attach itself to a single metal ion through six donor atoms. This theory is also in agreement with Singer-Sam et al., which suggests that Chelex 100 sequesters divalent heavy metals that would otherwise introduce DNA damage. An advantage of using Chelex 100 resin rather than TE buffer is that the Chelex 100 resin can be removed from the supernatant by centrifugation. This helps prevent any inhibitors or contaminants that may be bound to the resin from being introduced into the PCR. Additionally, samples that contain high concentrations of TE buffer may have a deleterious effect on the PCR by sequestering magnesium ions that are essential to Thermus aquaticus *(Taq)* polymerase. Therefore, it is advisable to use a PCR buffer with 2.0 m*M* $MgCl_2$ for amplifications from DNA stored in TE buffer with high concentrations of EDTA.
3. In a study performed by the Federal Bureau of Investigation (FBI), several extraction methods were compared. The data are a comparison of the two most common extraction methods in the field of forensic science.

   Chelex 100 and organic. A comparison of DNA yields was performed using the slot-blot method. Samples extracted from either method yielded a sufficient amount of DNA for PCR. For most substrates, excluding cotton and denim, the yield of DNA was relatively consistent. A possible explanation for lower yields with

Table 9.1. Results of concordance study in typing Chelex vs organic extraction at the HLA DQa locus

Sample type	*Number*	*%Concordance*
Bloodstains	56	100
Semen stains	9	100
Postcoital swabs	8	100
Buccal swabs	6	100
Hairs	5	100
TOTAL	84	100

the organic extraction of bloodstain on cotton may be the loss of DNA during the number of tube transfers that are required during the extraction process. The organic method resulted in a twofold difference in the concentration of DNA recovered from the bloodstain on denim, compared to the Chelex 100 method. This may be caused by the longer 56°C incubation time period (overnight for organic vs 2 h for Chelex 100), which allows more time for the cellular debris to dislodge from the fabric.

4. In a study performed by Walsh et al., 84 samples commonly encountered in forensics were evaluated for suitability of the DNA for amplification as well as for the quality of the results obtained. Included in these samples were bloodstains exposed to a variety of environmental conditions, blood and semen stains on several different fabric substrates, postcoital swabs, buccal swabs, and hair. Samples were originally extracted using the traditional organic method and analyzed at the HLA DQα locus. The extractions were later repeated using the Chelex 100-based procedure and reanalyzed. All samples produced typeable results with no extraneous alleles reported. As summarized, there were no discrepancies in the HLA DQα genotype obtained for any sample using either extraction method.
5. DNA has been successfully extracted from a variety of tissue samples that have been exposed to harsh environmental conditions. For example, 222 extractions were performed on samples recovered from the Waco, TX incident in 1994, wherein the samples were highly incinerated and in an advanced state of decomposition. Our strategy was to perform Chelex 100 extractions first on all of the samples. This procedure can be performed quickly, and, therefore results can be obtained in a short amount of time. In this case,

60% of the samples yielded sufficient DNA by Chelex 100 extraction to obtain results. The remaining 40% required an organic extraction to obtain results. Overall DNA recovery was minimal. More than 50% of the extracts contained <100 ng DNA. This may be attributed to the highly degraded nature of the DNA. One of the disadvantages of the Chelex 100 method is the limited sample size. The Chelex 100 procedure does not include a purification step and, therefore, if the sample contains inhibitors and contaminants, increasing the sample size increases the concentration of inhibitors and contaminants. Larger sample sizes can be used for the organic extraction method. In this instance, increasing the sample size increased the recovery of DNA. Chelex 100 can then be added to the organic extract to bind any contaminants that may still be present in the extract. To determine if inhibition is occurring when an amplification reaction fails or partial profiles are obtained, an aliquot of the sample extract can be added to the positive control to see if the results are inhibited. For example, during the fluorescence detection of STR profiles, the peak heights of the positive control may decrease in the presence of inhibitors. Inhibition can sometimes be overcome by using 1/10 or 1/100 dilutions of the original extract. Additionally, five units of *Taq* polymerase and/or 8 mL *bovine serum albumin* (BSA) can be added to the reaction to overcome inhibition.

6. Our laboratory has also been successful in extracting and analyzing DNA from samples recovered from aircraft accidents in which tissue samples were extremely charred as well as soaked with fuel. For example, results were obtained from an aircraft mishap in Alaska in which 24 individuals were killed. The aircraft crashed immediately on takeoff and was carrying approx 125,000 pounds of fuel. Our laboratory received 24 tissue samples and 20 reference bloodstain cards in order to confirm identifications using DNA analysis. All 44 samples were extracted within approx 3 h. Two samples did not produce results because of inhibition and were reextracted. The extractions were repeated using a smaller sample size and results were successfully obtained. All 44 samples were extracted and analyzed using PolyMarker analysis within 24 h. In addition, STR analysis was performed on four tissue samples and four reference specimens within an additional 24 h. Therefore, our laboratory was able to confirm the identifications of 16 individuals and provide strong evidence for identification of four

other individuals within 48 h. Without the use of the Chelex 100 extraction method, this would not have been possible.

7. It has been our experience that if blood is tightly bound to the substrate or ethanol fixed to the substrate, the initial wash step should be incubated at 56°C to help facilitate the diffusion of blood off of the substrate. Porphyrin compounds derived from heme in blood have also been shown to inhibit PCR. It has been suggested that these porphyrin rings are being washed away during the initial wash step or may bind to the Chelex 100 bead matrix itself. Additional water washes may be necessary in order to rid the sample of excess heme and inhibitors. For example, two of the 84 samples (bloodstain on a red sweatshirt and semen stain on black cotton) analyzed in the Typing Concordance Study failed to amplify initially using the Chelex 100 method. The bloodstain substrate was a red fabric that colored the extract red. This red dye apparently inhibited the amplification. An additional 3-mm^2 piece of bloodstain was allowed to soak for 30 min at room temperature and vortexed to dislodge cellular material from the fabric. The fabric substrate was removed, and the solution was centrifuged to pellet the cellular debris. The supernatant was removed and discarded. The cellular debris was washed three times with water followed by centrifugation. All but 50 ml of the last wash was discarded and 150 ml of 5% Chelex 100 was added. The remainder of the protocol was as described previously. The sample was then successfully amplified and analyzed.
8. The quality of each new manufactured lot of Chelex 100 should be assessed. A 5% Chelex 100 suspension should be made fresh for each set of extractions. According to the manufacturer of Chelex 100, the resin has a tendency to lose its chelating capacity after more than a few hours. The effectiveness of Chelex 100 is based on pH. The pH of the 5% Chelex 100 suspension should be between 10.0 and 11.0. Do not attempt to adjust the pH if the suspension does not fall within this range. A suggested method for assessing a new lot of Chelex 100 is to extract DNA from bloodstains or whole-blood samples (of known genotype) and analyze the extracts using the most sensitive typing system available. This will control for human contaminants. A "*spiked*" reagent blank (9 ml of reagent blank with 1 ng of known DNA) can also be analyzed. The "*spiked*" reagent blank ensures that the Chelex 100 itself is not inhibiting the PCR. All extracts and "*spiked*" reagent-blank controls must

yield detectable PCR product and generate the appropriate DNA profile. No PCR product should be present in the reagent blanks.

9. When pipetting the Chelex 100 suspension, the resin beads must be distributed evenly in solution. This can be done by gently mixing with a stir bar in a small beaker. The pipet tip used to draw up the suspension must have a relatively large bore, p 1000 (200,000 μm tip), to ensure that a 5% suspension is maintained.
10. A study was recently performed in our laboratory to evaluate the 56°C incubation period on our typing results. Fifty bloodstains were allowed to incubate at 56°C for 30 min and an additional 50 bloodstains were incubated at 56°C for 2 h. All 100 samples were successfully analyzed by STR analysis with no significant differences.
11. Specimens extracted with Chelex 100 yield single-stranded DNA and are unsuitable for quantitation methods that use intercalating dyes, such as ethidium bromide. Therefore, a quantitation method, such as slot-blot is suggested. In addition, the DNA is not suitable for RFLP analysis because the Chelex 100 procedure results in denatured DNA. Because of our case turnaround time, our samples are usually not quantitated prior to amplification, and therefore our laboratory routinely uses the following volumes of a bloodstain extract in the PCR: 5 ml for HLA DQα, 10 ml for PM, 10 ml for D1S80, 2 ml for STRs, and 2 ml for mtDNA sequencing. All of the afore-mentioned analyses can be performed multiple times on a single extract, since the final volume of a Chelex 100 extraction is 200 ml.
12. If the extracts are to be reanalyzed over a period of time, it is recommended that the supernatant be removed from the Chelex 100 resin and stored at -20°C (long-term storage). It has been suggested that the resin may break down over time, which in turn may release any previously bound inhibitors, or the resin itself may inhibit the PCR by chelating magnesium ions.
13. It is recommended that the sample selected for extraction be dissected from the innermost part of the tissue to avoid cros scontamination from comingled samples and inhibition from environmental factors.

PCR Analysis of DNA from Fresh and Decomposed Bodies

One of the greatest values of *polymerase chain reaction* (PCR) for the death investigator lies in the fact that even minute amounts of

DNA or extensively damaged (degraded) DNA can be successfully amplified and thus become amenable for typing procedures.

In medico-legal death investigations, the types of DNA recovered from a body can be divided into two areas: DNA evidence, which adheres to the surface of the body or is present within a body cavity (e.g., blood, semen, saliva, nasal secretions, hairs, shed scalp skin, urine, feces); and biological material, which belongs to the deceased (e.g., liquid blood, soft tissues, bones, teeth, fingernails) and can be used as reference samples. In general, the success of DNA profiling depends most on the environmental conditions the body was exposed to and on the proper preservation and collecting procedures.

There are many published methods for the extraction of DNA from forensic evidence for subsequent amplification. This section describes methods that are robust, extensively tested, and have been used successfully in difficult and high-priority cases. Since we deal with a variety of samples, the extraction methods will first be described, followed by notes for the different samples.

Materials

DNA extraction and quantitation

1. IX stain extraction buffer: 10 m*M* Tris-HCl, 10 m*M* EDTA, 100 m*M* NaCl, 39 m*M* DTT, 2% sodium dodecyl sulfate (SDS), pH 8.0. Short-time storage at room temperature (SDS precipitates at 4°C). Add proteinase K fresh from frozen aliquots of 20 mg/mL.
2. Phenol/chloroform/isoamylalcohol (25:24:1); in buffer 10 m*M* Tris-HCl, pH 7.5 .0, 1 m*M* EDTA-Na_2. Store at 4°C.
3. Water-saturated *n*-butanol. Prepare fresh before use.
4. Centricon 100 microconcentrator tubes.
5. QuantiBlot Human DNA Quantitation Kit or ACES 2.0$^+$ Human DNA Quantitation System.

   For recovery of sperm-cell and vaginal-cell DNA:
6. HEPES-buffered saline: 10 m*M* HEPES, 150 m*M* NaCl, pH 7.5. Store at 4°C.
7. Phosphate-buffered saline (PBS): 137 m*M* NaCI, 2.7 m*M* KCl, 1.5 m*M* KH_2PO_4, 8.1 m*M* Na_2HPO_4, pH7.5.
8. Sarcosyl: 20 and 10%. Store at 4°C.
9. TNE: 10 m*M* Tris-base, 100 m*M* NaCI, 1 m*M* Na_2EDTA, pH 8.0. Store at 4°C.
10. Dithiothreitol (DTT) 0.39 M. Add fresh from frozen aliquots.
11. 0.5 M EDTA, pH 8.0. Store at 4°C (for bone samples).

PCR and detection of PCR products

1. Standard PCR reagents (e.g., Multiplex PCR kits: AmpliType PM PCR Amplification and Typing Kit; GenePrint STR Systems PCR Amplification Kit).
2. SA 32 Electrophoresis apparatus. Gel dimensions: 310 × 0.4 mm.
3. Gel Slick and binding solution (3 μL methacryloxypropyl-trimethoxysilane in 1 mL 0.5% acetic acid in 95% ethanol) to prepare glass plates.
4. Denaturing polyacrylamide gel (4% T, 5% C, containing 7 *M* urea and 0.5X TrisBorate-EDTA buffer) (210 g urea, 267 mL dH_2O, 25 mL 10X TBE, and 50 mL 40% acrylamide:bis [19:1]).
5. 0.5X TBE (electrophoresis buffer).
6. Silver staining reagents:
   (a) Fix/stop solution (10% acetic acid);
   (b) Staining solution (2 g silver nitrate and 3 mL 37% formaldehyde in 2000 mL H_2O);
   (c) Developer solution (3 mL 37% formaldehyde, 400 μL 10 mg/mL sodium thiosulfate, 60 g sodium carbonate in 2000 mL H_2O).
7. Duplicating X-ray film.

Methods

Organic extraction of biological material with centricon purification

1. Biological material is incubated overnight at 56°C in 400 μL (up to 600 μL) IX stain-extraction buffer and 10 μL (up to 50 μL) proteinase K (20 mg/mL) in a sterile 1.5 or 2.0-mL tube with a screw cap. If swabs or cuttings are processed, a 2.2-mL microcentrifuge tube with a spin insert (with no membrane) or a Spin-EASE Extraction tube is used.
2. On the following day, an additional 10 μL (up to 50 μL) proteinase K (20 mg/mL) is added and the sample is incubated for an additional 2 h at 56°C.
3. Without removing the material, 700 mL phenol/chloroform/isoamylalcohol (25:24:1) is added, and the tube is vigorously shaken by hand for 2 min to achieve a milky emulsion. The tube is subjected to centrifugation at 10,000g for 3 min. If swabs or cuttings are processed, the material is removed with sterile forceps and placed into the spin insert, which is then placed into the tube from which the swab or cutting came and centrifuged at 10,000g

for 5 min. Then the spin insert with the swab or cutting is removed and discarded.

4. The aqueous phase (top layer) is transferred to a new tube with a screw cap, taking care not to transfer the interphase. The phenol-extraction step is repeated up to three times for materials with high protein content.
5. To purify the DNA, the aqueous phase (bottom layer) is transferred to a Centricon 100 microconcentrator tube containing sterile water, and the volume is brought up to 2 mL with sterile water. The sample reservoir is sealed with parafilm, and after punching a hole in the parafilm (using a sterile needle), the tube is subjected to centrifugation at 1000g for 30 min. Then 2 mL of sterile water is added to the sample reservoir, which is then sealed with new parafilm. Again the tube is centrifuged at 1000g for 30 min. The DNA is recovered by back centrifugation at 1000g for 5 min. The final sample volume is approx 25 μL.
6. Ten percent of the retentate is used to determine the quantity of human DNA by slot-blot analysis.

Organic extraction with centricon purification for the recovery of sperm-cell and vaginal-cell DNA

1. The swab or cuttings are placed into a 2.2-mL microcentrifuge tube with a spin insert (with no membrane). After addition of 450 μL HEPES-buffered saline and 50 μL 20% Sarcosyl, the tube is vigorously shaken at 4°C for at least 2 h to overnight and then briefly centrifuged. The swab or cuttings are removed with sterile forceps and placed into the spin insert. The spin insert is placed into the tube from which the swab or cuttings came and centrifuged at 10,000g for 5 min. The swab or cuttings are removed and placed into a new 1.5-mL tube with a screw cap.
2. The supernatant fluid in the tube is discarded, leaving behind approx 20 μL; 1 μL of the cell pellet is spotted on a microscopic slide and stained for the presence of sperm cells and epithelia cells.
3. The swab or cuttings are placed back into the original tube, 200 μL Tris-EDTANaCl, 50 μL 10% SDS, 245 μL sterile water, and 5 μL proteinase K (20 mg/mL) is added, and the tube incubated at 37°C for 2 h to isolate the DNA from epithelia cells. Again, the swab or cuttings are removed with sterile forceps and placed into a spin insert. The spin insert is placed into the tube from which the swab or cutting came and centrifuged at 10,000g for 5 min.

4. The swab or cuttings are removed and discarded.
5. The supernatant fluid is saved as "*epithelial-cell fraction.*"
6. The sperm-cell pellet is washed by adding 500 μL PBS, vortexing, and centrifuging at 10,000g for 5 min. This washing step is repeated three times.
7. To the washed sperm-cell pellet, 200 μL TNE, 125 μL 10% sarcosyl, 50 μL 0.39 M dithiothreitol (DTT), 115 μL sterile water, and 10 μL proteinase K (20 mg/mL) are added and the tube incubated at 37°C for 2 h to isolate the DNA from the sperm cells. This fluid is called "*sperm-cell fraction.*" Both fractions are extracted with an equal volume of phenol/chloroform/isoamylalcohol.

Organic DNA extraction from bone

1. The DNA is extracted from 5-g fragment of the femur bone. The bone is cleaned with sandpaper to remove the outer layer, broken into small pieces, and pulverized into a fine powder using liquid nitrogen. The bone powder is transferred into a sterile 50-mL polypropylene tube and decalcified in 40 mL of 0.5 M EDTA, pH 8.0, on a rotator at 4°C for 24 h. After centrifugation at 2000g for 15 min, the supernatant is discarded. The powder is washed with 40 mL of extraction buffer (0.5 M EDTA, 0.5% sarcosyl, pH 8.0) to remove excess calcium. Then the sample is centrifuged at 2000g for 15 min and the supernatant discarded.
2. The DNA is extracted by adding prewarmed (37°C) extraction buffer (0.5 *M* EDTA, 0.5% sarcosyl, pH 8.0) to a final volume of approx 7 mL. Then 100 μL of proteinase K (20 mg/mL) is added and the tube incubated at 37°C for 12 h. Subsequently, 100 μL proteinase K (20 mg/mL) is added and incubation continued at 37°C for an additional 12 h.
3. The solution is extracted two to three times with phenol/chloroform/isoamylalcohol (25:24:1).
4. One extraction with 20 mL water-saturated *n*-butanol is carried out to remove traces of phenol.
5. The aqueous phase is concentrated using a Centricon 100 microconcentrator tube that is subjected to several 30-min centrifugation steps at 1000g. Finally, the retentate is washed three times with 2 mL of sterile water. The final sample volume is approx 250 μL. Bone extraction is carried out independently in duplicate, and a sample containing no bone serves as a reagent negative control sample.

6. Ten percent of the retentate is used to determine the quantity of human DNA by slot-blot analysis.

Notes

1. Blood: Blood on the skin is removed with a cotton swab moistened with sterile water. The area is swabbed carefully in a circular motion for approx 30 s. The swab is air-dried for 6 h or immediately frozen, and DNA is extracted from the swab using the method described above.
2. Semen: Evidence is removed as described above. DNA is extracted from the swab in one tube using the differential lysis method described above.
3. Saliva: Bite marks or areas where a perpetrator might have kissed or sucked a victim (e.g., nipples) are swabbed as described above.
4. Nasal secretions: The material is extracted using the method described above or in the same manner as described for saliva stains.
5. Hair: DNA is isolated from 1 cm of the root portion from a single hair with attached sheath material using the method described above.
6. Fingernails: The fingernail is chopped into very fine pieces and DNA extracted using the method described above. Nails can be boiled for 5 min in sterile water and then chopped into fine pieces to help the nails digest faster. It is also possible to extract DNA without this step.
7. Fingernail debris: In a case where a victim has scratched the perpetrator, fingernail debris might contain nucleated cells or even small amounts of blood. Fingernail debris can be recovered by swabbing all nails of a hand with a single cotton swab moistened with sterile water.
8. Urine: Extraction and amplification of DNA from urine stains is seldom successful. Methods for isolating DNA are provided by several authors.
9. Feces: There is no reference that indicates that an individual was identified from fecal material. A method for preparation of fecal DNA suitable for PCR is provided by Deuter et al.
10. Liquid blood from a cadaver is not a reference material of choice, even if the cadaver is fresh, since after death blood clots form that trap nucleated blood cells. During the autopsy, often hemolyzed serum containing only a few nucleated blood cells is collected,

which makes DNA isolation cumbersome. In our experience, DNA extraction from 300 μL of cadaver blood using standard protocols often fails to yield enough DNA. If cadaver blood is the only reference material, best results are obtained by using approx 50 mL of blood and the organic extraction method provided by Maniatis.

11. Soft tissues are an excellent reference material, if the cadaver is fresh. The material should be stored frozen. Approximately 100 mg of soft tissue (preferable a fat-free lymph node from the neck or a piece of muscle tissue) are cut with a sterile scalpel blade on a microscope slide and processed. Fifty microliters of proteinase K (20 mg/mL) are added to the sample and the solution extracted two to three times with an equal amount of phenol/chloroform/ isoamylalcohol.
12. Bone: From fresh cadavers or decomposed bodies approx 5 cm of the femur bone should be routinely collected as reference material and stored frozen. From recovered skeleton remains any available bone may be used, but compact bone is preferred. The material should be removed by cutting a long bone in a wedge shape in order to keep the length of the bone intact for future measurements. DNA can be extracted using various methods. In our experience, it is necessary to start with approx 5 g of bone powder in order to extract enough human DNA (sometimes only a few nanograms). Before the bone is pulverized into a fine powder, the metal blender must be thoroughly cleaned with ethanol. During pulverization, the blender should be covered with a piece of cardboard. Special care must be taken not to contaminate the powder during the process. In all bone cases, the DNA extraction is carried out independently in duplicate (preferably from different bones of the body), and a sample containing no bone serves as a reagent-negative control sample. If no amplification is achieved, the Centricon-100 extract shoud be subjected to a silica purification as described by Boom et al. This procedure takes approx 1 h and has led to amplification of samples that did not yield any product without this step.
13. Teeth: Dental DNA yield can be maximized by crushing the entire specimen. A broken tooth is placed in 1.5 mL of buffer (0.5 M EDTA, pH 9.0; 0.01 g/mL SDS; 1 mg/mL proteinase K) and incubated for 1 d at 55°C. The solution is extracted two to three times with an equal amount of phenol/chloroform/isoamylalcohol (25:24:1). Then, one extraction with water-saturated *n*-butanol is

carried out to remove traces of phenol. The aqueous phase is subsequently purified by centrifugation through a Centricon 100 microconcentrator tube.

14. Centricon 100 purification: Each Centricon 100 microconcentrator tube is checked by adding 1.0 mL sterile water, sealing the tube with parafilm, punching a hole, and centrifuging the tube at 1000g for 3 min. In case of leaking (defect in the membrane), the water would pass through the membrane faster than in a normal tube. During the Centricon 100 purification step, it is important to remove the old parafilm and seal the tube with new parafilm every time sterile water is added. If water is added through the hole in the parafilm, contamination might occur. The Centricon 100 purification step should not be carried out in a centrifuge regularly used for centrifugation of blood samples. We could amplify DNA by swabbing the rotor of such centrifuges. The centrifuge should always be cleaned thoroughly with ethanol.
15. For storage, we transfer the retentate to 1.5 mL Saarstedt tubes with screw caps. Determination of the final sample volume is done by by weighing.
16. Compared to the Chelex method, we obtained better results from evidentiary material using the organic extraction.
17. All forensic samples are routinely amplified in the presence of BSA (albumin bovine fraction V) in the amplification mix (16 μg/ 100 μL) in order to overcome inhibition.

PCR Analysis from Cigaret Butts, Postage Stamps, Envelope Sealing Flaps, and Other Saliva-Stained Material

The *polymerase chain reaction* (PCR) has offered the forensic scientist a new range of sensitivity in the examination of forensic samples. PCR has been successfully used to amplify specific DNA fragments from extremely small amounts of DNA present on cigaret butts, postage stamps, envelope sealing flaps, and other saliva-stained materials. In addition to DNA typing results, it is at times desirable to confirm the presence of saliva by the simultaneous employment of an amylase assay.

Materials

Amylase assay

1. Amylase buffer: 50 m*M* KCl, 50 m*M* phosphate buffer, pH 6.8. Dissolve 3.728 g KCl in 1.0 L dH_2O (50 m*M* KCl). Solution A:

Dissolve 3.402 gKH_2PO_4 in 500 mL 50 m*M* KCl. Solution B: Dissolve 3.549 g Na_2HPO_4 in 500 mL 50 m*M* KCl. To 500 mL of solution A add approx 400 50 mL of solution B to bring the pH to 6.8. Store at 4°C.

2. α-Amylase Uni-Kit I Roche or α-amylase Granutest 3 Merck. Store at 4°C.
3. Filter photometer or spectrophotometer (405 nm).

DNA extraction and quantitation

1. 3X stain extraction buffer modified from: 30 m*M* Tris-HCl, 30 m*M* EDTA, 300 m*M* NaCl, 6% sodium dodecyl sulfate (SDS), pH 10.2. Short-time storage at room temperature (SDS precipitates at 4°). Add proteinase K fresh from frozen aliquots of 20 mg/mL.
2. IX stain extraction buffer: 10 m*M* Tris-HCl, 10 m*M* EDTA, 100 m*M* NaCl, 2% SDS, pH 8.0. Short time storage at room temperature (SDS precipitates at 4°C). Add proteinase K fresh from frozen aliquots of 20 mg/mL.
3. Phenol/chloroform/isoamylalcohol (25:24:1), in buffer, 10 m*M* Tris-HCl, pH 7.5 .01 m*M* EDTA-Na_2. Store at 4°C.
4. Water-saturated *n*-butanol. Prepare fresh before use.
5. Centricon 100 microconcentrator tubes.
6. QuantiBlotTM Human DNA Quantitation Kit or ACESTM 2.0^+ Human DNA Quantitation System.

PCR and detection of PCR products

1. Standard PCR reagents (e.g., Multiplex PCR kits: AmpliType PM PCR Amplification and Typing Kit; GenePrintTM STR Systems PCR Amplification Kit).
2. SA 32 Electrophoresis Apparatus.
3. Gel Slick and binding solution (3 μL of methacryloxypropyl-trimethoxysilane in 1 mL 0.5% acetic acid in 95% ethanol) to prepare glass plates.
4. Denaturing polyacrylamide gel (4% T, 5% C, containing 7 *M* urea and 0.5X Trisborate-EDTA buffer) (210 g urea, 267 mL dH_2O, 25 mL 10X TBE, and 50 mL 40% acrylamide:bis [19:1]).
5. 0.5X TBE (electrophoresis buffer).
6. Silver staining reagents:
   (a) Fix/stop solution: 10% acetic acid;
   (b) Staining solution: 2 g silver nitrate and 3 mL 37% formaldehyde in 2000 mL H_2O; and

(c) Developer solution: 3 mL 37% formaldehyde, 400 μL 10 mg/mL sodium thiosulfate, 60 g sodium carbonate in 2000 mL H_2O.

7. Duplicating X-ray film.

Methods

Amylase assay

Postage stamps and envelope sealing flaps

1. The evidence is handled with forceps at all times. One-half of a postage stamp with the attached part of the envelope or approx 1 cm^2 of an envelope sealing flap is cut into very small pieces and placed in a sterile 1 .5-mL Saarstedt tube with a screw cap. Alternatively, a 2.2-mL microcentrifuge tube with spin insert (with no membrane) or a Spin-EASE extraction tube can be used.
2. After addition of 400 μL amylase buffer, the tube is vigorously shaken at 4°C for at least 2 h to overnight and then subjected to centrifugation at 10,000g for 5 min.
3. For the determination of the enzymatic activity of α-amylase, the α-amylase Uni-Kit I Roche or the α-amylase Granutest 3 Merck Kit is used. The kits contain vials of reagents (2-chloro-4-nitrophenyl-β-D-maltoheptaoside, α-glucosidase, and β-glucosidase) and a solvent (50 m*M* KCl, 50 m *M* phosphate buffer, pH 6.8). The contents of one vial are dissolved using, respectively, 2.5 mL and 3 mL of the solvent.
4. To 1 mL of prewarmed (37°C) α-amylase reagent, 10 μL of the supernatant from the sample is added in a 1-cm light path, thermostated cuvet. The contents are mixed, and after 5 min the absorbance is measured against the solvent and again read after exactly 1, 2, and 3 min.
5. The AA/min is calculated. If AA/min exceeds 0.16, the sample is diluted 1:10 and the assay repeated. To determine the enzyme activity (U/L) in the sample, AA/min is multiplied with a factor provided in the kits.
6. A reaction is considered positive if the enzyme activity in the sample exceeds three times the enzyme activity of the blank reagent control.
7. A negative-control sample (containing no saliva-stained material) and a positive control sample (one half of a stamp licked by a known person) are processed in the same manner.

Cigaret butts, chewing gum, and other saliva-stained materials

In contrast to postage stamps or envelope sealing flaps, the actual determination of the presence of saliva on these evidentiary items may be deemed unnecessary, since it is almost certain to be present. However, the amylase test can be applied exactly as described above, since it neither consumes parts of the sample nor adversely affects the yield of DNA.

1. Cigaret butts are handled with forceps at all times. From the end of the cigaret butt that would have been in contact with the mouth, three cross-sectional slices, each 3 mm wide, are made using a sterile scalpel blade. The outer paper covering from the three sections is removed using sterile forceps, cut into small pieces and placed in a single 1.5-mL Saarstedt tube with a screw cap. Alternatively, a 2.2-mL microcentrifuge tube with a spin insert (with no membrane) can be used. If an amylase assay is desired, follow steps 2 of the procedure above.
2. A portion of the chewing gum is cut into very small pieces and placed in a single 1.5-mL Saarstedt tube with a screw cap or the 2.2-mL tube described above. If an amylase assay is desired, follow steps 2 of the procedure above.
3. Other saliva-stained materials are treated in the same manner.

DNA extraction and quantitation

1. If an amylase assay was required, 200 μL of 3X stain-extraction buffer and 15 μL proteinase K are added to the 390 μL amylase buffer (total vol 605 μL) and the tube is incubated overnight at 56°C.
2. If no amylase assay is required, 600 μL of IX stain-extraction buffer, pH 8.0, and 15 μL proteinase K, 20 mg/mL are added to the tube and the tube is incubated overnight at 56°C.
3. On the following day, an additional 15 μL proteinase K (20 mg/mL) is added and the sample incubated for an additional 2 h at 56°C.
4. Without removing the saliva-stained material, 700 mL phenol/chloroform/isoamylalcohol (25:24:1) is added and the tube vigorously shaken by hand for 2 min to achieve a milky emulsion in the tube. The tube is subjected to centrifugation at 10,000g for 3 min. If the 2.2-mL microcentrifuge tube with a spin insert is used, the material is removed with sterile forceps and placed into the spin insert. The spin insert is placed into the tube from which the

material came and centrifuged at 10,000g for 5 min. Then the spin insert with the material is removed and discarded.

5. The aqueous phase (top layer) is transferred to a new 1.5-mL Saarstedt tube with a screw cap, taking care not to transfer the interphase.
6. To the aqueous phase, 700 μL of water-saturated *n*-butanol is added in order to remove traces of phenol. The tube is vigorously shaken by hand for 2 min and then subjected to centrifugation at 10,000g for 3 min.
7. To purify the DNA, the aqueous phase (bottom layer) is transferred to a Centricon 100 microconcentrator tube. After the transfer the volume is brought up with sterile water to 2.0 mL. The sample reservoir is sealed with parafilm, and after punching a hole in the parafilm (using a sterile needle) the tube is subjected to centrifugation at 1000g for 30 min. Then 2 mL of sterile water is added to the sample reservoir and the reservoir sealed with new parafilm. Again the tube is centrifuged at 1000g for 30 min. The DNA is recovered by back centrifugation at 1000g for 5 min. The final sample volume is approx 250 μL.
8. To determine the quantity of human DNA, 10% of the retentate is used in slotblot analysis.

Notes

1. For postage stamps, postcards, and envelopes, methods for the detection of fingerprints should be applied before any DNA testing is carried out.
2. The saliva-stained material should be cut in small pieces (≈35 mm), to be completely submerged in the phenol phase during the phenol-extraction step. If the pieces are too big, removing the aqueous phase becomes difficult. When no spin insert is used, the stained material is better submerged in 1.5 mL tubes than in 2.0 mL tubes.
3. The amylase buffer is the same as the solvent provided in the amylase test kits.
4. Adding 200 μL of 3X stain-extraction buffer, pH 10.2, to 390 μL amylase buffer, pH 6.8, and 15 μL proteinase K, changes the pH to ≈8.0. This is equal to the pH of IX stain-extraction buffer. The 3X stain extraction buffer is modified to meet these requirements; also, it does not contain dithiothreitol (DTT). It must be prewarmed before use.

5. In contrast to a previously published method, a step is omitted in this new protocol. This step involved cleaning of the outside of the tube with ethanol and punching a hole with a sterile needle in the bottom of the tube. The solution was then transferred to a new tube by the piggyback method via centrifugation at 1000g for 5 min. After removing the upper tube, leaving behind the paper, the solution was extracted. In the new protocol, phenol extraction is carried out without removing the stained material. Alternatively, a microcentrifuge tube with a spin insert can be used.
6. Each Centricon 100 microconcentrator tube is checked by adding 1.0 mL sterile water, sealing the tube with parafilm, punching a hole, and centrifuging the tube at 1000*g* for 3 min. In case of leaking (defect in the membrane), the water would pass through the membrane faster than in a normal tube. During the Centricon 100 purification step, it is important to remove the old parafilm and seal the tube with new parafilm every time sterile water is added. If water is added through the hole in the parafilm, crosscontamination might occur. The Centricon 100 purification step should not be carried out in a centrifuge regularly used for centrifugation of blood samples. We could amplify DNA by swabbing the rotor of such centrifuges with cotton swabs. The centrifuge should be cleaned regularly and thoroughly with ethanol.
7. For storage, we transfer the retentate to 1.5-mL Saarstedt tubes with screw caps. Determination of the final sample volume is by weighing.
8. The success rate of the procedure described above on cigaret butts up to 10 yr old is $>>95\%$; also, we detected amylase activity and extracted and typed DNA from postage stamps up to 33 yr old.
9. Compared to the previously published Chelex method, we obtained better results from old evidentiary material using the organic extraction method described above.
10. All forensic samples are routinely amplified in the presence of bovine serum albumin (BSA) (albumin bovine fraction V; Sigma A 4503) in the amplification mix (16 μg/100 μL) in order to overcome inhibition.

10

Chromosomes in Forensic Science

Chromosome Aberration Analysis

Numerical and structural chromosome aberration analysis is widely used in many fields: in the diagnosis of genetic diseases, in screening of chemical(s) or drug(s) for toxicity, in environmental monitoring for genotoxicity, in biological assessment of radiation dose in accidental or occupational overexposures, in biomonitoring for genotoxic risk assessment, in genomics, and in many other applications. Routine chromosome aberration analysis uses metaphase spreads obtained from either cultured mammalian cells or from mitogen-stimulated short-term cultures of *human peripheral blood lymphocytes* (HPBLs). Metaphase spread-based chromosome aberration analysis depends on successful mitogen (e.g., phytohemagglutinin) stimulation of "*resting*" HPBLs into the cell cycle. Cell cycle progression is then arrested in metaphase using a spindle poison (e.g., colchicine). Chromosome spreads on glass slides are obtained after treatment with a hypotonic solution and fixation in acetic acid/methanol for analysis of quantitative or qualitative changes involving structural and/or numerical aberrations.

Metaphase spread-based chromosome aberration analysis is laborious, requires cytogenetic expertise, and is time-consuming. Confounding factors associated with metaphase spread-based chromosome aberration analysis resulting from cell cycle progression, such as induced cell killing and cell cycle delay, are known to interfere with assay results. In addition, metaphase spread-based quantitative aberration analysis is critically dependent on the availability of a large number of suitable metaphase spreads because often only 3–4% of cells are analyzable. The ability to analyze chromosome aberrations prior to DNA synthesis eliminates most of these inherent problems associated with cell cycle kinetics.

A method for inducing *premature chromosome condensation* (PCC) in "*resting*" HPBLs so as to obtain chromosome spreads prior to DNA synthesis for chromosome aberration analysis has been described. The method involves the fusion of HPBLs with mitotic cells. Mitotic cells are obtained from a mammalian cell culture, and *polyethylene glycol* (PEG) can be used as a fusogen to allow *mitosis-promoting factors* (MPFs) to diffuse from mitotic cells into resting lymphocytes and bring about PCC. This method is technically demanding and difficult, and the PCC yield is low and not consistent. Therefore, this method of obtaining chromosome spreads prior to DNA synthesis for chromosome aberration analysis has not been widely adopted in cytogenetics.

PCC can also be induced by incubating proliferating cells, such as mitogen-stimulated HPBLs or human tumor cell lines, in cell culture medium containing type 1 and type 2A protein phosphatase inhibitors (e.g., okadaic acid [OA] or calyculin A). This approach, when combined with whole-chromosome-specific hybridization probes, permits both the scoring of chromosomal damage in PCC spreads and the identification of other interphase cells with discrete chromosome domains or spots. For autosomes, normal (undamaged) cells display two fluorescent spots, one each corresponding to the paternally and maternally derived homologs, and cells with an aberrant specific chromosome usually show more than two spots. Irradiation, for example, causes a dose-dependent increase in proliferating interphase tumor cells with more than two spots. The method described earlier for inducing PCC in HPBLs using phosphatase inhibitors, such as OA or calyculin A, requires a mitogenic stimulation and involves a short-term HPBL culture before the PCC spreads are prepared on glass slides for analysis. Stimulation with mitogen results in an asynchronous culture, complicating chromosome-aberration analysis and lengthening the time required to prepare samples for analysis. Differentiated and nonproliferating cells, such as resting HPBLs do not respond to phosphatase inhibitor treatment and do not induce PCC.

The rationale, to be published elsewhere, for developing a method of inducing PCC in resting HPBLs is based on an understanding of the mechanisms of signal transduction events surrounding the regulation of cell cycle phases, DNA replication, chromosome condensation, and mitosis. Briefly, mitosis in proliferating cells is triggered by the specific activation of *cyclin D kinase* (cdk), and chromosome condensation is regulated by p34cdc2/cyclin B kinase activity, the hyperphosphorylation of histone H1, and the phosphorylation of histone H3. For example, treatment of BHK1 cells in G_1 phase with OA alone does not induce PCC, apparently owing to a lack of p34cdc2/cyclin B kinase activity. Recently, we demonstrated that incubation of resting HPBLs in a special cell culture medium induces PCC without mitogen stimulation. The medium contains p34cdc2/cyclin B kinase (a component of MPF), a phosphatase inhibitor (OA or calyculin A), and ATP (an enzyme system substrate that increases Ca^{2+}-activated K^+ channels). The method results in a high yield of PCC suitable for *fluorescence in situ hybridization* (FISH) of whole chromosomes and for detection of numerical and structural aberrations involving specific chromosomes. Chromosome aberrations can be rapidly analyzed in a large resting lymphocyte population directly collected from human peripheral whole blood and readily isolated on a density gradient. In this section we describe, step by step, this unique, simple, and rapid method for inducing PCC in resting HPBLs as well as an approach to studying numerical changes or structural aberrations involving specific chromosomes.

Materials

Isolation of HPBLs

1. Biological safety cabinet.
2. Benchtop centrifuge.
3. Polystyrene centrifuge tubes (15-mL capacity).
4. Pipets (1-, 2-, 5-, and 10-mL capacities).
5. Vortex mixer.
6. Lymphocyte separation medium.
7. Dulbecco's phosphate-buffered saline (PBS) without Ca^{2+} and Mg^{2+}.
8. Bone marrow karyotyping medium.
9. Disinfectant.

PCC induction

1. Benchtop centrifuge.
2. Water bath.
3. Light microscope.
4. Microscope slides.
5. Pipets.

6. Polystyrene centrifuge tubes (15-mL capacity).
7. Bone marrow karyotyping medium.
8. ATP (Sigma).
9. Colchicine (Sigma).
10. OA or calyculin A.
11. p34cdc2/cyclin B kinase.
12. Potassium chloride.
13. Glacial acetic acid (analytical reagent grade).
14. Methanol (200° proof, analytical reagent grade).

In situ hybridization, chromosome painting, and fluorescence microscopy

1. pH meter.
2. pH papers.
3. Diamond marker.
4. Glass Coplin jars.
5. Microcentrifuge.
6. Thermalcycler.
7. In situ hybridization machine.
8. Water bath.
9. Micropipets.
10. Cover slips.
11. Rubber cement.
12. Fluorescence microscope and imaging station.
13. Whole-chromosome–specific probe.
14. 20X SSC solution.
15. 2X SSC solution.
16. 2X SSC/0.1% NP-40 wash solution.
17. 70% Formamide/2X SSC (denaturation) solution.
18. Ethanol solutions.
19. 50% Formamide/2X SSC (formamide wash) solution.
20. 4,6-Diamidino-2-phenyl-indole (DAPI) in a mounting solution.

Methods

Isolation of HPBLs from whole blood

1. To a 15-mL conical centrifuge tube, transfer 3 mL of lymphocyte separation media, and carefully layer 3 mL of whole blood such that a density separation of the medium and the blood occurs.

2. Centrifuge at 400g for exactly 30 min at room temperature (~25°C) using a swinging bucket type of rotor.
3. Following centrifugation, carefully aspirate, with a Pasteur pipet, the upper layer to within 0.5 mm of the opaque interface (Buffy coat) containing mononuclear cells. Discard upper layer.
4. Using a Pasteur pipet, carefully transfer the opaque interface to a separate 15-mL centrifuge tube and discard the red blood cells.
5. Add 10 mL of PBS to the centrifuge tube and gently mix using a pipet.
6. Centrifuge at 200g for 15 min at room temperature.
7. Aspirate the supernatant and discard.
8. Using a Vortex mixer, gently break up the cell pellet, resuspend with 10 mL of PBS, and mix as above.
9. Centrifuge at 200g for 15 min at room temperature.
10. Repeat steps 7–9; discard supernatant.

PCC induction

1. Prepare incubation media: mix 2.96 mL of Karyomax, 30 μL ATP, 12 μL colchicine, 2.25 μL OA, and p34cdc2/cyclin B kinase.
2. Resuspend lymphocytes at approx 1–1.5 $\times$ 10^6 cells per milliliter in the above PCC incubation medium in a 15-mL centrifuge tube.
3. Incubate lymphocytes in the above media for 3 h at 37°C in a circulating water bath.
4. Centrifuge at 200g for 8 min.
5. Aspirate the supernatant, gently disrupt the cell pellet by hand vortexing, and add 2 mL of 0.06 M KCl (0.56%).
6. Leave the cell suspension at room temperature for 4–5 min.
7. Centrifuge, and carefully aspirate supernatant.
8. Gently disrupt the cell pellet by hand vortexing and add 3–4 mL of ice-cold 1:3 acetic acid/methanol fixative carefully down the side of the centrifuge tube. Leave the cell suspension in a refrigerator at 4°C overnight.
9. Centrifuge, aspirate the supernatant, disrupt the cell pellet, and add 3–4 mL of fresh fixative.
10. Leave the cell suspension at room temperature for 10 min.
11. Centrifuge, aspirate the supernatant, disrupt the cell pellet, and add 3–4 mL of fresh fixative as described above.
12. Centrifuge, aspirate the supernatant, disturb the cell pellet, and prepare concentrated cell suspension in fresh fixative.
13. Drop cell suspension onto acid-cleaned microscope slides.

In situ hybridization, chromosome painting, and fluorescence microscopy

1. Select an area suitable for hybridization on the slide and mark with a diamond marker.
2. Pipet 40 mL of 70% formamide/2X SSC solution into a Coplin jar, and place the jar in a water bath at 73°C. Ensure that the temperature inside the Coplin jar is 72 ± 1°C.
3. Immerse the slide in the denaturation solution for 3 min.
4. Dehydrate the slide in 70, 85, and 100% ice-cold ethanol by immersing the slide for 2 min in each alcohol grade.
5. Leave the slide immersed in 100% ethanol until the probe is ready.
6. Prepare the probe mixture as follows:
   (a) Bring the probe to room temperature for a complete thaw, and vortex.
   (b) In a microcentrifuge tube, mix 7 μL of hybridization buffer, 1 μL of probe, and 2 μL of distilled water.
7. Briefly centrifuge in a microcentrifuge to collect the contents at the bottom of the tube.
8. Denature the probe mixture using a thermalcycler or a water bath at 73°C for 5 min.
9. Hold the tube at 45–50°C until ready to apply to the slide.
10. Remove the slide from 100% ethanol and dry by touching the bottom edge of the slide to blotting paper and wiping the outside of the slide with a clean paper towel, followed by placement of the slide on a slide warmer to evaporate remaining alcohol.
11. Apply 10 μL of the denatured probe mixture to the target area marked with a diamond maker, immediately apply a cover slip, and seal with rubber cement.
12. Hybridize at 37°C overnight (8–16 h) either by placing the slide in a prewarmed, humidified box kept in an incubator or by using an in situ hybridization machine.
13. To each of three Coplin jars, labeled 1, 2, and 3, transfer 50 mL of 50% formamide/2X SSC and place each in a water bath at 46°C at least 30 min prior to use.
14. Transfer 50 mL of 2X SSC to another Coplin jar, and place it in a water bath at 46°C at least 30 min prior to use.
15. Transfer 50 mL of 2X SSC/0.1% NP-40 to another Coplin jar, and place it in the water bath at 46°C at least 30 min prior to use.

16. Carefully remove the cover slip from the slide, immerse the slide in the 50% formamide/2X SSC solution in Coplin jar 1, and agitate the jar frequently to wash the slide.
17. After 10 min, transfer the slide to Coplin jar 2, repeat the procedure as in step 16, and subsequently transfer the slide to Coplin jar 3 after 10 min.
18. Immerse the slide in Coplin jar 3, agitate the jar, remove the slide after 10 min, and dry the slide by touching the end of the slide onto blotting paper.
19. Transfer the slide to 2X SSC solution, agitate the jar frequently, and remove the slide after 10 min.
20. Immerse the slide in 2X SSC/0.1% NP-40. Agitate the jar and remove the slide after 5 min.
21. Let the slide dry in total darkness.
22. Apply 10 μL of DAPI (1000 ng/mL) counterstain in mounting medium and apply a cover slip.
23. These slides are suitable for observation under a fluorescence microscope equipped with filters for DAPI and fluorescin isothiocyanate (FITC). The slides are observed under an oil-immersion objective, at 1000× magnification, for aberrations involving a specific chromosome.
24. The quantitative analysis of chromosome aberrations is based on the following general criteria. The cells included in the analysis should show:
    (a) At least a partial separation of chromosomes with condensed chromatin material as determined by DAPI counterstain.
    (b) Two or more clearly separated chromosome-specific spots with bright green fluorescent signals.
    (c) Spots that are similar in fluorescent intensity.
    (d) An area representing about 15–100% of the area of spots observed in the controls.
25. Normal (undamaged) cells display two fluorescent spots, which indicate two copies of the chromosome corresponding to the painting probe employed. Cells with aberrant specific chromosomes are characterized by the presence of more than two spots, which possibly reflect fragments, dicentrics, or symmetrical translocations.

Notes

1. *Caution*: Adhere to biosafety procedures while carrying out the steps in this protocol. Use of a biological safety cabinet (class II,

type A/B3) is required. All liquid wastes should be treated as biologically hazardous. Therefore, liquid wastes should be aspirated into a conical flask containing 50% bleach to sterilize biohazardous liquids. Solid wastes should be treated as regulated medical wastes and should be disposed of in appropriately labeled burn boxes (8).

2. Store lymphocyte separation medium at 4°C under refrigeration, bringing it up to room temperature (~25°C) before use.
3. Store bone marrow karyotyping medium frozen at –20°C. Thaw it and heat to 37°C before use.
4. Clean microscope slides by immersing them in 4:1 methanol HCl solution for 4 h, rinsing thoroughly in running tap water, washing in soap, and thoroughly rinsing in distilled water five to six times. Store slides in distilled water at 4°C in a refrigerator.
5. Prepare 10 mM stock solution of ATP (molecular weight 551.1) by dissolving 0.0551 g of ATP in 10 mL of Karyomax. Store at 4°C in a refrigerator until used.
6. Prepare 0.25 μg/μL stock solution of colchicine (molecular weight 399.4) by dissolving 2.5 mg in 10 mL of Karyomax. Store it at 4°C in a refrigerator until used. Handle the carcinogen with care.
7. Prepare 1 mM solution of OA (molecular weight 804.9) by dissolving 25 μg in 31.1 μL of 200° proof ethanol. Store at –20°C. Handle the carcinogen with care.
8. Concentration of p34cdc2/cyclin B kinase varies with the lot. Therefore, modify the volume of Karyomax accordingly to get a final concentration of 50 U/mL. Store at –70°C. Activity reduces at a rate of about 50% per week.
9. Freshly prepare 0.56% potassium chloride solution by dissolving 0.56 g in 100 mL of distilled water.
10. Adjust pH of 20X SSC solution to 5.3 with HCl. The solution can be stored at room temperature. Discard stock solution after 6 mo, or sooner if found to be cloudy or contaminated.
11. Mix well 100 mL of 20X SSC (pH 5.3) with 850 mL of distilled water. Adjust pH to 7.0 ± 0.2 with NaOH. Add distilled water to bring volume to 1 L. The solution can be kept at room temperature. Discard stock solution after 6 mo, or sooner if the solution appears cloudy or contaminated.
12. Mix well 100 mL of 20X SSC (pH 5.3) with 850 mL of distilled water. Add 1 mL of NP40. Adjust pH to 7.0 ± 0.2 with NaOH. Add distilled water to bring the volume to 1 L. Solution can be

kept at room temperature. Discard after 6 mo, or sooner if it appears cloudy or contaminated.

13. Mix well 49 mL of formamide, 7 mL of 20X SSC, and 14 mL of distilled water in a glass Coplin jar. Measure pH using pH paper to verify a pH of 7.0–8.0. Prepare a fresh mixture for each use.
14. Prepare v/v solutions of 70, 85, and 100% ethanol with distilled water. Prepare a fresh solution for each use.
15. Mix well 105 mL of formamide, 21 mL of 20X SSC, and 84 mL of distilled water. Measure pH using pH paper to verify a pH of 7.0–8.0. Pour equal volumes of the solution into three glass Coplin jars with lids. Prepare the solution fresh every week, and store it covered in a refrigerator at 4°C.
16. Peripheral blood collected from healthy adult donors by phlebotomy into vacutainers containing EDTA is suitable. However, the Human Use Committee may require approved informed consent from the donors, as determined by the policies of the institute where the work will be carried out.
17. Treat solid waste as regulated biomedical waste, and dispose of it in an appropriately labeled burn box.
18. Expected recovery for a healthy adult donor is about 3–4.5 million mononuclear cells from 3 mL of whole blood.
19. The final concentration of OA in the incubation medium is 0.75 μM. Instead of OA, another phosphatase inhibitor, calyculin A, may be used at a final concentration of 50 nM and is equally effective in inducing PCC.
20. The concentration of the p34cdc2/cyclin B kinase varies with the lot. Therefore, modify the volume accordingly to get a final concentration of 50 U/mL. Although concentrations as low as 5 U/mL induce PCC, the yield is considerably lower.
21. Use of a blood cell counter for determining lymphocyte count is suggested but not required.
22. Prepare fixative and keep it ice cold until used.
23. After each of these steps involving a wash in fixative, the cells can be monitored for optimum fixation by preparing a test slide and observing under a light microscope. The fixed cells appear highly transparent under low-intensity light.
24. Perform a trial slide denaturation run. Following denaturation, stain with Giemsa and observe under a microscope. If the morphology is altered, then decrease the melting temperature by 2°C, or reduce the denaturation time.

25. The Coplin jars containing alcohol grades should be placed in an ice bucket at least 30–60 min before starting the experiment, to carry out the cold temperature reactions.
26. Aberrations can be studied using any whole-chromosome–specific probe. The manufacturer's original protocol for metaphase chromosomes is modified for applications involving PCC spreads. Protocols may vary for other whole chromosome probes. We suggest following the manufacturer's instructions and suitably modifying the protocol if needed.
27. Care should be taken not to trap air bubbles when applying the cover slip.
28. Alternatively, slides can be stored at –20°C in the dark for up to 1 wk without fading.
29. Cells with single green spots arising because of overlapping signals must not be included.
30. However, the area of spots in the control samples is not always uniform because of differential chromosome condensation and, in a few cases, angular presentation under the microscope. In such cases of ambiguity, cells may be excluded from analysis.

Chromatid Breakage as a Marker

Risk assessment is now recognized as a multidisciplinary process, extending beyond the scope of traditional epidemiologic methodology to include biological evaluation of interindividual differences in carcinogenic susceptibility. Modulation of environmental exposures by host genetic factors may explain much of the observed interindividual variation in susceptibility to carcinogenesis. These genetic factors include, but are not limited to, carcinogen metabolism and DNA repair capacity. This section describes a standardized method for the functional assessment of mutagen sensitivity. This in vitro assay measures the frequency of mutagen-induced breaks in peripheral lymphocytes. Mutagen sensitivity assessed by this method has been shown to be a significant risk factor for tobacco-related malignancies, especially those of the upper aerodigestive tract. Mutagen sensitivity may therefore be a useful member of a panel of susceptibility markers for defining high-risk subgroups for chemoprevention trials. This section describes methods for and discusses results from studies of mutagen sensitivity as measured by quantifying chromatid breaks induced by chromosome breaking agents, such as the γ-radiation radiomimetic DNA crosslinking agent bleomycin and chemicals that form so-called bulky DNA adducts, such as 4-NQO and the tobacco smoke constituent, benzo[a]pyrene, in short-term cultured peripheral blood lymphocytes.

Maintaining the integrity of the genome is essential to normal cell function. Disruption of this normally well-regulated process can lead to cell death or neoplasia. The notion that genetic susceptibility to cancer is related to genomic instability was initially supported by rare autosomal recessive disorders such as ataxia telangiectasia and xeroderma pigmentosum, which are associated with in vivo and in vitro chromosomal instability, defective DNA repair capaçity, and increased cancer risk. Hsu hypothesized that in the general population, susceptibility to chromosome damage in response to mutagens varies along a continuum, with recognized chromosome fragility syndromes such as Fanconi's anemia and ataxia telangiectasia being the most extreme. In response to environmental exposures, genetic damage would accumulate more quickly in people with an inherited susceptibility to DNA damage than in other similarly exposed people, and those with the inherited susceptibility might therefore be at higher risk for cancer. Hsu et al. developed a phenotypic assay of intrinsic cancer susceptibility, the *mutagen sensitivity assay*.

Mutagen sensitivity is an in vitro assay that gauges host susceptibility by measuring the frequency of induced chromatid breaks in short-term cultured lymphocytes after exposure to an array of mutagens. A series of studies has indicated that mutagen sensitivity is a promising environmental exposure-related cancer risk marker. This assay has been successfully expanded by replacing the initial test mutagen, bleomycin, with 4-nitroquinoline-1-oxide (4-NQO; a UV mimetic agent), γ-radiation, and benzo[a]pyrene diol epoxide (BPDE) to measure risks associated with different types of cancers. Different mutagens may act on cells through different molecular mechanisms and may activate different repair pathways. Bleomycin is radiomimetic and generates free oxygen radicals that can induce single-stranded and double-stranded breaks and subsequent mutations. Bleomycin- or γ-radiation-induced DNA damage requires base excision or recombinant DNA repair. BPDE is a metabolic product of benzo[a]pyrene, a major constituent of tobacco smoke. BPDE forms covalent "bulky" adducts upon interaction with DNA, which require the nucleotide excision repair pathway for their remediation. DNA damaged by 4-NQO also requires nucleotide excision repair. Because different cancer sites may be associated with different carcinogenic exposures, the relevancy of specific mutagen sensitivity assays might vary from site to site. It has been found that bleomycin sensitivity is associated with increased risk for environmentally related cancers; BPDE sensitivity is associated with increased risk for smoking-related cancers; 4-NQO sensitivity is associated with increased risk for skin cancer; and γ-radiation sensitivity is associated with increased risk for brain tumors and breast cancer.

This section discusses mutagen sensitivity as measured by quantifying bleomycin-, BPDE-, 4-NQO-, and γ-radiation-induced chromatid breaks in short-term cultured peripheral blood lymphocytes. Chromatid breaks occur in the late S and G_2 phases of the cell cycle and are detected at metaphase. Chromatid breaks are one of five types of chromosomal aberrations, which also include interchromosomal exchange, intrachromosomal exchange, interstitial deletions, and chromatid gaps. Briefly, interchromosomal exchanges involve either a symmetrical or an asymmetrical exchange. When a translocation results in two intact, unicentric chromosomes, a symmetrical exchange has occurred, and when it leads to the formation of a dicentric chromosome and an acentric fragment, an asymmetrical exchange has occurred. Intrachromosomal exchanges also include symmetrical and asymmetrical exchanges. Symmetrical exchange results in an inversion chromosome but usually causes no mitotic abnormality. An asymmetric exchange produces a ring chromosome and one or two acentric fragments. Interstitial deletion occurs when a chromatid fragment breaks off and the broken ends fuse. These deletions are usually rare. A chromatid *gap* is defined as a small lesion whose size is shorter than the diameter of the chromatid. A chromatid gap can occur when two broken ends of a chromatid join together. A chromatid *break* is defined as occurring when the size of the lesion is equal to or larger than the diameter of the chromatid. Using a slightly modified version of the Chatham Barrs Inn Conference (CBIC) nomenclature, chromatid breaks are also defined as follows: (1) when the sister chromatid is bent at the point of the lesion (or chromatid gap), or (2) when two "broken" ends do not face each other.

The following protocol provides instructions for conducting mutagen sensitivity assays and for reading and interpreting chromatid breaks.

Materials

Treatment and culture of lymphocyte cells

1. 5 mL Peripheral blood in green-top tube (sodium heparin as anticoagulant).
2. Blood culture media.
3. 25-cm^2 Culture flasks.

4. 37°C Cell culture incubator.
5. Treatment chemical working solutions.

Blood culture medium

1. 1X RPMI-1640 powder.
2. 20% Fetal bovine serum (FBS).
3. 100 U/mL Penicillin, 100 μg/mL streptomycin.
4. 2 mML-glutamine.
5. 24 mM (2 g/L) sodium bicarbonate ($NaHCO_3$).
6. 1.25% (v/v) Phytohemagglutinin.
7. 10 U/mL Heparin sodium salt solution, reconstituted in distilled, deionized H_2O.

Treatment chemical working solutions

1. 1.5 U/mL bleomycin in distilled, deionized H_2O. The working solution can be stored at −20°C.
2. BDPE: 12 mM benzo[a]pyrene-r-7, t-8-dihydrodiol-t-9,10-epoxide in anhydrous tetrahydrofuran. Dilute stock solution in dimethyl sulfoxide to a final concentration of 0.5 mM immediately before adding it to the blood culture.
3. 1.0 mM 4-NQO in acetone.

Irradiation treatment

1. ^{137}Cs source.

Harvesting of lymphocyte cells and slide preparation

1. Colcemid (demecolcine) working solution: 2 μg/mL colcemid in Hanks' balanced salt solution without Ca^{2+} and Mg^{2+}.
2. 15 mL Centrifugation tubes.
3. Centrifuge.
4. 0.06 M KCl hypotonic solution.
5. Carnoy's fixative: 3:1 (v/v) methanol and glacial acetic acid, mixed. Prepare fresh every day.
6. Preparative microscope slides.
7. Giemsa stain working solution: 4% Gurr's Giemsa stain in 0.01 M phosphate-buffered saline (PBS) stock solution (pH 7.0).

Methods

Initiation of lymphocyte cultures

1. Begin blood culture by adding 1 mL whole blood to 9 mL blood medium in 25-cm^2 tissue flask.

2. Culture cells at 37°C for 72–91 h, depending on specific mutagen treatment.

Treatment of lymphocyte cells

1. Bleomycin sensitivity assay: after 91 h, add 200 μL of 1.5 U/mL bleomycin (final concentration of 0.03 U/mL) and incubate cells for an additional 4 h at 37°C.
2. BPDE sensitivity assay: after 72 h, add 40 μL of BPDE (final concentration of 2 M) and incubate cells for an additional 23 h at 37°C.
3. 4-NQO sensitivity assay: after 72 h, add 100 μL of 4-NQO (final concentration of 10 μM) and incubate cells for an additional 23 h at 37°C.
4. γ-Radiation sensitivity assay: after 91 h, irradiate cells with 1.25 Gy from the 137 Cs source. To do this, the flasks containing the cell cultures in 10 μL medium are directly exposed to incident γ-radiation at a rate of 15.58 Gy/min (or 0.26 Gy/s) for 4.8 s. Incubate the cells for an additional 4 h at 37°C.

Harvesting of lymphocytes

1. After the appropriate length of incubation for the different assays, add 200 μL colcemid (final concentration of 0.04 μg/mL) to arrest mitotic cells; incubate at 37°C for 1 h.
2. Pour culture into a 15-mL centrifuge tube.
3. Spin for 5 min at 410 g.
4. Discard supernatant.
5. Suspend the cell pellet in 8 mL 0.06 M KCl hypotonic solution; mix thoroughly. Incubate at room temperature for 15 min.
6. Add 1.5 mL Carney's fixative solution to mixture, and mix well.
7. Spin 5 min at 410 g.
8. Discard supernatant.
9. Resuspend the cell pellet in fixative twice, bring volume up to 10 mL, spin, and discard supernatant.
10. Wash the cells with fixative twice more.

Slide preparation

1. Spin cells down at 410g, discard supernatant, and resuspend the cell pellet in appropriate amount of fixative solution to give a slightly cloudy suspension of cells.
2. Rinse the slides with distilled, deionized water.

3. Drop 4–6 drops of the suspension onto each slide; let the suspension air-dry (~1 min).
4. Code the slides with laboratory identification numbers and stain with 4% Gurr's Giemsa solution for 2–3 min.

Reading chromatid breaks

1. To view the induced chromatid breaks, two brightfield objectives are needed: low magnification (10–16×) for scanning, and high magnification (100×). Use a 100× dry objective that is specifically designed for preparations lacking cover slips.
2. When choosing metaphases for scoring chromatid breaks, randomly select full metaphases whose chromosomes are well spread with a minimum amount of overlap. This can be done at low magnification. At high magnification, avoid chromosomes that have overlapped or chromatids that have been twisted, which can be mistaken for chromatid breaks.
3. Read 50 metaphases per sample and calculate the mean number of breaks. Breaks are recorded as the average number of breaks per cell.

Recording chromatid breaks

1. Before recording chromatid breaks, establish detailed reading criteria and review examples of various types of breakage to ensure high-quality data. When recording chromatid breaks, be conservative. Record only frank chromatid breaks or exchanges. If multiple breaks are visible on the chromatid, count each break individually. Each chromatid exchange is considered as two breaks. Record the frequency of breakage as breaks per cell.
2. Enter the recordings consecutively. Using abbreviations to record the different aberrations is acceptable, but it must be done consistently.
3. Establish a quality control procedure for scoring chromatid breaks.

Notes

1. A premade colcemid working solution can be used, such as KaryoMAX Colcemid Solution. However, the final solution should be 10 μg/mL in the blood culture.
2. Take the blood medium from the freezer the day before the experiment and place it in the refrigerator. Do not let it stay in the refrigerator for more than 7 d.
3. The BPDE should be prepared and added to the blood culture in the dark because it is light sensitive.

4. Do not use the colcemid working solution for more than 20 d.
5. The solution lyses the red blood cells, and the suspension will turn brown.
6. Depending on the size of the pellet, add 0.5–2 mL of the fixative solution.
7. It is important to code the slides before reading to prevent any introduction of bias. More specifically, the technician reading the slides should not know the case-control status, drug dosage, or duration of treatment related to the slides.
8. The dry 100× objective will have the same resolution as the oil immersion lens. Using the "no cover slip" preparation will prevent the untidiness created by using the oil lens. Make certain that the same field is not observed twice.
9. Do not read cells with incomplete metaphase figures or metaphases with a distorted chromosome arrangement. Avoid reading of prophases and early prometaphases, because chromosomes in these phases show a more beaded morphology and are often more "gappy" than those in full metaphase. Do not read metaphases with crowded chromosomes. It is important to use cells with sister chromatids that are well separated and clearly distinguishable from one another.
10. Be careful when recording chromatid breaks. Breaks usually occur near the ends. If a particular chromosome is difficult to interpret, than consider the chromosome normal. Cells that have been understained tend to show more "gappy" chromosomes, whereas cells that are overstained tend to mask minor chromatid lesions. The heterochromatin regions of chromosomes 1, 9, and 16 usually stain lightly and thus can be misinterpreted as a gap or a break. In approx 1% of bleomycin-treated cultures, metaphases may have extensive (>12) chromatid breaks per cell. These metaphases should be discarded. It might be of interest to record chromatid gaps along with the chromatid breaks; however, they should be recorded separately. The accrued data can be compared with data from other investigators who do not differentiate between chromatid breaks and gaps.
11. It is important to have a well-trained technician to read the slides. The technician should have a basic knowledge of and some experience in cytogenetics. A trained technician will be able to read five to eight slides per day. To become familiar with chromatid breaks, human blood cultures treated with bleomycin (30 μg/mL) for 5 h can be used as test material.

Cytometric Analysis

The in vivo *micronucleus* (MN) test in bone marrow or peripheral blood erythrocytes is widely used as a short-term assay for the detection of agents able to induce chromosome aberrations in somatic cells and has also been shown to have good predictive potential for the identification of carcinogens and germ cell mutagens. The endpoint used is the scoring of *micronuclei* (MN) in bone marrow or peripheral blood erythrocytes of mice or rats. In this section, a detailed description of the flow cytometric micronucleus test will be given, as well as a more general description of the manual micronucleus assay. The DNA of MN is identified using the DNA-specific fluorescent stain Hoechst 33342; discrimination between polychromatic and normochromatic erthrocytes is based on staining with thiazole orange, a fluorescent probe with high RNA affinity. The use of flow-cytometric quantification of micronucleated polychromatic and normochromatic erythrocytes (MNPCE and MNNCE), beyond replacing manual enumeration, provides substantial advantages in terms of speed of analysis, as well as sensitivity. The general description of the MN assay briefly covers choice of animal species and strains, treatment regime, sampling times, and data interpretation. The description of the flow cytometric assay covers in detail erythrocyte preparation and purification, fixation, staining, data acquisition, and data analysis.

Micronuclei (MN) are small, nucleus-like structures present in the cytoplasm. They are formed by chromosomes, or fragments of chromosomes, that have failed to be incorporated into one of the daughter nuclei during a mitosis or meiosis. This failure occurs because these chromosomes or fragments have lost their connection to a centromere and thus cannot be properly segregated from the metaphase plate to either of the poles during anaphase. The lost material consists either of acentric fragments, formed from chromosome breakage, or whole chromosomes, left behind owing to damage to the mitotic spindle. In telophase, the lost chromosomal material may be enclosed in a nuclear membrane and, after cytokinesis, then appears as small round nucleus-like structures in either of the daughter cells. MN are present in low frequencies (~1–10 per million) in most cell types. Because they are visible and relatively easily scored in interphase cells, they have become a widely used endpoint for the monitoring of chromosome damage.

The in vivo MN test in bone marrow or peripheral blood erythrocytes is widely used as a short-term assay for the detection of agents able to induce chromosome aberrations in somatic cells and has also been shown to have good predictive potential for the identification of carcinogens and germ cell mutagens. The endpoint involves the scoring of MN in the bone marrow or peripheral blood erythrocytes of mice or rats. MN are formed in bone marrow and, in some cases, spleen erythroblasts, as the result of structural or numerical chromosome damage. During the final maturation of erythroblasts into young or *polychromatic erythrocytes* (PCE), the main nucleus is expelled. This phenomenon makes the scoring of MN in erythrocytes simpler than in other cell types and also opens the possibility of using automated scoring by flow cytometry. The bone marrow PCE migrate into the peripheral circulation, where they mature into *normochromatic erythrocytes* (NCE). MN are most often scored in bone marrow PCE or peripheral blood PCE (also termed *reticulocytes*). The baseline frequency of micronucleated PCE for most strains of mice and rat is between 1 and 3 per million.

As can be seen, damage induced during the last cell cycle of the erythroblast is, in most cases, best observable about 24 h after damage induction for bone marrow erythrocytes and an additional 20–25 h later in peripheral blood reticulocytes. It is, however, important to note that agent-specific factors such as a requirement for metabolic activation, or delays in cell cycle progression owing to toxic effects, may affect the length of these time spans. It is routine procedure to monitor the ratio of immature bone marrow PCE or peripheral blood reticulocytes as a measure of bone marrow toxicity, because excessive toxicity and concomitant cell cycle delay of damaged erythroblasts may result in false-negative assay results.

In this section, a detailed description of the flow cytometric MN test will be given. A full description of the *in vivo* MN assay is beyond the scope of this section; however, methodological guidelines for the conduct of this assay are periodically reviewed and published.

We have developed a flow cytometric approach to enumerating MN in PCE. The DNA of MN is identified using the DNA-specific fluorescent stain Hoechst 33342, and discrimination between PCE and NCE is based on staining with thiazole orange, a fluorescent probe with high RNA affinity. We have shown that the use of flow cytometric quantification of micronucleated *polychromatic* and *normochromatic* erythrocytes (MPCE and MNCE), beyond replacing manual enumeration, provides substantial advantages in terms of speed of analysis, as well as sensitivity. Because of the rapidity of the flow cytometric assay, the number of PCE screened per sample may easily be increased by a factor of 100, or from about 1000 to about 100,000, at an assay rate of about 1 sample every 5 min. Assuming a baseline frequency of MN in the population of scored PCE of 2 per million, the expected numbers of MN to be found are 2 and 200, respectively. MN frequencies tend to be Poisson distributed, giving standard deviations of about 1.4 and 14 respectively, or 70 and 7% of the number of MN enumerated. Thus, the flow cytometric technique is potentially as much as 10- fold more sensitive than the manual assay. This potentially high sensitivity is also realized in practice. Using both ionizing radiation and diverse chemical agents as inducers of MN, the flow cytometric assay has exhibited a sensitivity increase of about 10-fold in comparison with manual counting.

The flow cytometric MN assay has recently been adapted for the study of MN in human erythrocytes. Although these studies are still at an early stage, available data indicate that the high sensitivity shown in rodent studies may, to a large degree, be achievable in human studies.

Materials

Animal species and strains

1. The method has been applied to several strains of mice and rat, as well as wild-living species of rodents, e.g., wood mouse, yellow-necked mouse, and bank and field voles.
2. For the bone marrow erythrocyte test, mouse and rat as well as other species are acceptable; however, only mouse and rat have been extensively validated in the flow cytometric MN assay.
3. For the peripheral blood MN assay, the species used must not remove micronucleated erythrocytes in the spleen, leaving the mouse as the recommended species.
4. In the mouse, mature erythrocytes are also acceptable for MN analysis when the exposure duration exceeds 4 wk.
5. Among the mouse strains studied using the flow cytometric assay are CBA, C57Bl, Balb-C, and NMRI, and for rats, Fisher 344 and Sprague-Dawley.
6. Animal experiments are subject to local regulations.

Bone marrow and peripheral blood sampling

RPMI medium, Percoll, and fixative should be at room temperature at time of use.

1. Anesthetization equipment (anesthetic ether, CO_2 chamber, or equivalent).
2. Dissection instruments (scalpel, scissors, tweezers).
3. Heparinized blood collection tubes.
4. 1-mL Syringes with 0.4–0.6-mm needles.
5. RPMI-1640 medium.
6. Conical tubes (11/60 mm).
7. Centrifuge with swingout rotor and adaptors for 11/60-mm tubes.

Sample preparation

1. 1X, 10X Phosphate-buffered saline.
2. Percoll.
3. Adjustable micropipets covering 1–1000-μL range.
4. Percoll density gradient medium: 65% Percoll in PBS (58.5% Percoll, 6.5% 10X PBS, 35% PBS). May be stored for at least 1 wk at 4°C if prepared in a sterile fashion.
5. Centrifuge (as above).
6. Fluorescence-activated cell sorting (FACS) tubes.
7. Vortex.
8. Sorensen buffer A: 0.5 M KH_2PO_4 (6.805 g KH_2PO_4 to 1 L distilled water). Sorensen buffer B: 0.5 M $Na_2HPO_4 \cdot 2H_2O$ (8.903 g $Na_2HPO_4 \cdot 2H_2O$ to 1 L distilled water). Both buffers are stable for at least 6 mo at room temperature.
9. 70% Glutaraldehyde.
10. Sodium dodecyl sulphate stock solution: 1.5 mg/mL in distilled water; filter after preparation; stable for at least 6 mo at room temperature.
11. Fixative: 1% glutaraldehyde, 30 μg/mL sodium dodecyl sulfate (SDS; 50X dilution from stock solution) in 0.05 M PO_4 complete Sorensen's buffer, pH 6.8 (for pH 6.8, mix 53.4% Sorensen buffer A and 46.6% Sorensen buffer B). Make fresh every day.
12. 1 mg/mL Thiazole orange stock solution in methanol, stable for at least 1 yr when kept light protected at 4°C.
13. 500 μM Hoechst 33342 stock solution in distilled water. Stable for at least 1 yr when kept light protected at 4°C.
14. Staining solution: to 100 mL PBS, add 500 μL HO342 stock solution and 50 μL TO stock solution. Make fresh every day.
15. 37°C water bath.

Flow cytometry

1. Flow cytometer capable of simultaneous excitation at UV (minimum power 50 mW) and 488 nm (minimum power 100 mW) lines, preferably with spatially separated beams, e.g., FACSVantage SE equipped with Enterprise dual-wavelength (UV 351–364 and 488 nm) excitation laser. Recent data indicate that benchtop instruments with UV capability, e.g., the LSR from Becton-Dickinson Biosciences equipped with the HeCd UV laser, may also be used.
2. Filter set: 530/30-nm bandpass filter for detection of TO fluorescence emission; 424/44-nm bandpass filter for detection of HO342 fluorescence emission.
3. PBS or equivalent sheath fluid for flow analysis; PBS diluted 1:100–1:300 is recommended for sorting.

Methods

Study design and chemical treatment

For an extensive description of animal care and treatment regimes for the manual in vivo MN assay, as recommended by international expert working groups. The methods described for animal care and treatment below are based on these recommendations.

Because of the diverse properties of all possible substances that may be subject to testing, no unique treatment schedule can be recommended. Results from extended dose regimens are acceptable if they are positive. For studies showing negative results, there should be either demonstrated toxic effects or the limit dose should be used and dosing continued until sampling. Some basic recommendations for study design follow.

1. The size of the experiment (i.e., the number of cells scored per animal and the number of animals per group) should be based on statistical considerations: a doubling of the baseline frequency of micronucleated PCE or mature erythrocytes should be detectable compared with a control group with 95% confidence. Minimum recommended requirements for the manual assay are 2000 erythrocytes scored per animal, with at least four animals per dose group.
2. At least three dose levels should be used. They should be separated by a factor between 2 and the square root of 10. The highest dose tested should be the *maximum tolerated dose* (MTD). This dose is determined on the basis of mortality, bone marrow cell toxicity

as measured by the decrease in PCE frequency, or clinical symptoms such as weight loss or moribund animals. The MTD is usually determined in preliminary range-finding experiments with a smaller number of animals.

3. The highest or limit dose recommended in the absence of any signs of toxicity is 2 g/kg/d for treatment periods of 14 d or less and 1 g/kg/d for treatment periods greater than 14 d.
4. Controls given solvent (vehicle) only should be included at all sampling times. A concurrent positive control group, i.e., a group given a known MN-inducing agent at an effective dose should be included for each experiment. This is especially important for the interpretation of results in the case of a negative result for the substance being tested. Commonly used positive control substances include cyclophosphamide (monohydrate), mitomycin C, and triethylenemelamine. Positive control substances should be given at doses sufficient to induce a clear increase in MN frequencies but not so high that bone marrow toxicity detected as a reduced PCE frequency is apparent. Although the proper dosage for a positive control must be determined for each laboratory, doses in the range of 50 mg/kg for cyclophosphamide or 1 mg/kg for mitomycin C may give the desired results. These dosages are given for reference only.
5. In a typical experiment, three different dose groups, a vehicle control group, and a positive control group, each consisting of five animals, are treated at the same time. For the bone marrow MN test, animals are sacrificed and bone marrow sampled at 24 and 48 h after treatment. 24 h is the presumed ideal time window for the scoring in bone marrow PCE of MN induced in erythroblasts. The 48-h time is included to allow for delayed effects owing to, for example, the necessity for metabolic activation of the substance. For the peripheral blood MN test, sampling times should be delayed about another 24 h after treatment to allow for the transition of PCE from the bone marrow to the peripheral circulation, with 40–48 and 72 h being possible sampling times.

Collection of bone marrow cells

1. At time of sampling, anesthetize and sacrifice animals through cervical dislocation.
2. Dissect both femurs. Clean femurs and cut off outermost ends of each.

3. Into one end, insert a syringe filled with 1 mL RPMI-1640 cell culture medium and fitted with a 0.4–0.6-mm gauge needle. Forcefully flush the marrow into a conical tube containing another 1 mL of RPMI. Fill the syringe again with 1 mL of the cell suspension. Flush the femur again into the tube but from the other direction.
4. Repeat with second femur from the same animal.
5. Draw the cell suspension 5–10 times through the syringe to disperse cell aggregates. Let stand for about 1 min.
6. Transfer uppermost approx 1.8 mL to a new tube.
7. Centrifuge for 5 min at 600g.
8. Aspirate all but approx 100 μL of the medium.
9. Resuspend cells in remaining medium by gentle vortexing for 1–2 s (repeat if necessary).

Cell collection from peripheral blood

1. At time of sampling, anesthetize and draw approx 100–300 μL peripheral blood from animals by tail puncture, retro-orbital bleeding, or other suitable means into heparinized blood collection tubes.
2. Mix immediately by gentle vortexing, and again after about 1 min in order to avoid clotting.

Erythrocyte purification

1. Prepare 65% Percoll and add 1 mL each to appropriate number of conical test tubes. For each animal, prepare duplicate samples.
2. For bone marrow samples, layer 50 μL of the bone marrow cell suspension on top of the 65% Percoll in each tube.
3. For peripheral blood samples, add 6 μL of well-mixed peripheral blood on top of the 65% Percoll in each tube.
4. Centrifuge for 20 min at 600g with the centrifuge brake turned off.
5. Carefully aspirate the supernatant, including the majority of nucleated cells, being careful not to aspirate the red cell pellet.
6. Resuspend the pellet of red cells in 30 μL PBS by gentle vortexing.

Cell fixation

1. For each sample, add 1.25 mL of freshly made fixative to a FACS tube.
2. Suck the small volume of suspended red cells into an adjustable pipet set to a volume appropriate to accommodate the entire suspension (~50 μL).

3. During vigorous vortexing, quickly expel the cell suspension into the fixative, and continue vortexing for 5 s.
4. Keep samples at 4°C for at least 24 h and up to 7 d before staining.

Cell staining

1. Aspirate the fixative.
2. Loosen the cell pellet, which can be tightly packed, by vigorously shaking the test tube rack holding the tubes.
3. Add 1 mL of staining solution.
4. Stain for 1 h at 37°C in a water bath. Mix samples every 15 min by inverting the tubes.
5. Let stand for at least 2 h or overnight at 4°C before flow cytometric analysis.

Flow cytometry

1. Set UV laser power to at least 50 mW and 488 nm laser power to at least 100 mW for a FACS Vantage instrument.
2. Set the instrument to measure forward light scatter (FSC), side scatter (SSC), 530 nm fluorescence from TO (TOfl) excited by the 488-nm laser (usually the fluorescence isothiocyanate [FITC] channel) and 424 nm fluorescence from HO342 (HOfl) excited by the UV laser.
3. All four signals should be measured in peak height mode. Set the FSC channel to linear amplification, and the other three channels to logarithmic amplification.
4. Run the first sample. Owing to the high cell concentration, a low sample differential pressure is needed.
5. Set the threshold to FSC. Set the event rate to 3000–5000 events for peripheral blood samples or 1000–2000 events for bone marrow samples.
6. In the data acquisition program, make the following acquisition plots: an FSC-SSC density plot, an FSC-SSC dot plot, and a TOfl-HOfl dot plot. Set the FSC-SSC dot plot to accumulate all events.
7. Set the TOfl-HOfl dot plot to display about 10,000 events. Adjust the FSC and SSC gain to approximately center the cell population in the FSC-SSC plots.
8. Set the FSC threshold level to about one-fourth of full scale (~250 on a 1024-channel display).

9. Adjust the TOfl and HOfl gain to place the cell population in the TOfl-HOfl dot plot. A bimodal distribution in TOfl should be seen, whereby mature erythrocytes (NCE) have low TO fluorescence, and PCE have a higher fluorescence. The division between NCE and PCE should lie at about one-fourth of full scale. The appearance of cells will differ between bone marrow samples, in which PCE constitute some 50% of total erythrocytes, and peripheral blood samples, in which the PCE frequency is approx 1–3%. Additionally, a significant amount of residual nucleated cells should be seen in the upper right-hand part of the TOfl-HOfl dot plot in bone marrow samples.
10. Acquire a list mode file of at least 10,000 events with this setting. These files will be used for the analysis of PCE frequencies in order to detect bone marrow toxicity.
11. Running the same sample, change the threshold to TOfl, and set the threshold level to exclude NCE.
12. Adjust the flow rate to about 1000 cells/s for both bone marrow and peripheral blood samples. In the FSC-SSC dot plot, a bimodal population is now seen. One population (lower in FSC and SSC) represents single erythrocytes and one erythrocyte aggregates and nucleated cells.
13. Draw a region of interest around the single erythrocyte population. Gate the TOfl-HOfl dot plot on this region. In the TOfl-HOfl dot plot there should now be three visible populations: PCE, micronucleated PCE (MNPCE) differentiated from the PCE by their higher HO342 fluorescence, and residual nucleated cells in the upper right-hand region. Since MNPCE are rare, on the order of 1 per million of the erythrocyte population, only a few will be visible on the dot plot, even if it is set to display 10,000 events.
14. One way of verifying that the dots seen in the presumed MNPCE region are true events is to use so-called back-gating. Draw a region around the presumed MNPCE, taking care not to include any PCE without MN. Gate the hitherto unused FSC-SSC dot plot on this region. As the presumed MNPCE accumulate in this region, a population should form with the same FSC-SSC characteristics as the ungated PCE population in the FSC- SSC density plot. These are the true MNPCE. Events will also be seen with other FCS- SSC properties. These are false events and will be gated out during data analysis. However, if no distinct

population appears with the similar population characteristics as the main PCE population, there may be a problem with the sample.

15. Acquire a list mode file of 100,000 events in the single erythrocyte region with this setting. Now run all samples, acquiring both list mode files for each sample. Take care to place the PCE population in the same position for all samples by adjusting amplifier gains, as this greatly simplifies subsequent data analysis.

Flow sorting

It may be desirable to sort micronucleated cells for verification by microscopy or for downstream analysis such as fluorescence in situ hybridization (FISH).

1. For sorting, the FSC threshold should be used, so that all erythrocytes are "seen" by the instrument; otherwise the sort purity will be very low. This will slow down the sort when sorting MNPCE from peripheral blood, since running PCE at 1000 events/s means that 30,000–40,000 erythrocytes/s pass through the sorter. This rate is too high for sorting for most instruments.

Data analysis

Each sample is now represented by two list mode data files, one with all erythrocytes and one with PCE only (and some nucleated cells).

1. For analysis of PCE frequencies, first open a dot plot of HOfl vs TOfl in your flow cytometry data analysis program. Draw a region around all the erythrocytes and another region enclosing the PCE population, and determine the number of events in both regions.
2. Repeat for all total erythrocyte files.
3. Add the results from duplicate samples from each animal, and use these sums for the calculation of the PCE frequency for each animal. The frequency is generally around 50% in bone marrow and around 1–3% in peripheral blood for control animals, depending on animal strain and age.
4. For analysis of MNPCE frequencies, make an FSC-SSC density plot, and open one of the files containing PCE only. Identify the population of single PCE, and draw a region enclosing it.
5. Make a dot plot of HOfl vs TOfl showing all events. Gate this plot on the PCE region in the FSC-SSC plot in the same way.
6. Draw regions identifying PCE and MNPCE, and determine the number of events in these regions. When drawing the MNPCE region, take care not to include any PCE without MN.

7. Add these figures from duplicate samples from each animal, and use these sums for the calculation of the MNPCE frequency for each animal as % MNPCE = number of MNPCE × 1000/(number of PCE + number of MNPCE).

Data interpretation

The data evaluation will naturally depend on the design of the experiment. Preliminary data interpretation includes viewing dot plots for samples with abnormal appearance, e.g., strongly deviating positions or shapes of the cell populations. These should be excluded from the evaluation. Determining the existence and nature of a response in the frequency of MNPCE should be based on both biological and statistical considerations.

1. In a typical experiment with a control group, three treatment groups, and a positive control group, it should first be determined whether the negative control is within the range (± 3 standard deviations) of the laboratory's historical control data. If the laboratory has not yet generated sufficient control data, published literature values of control data may be of use.
2. It should also be determined whether the positive control shows the expected response, with a statistically significant elevation in MN frequency.
3. The dose–response rate of the treatment can then be statistically evaluated using a trend test.
4. Ideally, each treatment group should also be compared pairwise with both the concurrent and the historical controls.
5. For a clear negative result, the trend analysis and the pairwise comparisons should both be without significance. For a clear positive result, the trend test and at least one of the pairwise comparisons should be positive.

Notes

1. However, it is possible to perform the flow cytometric MN assay on rat peripheral blood by using the TO fluorescence intensity to identify the youngest of the peripheral blood PCE.
2. Temperature differences among medium, Percoll, and fixative may lead to partial erythrocyte lysis, which in turn gives problems when identifying erythrocytes in the FSC-SSC dot plot during data acquisition and analysis.
3. In general, the use of one gender is adequate for screening. However, if there is evidence indicating differences between males

and females in the toxicity of a certain substance, both sexes should be used.

4. Organic solvents such as DMSO are not recommended. Vegetable oils are acceptable as solvents or vehicles. Suspensions (as opposed to solutions) of the test chemicals are acceptable for peroral or intraperitoneal administration, but not for intravenous injection. Freshly prepared solutions or suspensions should be used unless stability data demonstrate the acceptability of storage.
5. Remaining cell aggregates and tissue pieces will thereby be removed, eliminating nozzle clogging problems during flow analysis.
6. Results of parallel samples are pooled for data analysis, reducing the effect of possible variations in sample preparation. In low-dose studies, in which high measurement precision is necessary, triplicate samples are recommended.
7. In bone marrow samples, nucleated cells are visible as a band on top of the Percoll and as a white or pink cloudiness on top of the red pellet. The latter phase can also be removed by careful aspiration, improving the identification of erythrocytes during flow analysis.
8. Immediate and complete mixing is important for a uniform shape after fixation. The SDS in the fixative swells the erythrocytes to uniform spheres for optimal flow analysis.
9. With increasing fixation time, the autofluorescence of the fixed erythrocytes slowly increases, reducing the discrimination between PCE and NCE.
10. Use of 1 mL is standard practice in samples from peripheral blood, as well as for bone marrow when the cell concentration is very similar in all samples. If there are large variations in cell concentration (easily visible in the fixed samples by estimating the size of the sedimented red cell pellet), the amount of staining solution should be adjusted accordingly.
11. A well-aligned instrument is imperative for optimal results.
12. Use of a high cell concentration during sample staining and analysis significantly enhances the quality of the results. High cell concentration when staining reduces nonspecific staining, improving discrimination between MNPCE and PCE. High cell concentration during flow analysis allows a low sample flow rate, which in turn improves especially the precision of the DNA (HO342) measurement.

13. Because of variations between samples, e.g., low PCE frequency in some samples, it may not always be possible to reach speeds of 1000 cells/s.
14. In bone marrow samples, this is usually a discrete population. In peripheral blood samples, the single erythrocyte population often overlaps with the population of doublets and nucleated cells. It is then best to reduce the size of the gate, losing some single erythrocytes, but also most nonspecific events. The shape of this region can be optimized during data analysis, in which the effect of different positions and shapes on the appearance and frequency of the MNPCE population in the HOfl-TOfl dot plot can be evaluated.
15. For a successful sort, one should bear in mind that the MNPCE are very rare. Given a baseline frequency of 2 per million MNPCE among all PCE, and a PCE frequency of 50% among all bone marrow erythrocytes, the frequency of MNPCE among all cells is on the order of 1 per million. In peripheral blood with a PCE frequency of approx 2%, the frequency of MPCE among all cells may be as low as approx 4×10^{-5}.
16. If one is sorting for subsequent probing by FISH an alternative, two-step fixation procedure is required. First the pellet is suspended as describe above, and 0.5 mL of PBS containing 5 μg/mL of SDS is added with simultaneous agitation. This step spheres the erythrocytes. After exactly 1 min, 2 mL of Millonig's phosphate-buffered formalin (0.105 M NaOH, 0.137 M KH_2PO_4 in 10% formalin: 0.42 g NaOH, 1.86 g KH_2PO_4, 90 mL distilled water, 10 mL 37% formaldehyde) is added. After gentle mixing, the samples are left for 2 h at room temperature (~22°C) before being stored at +4°C for at least 12 h before staining and analysis. The amount of TO stock solution in the staining buffer should then be reduced to 5 μL/100 mL owing to reduced autofluorescence of the fixed cells.
17. To avoid salt buildup when sorting on slides, it is advisable to sort using a low-salt sheath fluid for the sorter. Pure water does not work owing to its low conductivity, but using a standard sorter, it should be possible to use PBS diluted 100–300X with water.
18. Use of silane-coated slides improves the adherence of sorted cells:
    (a) Wash slides in detergent solution for 30 min.
    (b) Wash slides in running tap water for 30 min.
    (c) Wash slides in distilled water for 2×5 min.

(d) Wash slides in 95% ethanol for 2 × 5 min.

(e) Air-dry in a dust-free environment for 5 min.

(f) Add 6 mL aminopropyltriethoxysilane solution to 300 mL acetone.

(g) Dip slides into silane solution for 10 s.

(h) Wash twice briefly in distilled water.

(i) Dry overnight at 37°C in a dust-free environment.

19. Other alternatives require biological judgment, including control of PCE frequencies, to exclude the possibility of excessive bone marrow toxicity.

Genotoxicity Test

The comet assay or *single-cell gel* (SCG) test is a microgel electrophoresis technique that measures DNA damage at the level of single cells. A small number of cells suspended in a thin agarose gel on a microscope slide is lysed, electrophoresed, and stained with a fluorescent DNA binding dye. Cells with increased DNA damage display increased migration of chromosomal DNA from the nucleus toward the anode, which resembles the shape of a comet. In its alkaline version, which is mainly used, DNA single-strand breaks, DNA double-strand breaks, alkali-labile sites, and single-strand breaks associated with incomplete excision repair sites cause increased DNA migration. On the other hand, crosslinks (DNA–DNA or DNA–protein) can lead to decreased DNA migration. Variations of the comet assay have been established for the detection of specific DNA base modifications. Here we describe the basic methodology of the alkaline comet assay, establishing a sensitive protocol for obtaining reproducible and reliable data.

The comet assay (or *single-cell gel* [SCG]) test permits the sensitive detection of DNA damage at the level of single cells. In this microgel electrophoresis technique, small numbers of cells, such as cultured cells, isolated peripheral lymphocytes or cells isolated from various tissues are suspended in a thin agarose gel on a microscope slide. The cells are lysed with detergent and treated with high salt. Nucleoids are formed, containing non-nucleosomal but still supercoiled DNA. After electrophoresis and staining with a fluorescent DNA-binding dye, cells with increased DNA damage dis play increased migration of chromosomal DNA from the nucleoid toward the anode, which resembles the shape of a comet. In the alkaline version of the assay which is most often used, DNA strand breaks and alkali-labile sites become apparent, and the amount of DNA migration indicates the amount of DNA damage in the cell. The comet assay combines the simplicity of biochemical techniques for detecting DNA single-strand breaks and/or alkali-labile sites with the single-cell approach typical of cytogenetic assays.

The advantages of the SCG test include its simple and rapid performance, its sensitivity for detecting DNA damage, the analysis of data at the level of the individual cell, the use of extremely small cell samples, and the usability of virtually any eukaryote cell population. Apart from image analysis, which greatly facilitates and enhances the possibilities of comet measurements, the cost of performing the assay is extremely low. The comet assay has already been used in many studies to assess DNA damage and repair induced by various agents in a variety of cells *in vitro* and *in vivo*. The test has widespread applications in DNA damage and repair studies, environmental biomonitoring, and human population monitoring. The comet assay is widely used in genotoxicity testing *in vitro* and *in vivo*.

The alkaline version of the comet assay was introduced by Singh and coworkers in 1988. Performing electrophoresis at pH >13.0 enabled the detection of DNA single-strand breaks and alkali-labile lesions. Other versions of the assay were then developed by Olive and coworkers, which involved lysis in alkali followed by electrophoresis at either neutral or mild alkaline (pH 12.1) conditions to detect DNA double-strand breaks or single-strand breaks, respectively. Because most genotoxic agents induce many more single-strand breaks and alkali-labile sites than double-strand breaks, the alkaline version (pH >13.0) of the comet assay, although less specific, has the highest sensitivity for detecting induced DNA damage. Important improvements of the test procedure were introduced by Klaude and coworkers in 1996. The use of agarose-precoated slides in combination with drying of gels and fixation of the comets led to a further simplification and a much better handling of the test.

A broad spectrum of DNA-damaging agents cause increased DNA migration in the comet assay. In principal, the alkaline version of the comet assay detects all kinds of directly induced DNA single-strand breaks and any lesion capable of being transformed into a single-strand break at the alkaline pH used (i.e. alkali-labile sites). Breaks introduced into DNA can produce fragments or cause the supercoiled DNA to relax locally. Fragments and/or loops of DNA are then free to migrate toward the anode, thus forming the "*comet tail.*" The alkaline conditions allow DNA strands to unwind and also convert alkali-labile sites, such as apurinic and apyrimidinic sites formed when bases are lost, into DNA breaks. Therefore, the comet assay detects the DNA-damaging effects not only of ionizing radiation and radiomimetic chemicals with high sensitivity but also other types of primary DNA damage such as that induced by hydrogen peroxide and other radical-forming chemicals, alkylating agents, *polycyclic aromatic hydrocarbons* (PAHs) and other adduct-forming chemicals, various metals and UV irradiation. In addition to directly induced strand breakage, processes that introduce single-strand nicks in the DNA, such as incision during excision repair processes, are also detectable. In some cases (e.g., UV, PAHs) the contribution of excision repair to the induced DNA effects in the comet assay seems to be of major importance. Some specific classes of DNA base damage can be detected with the comet assay in conjunction with lesion-specific endonucleases. These enzymes, applied to the slides for a short time after lysis, nick DNA at sites of specific base alterations, and the resulting single-strand breaks can be quantified in the comet assay.

Using this modification of the comet assay, the induction and persistence of UV-induced pyrimidine dimers could be monitored in HeLa cells by incubating lysed DNA with a UV-specific endonuclease. Oxidized DNA bases have been detected with high sensitivity with the help of endonuclease III or formamidopyrimidine-DNA-glycosylase (FPG) *in vitro* and *in vivo*. Other types of DNA damage, such as pyrimidine dimers and bulky adducts, could be revealed by an indirect immmuno-fluorescence detection using lesion-specific monoclonal antibodies. A combination of the comet assay with *fluorescence in situ hybridization* (FISH) makes it possible to investigate the induction and persistence of DNA damage in specific chromosomal regions and genes.

Crosslinks (DNA–DNA or DNA–protein), such as those induced by nitrogen mustard, cisplatin, cyclophosphamide, or formaldehyde, may cause problems in the standard protocol of the test, because crosslinking may stabilize chromosomal DNA and inhibit DNA migration. However, the comet assay has also been used to detect crosslinking. One approach is to induce DNA migration with a second agent (e.g., ionizing radiation, methyl methanesulfonate) and to determine the reduced migration in the presence of the crosslinking agent. Crosslinks can also be detected by increasing the duration of unwinding and/or electrophoresis to such an extent that control cells exhibit significant DNA migration, demonstrating the effect of crosslinking by a retardation in the extent of DNA migration in comparison with the control. DNA–DNA and DNA–protein crosslinks can be distinguished by incubating the lysed DNA in *proteinase K* (PK) prior to electrophoresis. Exposure of crosslinked DNA to PK reduces or eliminates DNA–protein crosslinks and enhances migration, while having no effect on the amount of DNA–DNA crosslinks. These modifications of the standard protocol provide additional mechanistic information on the specific types of DNA damage induced by a DNA-damaging agent.

The purpose of this protocol is to provide information on the application of the alkaline comet assay for the investigation of DNA damage in mammalian cells in vitro. For establishing the method, we recommend starting with experiments using blood samples and the induction of DNA damage by a standard mutagen (ionizing radiation or an alkylating agent). The method described here is based on a protocol established by R. Tice according to the original work of Singh et al. and includes the modifications introduced by Klaude and coworkers.

Materials

Preparation of slides

1. Microscope slides (with frosted end).
2. Coverslips (24 × 60 mm).
3. Ethanol (absolute).
4. Microcentrifuge tubes.
5. Agarose (*low melting point* [LMP]).
6. Phosphate-buffered saline (PBS), Ca^{2+}, Mg^{2+} free.
7. Micropipetors and tips.
8. Lysing solution per 1000 mL: 2.5 M NaCl (146.1 g), 100 mM EDTA (disodinar salt; 37.2 g), 10 mM Tris-HCl (1.2 g). Titrate to 10.0 pH with approx 8 g solid NaOH; make up to 890 mL with dH_2O, and store at room temperature. Final lysing solution (100 mL): add fresh 1 mL Triton X-100 and 10 mL dimethyl sulfoxide (DMSO) to 89 mL lysing solution, and then refrigerate (4°C) for 60 min before use.

Preparation of cells

1. Heparinized peripheral blood.
2. RPMI-1640 media.
3. Ficoll/Hypaque solution.
4. Centrifuge.

Electrophoresis and staining

1. Horizontal gel electrophoresis unit.
2. Electrophoresis buffer: 300 mM NaOH/1 mM EDTA. Prepare from stock solutions: 10 N NaOH (200 g/500 mL dH_2O); 200 mM EDTA (14.89 g/200 mL dH_2O, pH 10). Store at room temperature. For 1X buffer (made fresh before each run; total volume depends on gel box capacity), mix 45 mL NaOH solution plus 7.5 mL EDTA solution, fill to 1500 mL, and mix well.
3. Neutralization buffer: 0.4 M Tris-HCl (48.5 g). Fill to 1000 mL with dH_2O. Set pH to 7.5 with HCl. Store at room temperature.
4. Ethanol (absolute).
5. Staining solution: ethidium bromide (10X stock: 200 μg/mL), 10 mg in 50 mL dH_2O. Store at room temperature. For 1X stock (20 μg/mL), mix 1 mL with 9 mL dH_2O and filter.

Evaluation of DNA damage

1. Fluorescence microscope (equipped with an excitation filter of 515–560 nm and a barrier filter of 590 nm).

Methods

Preparation of slides

1. Clean oily or dusty slides with ethanol before use, and label them with a solvent-resistant marker.
2. Agarose:
   (a) For bottom layer, prepare 1.5% normal melting agarose (300 mg in 20 mL PBS) and boil two to three times before use.
   (b) Dip the cleaned slides briefly into hot (>60°C) agarose. The agarose should reach halfway up the frosted part of the slide to ensure that the agarose will stick properly to the slide.
   (c) Wipe off the agarose from the bottom side of the slide, and place the slide horizontally. (This step has to be performed quickly to ensure a good distribution of the agarose.)
   (d) Dry the slides and store them at room temperature until needed. Avoid high-humidity conditions.
3. Prepare 0.5% LMP agarose (100 mg in 20 mL PBS). Microwave or heat until near boiling and the agarose dissolves. Place LMP agarose vial in a 37°C water bath to cool.
4. Add 120 μL of LMP agarose (37°C) mixed with 5000–50000 cells in approx 5–10 μL. (Do not use more than 10 μL). Add cover slip and place the tray in a refrigerator for approx 2 min (until the

agarose layer hardens). Using approx 10,000 cells results in approx 1 cell/microscope field (400× magnification). After adding the cells to the slides until the end of electrophoresis, direct light irradiation should be avoided to prevent additional DNA damage.

5. Gently slide off cover slip and slowly lower slide into cold, freshly made lysing solution. Protect from light and place in 4°C refrigeration for a minimum of 1 h. Slides may be stored for extended periods in cold lysing solution (but generally not longer than 4 wk). If precipitation of the lysing solution is observed, slides should be rinsed carefully with distilled water before electrophoresis.

Preparation and treatment of cells

1. Whole blood: mix approx 5 μL whole blood with 120 μL LMP agarose, and layer onto slide.
2. Isolated lymphocytes:
   (a) Mix 40 μL whole blood with 500 μL mL RPMI-1640 in a microcentrifuge tube, and add 150 μL Ficoll below the blood/medium mixture.
   (b) Spin for 3 min at 200g.
   (c) Remove 100 μL of the middle/top of the Ficoll layer, add to 1 mL medium, mix, and spin for 3 min to pellet the lymphocytes.
   (d) Pour off the supernatant, resuspend the pellet in 120 μL LMP agarose, and layer onto slide.
3. Cell cultures:
   (a) Monolayer cultures: gently trypsinize cells (for about 2 min with 0.15% trypsin; stop by adding serum or complete cell culture medium) to yield approx 1×10^6 cells/mL. Add 10 μL cell suspension to 120 μL LMP agarose, and layer onto slide.
   (b) Suspension cultures: add approx 20,000 cells in 10 μL or less volume to 120 μL LMP agarose, and layer onto slide.

In vitro treatment of cells

1. For in vitro tests, cells are usually incubated with the test substances for a defined period, then mixed with LMP agarose, and added to the slide. A modified protocol, which may be performed in combination with the standard comet assay, suggests treating after cell lysis. Under these conditions, the lysed cells are no longer held under the regulation of any metabolic pathway or membrane barrier.

Standardized positive control

For demonstration of a positive effect:

1. Mix 200 μL heparinized whole blood with 50 μL of a 2.5×10^{-4} M methyl methanesulfonate (MMS) solution (final concentration: 5×10^{-5} M), incubate for 1 h at 37°C and then use 10 μL for the test.
2. Alternatively, cells can be irradiated with 1 Gy γ-irradiation.
3. To evaluate whether the assay is functioning correctly, a treated (e.g., MMS or γ-irradiation), cryopreserved cell sample (e.g., isolated blood lymphocytes or a permanent cell line) can be used.
4. The treated cell population can be stored as 1-mL aliquots (about 10^5 cells/mL) in microcentrifuge tubes. Such a sample can be thawed and processed along with the experimental samples.
5. Data from these samples indicate the interrun variability.

Electrophoresis and staining

1. After at least 1 h at 4°C, gently remove slides from the lysing solution.
2. Place slides on the horizontal gel box near the anode (+) end, sliding them as close together as possible.
3. Fill the buffer reservoirs with freshly made electrophoresis buffer (4°C) until the liquid level completely covers the slides (avoid bubbles over the agarose). Alkaline treatment and electrophoresis are both performed in an ice bath (4°C).
4. Let slides sit in the alkaline buffer for 20–60 min to allow unwinding of the DNA and the expression of alkali-labile damage. For most experiments with cultivated cells, 20 min is sufficient.
5. Turn on power supply to 25 V (~0.8–1.5 V/cm, depending on gel box size), and adjust current to 300 mA by slowly raising or lowering the buffer level. Depending on the purpose of the study and the extent of migration in control samples, allow slides to run for 20–40 min. The goal is to obtain a little migration among the control cells to ensure sensitive test conditions. The optimal electrophoresis duration differs for different cell types and has to be established first.
6. Turn off the power. Gently lift the slides from the buffer, and place on a staining tray. Coat the slides dropwise with neutralization buffer, and let sit for at least 5 min. Repeat two more times.

7. Drain slides, dry the bottom side, incubate for 5–10 min in absolute ethanol, and let them dry (inclined) at room temperature. Slides can be stored for a longer time before staining. To stain, add 50 μL 1X ethidium bromide staining solution, and cover with a cover slip.
8. Slides are stained one by one and evaluated immediately. It is possible to rinse stained (evaluated) slides in distilled water, remove the coverslip, let the slides dry, and stain them at a later time point for re-evaluation.

Evaluation of DNA Effects

For visualization of DNA damage, observations are made of ethidium bromidestained DNA at 400× magnification using a fluorescence microscope equipped with an excitation filter of 515–560 nm and a barrier filter of 590 nm. Generally, 50 randomly selected cells per sample are analyzed. Depending on the size of the cells being analyzed, other magnifications (e.g., 250×) can be used.

In principle, evaluation can be done in four different ways:

1. The percentage of cells with a tail vs those without is determined.
2. Cells are scored visually according to tail size into five classes (from undamaged, 0, to maximally damaged, 4). Thus, the total score for 50 comets can range from 0 (all undamaged) to 200 (all maximally damaged).
3. Cells are analyzed using a calibrated scale in the ocular of the microscope. For each cell, the image length (diameter of the nucleus plus migrated DNA) is measured in microns, and the mean is calculated.
4. An image analysis system linked to a gated CCD camera is used to quantitate DNA image length, head length, tail length, and tail intensity. The statistical variants usually used include DNA migration (image length, tail length), tail intensity, and tail moment. It should be noted that the calculation of tail moment (DNA migration × tail intensity) in different image analysis systems may not be based on the same parameters.

For the statistical analysis of comet assay data, a variety of parametric and nonparametric statistical methods are used. The most appropriate means of statistical analysis depends on the kind of study and has to take into account the various sources of assay variability. For a powerful statistical analysis of in vitro test data, appropriate replication and repeat experiments have to be performed. When migration length is used as the measure of DNA damage, the median of the 50 cells per experimental point and the mean from repeat experiments should be determined. Mean migration should not be used since a normal size distribution is not observed. Analyses are mainly based on changes in group mean response, but attention should also be paid to the distribution among cells, which often provides additional important information.

Notes

1. Many technical variables have been modified, including the concentration and amount of LMP agarose, the composition of the lysing solution and the lysis time, the alkaline unwinding, the electrophoresis buffer and electrophoretic conditions, DNA-specific dyes for staining, and so on. Some of these variables may affect the sensitivity of the test. To allow for a comparison obtained in different laboratories and for a critical evaluation of data, it is absolutely necessary to describe the technical details of the method employed clearly.
2. Although the protocol described here detects a broad spectrum of DNA-damaging agents with high sensitivity, modifications have been suggested that further increase the sensitivity and may be advantageous for certain applications. These modifications include the addition of radical scavengers to the electrophoresis buffer (to reduce damage during prolonged electrophoresis), the addition of PK to the lysing solution (to remove residual proteins that might inhibit DNA migration), and the use of the DNA dyes SYBR Green-I or YOYO-1 (to increase the sensitivity for the detection of migrated DNA).
3. Many other cell types have been used, and it is a strength of the comet assay that virtually any eukaryote cell population is amenable to analysis. The comet assay is particularly suited for the investigation of organ- or tissue-specific genotoxic effects in vivo, the only requirement being the preparation of an intact single cell suspension.
4. It is strongly recommended to include some measure of cytotoxicity in every study and to specify the limits of cytotoxicity used in a test. Acute lethal effects can easily be determined by various viability tests such as Trypan blue exclusion, ATP levels, or fluorochrome-mediated assays. However, as cell survival may be significantly reduced in the absence of acute cytotoxicity, tests indicating long-term survivability (e.g., plating efficiency) should

also be considered. The comet assay has not yet been sufficiently validated and may be sensitive to nongenotoxic cell killing. Upon cell death, elevated DNA migration may be induced by extensive DNA fragmentation. However, data suggest that false-positive results owing to cytotoxicity may be cell type-specific. Although excessive cytotoxicity in V79 Chinese hamster cells or L5178Y mouse lymphoma cells did not result in positive effects in the comet assay, cytotoxicity was reported as a possible confounding effect in TK-6 cells or rat lymphocytes. However, the comet assay has the advantage that dead or dying cells can be identified on microscope slides by their morphology. Such cells exhibit extensive DNA fragmentation, are without a visible nucleus, and nearly all of their DNA is in the tail. For the evaluation of genotoxic effects, it is recommended to record these cells and use them as an additional parameter of cytotoxicity, but to exclude them from evaluation under the principle that they represent dead cells.

5. If specific types of base damage are to determined by using lesion-specific endonucleases, the standard protocol has to be modified in the following way: after at least 1 h at 4°C, gently remove slides from the lysing solution and wash three times in enzyme buffer. Drain slides and cover with 200 μL of either buffer or enzyme in buffer. Seal with a cover slip, and incubate for 30 min at 37°C. Remove the cover slip, rinse slides with PBS, and place them on the electrophoresis box.

Computerized Image

Single-cell gel electrophoresis (SCGE) or the *comet assay* is a powerful tool for the detection of DNA single- and double-strand breaks and base damage and for investigating the kinetics of DNA strand break rejoining in human and animal model systems. It is a versatile technique that can be applied in various areas of biomedical research. This section highlights the importance of computerized analysis and data processing for the comet assay and describes the criteria used for manual evaluation of comets and their limitations compared with the computer-based analysis. It describes in detail SCGE-Pro, a semi-automatic software developed in our laboratory for comet evaluation and data processing. For comparison, some of the commercially available software for analysis of data from the comet assay is also described.

Single-cell gel electrophoresis (SCGE) or the *comet assay* can be used for detection of DNA damage and repair at the single-cell level and provides a unique opportunity to investigate intercellular differences in any eukaryotic cell population. During the early development of this assay, the problems inherent in manual evaluation of comets were major stumbling blocks for the widespread acceptance and application of the technique. Measurements of comet characteristics using an ocular micrometer were tedious and time-consuming. Meanwhile, there has been rapid development in the field of imaging devices/sensors, owing to the increasing availability of low-cost, highspeed computational facility and denser memory chips, which has led to the development of a number of imaging techniques and software for biological applications. Basically, *digital image processing* (DIP) has four components: image acquisition, processing, storage, and display. During recent years, a number of types of imaging software have been developed for visualization and measurement of various comet characteristics, e.g., total/tail area, DNA content, percentage of DNA in head/tail, head diameter, tail length, and so on. The commercial availability of various imaging software packages for evaluation of the comet assay has created considerable interest in laboratories across the world engaged in genotoxicity evaluation of physical and chemical mutagens and carcinogens. This assay has been in applied in many areas of biomedical research, including genetic toxicology, radiation biology, human biomonitoring, clinical and molecular epidemiology, and, as a predictive assay, cancer radiotherapy.

The comet assay is highly sensitive and can be used to detect DNA double-strand breaks under neutral conditions, as well as DNA single-strand breaks, alkali-labile sites, and incomplete DNA repair sites under alkaline conditions (by converting them to double-strand breaks). In addition, specific types of DNA base damage can be detected and quantified using endonuclease III and formamidopyrimidine-glycosylase (FPG), and UV-induced pyrimidine dimers can be detected and quantified using T4 endonuclease V. The assay has been further modified to detect agents that do not produce DNA strand breaks except as transient intermediates during nucleotide excision repair by incubating cells with DNA polymerase inhibitors, such as cytosine arabinoside or aphidicolin, and it has also been combined with *fluorescence in situ hybridization* (FISH) to measure gene-specific repair relative to total DNA or *loss of heterozygosity* (LOH) for a single gene.

This section describes SCGE-Pro, digital imaging software developed in our laboratory for automated image analysis and data processing of the comet assay. It also describes various criteria used for manual scoring of comets and their limitations. Besides SCGE-Pro, a number of other types of software available commercially for evaluation of the comet assay.

Materials

Hardware

A digital imaging system for data capture from the comet assay consists of the following components: a fluorescence microscope, a video camera, a frame grabber (in the case of an analog camera), and a suitable computer with a printer. A high-resolution digital camera can also be used for image acquisition. The various components of the imaging system can be obtained from any reliable vendor. The following examples are derived from our own system.

1. Fluorescence microscope: a Zeiss Axioplan microscope with epifluorescence facility (HBO 50 high-pressure mercury lamp) and suitable filter sets.
2. Video camera: a high-performance color video camera, JVC KY-F55BE 3CCD. This camera has a 1/3-inch 440,000-pixel CCD with on-chip lens, and it delivers high-quality pictures with a signal-to-noise ratio of 58 dB and sensitivity as high as 2000 lux at F5.6. It has a horizontal resolution of 750 lines. It also incorporates a comprehensive range of automatic functions including automatic level control, continuously variable electronic shutter, and full-time auto white balance. It also has outputs for composite video, RGB, and composite sync signals.
3. Video frame grabber: Integral Flashpoint Intrigue frame grabber. The FlashBus MV uses the PCI bus for real-time transfer of video to system memory. The PCI bus has a theoretical data transfer rate fast enough for real-time transfer of video data. The actual performance of the FlashBus MV also depends on other factors such as CPU memory, interaction among cards, operating system used, bus implementation, BIOS versions, and so on. The Integral Flashpoint Intrigue frame grabber accepts color composite video output of the camera. It digitizes each of the RGB planes at a tonal resolution of 24 bits per pixel and has a spatial resolution of 768 × 576 per frame.
4. Computer and related accessories: a complete color image requires 640 × 480 × 24 bits (921,600 bytes) of data space. Thus, complex operations on large images require large storage space and a fast computer. For our software, the ideal computer configuration

requires a Pentium-III computer with a super VGA 17-inch color monitor, CD-ROM drive, 40 GB hard disk, CD writer for image storage, and printer.

Software

1. SCGE-Pro.
2. LAI's Automated Comet Analysis System.
3. Komet 5.
4. Comet Imager and CometScan.
5. Comet assay II.
6. AutoComet.
7. Fenestra Comet.

Methods

Exposure of cells to any physical or chemical mutagen produces DNA strand breaks or base damage, which can be easily quantified with the comet assay. Briefly, in this assay, the cells of interest (which may have been exposed *in vitro* or *in vivo*) are suspended in agarose on microscope slides and lysed with any detergent or high salt solution; then the liberated DNA is electrophoresed under neutral or alkaline conditions. Depending on their size and total negative charge, the DNA fragments migrate different distances toward the anode. After electrophoresis, the cells are stained with a DNA-specific dye and observed under a fluorescence microscope. Under these conditions, individual cells appear as comets with brightly fluorescing nuclei and a "tail" of diminishing fluorescence intensity. The distance migrated by DNA fragments from the nucleus, i.e., *tail length* (TL), is considered to be a measure of genetic damage. Using digital imaging software, other characteristics of these comets, e.g., tail moment (defined as the product of percentage of DNA in the tail and tail length), percent DNA in the tail (%DNA-T) or head (%DNA-H), can also be measured, which are considered to be more consistent and reliable indicators of DNA damage.

Manual evaluation of comets

After staining the cells with a suitable DNA-specific dye, comets are observed at 25× or 40× under a fluorescence microscope with suitable filters. The objectives of the microscope should be calibrated using the stage and ocular micrometer. The length of the comet is measured in microns and recorded. *Apoptotic* or *dead cells* should be recorded separately. Some laboratories use visual methods to score comet slides. By this method, the cells are initially classified as

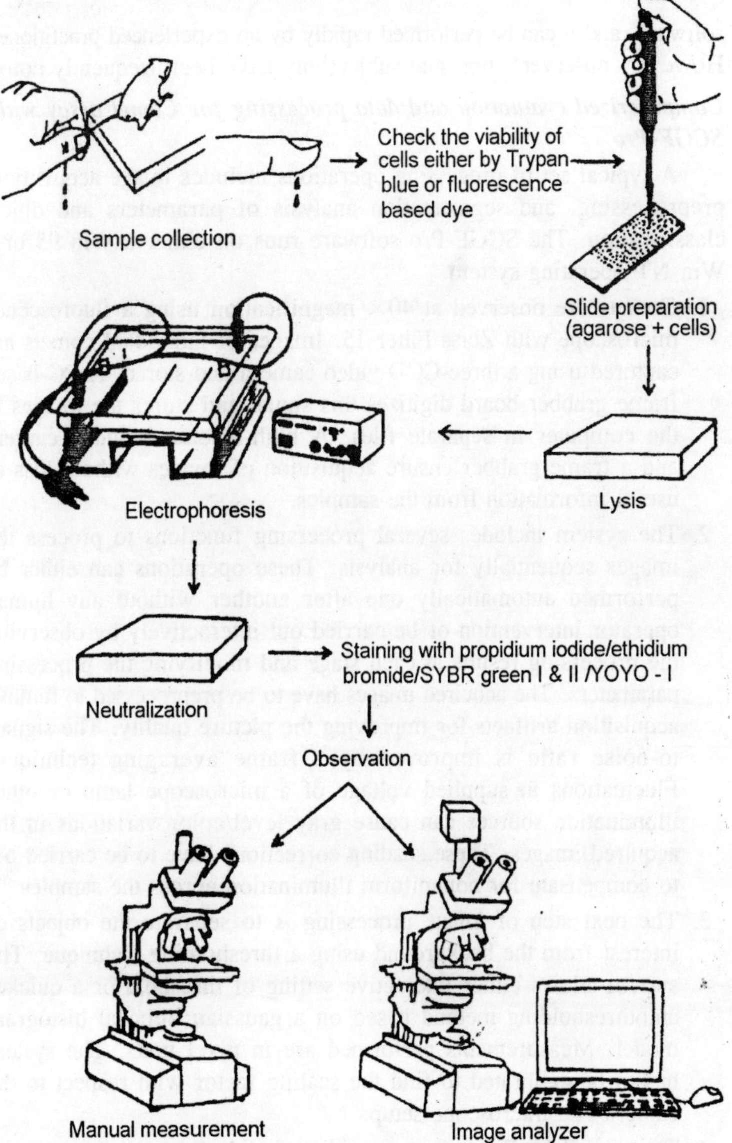

Fig. 10.1. Schematic presentation of comet assay.

undamaged or damaged, and then the degree of damage is estimated by assignment to categories, such as type I (no damage) to type V (highly damaged). This type of visual scoring does not require any software, and it can be performed rapidly by an experienced practitioner. However, observer's bias and subjectivity have been frequently noted.

Computerized evaluation and data processing for Comet assay with SCGE-Pro

A typical set of processing operations includes image acquisition, preprocessing, and segmentation analysis of parameters and object classification. The SCGE-Pro software runs on either a Win 95 or a Win NT operating system.

1. Comets are observed at 40× magnification using a fluorescence microscope with Zeiss Filter 15. Images of individual comets are captured using a three-CCD video camera and stored. A PC-based frame grabber board digitizes this signal and stores the images in the computer in separate files. A high-resolution video camera and a frame grabber ensure acquisition of images without loss of useful information from the samples.
2. The system includes several processing functions to process the images sequentially for analysis. These operations can either be performed automatically one after another without any human operator intervention or be carried out interactively by observing the processing results at each stage and modifying the processing parameters. The acquired images have to be preprocessed to remove acquisition artifacts for improving the picture quality. The signal-to-noise ratio is improved by a frame averaging technique. Fluctuations in supplied voltage of a microscope lamp or other illumination sources can cause gray level/color variations in the acquired images. These shading corrections have to be carried out to compensate for nonuniform illumination across the samples.
3. The next step of image processing is to separate the objects of interest from the background using a thresholding technique. The system allows either interactive setting of threshold or a quicker autothresholding method based on a gaussian bimodal histogram model. Measurements performed are in pixel units. The system has to be calibrated to find the scaling factor with respect to the camera and microscope setup.
4. The total Sybr Green II or propidium iodide fluorescence intensity is taken as total DNA content in the comet. The software allows quantitative measurements of total fluorescence of the comet, fluorescence of the tail, and length of migrated DNA fragments, and it calculates tail moment. The system has to be calibrated at 25×, 40×, or 100× before making any measurements, depending

on the magnification used during image acquisition. For measuring the DNA content in the tail region, both lower threshold and upper threshold have to be set to the same level as in the case of total DNA measurement in the comet. This mode allows more distinct discrimination between the head (nucleus) and tail of the comet. This is a unique feature, allowing for more accurate measurements. The data are automatically stored in an application-specific format in the result file, which can be imported to Microcal Origin version 5 for various statistical calculations and graphical representations.

Overview of commercially available software for evaluation of the Comet assay

1. LACAAS is a modular system of hardware and software that provides all the features and components required for efficient and rapid automated analysis of large sets of fluorescent single-cell comets. It has a proprietary image capture system, which provides extended dynamic range capabilities, which are essential for accurate image analysis. Measurements and analysis of cellular fluorescent intensities yield measures of cellular DNA content, distribution, and damage. This software operates under the Windows operating system on Pentium computers. The software eliminates user subjectivity by providing fully automated delineation and analysis of head and tail regions of the comets. It provides multiple quantitative measures of each cell analyzed, e.g., TL, area, moment of inertia, cellular DNA content, percent of cellular DNA in the tail, and so on. It also provides password-protected multilevel access, data audit features, and other features.
2. The Komet system has been designed specifically for image acquisition and sample analysis for the comet assay. This is one of the oldest systems developed for computerized evaluation of the comet assay. Komet 5 is currently the leading DNA damage analysis software for the comet assay. It has the following key features: two-click capture and analysis of comets, fully automatic or interactive computation of head/tail %DNA, Olive tail moment, analysis of the comet at different magnifications, and powerful Microsoft Excel Macros for quick manipulation of data. The system supports a wide variety of video cameras, e.g., Hitachi KMP1, Cohu 4910, or Pulnix TM745. The user also has the ability to choose from a variety of digital CCD cameras, e.g., PCO SensiCam, Hamamatsu Orca, or Roper Cool snap/HQ.

3. MetaSystems provides two different products for evaluation of the comet assay, Comet Imager and CometScan. Comet Imager is an interactive system that allows fast and reliable analysis of comets under normal lab conditions with moderate throughput and moderately expensive hardware requirements. CometScan is a fully automatic system based on the Metafer automated scanning platform and provides the facility for completely unattended evaluation of comet slides.
4. Comet assay II is an advanced image analysis system developed for quantification of DNA damage by the comet assay. This system consists of an image capture card, a highsensitivity CCD video camera, and Windows-based software. It has a three-button mouse to position a rectangular frame around the cell to be measured. A single button press then starts analysis, including correction of any variation in background intensity, followed by measurements of head and tail fluorescent intensities of the comet. This system has a special feature that allows the user to perform measurements on live or frozen images, and an interactive editing function that is useful in the case of severely damaged cells. The software provides measurements of various characteristics, such as tail moment, TL, head length, %DNA-H, %DNA-T, cell area, total intensity, and mean gray level. It provides password protection to restrict access to the software and prevent unauthorized changes.
5. AutoComet is a fully automated computer-controlled optical microscopy system for SCGE. The microscope is provided with a motorized stage, motorized focus, and epifluorescence illumination system. The system has been optimized for automatic detection and measurement of comets.
6. Fenestra Comet is an automatic digital imaging software for evaluation of the comet assay. The software allows for a full range of densitometric and geometric parameter measurements. It also allows measurement of two other important parameters; skewness and kurtosis, which provides information on comet morphology.

Statistical analysis

Different investigators have used different statistical methods for evaluation of data from the comet assay. If the data have been obtained manually, increase in TL is considered the best criterion of genetic damage. However, mean TL should not be used, because the distribution is not normal; instead, the median TL of 50 cells per experimental point should be used. In our studies, data files from the SCGE-Pro software can be imported to Origin ver.5 for various statistical analyses and graphics. We use one-way ANOVA for statistical analysis. Values are considered significant at $p < 0.05$. There is no general agreement on any specific statistical method to be used for comet assay. However, the choice of statistical method depends on the type of distribution obtained with the comet data. In the case of a normal distribution, parametric methods can be used, whereas when the data appear to be Poisson or binomially distributed, nonparametric methods should be used.

Comet–FISH Technique

The comet–FISH technique described in this protocol is a tool to detect genome region-specific DNA damage and repair. It is a combination of two established techniques, the comet assay (or single-cell gel electrophoresis, or the single-cell gel test), to separate highly fragmented from moderately or nonfragmented DNA and to measure it, and *fluorescence in situ hybridization* (FISH), to specifically label DNA sequences of interest. Comet–FISH exists in two versions, based on the neutral and the alkaline comet assays. The neutral version of the comet assay detects double-strand breaks, while the alkaline version detects both double- and single-strand breaks as well as abasic sites or sites of incomplete repair. This section also details cell preparation and production of the hybridization probes adapted to the comet–FISH technique. Finally, microscopic analysis of comet–FISH results is described, and possible procedures of quantification of the specific DNA damage are presented.

The comet assay technique offers a relatively simple and fast means of measuring the relative amount of DNA damage in individual cells. The assay can easily be modified to fit the specific requests of the experiment to be performed. For example, comparison of results from the alkaline and neutral versions of the comet assay discriminates between single- and double-strand breaks. Since semiautomatic, quantitative software has become available and especially since fully automated commercial systems have recently become available, the quantitative analysis of DNA damages has become routine. The test is highly sensitive, especially with the modifications described by N. P. Singh, using the alkaline version. It is also highly versatile with respect to the cell type amenable to investigation, from mollusk cells to human tissue and from bacteria to plant cells.

The comet assay has several disadvantages. So far, no general protocol can be provided, and the comparison of data from different laboratories is difficult, because no standardization is available. Also, numerous parameters affect the results and sensitivity in a comet assay experiment, for example, lysis or electrophoresis conditions and even the geometry of the electrophoresis tank. Therefore, parameters must be kept constant during a series of experiments to reduce possible sources of variation.

Comet–FISH is a modification of the comet assay that includes a hybridization step after electrophoresis and therefore allows specific labeling of sequences within the comet. The comet assay alone gives information about the level of overall DNA damage, whereas the combination with *fluorescence in situ hybridization* (FISH) allows allocation of the sequence examined to the damaged or undamaged part of the comet and therefore gives additional information on specific sequences or genome regions. The combination of the comet assay with FISH was first published by Santos et al. in 1997 and was simultaneously developed in two other laboratories to tackle different experimental questions. The FISH protocol has been adapted to the experimental constraints of comets embedded in agarose from standard FISH techniques. Therefore, e.g., no thermal denaturation can be used for strand separation (denaturation) of the target DNA, but chemical denaturation has to be applied, which does not damage the gel matrix. However, even for chemical denaturation, the parameters have to be chosen in such a way that the gel matrix is not damaged. Also, other steps such as post-hybridization washes, signal amplification, and microscopic analysis need to be adapted in the comet–FISH technique when specimens are embedded in a 3D gel matrix. Moreover, the hybridization efficiency can be increased using DNA probes optimized for comet–FISH, in such a way that faster probe diffusion into the gel is achieved. These probes need to have a higher DNA concentration and a reduced size compared with the probes used for conventional FISH on metaphase chromosomes.

The comet–FISH technique has been used to tackle a number of different questions. First, it has been used for localization of specific genomic regions on stretched DNA fibers, to gain information on the spatial organization of genomic elements. This method uses the technique to detect region-specific repair in the comet assay. Also, the site-specific introduction and persistence of radiation-induced damages has been monitored using comet–FISH. In contrast to DNA sequencing of large genomic loci, comet–FISH is less time- and less cost-intensive, if DNA damage and repair are analyzed. Comet–FISH has been applied not only to animal cell culture but also to plant cells. Recently, the comet–FISH technique has been used to discriminate between DNA double-strand breaks and single-strand breaks and to study the region-specific effects of oxidative damages induced by different nutrition compounds.

Comet--FISH is still in its infancy. New applications were discussed during the 6th Comet Assay Workshop in Ulm, 2001, for example, the use of comet–FISH to detect sites where DNA is anchored to the nuclear matrix, screening for chromosomal translocations within the comet assay, or enhanced detection of gene-specific DNA damage and repair using a two-color approach with one probe flanking the 3' and one flanking the 5' end of a gene of interest. These new applications are supported by modern analysis methods such as (semi-)automated, computer-aided comet evaluation and new quantification parameters to describe the relationship between total DNA damage and the damage of specific sequences.

The following protocol describes the two versions of comet–FISH routinely used in our laboratory. The first is based on the alkaline version of the comet assay described by R. Tice et al., and the second is based on the neutral comet assay published by P. Olive. These two protocols are additionally given as general guidelines for those who are not very familiar with the comet assay itself. Those readers already experienced with the comet assay should be able to adapt the comet–FISH procedure to their own comet assay protocols.

Materials

DNA probe preparation

1. Cot-1 DNA.
2. Polymerase chain reaction (PCR) Core Kit.
3. DNase/polymerase mix, or nick translation kit; store at –20°C.
4. Labeled nucleotides, e.g., digoxigenin-11-dUTP; store at –20°C.
5. Unlabeled nucleotides; store at –20°C.
6. Hybridization buffer: 50% formamide, 1X SSC, 10% dextran sulfate; store at room temperature in aliquots of 1 mL.
7. Chromosomes in metaphase state fixed on a slide.

Cell preparation

1. Phosphate-buffered saline (PBS) buffer; store at room temperature.
2. Medicon disaggregation system, 50 μm, nonsterile.
3. Ficoll; store at 4°C.

Comet assay and comet–FISH

1. Fully frosted.
2. 24 × 60-mm Cover slips.
3. Metal plate size: approx 30 × 20 × 2.5 cm^3, made from aluminum.
4. Ground layer agarose: 0.5% normal melting point agarose in PBS (50 mM phosphate).
5. Middle layer agarose: 1.0% normal melting point agarose in PBS (100 mM phosphate). Make 50 mL, melt, and store in aliquots of 1 mL at 4°C until use.
6. Top layer agarose: 1.0% low melting point agarose in water.
7. Neutral lysis buffer: 1% N-lauryl-sarcosinat, 1% Triton X-100, 0.5% dimethyl sulfoxide (DMSO), 10 mM Tris-base, 150 mM NaCl; adjust pH to 8.0.
8. Alkaline lysis buffer (for 1 L): 2.5 M NaCl, 0.1 M EDTA, 0.01 M Tris-base, 0.2 M NaOH, 1% sodium dodecyl sulfate (SDS); adjust pH to 10.0 with NaOH in a volume of 890 mL. This solution can be stored at room temperature for several weeks. Prior to use, mix 1 mL of Triton X-100, 10 mL DMSO with 89 mL of the prepared lysis solution and chill to 4°C. *Caution*: SDS and NaOH may cause skin irritations and eye injuries, wear protective gloves and eye goggles.
9. Electrophoresis tank e.g., Hofer Supersub with integrated cooling circuit and recirculation.
10. Neutral electrophoresis buffer (1X TBE): 90 mM Tris-HCl, 2 mM Na_2-EDTA, 90 mM borate: adjust pH to 8.0.
11. Alkaline electrophoresis buffer: 0.3 M NaOH, 1 mM Na_2-EDTA; make fresh on the day of use from the stock solutions and chill to 4°C. Caution: wear protective gloves and eye goggles.
12. Neutralization buffer: 0.42 M Tris-HCL 0.08 M Tris-base, pH 7.5; store at room temperature for up to 6 mo.
13. SybrGreen fluorescence dye. Caution: SybrGreen is a potential mutagen; handle with gloves and care.
14. Antifade.
15. Counterstaining solution: 1 μL Sybr Green stock solution, 500 μL water, and 500 μL antifade; store in the dark at –20°C in 500 μL aliquots.
16. Plastic cover slip.
17. PBD buffer: 94 mM $Na_2HPO_4 \cdot 2\ H_2O$, 6 mM $NaH_2PO_4 \cdot 1\ H_2O$, 0.06% Triton X-100.

18. Posthybridization wash buffer: 0.5–3X SSC buffer depending on the probe.
19. 1X SSC: 150 mM NaCl, 15 mM Na-citrate, pH 7.0; make as 20X stock and store at room temperature. Stock: 3 M NaCl, 0.3 M Na-citrate.
20. Blocking reagent.
21. Enzyme-coupled antibodies, e.g., anti-digoxigenin-alkaline peroxidase (DIG-AP), antibiotin-AP or TUNEL-AP (= anti-fluorescein isothiocyanate [FITC]-AP); all from Roche.
22. HNPP (2-hydroxy-3-naphtoic acid-2'-phenylanilide phosphate) detection kit:
    - (a) HNPP buffer 1: 0.1 M Tris-HCl; 150 mM NaCl, pH 7.5.
    - (b) HNPP buffer 2: 0.5% blocking reagent in HNPP buffer 1.
    - (c) HNPP buffer 3: 0.05% Tween-20 in buffer 1.
    - (d) HNPP buffer 4: 0.1 M Tris-HCl, 0.1 M NaCl, 0.01 M $MgCl_2$; adjust to pH 8.0.
    - (e) Buffers 1 and 4 can be made in larger amounts and stored at room temperature for at least 3 mo.
    - (f) Buffers 2 and 3 should be made fresh on the day of use.
    - (g) HNPP solution: 10 mg/mL ready made; 25 mg/mL Fast Red solution in water. (Make small amounts and store in the dark at 4°C for 1 mo.)
    - (h) HNPP/Fast Red solution: 10 μL Fast Red, 10 μL HNPP solution in 1 mL HNPP buffer 4, sterile-filtered. (Store in the dark at 4°C for 1–2 wk; check for precipitation before use.)
23. Microscope objectives: Plan Neofluar 25×/NA 0.8 oil and Plan Neofluar 40×/NA 1.3 oil.
24. Filter sets appropriate for the detection of two colors, e.g., filter set no. 10 and filter set no. 14, both from Carl Zeiss.

Methods

Sample preparations

1. Preparation of a single-cell suspension.
2. Cell cultures: preparation of samples for the comet assay from blood samples has been described already.

Tissue preparation

Tissues can be disaggregated in many ways for use in the comet assay, including enzymatic or mechanical techniques. A fast and reliable procedure adapted from flow cytometry is as follows:

1. Wash the Medicon vessel twice with 1 mL of PBS and rotate the blade of the Medicon by hand for 1 min each time.
2. Remove the PBS from the lower part of the vessel, place your pieces of tissue (e.g., four pieces, 3 × 3 × 3 mm^3 each) in the upper Medicon chamber, and rotate by hand for 2 min.
3. Remove the first fraction of the cell suspension from the lower part using a 25-gage needle and a syringe.
4. Rotate again with 1 mL fresh PBS, and remove the suspension cells from the lower part.
5. Filter through a 30-μm nylon mesh.

Peripheral blood

The preparation of samples for the comet assay from blood samples has been described already.

Slide preparation

The preparation of slides for comet–FISH is slightly different from the method described already, as the mechanical stress is greater than in the standard comet assay.

1. Boil ground layer agarose and distribute 100 μL of the agarose suspension as a thin layer on the frosted slide using a second slide as a tool.
2. Air-dry completely; slides can be stored in this stage for several months.
3. Add the middle layer the day before the comet assay is performed. Melt the agarose suspension, cool to approx 50°C, drop 400 μL of the suspension carefully on the precoated slides, and quickly cover with a cover slip.
4. Place on a chilled metal plate, in even position.
5. Store the slides in a moistened chamber at 4°C overnight after solidification of the agarose.

Preparation of hybridization probes

Instead of using self-made DNA probes for in situ hybridization, commercially available DNA probes can be used, but a larger amount is required than is usually suggested for metaphase spread hybridizations in the protocols of the suppliers. Otherwise hybridization probes can be self-made if the desired target DNA is available in the form of a clone or can be amplified with PCR. As short probe lengths are preferred for hybridization on comets, the method of choice for probe labeling is nick translation.

1. Prepare cloned DNA or PCR fragments >500 bp by your preferred method.
2. Dilute DNA to a final concentration of 1 μg/μL in 10 mM Tris-base, 1 mM EDTA, pH 8.0.
3. Prepare on ice: 5 μg isolated DNA, 20 μL DNase/polymerase I enzyme mixture, 25 μL nucleotide mix (2 mM dATP, dCTP, dGTP, 1.8 mM dTTP; 0.2 mM DIG-dUTP—or equivalent); 25 μL 10X buffer: 500 mM Tris-HCl, pH 7.8, 50 mM $MgCl_2$, 100 mM 2-mercaptoethanol, 100 μg/mL nuclease-free bovine serum albumin (BSA) water to 250 μL.
4. Incubate at 37°C for 1–2 h; check the typical probe length of 5-μL aliquots on a 1.5% agarose gel.
5. The optimum is reached when the probe length ranges from 150 to 500 bp and the size of the majority of the probes is around 250 bp.
6. Add 25 μg salmon sperm DNA, 25 μg Cot-1 DNA, 1/10 vol of 4 M NaOAc, and precipitate with 2.5 vol ice-cooled ethanol for 2 h minimum in the refrigerator.
7. Spin at maximum speed in a table top centrifuge at 0°C for 30 min.
8. Remove the supernatant carefully, apply 500 μL 70% ethanol, and spin again at maximum speed for 15 min.
9. Remove the supernatant carefully, dry briefly, and dissolve pellet in 150 μL hybridization buffer. Store in the dark at –20°C.
10. Take 15 μL (450 ng) of these probes per hybridization. Before the probes are used, denature them at 72°C for 5 min and prehybridize at 37°C for 20 min.

Determination of hybridization conditions

For a successful experiment it is necessary to control differences in hybridization conditions on metaphase spreads to ensure stringency and selectivity of the comet hybridization. Therefore, hybridize the probe as described above or as suggested by the manufacturer and adjust the post-hybridization washes until a reproducible and stringent hybridization pattern is visible on the majority of the metaphase spreads. Optimized washing conditions should be transferred to the comet–FISH procedure.

Comet assay

1. Melt the top layer agarose and place in a water bath at 40°C.
2. Adjust the cell density of your cell suspension to 10^6 cells/mL with PBS.

3. Equilibrate the cell suspension to 40°C.
4. Mix 1 vol of cell suspension with 4 vol of agarose, and pipet up and down several times.
5. Carefully remove the cover slip of the slides bearing the middle layer that have been stored in the moistened chamber overnight.
6. Equilibrate the slides briefly to approx 40°C; be sure not to dry the agarose.
7. Quickly apply 100 μL of the cell suspension to the still moistened middle layer and quickly cover with a cover slip.
8. Place on a chilled metal plate to cool down the slides.
9. Remove the cover slips carefully after 5 min.

Neutral Comet assay

1. Place the slides in prechilled lysis solution for 1 h in the fridge.
2. Wash the slides briefly in electrophoresis buffer.
3. Transfer the slides to the electrophoresis tank, and align them perpendicularly to the electrodes.
4. Apply an electric field of 1 V/cm and adjust the current (A) by the buffer level (~2 mm above the slide surface) inside the electrophoresis tank.

Hybridization to Comets

1. Store slides in ethanol for 3–15 d at 4°C.
2. Drain the slides briefly and place them in water for 10 min.
3. Denature in 0.5 M NaOH at room temperature for 25 min. Caution: NaOH causes eye irritation; wear gloves and safety goggles.
4. Dry the slides in an ethanol series (70, 85, 95%) for 5 min each at room temperature.
5. Air-dry the gels completely.
6. Add the prepared hybridization probe (~450 ng labeled DNA) after the alcohol has completely evaporated.
7. Seal with a plastic cover slip.
8. Place in a moistened chamber at 37°C.
9. Hybridize overnight. The time needed for hybridization depends on the size of the individual hybridization probe molecules and the amount of probe material added.
10. Prepare a water bath and equilibrate a cuvet with post-hybridization washing solution to 72°C.
11. Remove the plastic cover slip carefully.

12. Place the cover slip in the cuvet and incubate for 2 min without agitation.
13. Quench the slides quickly in ice-cooled PBD buffer for 5 min.

Signal detection

We recommend using a signal-enhancing system for the detection of the hybridization signals on comets. The strongest enhancement can be achieved using enzymecoupled antibodies that convert a nonfluorescing substrate to a fluorescing one. Although other detection systems also work, the HNPP fluorescence-enhancing system offers strong enhancement, so even weak signals can be seen under the microscope.

1. Block slides by incubation in PBS containing 1% blocking reagent for 15 min at room temperature.
2. Add 50 μL of the enzyme-coupled antibody; 1:500 diluted in HNPP buffer 2.
3. Seal with a plastic cover slip and incubate in a moistened chamber at 37°C for 1 h.
4. Prepare the HNPP detection mix containing the Fast Red and the HNPP compound: 10 μL Fast Red solution, 10 μL HNPP solution in 1 mL HNPP buffer 4.
5. Remove the cover slip carefully.
6. Wash slides three times in HNPP buffer 3, 10 min each.
7. Wash slides twice in HNPP buffer 2, 10 min each.
8. Drain off excessive buffer, but do not allow the gels to dry.
9. Apply 100 μL of the prepared HNPP mix.
10. Seal with a plastic cover slip and incubate in a moistened chamber at room temperature for 30 min. For small hybridization targets, to enhance the amplification apply in a second step fresh Fast Red/HNPP solution and reincubate the slides.
11. Wash the slides twice for 10 min in HNPP buffer 3 at room temperature.
12. Wash once in water for 10 min at room temperature.
13. Drain off excessive buffer, but do not allow to dry completely.
14. Counterstain the total DNA by adding 30 μL of staining solution.
15. Cover with a glass cover slip.

Microscopy and image analysis

1. Use 25–40× high-aperture oil objectives.
2. Acquire each color channel as a separate monochrome image using appropriate high-quality bandpass filters. For the procedure

described, we use an FITC filter to detect the comet and a Texas Red filter to record the signals. Overlay image channels in a pseudocolor image.

3. Analyze, if possible, the comet images alone (total DNA stained) with comet assay analysis software; count the number of hybridization signals in the tail (if specific probes are used) of the corresponding image channel.

Notes

1. The concentration of the SSC determines the hybridization stringency. The lower the amount of SSC, the higher the stringency is. A concentration of 1X SSC is a good starting value. Evaluate the hybridization quality on metaphase spreads until the required stringency is achieved, and then transfer the conditions to the comet–FISH experiments. The use of formamide, especially in higher concentrations, in the washing buffer can cause the gels to slip from the slides.
2. For reliable evaluation and interpretation of the comet–FISH results, the use of cells with a stable karyotype during the experiment is required when specific hybridization probes are used (e.g., centromere or gene-specific probes). This is necessary since determination of the hybridization efficiency and stringency requires knowledge of the copy number of a specific sequence.
3. In standard comet assay experiments, it is useful to determine the cell viability and the cell number after cell isolation. Also, microscopic control of the morphology may be useful.
4. Use a water level from the electrophoresis tank to ensure levelled poisoning, as unlevelled placement will lead to uneven gels, which will result in inhomogeneities of the DNA movement and the comets.
5. Target sequences in comet–FISH are similar to those in standard FISH. This means that loci down to 5–10 kbp can be efficiently labeled. Other groups have also reported of the successful use of oligo DNA as a probe to label loci less than 1 kbp.
6. This step is important since a cold middle layer will lead to an unequal distribution of the top layer agarose by untimely gelling. The optimum is achieved when the middle layer is still wet but warm.
7. Check that the top layer still attaches to the gel sandwich by scraping the cover slip over a pipet tip. If top layer does not attach properly to the gel sandwich, increase the gelling time; if necessary, place gels in a refrigerator.

8. Because the current depends on the electrophoresis tank, no specific value can be given, but record the current for one experiment in order to readjust correctly to the same buffer level and ampere values in the following experiments.
9. This is the second critical point during the preparation, as gels may lose contact during drying. We recommend checking this step with some additional slides, so no hybridization probe or specimen is lost if you lose a gel in the beginning.
10. This temperature may differ if you are using commercial probes but should not exceed 42°C.
11. Objectives with higher resolutions and lower working distances lead to weaker signals and complicate the detection of comets if they are distant from the objective inside the agarose layer.
12. The signal may be integrated during recording; therefore a cooled CCD camera with on-chip integration is preferred; alternatively, a video camera connected to a frame grabber can be used, and low-intensity signals can be recorded by computer integration.
13. Analysis of comet–FISH experiments has not been standardized. Specific hybridization signals are located in the head or tail region and therefore the comets are counted as damaged or undamaged with respect to the specific sequence. Diffuse hybridization results have been analyzed by performing a second comet analysis on the signal channel. Semiautomated systems are currently under development, e.g., Komet++ from Kinetic Imaging, for the quantification of specific DNA damage using comet–FISH.

Pulsed-Field Gel Electrophoresis

This assay quantifies the amount of DNA *double-strand break* (DSB) damage in attached cell populations embedded in agarose and assayed for migratory DNA using *pulsed-field gel electrophoresis* (PFGE) with ethidium bromide staining. The assay can measure pre-existing damage, as well as induction of DSB by chemical (e.g., bleomycin), physical (e.g., X-irradiation), or biological (e.g., restriction enzymes) agents. By incubating the cells under physiological conditions prior to processing, the cells are allowed to repair DSB, primarily via the process of nonhomologous end joining. The amount of repair, corresponding to the repair capacity of the treated cells, is then quantified by determining the ratio of the fractions of activity released in these repaired lanes in comparison with the total amount of DNA fragmentation following determination of a optimal exposure for maximum initial fragmentation. Repair kinetics can also be analyzed through a time-course regimen.

Of all the forms of DNA damage, *double-strand breaks* (DSBs) induced from exogenous sources, such as ionizing radiation and chemical agents, or endogenous sources, such as oxidative stress, may be the most deleterious, for if they are unrepaired or misrepaired, they can lead to carcinogenic transformation or cell death.

DSBs (and some proportion of single-strand breaks, when they are clustered closely enough) result in high-molecular-weight DNA fragments that can be liberated from the cell and resolved by electrophoresis. This technique can be thought of as a bulk method for performing the comet assay, although with several advantages over that assay: thousands to millions of cells are analyzed, rather than hundreds; a single measurement for the population is derived, rather than hundreds; and, multiple samples, including controls, can be analyzed on the same gel. Application of *pulsed-field gel electrophoresis* (PFGE) also allows for a greater separation of DNA sizes, giving a better characterization of the nature of the underlying DNA damage.

Both the comet assay and the PFGE assay have been used extensively to study DNA repair, by observing the reduction in migrating DNA when cells are allowed a period of repair following genotoxic insult. These assays are therefore functional measures of DNA DSB repair.

From experiments using cell extracts from *Xenopus* eggs, Chinese hamster ovary cells, and human cells to repair plasmids containing breaks (e.g., the prokaryotic lacZ gene), as well as the transfection of damaged plasmids into DNA repair-deficient/proficient cell lines, two distinct DSB pathways—*homologous recombination* (HR) and *nonhomologous end joining* (NHEJ)—have been identified. In HR, the major DSB repair pathway in yeast, a homologous chromosome, or more frequently, a sister chromatid, is used as a template to repair the damaged copy of the sequence in an error-free manner. In contrast, NHEJ, the most prevalent pathway for DSB repair in vertebrates, is independent of sequence homology. In this process, the two ends of the breakpoint are religated together after limited modulation at the termini. Thus, small inserted sequences, as well as deletions, are often introduced by this repair process, making NHEJ an inherently error-prone pathway.

Although these cell extract and transfection techniques have provided valuable information, results from the cell extract experiments are often inconsistent, and there is always the possibility that repair processes in plasmids do not reflect normal DSB repair in genomic

DNA in intact cells. Thus, an *in vitro* assay has been developed that quantifies the amount of repaired genomic DNA DSBs in attached mammalian cells. Repair capacity is only measured under conditions of maximum damage, which are likely to differ between cell lines and cell types. Thus, an optimal dose for DSB damage is initially determined, and then, after applying this optimal dose, DSB repair can be examined over time by determining the ratio of remaining DNA fragmentation in comparison with the unrepaired control.

Cells with deficiencies in DNA protein kinase (DNA-PK; believed to regulate the accessibility of DNA ends and possibly recruit repair factors in the NHEJ pathway), as well as mouse fibroblasts deficient in Ku80 (another NHEJ-related protein involved in the protection and alignment DNA ends), have decreased repair capacity in this assay. Deficiencies in the BRCA2 gene, associated with HR pathways through Fanconi's anemia genes, have not been detected using this assay. Whether patients with Fanconi's anemia, ataxia telangiectasia, Bloom's syndrome, Nijmegen breakage syndrome, Berlin breakage syndrome, and Werner's syndrome, cancer-prone syndromes attributed to deficiencies in DNA DSB repair, are associated with the NHEJ pathway is unknown. Characterization of these processes is critical to our understanding of human disease as well as cellular responses to genotoxic stress.

Finally, there are two modifications that might allow the PFGE assay to analyze other types of DNA damage. Taking a cue from the comet assay, this assay could be extended to analysis of the majority of single-strand breaks by converting them to DSBs by alkaline treatment. By running cell samples processed under both neutral and basic pH side by side, the contribution of single-strand breaks can be observed as the quantitative difference in DNA migration. Next, by allowing a longer period between in vitro exposure and analysis, this assay could be used to quantitate the amount of "*complex*" or irreparable DNA damage associated with high-energy radiation.

Materials

Generation of double-strand breaks

1. T-25 (25-cm) cell culture flasks.
2. Appropriate growth media for each cell type, with appropriate amount and type of serum.
3. Cell culture incubator.
4. Irradiation source.

Cell sample (agarose plug) preparation

1. Trypsin (or other means of harvesting cells).
2. 15-mL Conical tubes.
3. Appropriate cell culture medium (serum-free).
4. Hemocytometer or Coulter counter.
5. 1-, 5-, and 10-mL Pipets and pipet aid.
6. 20-, 200-, and 1000-μL Micropipetors and appropriate pipet tips.
7. Benchtop centrifuge.
8. 50–56°C shaking water bath.
9. 1% InCert agarose solution. Incubate at 50–56°C to prevent solidification.
10. 100-μL Plastic plug molds taped on the bottom.
11. Lysis solution: 10 mM Tris-HCl, pH 8.0, 50 mM NaCl, 0.5 M EDTA, 2% N-lauryl sarcosyl, 0.1 mg/mL proteinase K.
12. Wash buffer: 10 mM Tris-HCl, pH 8.0, 0.1 M EDTA.
13. RNase solution: 10 mM Tris-HCl, pH 7.5, 0.1 M EDTA, 0.1 mg/mL RNase. Make 2.5 mL per sample fresh each time.

Pulsed-field gel electrophoresis (PFGE)

Although a number of PFGE apparatus have been developed, *clamped homogenous electric field* (CHEF) and *asymmetric field inversion gel electrophoresis* (AFIGE) are most often used for DSB analysis.

1. CHEF: CHEF DRII apparatus with refrigerated water bath and circulating pump.

   AFIGE: Horizontal gel electrophoresis system, model H4 with refrigerated water bath and circulating pump.
2. Seakem agarose.
3. 0.5X TBE: 45 mM Tris-HCl, pH 8.0, 45 mM boric acid, 1 mM EDTA. Prepare a 5X stock solution in large volumes (~500 mL); can be stored indefinitely at room temperature.
4. 10 mg/mL Ethidium bromide (made up in 10-mL lots, kept wrapped in aluminum foil in the refrigerator).
5. FluorImager

Methods

Generation of double-strand breaks

1. Cells should be firmly attached, semiconfluent, and in log phase growth when exposed to *ionizing radiation* (IR). Thus, they should

be plated at least 48 h prior to exposure and the T-25 flasks seeded with the appropriate number of cells to attain these conditions.

2. Cool cells on ice to 4°C prior to irradiation.
3. Expose cells in T-25 flasks to a source of ionizing radiation at doses ranging from 10 to 100 Gy (or at optimized dose, if this has been predetermined). Include one flask as an unexposed control to determine background DNA fragmentation levels.

Cell sample (agarose plug) preparation

1. Harvest cells, by trypsinization or other appropriate technique on ice in 15-mL conical tubes. This process may take 5–10 min. Centrifuge the cells for 5 min at 800g. Wash the cells once in serum-free medium.
2. Resuspend the cells in serum-free medium and count the cells, using a hemocytometer or Coulter counter. Aliquot the cells at a concentration of 1×10^6 or multiples of 1×10^6 (e.g., 2×10^6, 3×10^6) into 15-mL conical tubes and spin for 5 min at 800g.
3. Remove excess media with a pipet without disrupting the cell pellet. Add 30 μL of serumfree media to the 15-mL conical tubes for each 1×10^6 cells. Triturate the cell suspension to ensure that no clumps are present.
4. Mix the cell suspension with an equal volume of 1% agarose incubated at 50°C. The final concentration of agarose should be 0.5% with 1×10^6 cells per 60 μL of serum-free medium and agarose solution.
5. Pipet the 60 μL (or 60-μL aliquots) into the precooled 100 μL plastic plug molds, and incubate on ice for 5 min until the plugs solidify.
6. Extrude the solidified plugs from the molds into a 15-mL conical tube by removing the tape from the bottom of the molds and pipeting lysis buffer directly over the plug.
7. Add 2 mL lysis solution and incubate at 4°C for 45 min.
8. Transfer the plugs to 50°C for 16–18 h in a moderately shaking water bath.
9. Wash the plugs once with 2 mL washing buffer. Incubate in 2 mL of fresh washing buffer for 1 h at 37°C in a moderately shaking water bath.
10. Transfer the plugs to 2 mL RNase solution and incubate for 1 h at 37°C.

11. Plugs can then be stored in 5 mM EDTA buffer at 4°C indefinitely.

Preparation for plug gel electrophoresis

1. Cast a 0.8% agarose gel in 0.5X TBE with the appropriate comb when using the Bio-Rad CHEF-DRIII or a 0.5% agarose gel when using AFIGE. Allow the gel to solidify for approx 1 h.
2. Remove the comb after solidification, and load the plugs into the wells. Seal the wells with agarose to ensure that the plugs are not released from the wells during electrophoresis.
3. Place the gel into a precooled (10°C) electrophoresis box with 0.5X TBE.
4. Electrophorese for 23 h at 200 V with 60-s pulses for the first 8 h, followed by 120-s pulses for 15 h with the Bio-Rad CHEF-DRIII. Using AFIGE, cycles of 1.25 V/cm for 900 s in the forward direction and 5 V/cm for 75 s in the reverse direction should be used.
5. Stain the gel for 1 h with 0.5 μg/mL ethidium bromide.
6. Expose the gel to a FluorImager for analysis.
7. Quantitate the DSBs present by determining the ratio between the fraction of activity released from the plug (FAR) vs the total DNA in both the plug and in the lane: FAR = lane counts/(plug + lane) counts.
8. For quantification of damage, FAR should be compared with a standard control or curve. For quantification of repair, the amount of migratory DNA in the experimental lane may be subtracted directly from that in the control (no repair incubation), provided that the total amounts of DNA in both plugs/lanes are similar.
9. To examine repair capacity, first determine the optimal dose of radiation (the dose that provides the maximum fragmentation), and then plot dose vs FAR.

Analysis of the time-course of DSB repair

1. Prewarm medium supplemented with serum to 42°C (sufficient to replace media in all experimental flasks).
2. Cool cells on ice prior to irradiation and expose each flask to the optimal IR dose.
3. Replace medium in each flask with prewarmed medium (which rapidly restores the cultures to 37°C, at which temperature repair is activated):

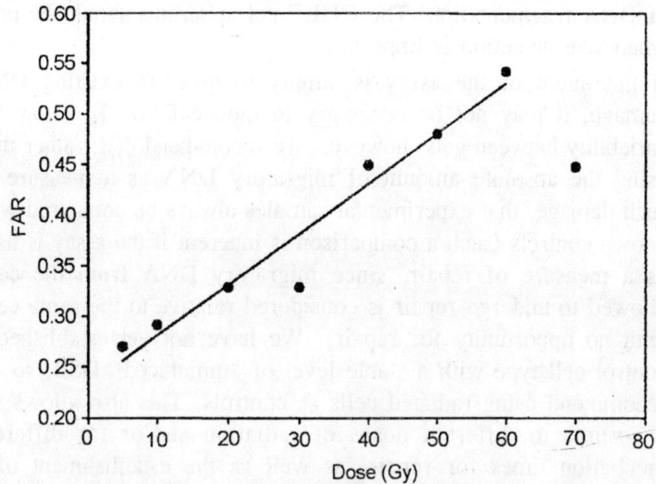

Fig. 10.2. Regression analysis of DNA fragmentation, quantified as the fraction of activity in the lane, vs dose to determine the optimal dose to be used to examine repair kinetics.

(a) Return flasks to the incubator for various times to allow for repair (time points: 0, 10, 20, 30, 60, 120, 128, 240, and 360 min).

(b) After the predetermined repair incubation periods, remove the flasks, harvest the cells, and place on ice for 5–10 min.

(c) Process samples as described above.

Notes

1. Direct DSB agents such as bleomycin, toposimerase II inhibitors, and carcinostatin, as well as enzymes that cleave DNA, such as BamH1, Pvu11, Hinf1, and HaeIII transfected into cells can be utilized as alternate sources of DBS damage.
2. PFGE separates larger DNA pieces than standard constant field electrophoresis by alternating the direction of the electric field at regular intervals, forcing the DNA to reorient itself constantly in new directions, resulting in far superior size separation. A number of PFGE apparatus have been developed, including *orthogonal field agarose electrophoresis* (OFAGE), *transverse alternating field electrophoresis* (TAFE), CHEF, and AFIGE. The choice depends on the type of equipment available, keeping in mind that CHEF and AFIGE have been most often used for DSB analysis. The AFIGE apparatus produces more uniform DNA fragments and should be used when the analysis does not require the precise size

of DNA fragmentation. The CHEF gel apparatus should be used when size detection is important.

3. If the intent of the assay is simply to quantify existing DNA damage, it may not be necessary to induce DSB. To allow for variability between gels, however, we recommend that, rather than using the absolute amount of migratory DNA as a measure of such damage, that experimental samples always be compared with known controls (such a comparison is inherent if the assay is used as a measure of repair, since migratory DNA from the cells allowed to undergo repair is considered relative to the same cells with no opportunity for repair). We have not yet established a control cell type with a stable level of "uninduced" DSB, so we recommend using radiated cells as controls. This also allows for exposures to different doses of radiation and/or for different incubation times for repair, as well as the establishment of a standard curve for the control cells.
4. If the intent of the assay is to measure repair capacity, an induction dose for maximum DNA DSB damage must first be determined by processing samples subjected to a range of IR dosages, as given above, then optimizing the incubation time for repair according to the protocol given above.

   Using this maximum dose provides damage and a damage signal (migratory DNA) on PFGE that makes sure the entire repair capacity of the cells is engaged. This dose is always a lethal dose, however, and it would be useful to confirm results from such experiments at sublethal levels of exposure and DNA damage.
5. DNA from cells in S phase migrate three to four times more slowly than from cells in G_1 or G_2 phase. Thus, cells should be analyzed once they reach the plateau phase, increasing the number of cells in G_1/G_0 and decreasing the variability in fragmentation. This phenomenon occurs not only in this assay but also in other techniques that measure DNA fragmentation.
6. Cells and plugs used during this assay should remain on ice at all times to decrease repair except during the predetermined repair incubation period as given above.
7. These electrophoresis conditions have been optimized for resolution of migratory DNA after a maximal induction of DSB. Different conditions may need to be developed for the lesser damage observed in unexposed cells or cells exposed to less efficient inducing agents than IR.

11

Microdissection in Forensic Science

Forensic science is aimed at detecting and analysing evidential material at crime scenes. Collection and careful laboratory analysis of any trace material is an extremely important activity in order to obtain as many pieces of information as possible. Considerable skill is involved in conducting searches at crime scenes. Frequently, particularly where sexual assault has occurred, crime scene investigators encounter mixed biological traces. The ability to isolate different cell populations (i.e. vaginal/sperm cells, epithelial/white cells, white/sperm cells, etc.) is therefore desirable to ensure the successful outcome of an investigation. Laser microdissection techniques have recently been introduced into forensic analysis and have proved to be very powerful in the isolation of specific cells from complex mixtures of biological material. It has also increased the types of samples that can be collected from crime scenes and usefully analysed.

Laser microdissection techniques fall within the field of microgenomics, which has been referred to as 'a quantitative molecular analysis of nucleic acids or proteins obtained from a single cell or a tiny amount of cells, which were isolated, collected and examined according to precise micromanipulating techniques'.

Micro-isolation and *micromanipulation* techniques are essential when undertaking laser microdissection techniques. Laser capture and laser cutting are the main techniques applied to perform cell micro-isolation.

Emmert-Buck and colleagues (1996) developed the first laser capture microdissection device, which was patented by Arcturus in the following year. It was based upon the heating and fusion of a thermo-sensitive plastic polymer that is modified by low-energy laser pulses (with near-infrared wavelength). This is also a useful device when dealing with RNA because of its sensitivity to high temperatures. However, the drawback is that the method lacks sufficient precision to isolate target cells from the matrix.

Laser cutting is preferable because the precision of the laser allows the isolation of single cells or a group of cells from more complex biological matrices such as tissue sections or hair shafts.

Modern laser cutting devices exploit a solid-state UV laser beam with a wavelength between 337 nm and 370 nm. Such a beam is able to behave like an electromagnetic knife and can destroy whatever it meets, including the biological substrate where cells are usually found. The cutting is done with great precision down to a single micrometre.

The cell sample is focused with the aid of a microscope through which the operator can select the target and then cut using the laser beam. The three main laser cutting systems may be defined by the collection method used:

1. Collection by gravity.
2. Collection by an adhesive polymer applied on a tube cap.
3. Collection through catapulting or energetic pulse.

Laser microdissecting instruments are coupled to different microscope systems depending on the collection method to be used. For example, a conventional upright microscope may be used for gravity-based collection, while an inverted microscope is used for the other two systems of collection.

In the case of gravity-based collection the operator can observe the target cells through the microscope at an appropriate magnification that enables the selection and cutting of the target with the aid of specific imaging software. The last laser pulse will allow the target sample to be collected under gravity into the tube cap placed immediately under the microscope. The successful removal of the sample can be confirmed by re-focusing the microscope onto the tube cap. A disadvantage of this system is that it does not allow for the possibility that the wrong sample can be cut off, which would be extremely important in forensic medicine where non-repeatable analyses are carried out.

The micro-isolation device based on the adhesive polymer allows visualization of the target sample through an inverted microscope and then, after cutting, collection by direct contact between the specimen and the tube cap where the polymer is located; in this way the target sample is torn away from the specimen. The adhesiveness of the polymer ensures that the sample is removed and its presence is confirmed by microscopy. A disadvantage of this system is that the contact between the slide and the cap could cause transfer of contaminating material. With catapulting microdissection, an inverted microscope is coupled to a high-resolution CCD camera showing the collected sample on the collection tube cap where a laser pulse has pushed it. There is no contact between specimen and collection tube and hence no need for any adhesive polymer to retain the cut sample, which can be easily visualized by the microscope. Moreover, the collection tube is positioned within a few microns of the specimen from which the target sample will be cut, which makes sample collection a very precise and contamination-free activity.

The choice of method will depend on the specific biological problem under investigation and individual preferences. The choice of microdissecting device/collection method is the starting point and there are several additional steps that must be taken into consideration in order to achieve good results in forensic medicine. These are summarized as follows:

1. Requirement for a dedicated 'isolated' laboratory exclusively for the use of microdissecting activity.
2. Requirement for *personal protective equipment* (PPE).
3. Specific collection tubes that are sterilized and, if possible, made of lowbinding plastic.
4. Ultraviolet-sterilized environment.
5. Isolated air supply in microdissection room.
6. Requirement for humidity and temperature monitoring.
7. Rigorous quality control of instrumentation.
8. Dedicated histological reagents.
9. DNA typing of all operators involved in the analysis chain.
10. Dissection and processing of control material not concurrent with target sample.
11. Performing analysis on duplicate samples if possible.

Histological, Biochemical Analysis

The aim of laser micro-isolating applications is to isolate specific nucleated cells and extract DNA for STR typing in order to determine a DNA profile. The first step is to make a cell smear on a microscope glass in order to visualize the specimen under the microscope lens.

The method for specimen preparation depends on the nature of the biological material to be analysed. In any case, the material of interest must be collected on a supporting synthetic polymeric membrane – *polyethylene terephthalate* (PET) or *polyethylene naphthalate* (PEN) – that may be mounted onto a glass slide or a metallic frame. In this way, during the laser cutting of an area containing a distinct cell type, a fragment of supporting membrane is collected together with the sample of interest into the microtube. The presence of the membrane does not interfere with the analytical procedures. Prior to specimen mounting, in order to avoid nucleic acid contaminations of the membrane, all procedures take place in a dedicated DNA-free area, and the membrane is sterilized by autoclaving and/or UV treatment. The latter is particularly useful because it eliminates electrostatic charges from the membrane, thus avoiding adhesive effects on the laser-cut fragment that could interfere with harvesting the cells.

In forensic analysis, a wide range of material, such as blood, organic fluids, hair or a mixture, may be collected on the membrane and subsequently subjected to morphological identification by laser-based methods. Specific identification of cell type, such as spermatozoa, epithelial cells from mucosae or skin, leucocytes or cells from hair follicles, frequently requires the use of several microscopic procedures.

The cell smear can be stained or left unstained. In the former case the operator must employ a stain that will not damage nuclear DNA, whereas in the latter case phase-contrast microscopy is used. It is often preferable to work on stained samples if the forensic laboratory is supported by a histological service that can perform the most appropriate cytological/histological staining. Good slide preparation and cellular morphology is essential to correctly distinguish different cell types. It will also ensure that the quality of DNA is sufficient to produce an unambiguous result. Many staining procedures have been investigated, leading to the identification of Papanicolau, Haematoxylin/ Eosin and Giemsa as the basis of the best staining protocols for forensic applications. For the great majority of specimens, the optimal balance between morphology and DNA integrity is usually obtained by air fixation and Giemsa staining. The above-mentioned stains do not intercalate DNA nor are they able to fragment the DNA backbone. Importantly they do not cause *polymerase chain reaction* (PCR) inhibition either. Other chemical staining agents, such as Nuclear Fast Red-Picroindigocarmine, may influence DNA preservation in spermatozoa and result in poor *single random repeat* (STR) DNA profiles. No matter which stain is used, in order to avoid contamination all the staining steps must be performed by dispensing the reagents on the surface of the specimen, which is then placed horizontally into an incubation chamber. Before starting the microdissection procedure, it is very important to verify that the specimen is dry, especially when membrane-coated slides are utilized, because any moisture present between the glass surface and the membrane may interfere with the detachment of the cut portion. An important step shared by all microdissection procedures is inspection of the cap of the microtube to confirm that the cut fragment has been collected. To facilitate the identification of membrane fragments, it is useful to leave a margin around the cell, drawing an irregular distinguishable outline.

Extraction of DNA from cell samples collected by laser microdissection is another delicate step. Different extraction protocols will be required according to the kind of specimen the operator is dealing with. Cell types differ in their biochemical and ultrastuctural properties: for example, amounts of fatty acids, phospholipids and proteins, the presence or absence of a cell wall, etc. Certain types of cell are more resistant to lysis, which is the primary step in DNA extraction. Lysis/DNA extraction takes place in a pH-controlled aqueous buffer with a hydrophobic environment useful for membrane disruption and in the presence of a protease.

Because forensic specimens are often typified by very low concentrations of potentially degraded DNA, consideration must be given to different extraction protocols at the outset of each case so that the best method can be employed.

A wide range of extraction kits/products are commercially available. Not all are suited to laser microdissected samples because of the small physical dimensions of the samples, the small amounts of DNA and the presence of PCR inhibitors, etc. Three types of reagents have emerged as being most suited to DNA extraction from laser microdissected samples (Chelex, ion exchange chromatography and magnetic resin) and modified protocols have been developed in all cases.

Chelex

A resin capable of chelating bivalent ions present in the cell lysate; such ions are potential PCR inhibitors and nuclease co-factors. The advantage of this method is that the whole lysate may be treated without further cleavage, although this is not a purification system. The concentration of the resin solution depends on the kind of cell sample under investigation, while the amount of resin required is usually limited in the case of laser microdissected samples. The extraction volume is related to the number of microdissected cells and can be decreased to a few microlitres in the case of DNA extraction from a single cell.

Ion Exchange Chromatography

This is a good purification system that can be used for some difficult samples. It is based on alkaline lysis and the separation of cellular debris from DNA using an ion-exchange silica column. Its application to laser microdissected samples is dependent on the number of cells available (down to 8–10 haploid cells), but it is not so useful when DNA extraction is performed on five cells or less. A potential drawback is that DNA damage could occur as a result of the alkaline environment, which is very important when working in low copy number conditions. DNA extracted from 1–10 microdissected cells needs to be dissolved in very small volumes of buffer solution because it will greatly influence the quality of the subsequent PCR.

Magnetic Resin

A purification system based upon the separation of cell debris from DNA by magnetic beads suspended in the same solution as the cell lysate. The chemistry of the system is most suited to laser microdissected spermatozoa and hair bulbs. As a consequence of the buffer composition, complete recovery when working with a very restricted number of cells (one or two) is seldom possible. Moreover, it is a very challenging method that requires great operating skill, otherwise DNA may become degraded. This has been noticed especially when dealing with telogen laser microdissected hair bulbs, where old and totally keratinized cells are present and their DNA is already partially fragmented.

Laser microdissection allows operators to isolate specific cells from minute samples to determine DNA profiles, gender and species of origin. As laser microdissection generates DNA templates at the lower limits of concentration, it is essential to consider the stoichiometry of the PCR.

There are two PCR strategies in general use. First, DNA can be separated into several aliquots and individually amplified. This is the traditional method of nucleic acid amplification, which can be applied to laser microdissected samples. This approach allows the detection of allelic drop-out since multiple aliquots are available for analysis. Second, the operator performs a single reaction of amplification, using all the DNA solution extracted from the forensic specimen. In principle any allelic drop-out observed is likely to be a biologically related phenomenon rather than an artefact of the PCR.

An intermediate situation between a complete STR-typed allelic profile and one affected by allelic drop-out can occur as a consequence of the reduced amount of DNA template in the PCR solution. When examining genotype peak heights it is important to discriminate, within an apparent heterozygous genotype, whether unbalanced alleles are due to the presence of a stutter product at that locus. Only a precise determination of allele peak areas or, even better, an initial design of a duplicate reaction set for each sample can assist in this situation.

In summary, operators aiming to perform analysis of low copy number DNA by the laser microdissection technique should take into account the following guidelines:

1. Adjust the protocols in order to work on low volumes.
2. Reach the maximum grade of purity of the extracted DNA; additionally evaluate the possibility to increase the injection time during capillary electrophoresis in order to reduce the influence of low-molecular-weight particles.
3. Duplicate the PCR assay on the same sample in order to potentially minimize any stochastic effect.
4. Avoid unnecessarily increasing the number of PCR cycles; the Taq polymerase concentration can be increased within the PCR reaction mix.

12

LIPID-PROTEIN ANALYSIS

In the four decades since the first description of the plasma lipoprotein transport system, there has been an explosion of knowledge about its component parts, operation, and regulation. Increasingly, the medical community has become aware that defects in lipoprotein metabolism are intimately involved in the pathogenesis of *coronary vascular disease* (CVD), the major cause of death in most Western countries. Investigations have been made on a broad front, ranging from intensive clinical investigations to fundamental studies on apolipoproteins, the nature and metabolism of lipoprotein, and the action of enzymes and receptors that control the course of lipoprotein metabolism.

The first step in diagnosis of hyper- and hypolipoproteinemias is to define a phenotype (plasma lipoprotein pattern) by chemical analysis of plasma lipids and lipoproteins. Lipoproteins have been separated in at least five different ways, depending on physical, chemical, and immunological properties of the lipid–protein complexes. Lipoproteins are macromolecules with lower hydrated densities than the other plasma proteins, therefore *ultracentrifugation* (UC), which is also the reference method, has been used to separate various fractions on the basis of differential density. Lipoproteins can also be separated by gel electrophoresis based on their differing surface charge and molecular size. They also form insoluble complexes with polyanions and divalent cations and will precipitate by appropriate choice and concentration of polyanions and metal ions. Lipoproteins may also be separated on the basis of their molecular size by gel or membrane filtration or isolated by reaction with antibodies to apolipoproteins. Quantification of the various apolipoproteins is predominantly performed by immunoassays.

The aim of this chapter is to provide a short introduction in the topic of lipoprotein metabolism and the clinical relevance of lipoproteins, followed by details of the potential analytical impact of *capillary electrophoretic* (CE) techniques in this important field. CE methods required for studies on the molecular biology of lipoproteins have not been included.

BIOMEDICAL BACKGROUND

Structure, Classes, and Metabolism of Lipoproteins

Medieval physicians first observed lipoproteins (milky serum) in association with diabetes mellitus, nephrotic syndrome, and overindulgence of alcohol. In the early 1900s studies focused on the metabolism of plasma cholesterol and triglycerides. This approach quickly gave way to the study of the various lipoprotein classes after it was recognized that lipids and cholesterol were merely cargo and that apolipoproteins on the surface of lipoprotein particles were involved in their metabolism.

All of the major lipoprotein particles consist of a shell of amphipathic proteins (apolipoproteins), unesterified cholesterol and phospholipids (hydrophilic on one face and hydrophobic on the other), and a core of triglycerides and cholesterol esters. They are classified according to increasing density; chylomicrons (<0.95 g/mL), *very low-density lipoproteins* (VLDL, 0.95–1.006 g/mL), *intermediate-density lipoproteins* (IDL, 1.006–1.019), *low-density lipoproteins* (LDL, 1.019–1.063), and *high-density lipoproteins* (HDL, 1.063–1.210). Chylomicrons, which are synthesized by and released from the intestinal epithelial cells, consist of more than 80% of triglycerides and are responsible for transporting dietary fat. After release from the epithelial cells, the chylomicrons are metabolized to remnants that are composed mainly of cholesterol. The remnants bind to the hepatic chylomicron-remnant receptor and enter the liver cells, where the proteins are catabolized and cholesterol released. VLDL is a large triglyceride rich particle synthesized by the liver. Normally most of the VLDL is converted to smaller LDL particles through the "*VLDL remnants*" known as IDL. LDL, a small cholesterol-rich lipoprotein containing only apolipoprotein B-100, has a longer half-life than its precursors, VLDL and IDL. LDL accounts for about 70% of total cholesterol in plasma and is removed from plasma by LDL receptors, which are specific for Apo B-100. The rate of uptake determines plasma LDL concentration and therefore the measured plasma cholesterol concentration. LDL delivers cholesterol to all nucleated cells via endocytosis by the LDL-receptor.

HDL, on the other hand, plays an important role in reverse cholesterol transport. A gradient of reverse cholesterol transport is maintained, either by the liver taking up HDL or by transfer via *cholesterol ester transferase protein* (CETP) of HDL cholesterol ester to Apo B-containing particles, which are also subject to rapid uptake by the liver. Lipoprotein (a) (Lp [a]), whose function is unknown, is also produced by the liver, is similar to LDL, but distinct due to the presence of Apo(a), a glycoprotein with significant homology to plasminogen.

Most lipoprotein classes can be separated as discrete subpopulations, e.g. HDL exist in plasma as HDL_1, HDL_2, and HDL_3. These differ in density, size, composition, and physiological function. In normal human plasma, the two major subpopulations are HDL_2 and HDL_3. LDL, however, has been separated into at least 12 subfractions with particle size decreasing with increasing density. The smaller, denser LDL particles seem to be more atherogenic than the larger, lighter particles. Based on the experimental findings, smaller LDL particles have been found to be more susceptible to oxidation in vitro, have a lower binding affinity for the LDL receptors and a lower catabolic rate. They also have a higher concentration of polyunsaturated fatty acids and potentially interact more easily with proteoglycans of the arterial wall. For IDL two subpopulations of overlapping density have been isolated. Both subpopulations seem to be precursors of two different LDL subclasses. The VLDL subpopulation can be divided into two subspecies, large triglyceride-rich particles and smaller cholesterol ester enriched particles. Each of these various classes and subpopulations of lipoproteins play a more or less pivotal role in the pathogenesis of atherosclerosis, some as a risk factor, other as a protective factor.

Clinical Relevance and Evaluation of Atherosclerotic Risk

In the 20th century, *coronary vascular disease* (CVD) has been the major cause of death in the United States. Despite a 26.7% decline in death rates from CVD during the last decade, CVD is still the major cause of death in the Western world. In 1995, about one million Americans died of heart and blood vessel diseases (455,152 male deaths and 505,440 female deaths), whereas cancer killed a total of 538,455. The cost of cardiovascular diseases and stroke in 1998 has been estimated at $274.2 billion.

Atherosclerosis is the principal cause of CVD. It is a chronic disease characterized by the focal accumulation of plaque (consisting of cholesterol, lipids, leukocytes, macrophages, smooth muscle cells, and extracellular matrix) in the vessel wall that ultimately leads to obstruction of the lumen through gradual progression, plaque rupture with intraluminal thrombosis, or both. If left untreated, atherosclerosis can lead to peripheral vascular disease, heart attack, or stroke. Unfortunately, it is a "silent" disease developing without any symptoms over a long period of time, possibly beginning in childhood. Consequently, early diagnosis to identify individuals at risk is essential.

The importance of serum lipoprotein disturbances as an etiological factor in the development and potentiation of atherosclerosis is now supported by a considerable body of evidence, direct as well as circumstantial, amassed from epidemiological and population studies. Individuals with atherosclerotic CVD usually have one or more of the four lipoprotein abnormalities: (1) increased LDL, (2) decreased HDL usually associated with increased levels of VLDL, (3) increased level of IDL and chylomicron remnants, and (4) high levels of Lp(a). These abnormalities can be explained by genetic variations in proteins controlling lipid transport: apolipoproteins, processing proteins (lipoprotein and hepatic lipases, cholesterol ester transferase protein, lecithin:cholesterol acyl transferase), and receptors (LDL, chylomicron remnants, and scavenger). LDL oxidation, generated by endothelial cells during LDL transport through arterial walls may also play a proatherogenic role. A new, recently recognized factor associated with a high risk of atherosclerosis is mild hyperhomocysteinemia. HDL appears to play a protective role by removing cholesterol from peripheral tissues and preventing lipid accumulation in arterial wall. Other main risk factors are hypertension, increasing age, physical inactivity, obesity, smoking, and diabetes mellitus.

Lipoprotein metabolism is of particular interest to clinicians involved in diagnosis and treatment of atherosclerosis. Progress resulting in easy-to-handle methods and more detailed informations about the quantitative composition of the various lipoproteins should increase our knowledge and, hopefully, point toward new lines of protection and/or therapy. New analytical methods should facilitate the development of improved screening strategies to help identify individuals that have an increased risk of atherosclerosis.

Conventional Lipoprotein Analyses

In addition to careful history and physical examination, laboratory tests are very important in recognizing and classifying disorders of lipoprotein metabolism by describing lipoprotein profiles and their relation to the risk of CVD. However, measurement of lipids and lipoproteins are among the more difficult and sophisticated clinical laboratory tests and has always presented a challenge to the laboratory.

As a heterogeneous mixture of lipids and proteins, the lipoproteins are not easily defined because significant overlap can exist in the physical properties of the major lipoprotein classes. For example, physical separation, such as chemical precipitation or UC, is the basis for measuring HDL. However, an easy method for the direct measurement of HDL in blood does not exist.

After visual observation of the specimen, the next most useful and reliable tests are determinations of triglyceride and total cholesterol concentrations. These are used as a decision point for the logical progression in the evaluation of a patient suspected of having an abnormality of plasma lipids. However, triglyceride and cholesterol values alone do not address the equally important lipoprotein deficiency states (e.g., decreased HDL levels). It also carries the uncertainty that the atherosclerotic risk will be overestimated in patients with a high cholesterol because of a high HDL cholesterol.

Routine lipoprotein profile consists of measurement of serum cholesterol, triglycerides, LDL-cholesterol (LDL-C), and HDL-cholesterol (HDL-C). This is supplemented in special clinical settings by Lp(a), Apo A-I, and Apo B-100 determination. The routine procedure for lipoprotein quantification is to determine HDL-C in the supernatant after precipitation of apolipoprotein-B-containing lipoproteins (VLDL and LDL), e.g., with dextran sulfate. Convenient methods for directly measuring LDL suitable for mass screening are in progress, but not available yet. Currently most routine clinical laboratories estimate LDL-C indirectly using the Friedewald formula: LDL-cholesterol = [total cholesterol] – [total triglycerides/2.2] – [HDL-cholesterol] (mmol/L). This equation holds for triglyceride levels up to, but not above 4.5 mmol/L (400 mg/dl) and becomes inaccurate with increasing IDL levels. This situation occurs in familial dysbetalipoproteinemia, diabetes mellitus, chronic renal failure, atherosclerotic vascular disease, and primary biliary cirrhosis. In general, when classifying subjects into categories of CVD risk, LDL cholesterol calculation methods should be used with caution. Perhaps a better, though less used method to quantify HDL-C, Lp(a)-C, VLDL-C, and LDL-C is agarose gel electrophoresis with enzymatic staining for cholesterol. All four lipoprotein fractions can be obtained in one run and quantified by a densitometric scan. This procedure is more time-consuming than precipitation methods, however the method distinguishes between Lp(a)-

C and LDL-C and is more accurate than precipitation with respect to LDL-C.

Apo A-I and Apo B are usually measured by immunochemical methods. One drawback of immunochemical assays is the influence of the antiserum used, as antibody specificity can lead to appreciable differences in apolipoproteins quantification. Even introduction of an international reference material did not reduce inter-laboratory variability.

Epidemiological studies have also suggested that individuals with lower HDL_2-C levels are predisposed to early development of CVD. Thus a significant amount of work has been directed to adapting the polyanion-precipitating reagent technique to HDL subfraction analysis. So far, however, no high-throughput method for the analysis of lipoprotein subfractions in clinical routine exists.

In order to understand the complexity of lipoprotein metabolism, methodological advances are required to produce homogeneous lipoproteins in their native forms and to characterize these with respect to both particle size and composition. CE possesses the potential to contribute substantially to a sophisticated diagnosis, prevention, therapy and understanding of atherosclerotic diseases.

Lipoprotein and Apolipoprotein Analysis in Research and Clinical Settings by Capillary Electrophoresis

Sample Matrix

The matrices of the samples analyzed for lipoprotein and apolipoprotein determination are frequently very complex, e.g., a high total protein concentration, a high content of lipids, a high ionic strength, and so on. Thus, when developing methods it is necessary to focus not only on component separation but also on possible matrix effects. Thus, methods quantifying lipoproteins and apolipoproteins in or isolated from biological specimens have to be sensitive, selective, reproducible, robust, and, for routine clinical use, able to allow a high sample throughput and yield reliable results even in complex matrixes.

A major difficulty in the analysis of highly hydrophobic apolipoproteins is poor solubility or even insolubility in aqueous buffers. This problem can be solved by the use of detergents or organic solvents in the sample buffer (e.g., 20–70% 2-propanol). When using buffers containing organic modifiers, it is crucial to remember that increasing concentrations of organic modifiers decreases the electroendosmotic flow in CE. Thus, at concentrations of 50% of organic solvent, highly hydrophopbic proteins migrate very slowly, resulting in long analysis time and causing peak broadening and reduced mass flow to the detector.

The use of detergents to dissolve lipoproteins can also cause problems. This is because the binding of detergent to proteins, including apolipoproteins, alters the Stoke radius and with ionic detergents, the charge of the protein. The number of protein binding sites and the amount of detergent bound in apolipoprotein–detergent complexes are also very important. When using detergents it is important to realize that the lipids released in the delipidation process can interact with the surfactants in the running buffer. This can produce lipid-loaded micelles generating additional peaks and background in the electropherogram. This phenomenon is critical in the CE analysis of the apolipoproteins of VLDL and LDL but can be ignored for HDL.

Lipoproteins

Capillary isotachophoresis

Currently, the major classes of lipoproteins are separated electrophoretically based on their charge, as well as their size, shape, and interaction with supporting medium. The lipoproteins are detected after electrophoresis by nonspecific lipid staining, precipitation with polyanions, or enzymatic cholesterol staining.

In the 1970s and 1980s isotachophoresis in open polytetrafluorethylene-tubes was the dominating "*capillary*" technique. It is also the primarily method in the analysis of the various lipoprotein classes by CE. *Capillary isotachophoresis* (CITP) is based on the same principle as CZE, except that a discontinuous buffer system is used. This condenses lipoproteins in zones between the leading and terminating constituents. For better separation performance, spacer compounds can be added. Quantification is based on the measured zone length, which is proportional to the amount of sample present.

Analysis of lipoproteins in "*capillaries*" was first described in 1981 by Bon et al., demonstrating the preparative isotachophoretic separation of HDL_2 and HDL_3 in a 30-cm long plastic column. In this method the two HDL subclasses were separated into six and ten subfractions. Since then the application of CITP to the analysis of lipoproteins and their subfractions has been intensively evaluated. A mixture of spacers, such as different mixtures of aminoacids, dipeptides, modified nucleosides, 3-(n-morpholino)-2-hydroxypropanesulfonic acid, and so on, have been tested, enhancing separation. Both the composition and concentration of the various spacers define the position of the separated lipoprotein subfractions in CITP. In the first communication on the CITP separation of lipoproteins by Schmitz et al., the resolution of the subfractions was better than the traditional electrophoresis techniques. However, without spacers the separation was not adequate. Since then, with a mixture of spacers and different leading and terminating electrolytes, the same group separated 14 distinct lipoprotein subfractions using whole serum or plasma. Six HDL fractions, chylomicrons, large triglyceride-rich VLDL, small VLDL, IDL, and four LDL fractions were detectable. Visualization of the bands was achieved by pre-incubation (30 min at 4°C) of the serum or ethylenediaminetetraacetic acid (EDTA)-plasma with the nonpolar dye Sudan Black B before injection onto the capillary. The detection was at 570 nm.

CITP-analysis of lipoprotein subclasses isolated by UC from normal, hypercholesterolemic, and hypertriglyceridemic subjects showed that mobility of subclasses does not always correspond to the flotation properties of these lipoproteins. It was also found that the concentration of the different fractions varied between individuals. Additionally, CITP was able to classify the typical phenotypes of hyperlipoproteinemia according to the Frederickson classification and World Health Organization (WHO) recommendation. The effects of therapeutic interventions have also been analyzed using CITP. It was possible to observe the effects of a 3- hydroxymethylglutaryl (HMG)-CoA reductase inhibitor alone and in combination with bile-acid sequestrants on individual lipoprotein subpopulations. Subpopulations of Apo B-containing lipoproteins in the electropherograms were also shown to be significantly reduced by the HMG-CoA reductase inhibitor. By taking bile-acid sequestrants in addition to the HMG-CoA reductase inhibitor, a further reduction of the Apo B-containing lipoproteins was seen in the CITP separation pattern.

Recently, two new approaches of CITP to detect lipoproteins have been described. One, developed by Zorn et al., is to use enzymatic specific staining of the cholesterol or the triglyceride present in the lipoproteins. The other method by Schmitz et al., introduced a lipophilic fluorescent dye to stain the lipoproteins. Both investigations have been driven by the fact that the lipophilic dye Sudan Black B shows no saturation in lipoprotein staining.

Following staining of the lipoproteins with cholesterol-specific (cholesterol dehydrogenase and 4-nitrobluetetrazolium) as well as triglyceride-specific staining (glycerol, dihydroxy-acetone, gyceraldehyde,

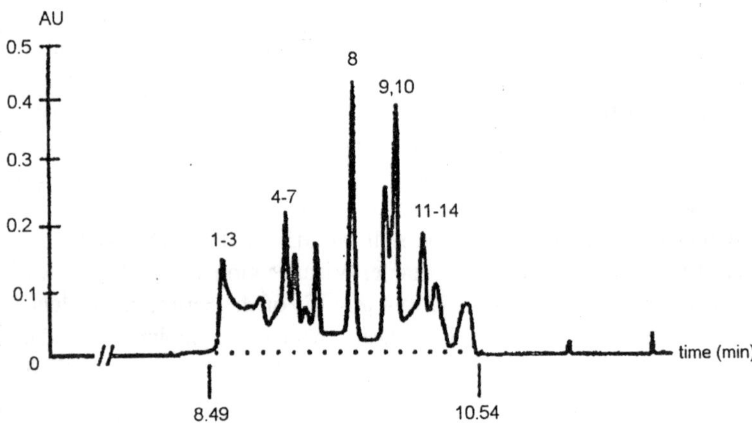

Fig. 12.1. Capillary isotachophoretic serum lipoprotein profile.

and 4-nitrobluetetrazolium) 14 lipoprotein subfractions were separated by CITP with detection at 566 nm. Peaks 1–5 have been identified as HDL subfractions, peaks 8–14 belong to LDL subfractions, and peaks 6–8 include the VLDL fraction and chylomicrons. Peak 8 contains one VLDL and one LDL-fraction. Using triglyceride-specific staining the peaks of the VLDL and chylomicrons dominate whereas cholesterol-specific staining causes an increased intensity of the peaks 1–6 (HDL) and 8–14 (LDL).

Following a high lipid diet the electropherograms demonstrate a clear increase in the triglyceride content of peak 6 and 7 (chylomicrons and VLDL) with no significant changes in the HDL and LDL region. After 8 h the triglycerides in subfractions 6 and 7 (VLDL and chylomicrons) shifted to subfractions 8–14 (LDL). In addition, the transition from hypothyroidism to hyperthyroidism also showed a decrease in the cholesterol content of all lipoprotein fractions with the cholesterol-specific staining.

Various fluorescence tagged phospholipid analogs can also be used for specific labeling and quantification of individual lipoprotein classes. The compound, 7-nitrobenz-2-oxa-1,3-diazole ceramide (NBD-ceramide), was identified as a good compromise, with respect to saturation and to specific surface area- or particle size-dependent staining. NBD-ceramide, an uncharged, lipophilic dye, labels the phospholipid/ cholesterol membrane.

The addition of nonfluorescent spacers allows the discrimination of 9 individual lipoprotein subpopulations monitored with *laser-induced fluorescence* (LIF) detection (ex. 488 nm; em. 510 nm). Four peaks are the result of HDL subpopulations, one represents chylomicrons, and four represent Apo-B containing particles, including VLDL, IDL, and LDL. An interesting aspect is that analytical CITP is currently the only automatic technique to quantify chylomicrons and IDL particles in human serum. This could be applied to the investigation of the VLDL/IDL subpopulations in patients with CVD. The ineffective conversion of VLDL/IDL to LDL by hepatic lipase in CVD patients could also be detected by CITP using LIF detection. Thus CITP allows estimation of highly atherogenic IDL particles simultaneously with HDL and LDL cholesterol levels, improving the estimation of atherosclerotic risk factors.

Results of lipoprotein analysis by CITP of 52 patient samples were compared with routine techniques for HDL and LDL quantification. Comparison of the results gave correlation's of $r = 0.9$ and 0.91, respectively, for HDL-C and LDL-C (equations: $HDL_{CITP} = 3 +$ total cholesterol $\times$ relative peak $area_{HDL}/1.53$; $LDL_{CITP} = -25 +$ total cholesterol (relative peak $area_{LDL}/\ 0.73$). CITP enables the simultaneous quantification of HDL- and LDL-cholesterol within 7 min and can be performed on whole serum, plasma, or other biological fluids. Furthermore, CITP analysis of serum lipoprotein patterns may significantly improve the diagnosis of disorders in lipoprotein metabolism.

In addition to quantification of various lipoprotein subpopulations, CITP allows insight into plasma lipoprotein metabolism. This is done by estimation of the major lipolytic enzyme activities by looking at the appropriate precursor and product. This means the ratio between precursor and product lipoprotein peaks is influenced by a specific lipolytic enzyme thus allowing estimation of lipoprotein conversion rates.

Currently it is difficult to directly quantify HDL by conventional techniques. Most laboratories estimate HDL levels by measuring cholesterol after precipitation of VLDL and LDL with various polyanions (e.g., heparin and manganese chloride). Using CITP prestained (Sudan Black B-, enzymatic-, or fluorescence-stained) serum, lipoproteins can be separated into 9–14 subpopulation and quantified within 7–15 min. The ability of CITP to separate the various lipoproteins is far superior to the results of the current routine procedures. Whether interpretation of this very complex lipoprotein separation pattern adds anything to every day clinical practice has yet to be determined.

CITP has the potential to improve the classification of lipoprotein patterns and to relate it to the risk of CHD. It could permit new insight into pathobiochemistry, etiology, and diagnosis of disorders of lipoprotein metabolism. Furthermore, it has the potential to be used for lipoprotein monitoring during drug therapy, as well as micro-preparation of various lipoprotein subpopulations for further investigations.

Micellar electrokinetic capillary chromatography and capillary zone electrophoresis

Micellar electrokinetic capillary chromatography (MEKC) and *capillary zone electrophoresis* (CZE) represent other options for the analysis of lipoproteins. The addition of a micellar agent, such as *sodium dodecyl sulfate* (SDS), to the running buffer allows the solubilization of neutral, hydrophobic analytes as well as ion pairs with opposite charge. Two basic principles have to be kept in mind when analyzing lipoproteins by MEKC or CZE: (1) operating at pH values above the *pI* of the lipoprotein particles, leads to negatively charged lipoproteins, keeping them from coming in contact with the surface of the fused silica capillary due to repulsion by the negatively charged surface, and (2) the addition of a detergent like SDS to the running buffer at a concentration that will not cause delipidation, enhances the migration of the lipoprotein particles due to incorporation of the detergent.

Cruzado et al. tested various buffers and detergent additives, as well as organic modifiers to achieve an adequate MEKC separation of the various lipoprotein fractions. They found that at high pH values HDL and LDL were found to have nearly identical mobilities in different buffers and ionic strengths. Addition of SDS or acetonitrile was found to influence significantly the electrophoretic behavior of HDL (high surface polarity) and LDL (low surface polarity). Decreasing the polarity of the running buffer by the addition of acetonitrile resulted in the retaining of an increased amount of SDS by the more hydrophobic LDL particles over the HDL particles. This increases the difference in electrophoretic mobility of both particles. Other lipoproteins like Lp(a) and its reduction products, Lp(a$^-$) and Apo(a), can also be separated with sodium borate buffer containing SDS and acetonitrile. Under these conditions, LDL and HDL have consistent electrophoretic mobilities that are significantly different from both Lp(a) and Lp(a$^-$).

Oxidative modifications of LDL appear to be the pathophysiological mechanism implicated in early atherogenesis. Oxidized LDL may also induce several pro-atherogenic mechanisms, such as the regulation of vascular tone by interfering with nitric oxide, in addition to the stimulation of cytokines, chemotactic factors, and transcription factors. In view of increasing interest in the role of LDL oxidation in the pathogenesis of atherosclerosis, there is clearly a need for improved methods to evaluate lipoprotein oxidation. A recent report by Stocks and Miller described a sophisticated CZE procedure using methylglucamine-Tricine buffer to monitor the in vitro oxidation of LDL, which can be initiated by incubation with transition metal catalysts such as Cu^{2+} ions or by exposure to free- radical generating agents. LDL oxidation is characterized by an increase in the electrophoretic mobility as previously shown in agarose gels and an increase in absorbance at 234 nm. CZE showed a marked improvement in peak resolution and recovery of LDL relative to earlier MEKC methods. The procedure provides a rapid, sensitive, and precise way of measuring the electrophoretic mobility of LDL (one of the more reliable indicators of LDL modification) with a very high precision (coefficient of variation $< 1\%$). The progressive increase in the electronegativity of LDL particles that occurs during Cu^{2+}-catalyzed auto-oxidation of LDLs, or during reaction with malondialdehyde, can be readily monitored by CZE. In addition, the spectral changes, induced by an increase in absorption at 234 nm resulting from the oxidation of fatty acids and cholesterol, can be monitored simultaneously. However, the applicability of the CE technique for the investigation of changes in LDL in vivo has yet to be proved.

Although MEKC is a much easier procedure to run than CITP, the resolving power is not as good. Similar to lipoprotein analysis by agarose gel electrophoresis, the lipoproteins HDL, VLDL, LDL and Lp(a) can be separated as single peaks, but the subfractions cannot be detected. So far experiments have been performed only with mixtures of UC-isolated lipoproteins. Because the plasma HDL content is usually quantified indirectly as HDL-cholesterol, the MEKC analysis of lipoproteins in serum, prestained plasma, or directly by UV detection, would have a potentially great impact on the routine clinical laboratory diagnosis of dyslipidemias. Contrary to precipitation procedures, the linear relationship of protein concentration to absorption between 195–230 nm guarantees valid quantification. This is because the signal is mainly dependent on the absorption of the peptide bond concentration as long as "Beer-Lambert law" is valid.

The conventional way to measure the increase in absorption of oxidized LDL spectrophotometrically can lead to conflicting results, as the compounds added to inhibit or promote oxidation can also contribute significantly to UV absorption. Using electrophoretic separation of the oxidized LDL particles by CZE, these effects can be avoided.

Apolipoproteins

Apolipoproteins play a pivotal role in lipid homeostasis. Recent publications have suggested that cardiovascular risk profile may be more reliable based on apolipoprotein levels rather than lipid composition of the lipoproteins. Usually apolipoprotein levels are measured by automated immunoturbidimetric or immunonephelometric assays. For smaller amounts of sample (e.g., in biomedical research) radial immunodiffusion, rocket electroimmunoassay, enzyme-linked immunosorbent assay, or radioimmunoassay can be used. A general drawback of all immunological determinations of apolipoproteins is caused by the differences in the antibody specificities and epitope recognition. In addition, lipids may mask antigenic sites affecting immunoreactivity. Thus, quantification of apolipoproteins is influenced by the antisera, sample, and methodology used in a particular assay system. This can result in appreciable differences in the amount of each apolipoprotein measured. Examples of completely different, antibody-independent ways to quantify apolipoproteins are: (1) the semi-quantitative densitometric evaluation of stained protein bands on a gel, and (2) to measure the direct UV signal of the polypeptide bonds at 195–230 nm. In general, the most popular techniques to separate and detect proteins directly nowadays are high-performance liquid chromatography (HPLC) and CE.

Surfactants are the main features of CE analysis of apolipoproteins, because the electrophoretic behavior of apolipoproteins is strongly influenced and can be modified by addition of detergent or organic solvents to the running buffer. At concentrations of ≥3.5 m*M* SDS, lipoproteins are delipidated. Knowing this, careful attention should be paid to the fact that lipids released in the delipidation process can associate with the surfactants in the running buffer, producing lipid-loaded micelles. This can generate additional peaks and increased background in the electropherogram. This phenomenon is crucial for the apolipoproteins of VLDL and LDL but can be ignored for HDL.

Tadey and Purdey performed the fundamental experiments at the beginning of the 1990s. They investigated the influence of various detergents and detergent concentrations, as well as pH on the MEKC separation profile and the migration behavior of apolipoproteins A-I, A-II, B-100, B-48, and C-III from HDL, VLDL and LDL. The analyses were performed on UC-isolated lipoproteins. Optimal resolution of HDL and LDL apolipoproteins can be achieved by the use of anionic surfactants. Both anionic and cationic detergents (SDS and cetyltrimethylammonium bromide) improve the separation profile of VLDL apolipoproteins. Seven different components of VLDL could be distinguished (not all have yet been identified).

Since then a number of reports using CE to analyze apolipoproteins has followed. The apolipoproteins from HDL (Apo A-I and Apo A-II) gave a very fast and clear-cut separation. Using MEKC Apo A-I is separated into two peaks (one major and a small peak) and Apo A-II can be separated into four different fractions. The heterogeneity in Apo A-II has been previously observed by *isoelectric focusing* (IEF)

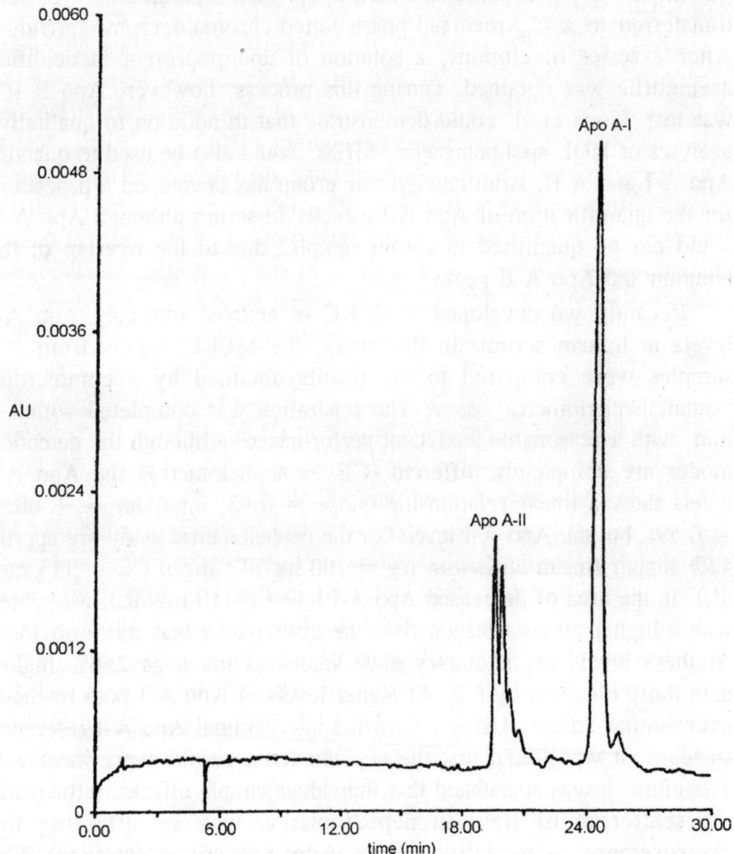

Fig. 12.2. Capillary electropherogram of a mixture of apolipoprotein A-I and A-II.

showing one major and several minor isoforms. Cruzado et al. confirmed this by a detailed characterization of the apolipoproteins from HDL by using a combination of MEKC, reversed- phase HPLC (RP-HPLC), and matrix assisted laser desorption/ionization mass spectrometry (MALDI-MS). They also looked at electropherograms of HDL before and after delipidation and found no differences, meaning that prior delipidation is not required for analysis of these apolipoproteins. On the other hand, delipidation of VLDL and LDL increase the background and generates additional peaks due to the interaction of the released lipids and the surfactant in the buffer. This high background prevents the detection of low level apolipoproteins (e.g., Apo E or Apo Cs). To circumvent this problem, they developed a multiple- step procedure in which lipoprotein separated by UC were transferred to a C_{18} reversed-phase liquid-chromatography cartridge. After a series of elutions, a solution of apolipoprotein in acidified acetonitrile was obtained. During this process, however, Apo B-100 was lost. Goux et al. could demonstrate that in addition to qualitative analyses of HDL apolipoproteins, MEKC could also be used to quantify Apo A-I and A-II. Additionally, our group has developed a procedure for the quantification of Apo A-I directly in serum although Apo A-II could not be quantified in serum samples due to the overlap of the albumin and Apo A-II peaks.

Recently we developed a MEKC to analyze routinely Apo A-I levels in human serum. In this study, the MEKC results from 100 samples were compared to the results obtained by a commercial immunonephelometric assay. The separation was completed within 8 min, with a reasonable analytical performance. Although the detection modes are completely different (CE vs nephelometry) the Apo A-I levels show a linear relationship (slope = 0.93; intercept = + 60; r = 0.59), but the Apo A-I levels for the nephelometric assay are approx 42% higher (mean nephelometry = 160 mg/dL; mean CE = 113 mg/dL). In the area of decreased Apo A-I levels (≤110 mg/dL), associated with a higher atherosclerotic risk, the discrepancy was more obvious. At these levels nephelometry gave values as much as 250% higher than those obtained by CE. At higher levels of Apo A-I both methods gave similar values. Using a certified international Apo A-I reference standard, it was found that the nephelometric results were incorrect. Therefore, it was speculated that individual sample effects, influencing the scattering of light in nephelometry, may be affecting the measurement, especially at low Apo A-I concentrations. The immunonephelometric assay may also be influenced by various

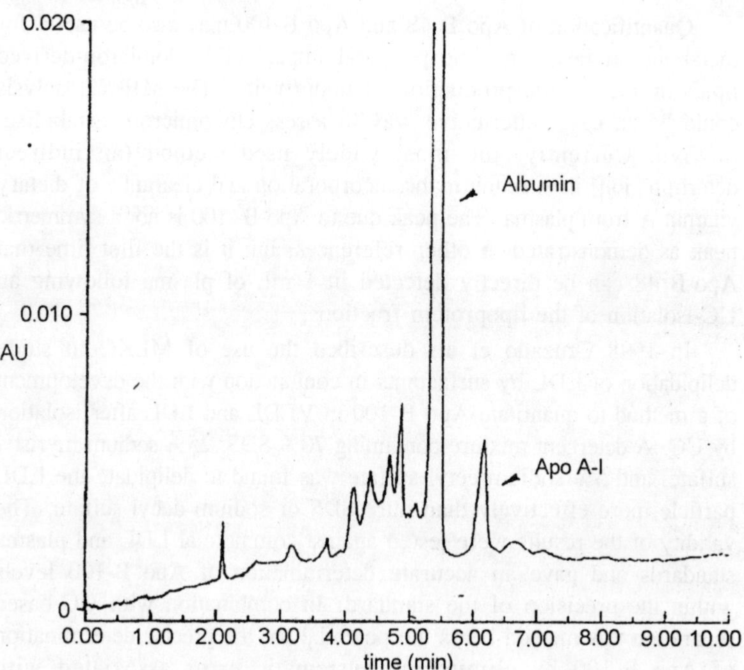

Fig. 12.3. Serum sample separated by micellar electrokinetic capillary chromatography.

polymorphic apolipoprotein forms (over- or underestimation of a specific variant), turbidity of any kind, unspecific binding of the antibody, cross-reactivities, or influences of the sample background. Interference due to hemolysis (free hemoglobin ≤3 g/L) or hyperbilirubinemia (bilirubin ≤714 μmol/L) did not affect the CE results. Also highly lipemic sera (triglyceride ≤27.1 mmol/L), which can not be analyzed by routine immunoassays, gave a well-separated and easy to quantify Apo A-I peak in CE.

Very recently Stocks et al. compared the levels obtained by CZE and MEKC of Apo A-I and Apo A-II isolated by UC from 17 human HDL samples to rocket immunoelectrophoresis. Both, the commercial MEKC kit and CZE gave values for Apo A-I and Apo A-II concentrations in human HDL that were in good agreement with those obtained by rocket immunoelectrophoresis. In addition, they showed that the patterns and migration times of rabbit, rat, bovine, and human HDL apolipoproteins (Apo A-I, Apo A-II, Apo A-IV and Apo E) are identical. This is a very important point especially for research projects dealing with animals, because species-specific antibodies that can be difficult to obtain are needed for reliable immunoassay results.

Quantification of Apo B-48 and Apo B-100 may also be useful for metabolic studies, e.g., the potential impact of chylomicron-derived lipids on the hepatic production of lipoproteins. The MEKC analysis could be an easy, alternative way to assess chylomicron metabolism in vivo. Currently, the most widely used method (an indirect determination) is to monitor the incorporation and clearance of dietary vitamin A from plasma. The peak due to Apo B- 100 is not a symmetric peak as demonstrated in other references, but it is the first time that Apo-B 48 can be directly detected in 1 mL of plasma following an UC-isolation of the lipoprotein fractions.

In 1998 Cruzado et al. described the use of MEKC to study delipidation of LDL by surfactants in conjunction with the development of a method to quantitate Apo B-100 in VLDL and LDL after isolation by UC. A detergent mixture containing 70% SDS, 25% sodium myristyl sulfate, and 5% sodium cetyl sulfate was found to delipidate the LDL particle more effectively than pure SDS or sodium decyl sulfate. The validity of the results were tested against commercial LDL and plasma standards and gave an accurate determination of Apo B-100 levels within the precision of the standard. In combination with UC-based separation this method bears the potential for the precise determination of Apo B-100 by eliminating systematic error associated with precipitation, resolubilization, losses associated with lipid removal, and variability in chromogenicity and immunoreactivity within the Apo-B-100 protein.

Immunoassay or CE: which method is better? There are a number of pros and cons for both techniques. Currently immunoassays are the generally accepted methods for the routine quantification of apolipoproteins in the clinical and research laboratories. Although reproducible within a particular laboratory, the inter-laboratory comparability is not good. With CE the major drawback is sequential operation that can be overcome by the use of a multi-capillary instrument. Currently a CE instrument with seven capillaries in parallel for routine serum protein analysis is offered on the market. On the other hand, for laboratories running smaller numbers of samples, a sequential CE instrument is adequate for the overnight analyses of ≥30 apolipoprotein samples. As described earlier, the CE methods should give comparable results between laboratories. However, the apolipoprotein results by CE are not identical to those using nephelometry. In a time with increasing health care costs and lower budgets for research, the price per result also has to be considered. Since the costs of an analysis using CE are extremely low, when compared to immunoassay, apolipoprotein determination using CE should be considered as an economical alternative.

Future Perspectives

Lipoproteins, in addition to apolipoprotein identification and quantification, will continue to play an important role in the understanding of the pathogenesis of atherosclerosis for many years. Further development efforts will be directed towards the development of increasingly affordable, rapid, reliable, and automated technologies. CE with its various modes has several advantages when compared to the current procedures for lipoprotein and apolipoprotein analyses. These advantages are extreme analytical flexibility, using small quantities of low cost separation buffer, ability to use of a variety of detection modes, small sample size (nanoliter), high speed, efficiency, and reproducibility. It is also possible to install fully automated procedures. Furthermore, CE allows a rapid change from one buffer system to another: in other words, change from one analytical procedure to another.

In this chapter it becomes obvious that use of CE for lipoprotein analysis is still in its infancy. LDL, which is routinely only detected as one fraction, can be subdivided in up to six fractions by CITP that may yield new insights in the pathophysiology of the LDL-subfractions. It is possible that new areas in the study of atherogenesis may be achieved by the analysis of HDL subfractions. Since CE first separates then detects the lipoproteins, immunoassay problems caused by antibodies are eliminated. In addition, since multiple apolipoproteins can be determined in one run, CE is a good alternative to procedures like gel electrophoresis or UC. In the future, with a multi- capillary instrument and with on-line sample pretreatment, it could well be competitive to automated special analyses. For broader acceptance of lipoprotein and apolipoprotein analysis by CE, three things are needed: (1) The development of chemical reagent kits, instruments, and software suitable for daily clinical laboratory use; (2) an increase of sensitivity and sample throughput; and (3) comparison and evaluation of various applications with current laboratory methods under daily laboratory conditions. In addition special attention needs to be paid to accuracy, reproducibility, speed, and susceptibility to disturbances (methods, capillaries, CE instruments). Other important criteria are ease of use in routine work situations, possibly automation, low cost per test, inexpensive and long-lasting reagents, widely accessible methodology, and clinically relevant reference ranges. Until now the number of reports evaluating these applications in comparison to the traditional procedures is low, however, this is likely to change in the near future.

Taken together, high-efficiency separations based on charge-to-mass ratio have been achieved through a combination of buffer modifiers and uncoated or permanently coated capillaries. Use of dynamically coated capillaries and separations based on the molecular weight have not yet been tested, but may further improve separation of the lipoproteins. CE offers more than simple improvement in quantitative and qualitative analyses of lipoprotein and apolipoproteins. It also offers the possibility of monitoring the reaction rates of apolipoproteins with different surfactants, lipoprotein degradation, lipoprotein metabolism, as well as therapeutic effects on lipoprotein classes. The use of CITP in the analysis of lipoproteins may facilitate the development of new clinical screening methods, possibly leading to new diagnostic markers or patterns, better prognostic evaluation, and new therapeutic modalities. Of course, as with all new developments, it is likely that some things may not turn out to be as important as expected. But I am also confident that many as yet unanticipated discoveries will be made as a result of the increased performance of this analytical technique. Nevertheless, the impact that these additional CE applications will have on diagnosis and treatment of atherosclerosis greatly depends on the success of transferring them from the academic research laboratories to the commercial marketplace.

13

Bone Markers

Analysis of the knee for forensic identification has often been overlooked in favor of studies of skeletal elements that have more individualizing features than the knee. However, there may be instances when careful analysis of the knee can provide clues to a person's identity.

All the musculoskeletal tissue at the knee should be examined carefully for evidence of antemortem injuries, repetitive stress, and surgical modifications, which, it is hoped, correlate with a specific overuse syndrome or ideally with a putative victim's medical record. In skeletonized remains, osteologic evidence (and perhaps some nonabsorbable sutures) may be the only evidence remaining for analysis. In other cases, analysis of the connecting ligaments and capsular structures often can provide answers to the puzzle of victim identification. Therefore, these structures should never be removed during hasty attempts to expose the bone.

This chapter will help forensic experts become familiar with the most common anatomic terminology and conditions involving the knee and provide a condensed anatomy atlas of that region. All illustrations depict the right knee.

Osteology

Femur

The femur is the longest bone of the human body. It consists of a rounded proximal head that articulates with the acetabulum at the hip, a nearly cylindrical shaft, and a distal metaphysis that forms two large rounded condyles that articulate with the tibia. Because of its relationship with the osteology of the knee, the distal portion of the

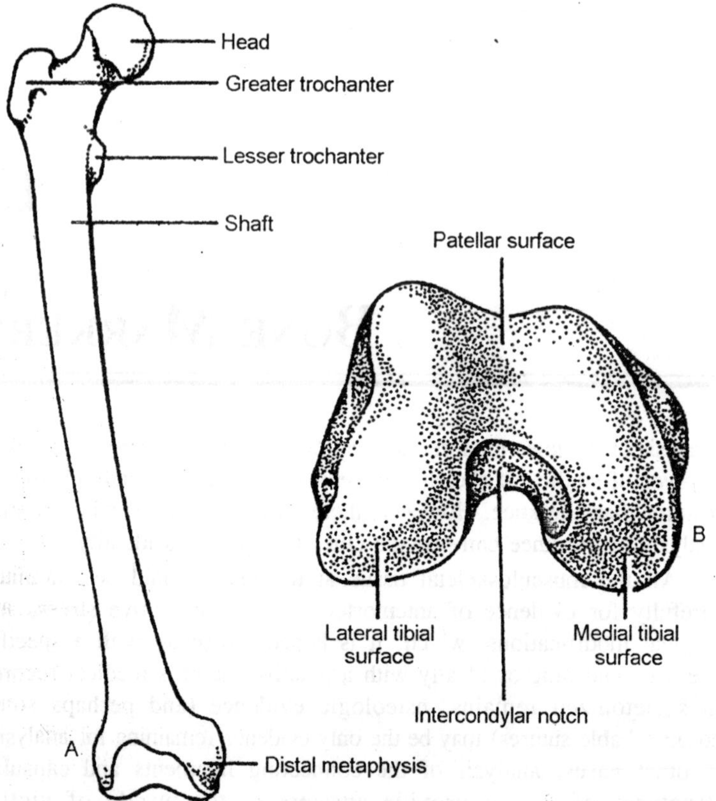

Fig. 13.1. Anterior femur. (A) Anterior view of the entire femur; (B) The distal articular surface shows how the patellar surface blends into medial and lateral tibial surfaces.

femur will be the focus of this section. This distal portion is widely expanded to provide a large surface for the transmission of body weight to the top of the tibia. It is made up of two large condyles that are partially covered by articular cartilage. These two condyles are separated posteriorly by the intercondylar notch but are united anteriorly, where they provide an articular surface for the patella.

Articular surfaces

The patellar and the tibial surfaces are the two major divisions of the distal articular surface. The patellar surface is concave from side to side and has a groove along its long axis. It is higher on the lateral side and is separated from the tibial surfaces by two relatively indistinct grooves. The tibial surface is further divided into medial and lateral

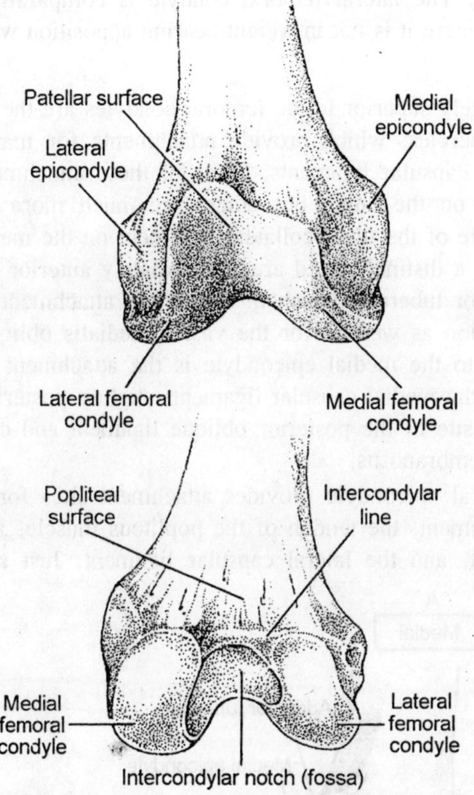

Fig. 13.2. Anterior and posterior views of the distal femur.

parts. Anteriorly the tibial surfaces are continuous with the patellar surface, but posteriorly they are separated by the intercondylar notch or fossa. Normally, all of these articular surfaces are covered with a thick layer of cartilage that protects the underlying bone.

Condyles

The femoral condyles are convex from side to side and front to back, and both project posteriorly past the plane of the posterior shaft of the femur. The medial femoral condyle is larger and rounder than the lateral condyle and projects downward and medially to such an extent that the lower surface of the lower end of the bone appears to be practically horizontal when seen from the side. The lateral femoral condyle is less prominent but is longer from front to back. It is wide and steeply sloped medially to laterally, where it creates a large weight-bearing surface against the interspinous eminence of the lateral tibial plateau. The lateral femoral condyle is comparatively narrow posteriorly, where it is not in weight-bearing apposition with the tibia.

Epicondyles

Immediately superior to the femoral condyles are the epicondyles and their tubercles, which provide attachments for many muscles, tendons, and capsular ligaments. Some of these attachment sites are well defined on the bone, but others are much more subtle. The attachment site of the tibial collateral ligament on the medial femoral epicondyle is a distinct raised area immediately anterior and inferior to the adductor tubercle, which in turn is the attachment site for the adductor tendon as well as for the vastus medialis obliquus muscle. Just inferior to the medial epicondyle is the attachment site for the mid third of the medial capsular ligament; slightly posterior to this is the insertion site of the posterior oblique ligament and capsular arm of the semimembranosus.

The lateral epicondyle provides attachment sites for the fibular collateral ligament, the tendon of the popliteus muscle, fibers of the iliotibial tract, and the lateral capsular ligament. Just superior and

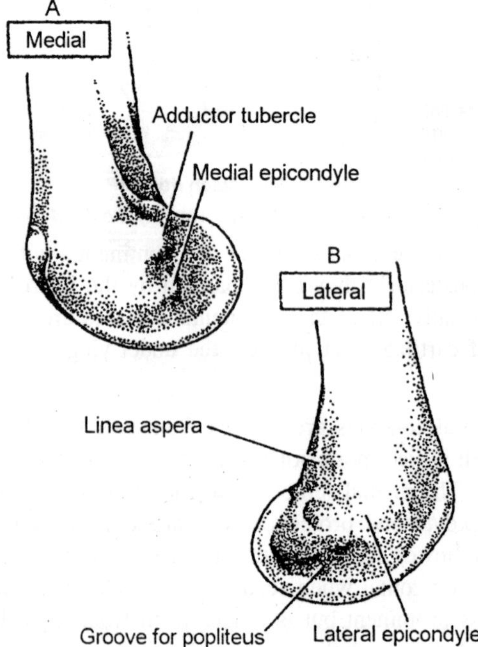

Fig. 13.3. The epicondyles of the femur: lateral and medial views.

posterior to the epicondyle is the most distal extent of the linea aspera. This raised area of bone provides attachment sites for the iliotibial tract, the vastus lateralis, and the short head of the biceps. Between the lateral epicondyle and the linea aspera is the attachment site for the lateral head of the gastrocnemius.

The so-called "*cheek*" of the femur provides an attachment site for the synovial membrane and separates both medial and lateral epicondylar areas of bone from the articular surfaces.

Intercondylar notch

The intercondylar notch separates the medial and lateral femoral condyles and is the attachment site for the cruciate ligaments, the ligaments of Wrisberg and Humphrey, and the frenulum of the patellar fat pad. A large portion of the notch is rough and pitted by vascular foramina, but it is relatively smooth where it provides attachment for ligaments. To accommodate the ligaments, the notch is widened posteriorly where it is not in apposition with the tibia. In the most posterior superior portion, the notch connects to the intercondylar line, a distinct ridge of bone that provides attachments for the oblique popliteal ligament and the posterior portion of the arcuate ligament.

Popliteal surface

A large portion of the posterior distal femur is described as the popliteal surface. It is the floor of the upper part of the popliteal fossa of the knee and is covered by fat, which separates it from the popliteal artery. It is a relatively flat, slightly concave surface that is deeply pitted with vascular foramina. Lateral to this is a raised area of bone where the plantaris, the lateral head of the gastrocnemius, and the arcuate ligament attach. At the most medial edge of the popliteal surface, the bone expands to provide an attachment site for the medial head of the gastrocnemius, the adductor aponeurosis, and the semimembranosus retinaculum.

Tibia

The tibia is the larger of the two bones of the lower leg and, except for the femur, is the longest bone of the skeleton. The proximal end is flattened and expanded to provide a large surface for bearing body weight transmitted through the lower end of the femur. The shaft is prismoid in section, especially in the proximal third. The distal end is smaller than the proximal end, and there is a stout process—the medial malleolus—at the end. The proximal end forms a large portion of the knee joint.

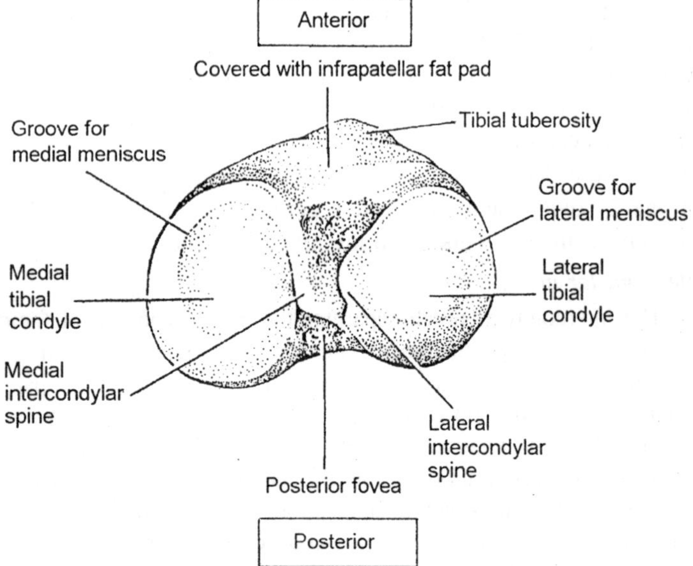

Fig. 13.4. Proximal surface of the tibia: superior view.

Articular surfaces

The uppermost portion of the tibia is expanded, especially in the transverse axis, into two prominent condyles. The articular surface of the larger medial condyle is concave and essentially ovoid. It is flattened where it comes in contact with the medial meniscus, and the imprint of the medial meniscus can frequently be seen on the bone. The articular surface of the lateral tibial condyle is more circular in outline and likewise bears a flattened imprint of the corresponding lateral meniscus. Both articular surfaces are normally covered with thick cartilage, and they rise sharply in the center of the joint to form their respective sides of the intercondylar eminence.

As the anterior articular margins of the two articular surfaces recede from each other, the middle of the tibial plateau broadens into a fairly flat, smooth area that is devoid of cartilage. The infrapatellar fat pad covers this portion and separates it from the patellar ligament. The medial and lateral menisci insert between this smooth, flat area and the articular surfaces just posterior to this fat pad. The area of attachment for the anterior cruciate ligament fits between the meniscal attachments and the intercondylar spines or eminences. Immediately posterior to the intercondylar eminences are attachment sites for the posterior horns of the medial and lateral menisci. Behind these, the posterior intercondylar area slopes sharply downward into a fovea and provides an attachment site for the lower end of the posterior cruciate ligament. The posterior intercondylar area ends in a ridge to which the posterior capsular structures are attached.

Tibial tuberosity

A large tuberosity that is divided into a lower roughened region and a smooth upper region is present on the anterior surface of the proximal tibial shaft. The patella ligament inserts on the lower region. The upper surface of this tuberosity is tilted backward relative to the long axis of the shaft, but the inferior surface projects forward in a triangular protuberance.

Condyles

On the lateral side of the tuberosity, the tibia first forms a ridge that provides attachment sites for the lateral capsule and fibers from the iliotibial tract. The strongest, direct attachment for the iliotibial tract, however, is on the lateral tibial tubercle. A prominent ridge just posterior to the tubercle provides an attachment site for the lateral capsular ligaments.

The lateral tibial condyle is somewhat flattened below and articulates with the head of the fibula posteriorly. The fibular facet is directed downward and laterally to match the articular surface of the head of the fibula. The posterior edge of the fibular facet is on the posterolateral portion of the proximal tibia, just below the posterolateral tibial plateau. The most posterior third of the lateral condyle has an acute posterior slope just medial to the plateau.

The medial tibial condyle projects much farther posteriorly than does the lateral condyle, and the entire nonarticular surface provides an extensive attachment site for the tendon and retinaculum of the semimembranosus. The superior posteromedial edge of this condyle has a distinct groove for the direct arm of the semimembranosus, and the tibial attachment for the posterior oblique ligament and the mid third of the medial capsular ligament is just above this groove.

The most medial portion of the medial tibial condyle is raised to create a smooth projection that secures a bursa over which the tibial collateral ligament glides. This ligament produces a distinct ridge that extends down the medial shaft of the tibia. As the distal condyle blends into the shaft, it drops off sharply and angles anteriorly to produce the medial surface of the tibial tuberosity and provide an attachment site for the tendons of the sartorius, gracilis and semitendinosus.

Posterior surface

The proximal tibia expands posteriorly and angles obliquely from the medial to lateral direction. Distally it ends abruptly as the shaft drops off to form a deep depression to accommodate the bulk of the popliteus muscle. Medial and posterior to the fibular facet, the tendon of the popliteus produces a distinct groove on the bone. The posterior border of the tibial plateau ends in a sharp ridge medial to this popliteal groove, and the posterior popliteal ligament inserts in the area inferior to the ridge. A deep fovea in the central part of the posterior proximal tibia marks the lower site of attachment for the posterior cruciate ligament. A distinct osseous ridge extends from just below the posterolateral tibial plateau and runs obliquely toward the medial border of the tibial shaft, the bony origin of the soleus muscle.

Fibula

The fibula, the lateral bone of the leg, is more slender than the tibia. It does not share in the transmission of body weight but functions primarily as an anchor for the muscles of the lower leg. The shaft, which has a variable shape that is molded by the muscles to which it gives attachment, ends distally as the lateral malleolus.

The head of the fibula is the only portion that contributes to the structure of the knee joint. The shape of the head is extremely variable, and all its diameters are expanded in relation to the shaft. Its upper surface contains an articular facet that joins onto the inferior lateral tibial condyle, but the exact location of the articulation with the tibia is not constant. The styloid process projects upwards from the lateral part of the superior surface of the head and is the site of attachment for the arcuate ligament. Anterior to this is a small depression that marks the attachment of the fibular collateral ligament. Short, strong ligaments totally surround the tibiofibular articular surfaces and create what is an almost immovable "*plane joint*" between the two bones. The tendon of the combined long and short heads of the biceps femoris inserts on the anterior surface of the head of the fibula.

Patella

The patella is a large sesamoid bone within the quadriceps femoris tendon that articulates with the patellar surface of the distal femur. The anterior surface is flattened, with just a slight convex curve. The surface is perforated with many nutrient foramina and is marked with numerous rough, longitudinal striae. The inferior half is roughly triangular and the superior border is rounded. The medial and lateral borders are relatively thin but provide substantial areas for

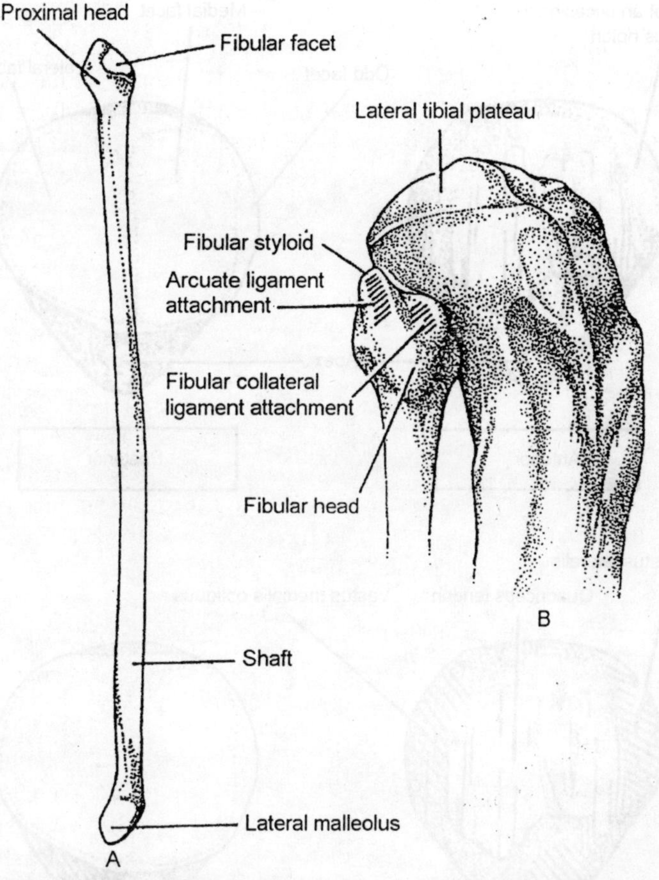

Fig. 13.5. The fibula. (A) Anterior view of the entire fibula; (B) Lateral view of the fibula and its relation to the tibia.

musculotendinous attachments. The superolateral border is the site of attachment of the vastus lateralis tendon, where a distinct notch often is present or even an accessory ossification center.

An articular surface covers most of the posterior patella and molds to fit smoothly against the femur. It made up of a large medial and lateral facet; a central ridge; and a single, small, medial facet that is sometimes referred to as the "odd" facet. The lateral facet is the largest and deepest of the three facets.

Just inferior to the articular surface is an area known as the apex. The inferior border of the apex is roughened and provides attachment for the patellar ligament. Its superior surface is covered

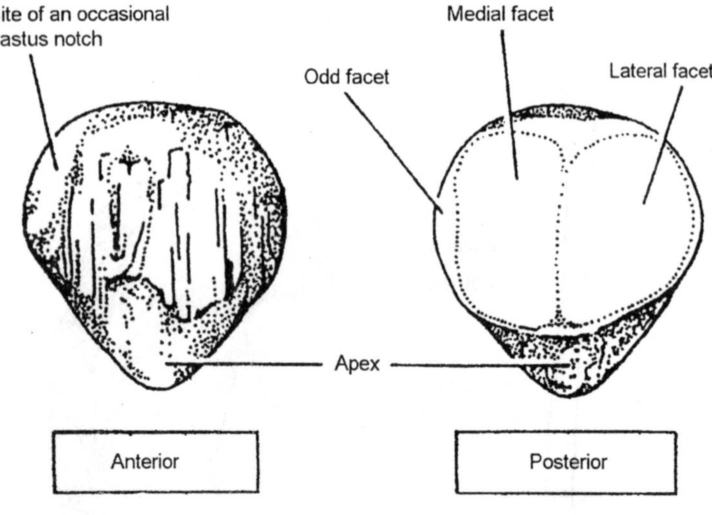

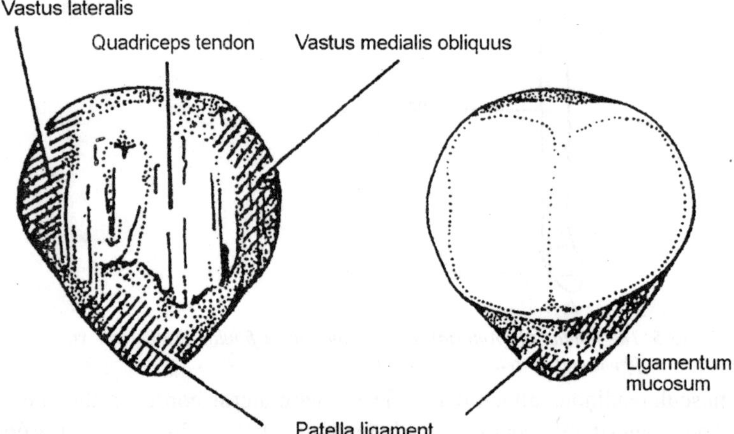

Fig. 13.6. Anterior and posterior views of a right patella. The top two views show the bony topography of the patella. The bottom two views indicate the attachment sites of soft tissues.

by the infrapatellar fat pad and an extension of synovium termed the ligamentum mucosum or frenulum.

Fabella

Fabella, a term derived from the Latin word for "*little bean*," is a sesamoid bone buried in the lateral head of the gastrocnemius muscle near the musculotendinous junction. The fabella is approximately 13.5

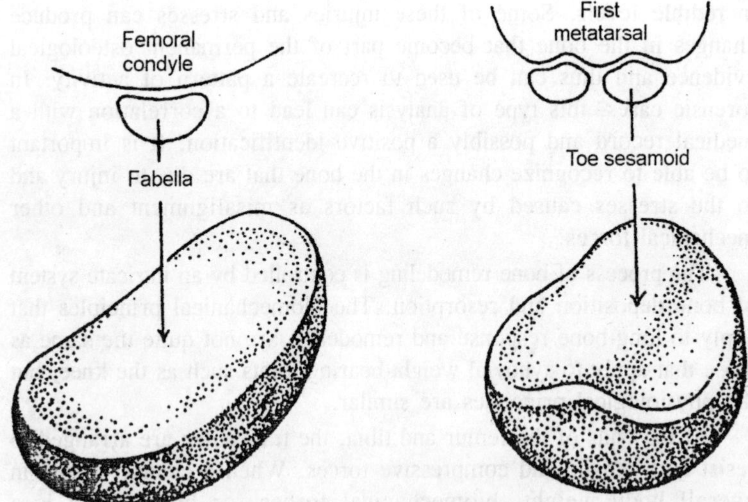

Fig. 13.7. Articular surfaces of a fabella and a toe sesamoid.

mm long and 3.5 mm wide on average but can be as large as 22 mm × 14 mm. Data on the occurrence of a fabella vary greatly; the reported frequency ranges from 9.8 to 22% in the normal population and up to 35% in patients with clinically significant osteoarthritis of the knee. Among individuals who have a fabella, it is bilateral in 71 to 85%.

The anterior surface of the fabella is covered with cartilage and forms an articulation with the posterior surface of the lateral femoral condyle. The fabella articulates with only a portion of the lateral femoral condyle when the knee is in extension, and the concave curve of the fabella touches only a small arc of the condyle. This limited contact area produces a fabella articular surface that curves very gently in both a superior–inferior and a medial–lateral direction. The overall shape of the fabella is variable, but the curve of the anterior articular surface is very consistent and its most distinguishing feature. This curve distinguishes a fabella from a toe sesamoid. Where the toe sesamoid forms a joint with the first metatarsal, the curve is opposite that of the fabella–femur articulation.

Skeletal Evidence of Knee Injury and Stress

The knee is the largest and one of the strongest joints in the human body. It is a major weight-bearing joint and is subjected to stress and injury even during sedentary daily living. During athletic competition and other strenuous activity, the stress is increased to incredible levels. Some of these injuries and stresses can produce changes in the bone that become part of the permanent osteological evidence and thus can be used to recreate a pattern of activity. In forensic cases, this type of analysis can lead to a correlation with a medical record and possibly a positive identification. It is important to be able to recognize changes in the bone that are due to injury and to the stresses caused by such factors as misalignment and other mechanical forces.

The process of bone remodeling is controlled by an intricate system of bone deposition and resorption. The biomechanical principles that apply to long-bone response and remodeling are not quite the same as those that apply to synovial weight-bearing joints such as the knee, but the physiological principles are similar.

At the ends of the femur and tibia, the trabeculae are arranged to resist both tensile and compressive forces. When a change occurs in overall body weight, biomechanical forces, or both, there is a corresponding thickening or thinning of the trabeculae. This change in trabecular thickness, rather than cortical bone remodeling, is the primary stress response at the joint.

Other forces and factors in and around the articular surfaces of weight-bearing joints affect the response to injury and stress. In addition to bone, cartilage is the primary connective tissue involved in and around large synovial joints. Articular cartilage covers the gliding and load-bearing surfaces of the bones; fibrocartilage attaches ligaments and tendons to the bones, and fibroelastic cartilage constitutes the bulk of the interarticular menisci.

The articular cartilage is continuous with the synovium, or synovial membrane. This synovium is a vascular mesenchymal tissue that lines the joint space and produces the joint fluid that serves to lubricate, nourish, and remove cellular debris within the joint capsule.

Trauma to a large synovial joint affects primarily the ligamentous, capsular, and cartilaginous structures, but these in turn can affect the osseous structures because of the action and interaction of all anatomic and biomechanical parts. Trauma to the synovial membrane and cartilaginous surfaces is a contributory factor to the later onset of degenerative arthritis. Miltner et al. pointed out that this synovial membrane becomes congested with small hemorrhages, resulting in the formation of pannus at the osteocartilaginous junction. This causes fibrillar degeneration of the surface layers of cartilage on the side of injury and cell damage and fissuring of the intermediate layer of cells on the opposite side. This latter change is the primary culprit in the onset of late traumatic arthritis.

Ligament injuries may be complete or incomplete. Complete ligament injury will result in demonstrable instability that if left untreated may become permanent and cause irreparable damage to cartilaginous and osseous structures. Repeated microtrauma can lead to the same sequence of hemorrhage, pannus, and fibrillar degeneration.

Postmortem evidence of these injuries and instabilities can be seen in and around the ends of long bones. They are sometimes overlooked or attributed to the general condition of "*arthritis.*" For forensic identification experts, however, it is important to be able to recognize and classify evidence of knee injuries and specific stress that may offer clues leading to identification of the victim.

As a consequence of diagnostic coding protocols that have been established by the health insurance industry, the recognition and exact classification of an injury is often necessary to trace an individual's medical history. The ability to provide autopsy documentation that an individual at one time likely sustained an "acute avulsion of the anterior cruciate ligament" or a "lateral tibial plateau fracture" will prove to be an advantage when attempting to match damaged, decomposed, or skeletal remains with the medical records of missing persons.

Conclusions

Evidence of antemortem injuries and stress usually remains as permanent osteological features in the bone. If recognized and correctly classified, this evidence can become a critical element in the process of victim identification. The first step is to recognize the anatomic or mechanical causation of the defect to identify individual clinical diagnoses that can perhaps be linked to these defects. The second step is to correlate these findings with the medical histories or medical records of suspected missing persons who match the additional criteria of age, race, sex, and stature. The ultimate goal in forensic analysis is, of course, to identify the skeletal remains, and more often than not the final identification will be based on dentition or DNA. Sometimes, however, evidence from the postcranial skeleton can provide critical clues leading to putative identification based on clinical history. In some cases, individual features of the knee can provide the investigator with enough evidence to make a positive identification if there is comparative documentation such as a radiograph, computed tomography, or magnetic resonance imaging.

14

LINEAGE MARKERS

Genetic lineage markers comprise polymorphisms that are present on the maternally inherited mitochondrial genome and the paternally inherited Y chromosome. The analysis of lineage markers is limited in most forensic casework because they do not possess the power of discrimination of autosomal markers. Even so, there are some features of both mtDNA and the Y chromosome that make them valuable forensic markers.

MITOCHONDRIA

The mitochondria are organelles that exist in the cytoplasm of eukaryotic cells. They carry out the vital job of producing approximately 90% of the energy required by the cell through the process of oxidative phosphorylation.

Inheritance of the Mitochondrial Genome

Mitochondria contain their own genome (mtDNA) which is maternally inherited. This was discovered in the 1950s after unusual patterns of inheritance of certain phenotypes were explained by the existence of extra nuclear genomes that did not obey Mendel's laws of inheritance.

During fertilization of an ovum, the sperm penetrates the egg and the sperm midpiece, which contains between 50–75 mitochondria, enters the egg along with the head. The egg has around 1000-times more mitochondria than the sperm. Although some paternal mtDNA enters the ovum it is actively removed. The process is not always completely effective and very rare cases of paternal mtDNA inheritance have been documented.

Copy Number

The mtDNA genome is present in multiple copies – individual cells can contain hundreds of mitochondria and a single human mitochondrion can contain several copies of the genome. Somatic cells, therefore, have thousands of copies of the mitochondrial genome and approximately 1% of total cellular DNA comprises mtDNA. This compares with only two copies per cell of the nuclear genome.

mtDNA Genome

The human mitochondrial genome is a 16569 bp circular molecule. It encodes for 22 *transfer RNAs* (tRNAs), 13 proteins and two ribosomal RNAs (the 12S and 16S rRNA). The majority of mitochondrial proteins is encoded by the nuclear genome as, over hundreds of millions of years, following the formation of the symbiotic relationship between eubacteria and eukaryote cells, most of the genes have been transferred from the mitochondrial to the nuclear genome. Analysis of the human mtDNA genome revealed a very economic use of the DNA and there are very few non-coding bases within the genome except in a region called the *D-loop*. The D-loop is the region of the genome where the initial separation, or displacement, of the two strands of DNA during replication occurs. The regulatory role of the D-loop has led to the other name by which it is known – the control region. It is approximately 1100 bp long.

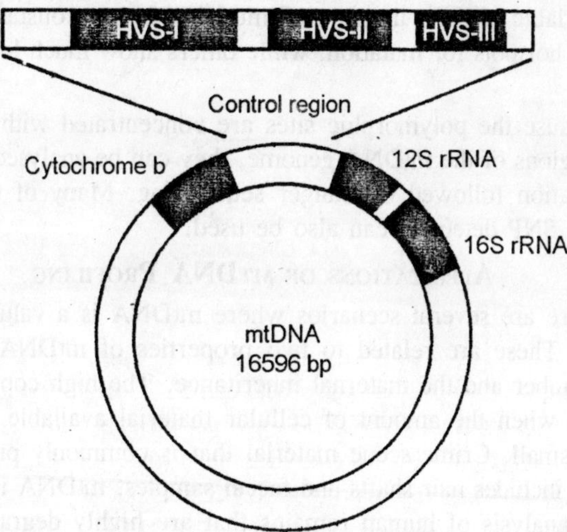

Fig. 14.1. The mitochondrial genome is circular and 16569 bp long. It encodes for 13 proteins, 22 transfer RNAs and two ribosomal RNAs.

Polymorphisms in mtDNA

The mtDNA genome accumulates mutations relatively rapidly as compared with the nuclear genome. The high mutation rate is due in part to the exposure of the mtDNA to reactive oxygen species that are produced as by-products in oxidative phosphorylation. Direct analysis of mother-to-children transmissions has estimated that a mutation in the hypervariable regions is passed from mother to child approximately once in every 30 to 40 events. In the vast majority of cases where a mutation is detected, there is only one base change between the mother and child.

Hypervariable Regions

In most forensic investigations the aim of DNA profiling is to differentiate between individuals, therefore the most polymorphic regions are analysed. Following the sequencing of the human mtDNA genome it was apparent that the D-loop was not under the same functional constraints as the rest of the genome. Some blocks within the control region are highly conserved but large parts are not. Two main regions are the focus of most forensic studies, these are known as hypervariable sequence regions I and II (HVS-I and HVS-II) and they contain the highest levels of variation within the mtDNA genome. Both the hypervariable blocks are approximately 350 bp long. A third hypervariable region, HVS-III has also been used in some cases. Within the hypervariable regions the rate of mutation is not constant and some sites are hotspots for mutation, while others show much lower rates of change.

Because the polymorphic sites are concentrated within relatively small regions of the mtDNA genome, they can be analysed using PCR amplification followed by Sanger sequencing. Many of the methods used for SNP detection can also be used.

Applications of mtDNA Profiling

There are several scenarios where mtDNA is a valuable genetic marker. These are related to two properties of mtDNA – the high copy number and the maternal inheritance. The high copy number is valuable when the amount of cellular material available for analysis is very small. Crime scene material that is commonly profiled using mtDNA includes hair shafts and faecal samples. mtDNA is also useful for the analysis of human remains that are highly degraded and not amenable to standard STR typing. The maternal inheritance is a useful trait for human identification when there are no direct relatives to use

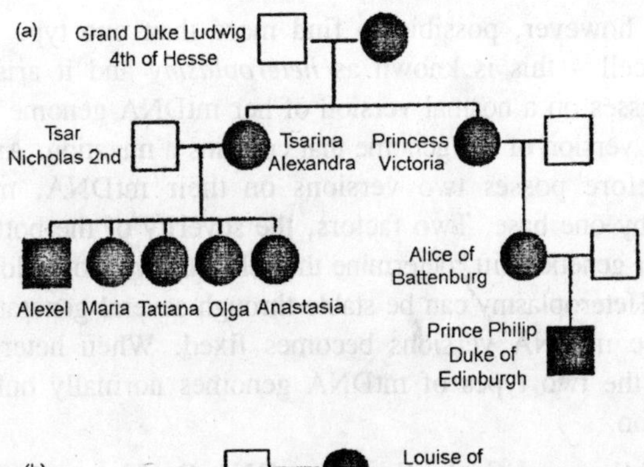

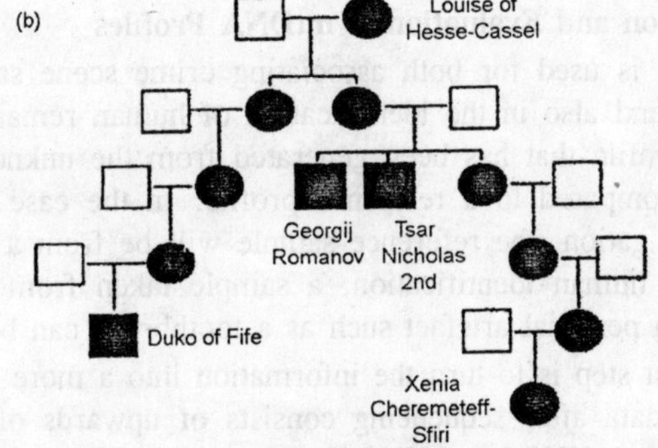

Fig. 14.2. The family tree of the Romanov royal family. (a) The maternal lineage of the Tsarina and her children. (b) The maternal lineage of Tsar Nicholas.

as a reference sample – the identification of some of the Romanov family using Prince Philip as a reference sample provides a powerful illustration of the use of maternal inheritance.

A series of historical cases has followed that demonstrates the application of mtDNA when linking relatives to human remains.

Homoplasmy and Heteroplasmy

Normally an individual contains only one type of mtDNA – this is termed *homoplasmy*. Mutations will inevitably occur within some of the thousands of copies of mtDNA within a cell and if these mutated copies of the genome were passed on to future generations, a mixture of different mtDNA genomes would occur. The process that maintains homoplasmy as the norm is not precisely understood but at some point a genetic bottleneck occurs before the formation of a mature oocyte. The bottleneck allows only a few mtDNA molecules to pass into the oocyte during its formation, thereby reducing the possibility of passing on a mixture of wild type and mutant genomes.

It is, however, possible to find more than one type of mtDNA within a cell – this is known as *heteroplasmy* and it arises when a mother passes on a normal version of her mtDNA genome (wild type) and also a version of the genome that contains a mutation. An individual will therefore posses two versions on their mtDNA, maybe only differing by one base. Two factors, the severity of the bottleneck and subsequent genetic drift, determine the relative levels of wild to mutated mtDNA. Heteroplasmy can be stable through several generations before one of the mtDNA versions becomes fixed. When heteroplasmy is detected, the two types of mtDNA genomes normally only differ at one position.

Interpretation and Evaluation of mtDNA Profiles

mtDNA is used for both associating crime scene samples with individuals and also in the identification of human remains. In both cases the profile that has been generated from the unknown sample has to be compared to a reference profile. In the case of a crime scene investigation, the reference sample will be from a suspect. In the case of human identification, a sample taken from a maternal relative or a personal artefact such as a toothbrush can be used.

The first step is to turn the information into a more manageable form. The data after sequencing consists of upwards of 350 DNA bases from both HVS-I and HVS-II and around 150 bases from HVS-III. Once the sequencing data have been checked to ensure that there is confidence in the sequence data and no errors, it is compared to the Cambridge Reference Sequence (CRS). The CRS was the first complete sequence of the mtDNA genome to be published in 1981. Differences between the questioned sequence and the CRS are noted and only these differences are recorded. The mtDNA profile is called a *haplotype*.

Declaring a match is straight forward but exclusions can be more problematic. When a questioned sample and a reference sample differ at only one position the likelihood of that one base difference occurring though a mutation has to be assessed. In such an instance the results are usually classified as inconclusive – when there are two or more differences between a questioned and known sample it is normally classified as an exclusion.

If a match is declared, the statistical significance of the match has to be assessed. The mtDNA genome is inherited as a single locus and this limits the evidential value of the marker in forensic cases. Haplotype frequencies have to be measured directly by counting the occurrence of a particular haplotype in a database and reporting the size of the database. When databases are relatively small, for example 100, many of the less common haplotypes that are within a population will not be represented. There are mechanisms that compensate for the limitations of reference databases, such as minimum haplotype frequencies, and employing standard error calculations and correction factors to allow for subpopulations.

When reporting the results of mtDNA analysis, the caveats associated with mtDNA have to be clearly explained so that there is no confusion with 'standard' (autosomal STR typing) analysis. In particular that 'it is inherited only from one's mother, and therefore all individuals who are related by a maternal link will have the same mtDNA profile', and that 'it varies less between individuals, and therefore more individuals chosen at random from the population will have the same mtDNA profile' should be made very clear.

Y Chromosome

In humans the Y chromosome is approximately 60 Mb long (million base pairs) long and contains just 78 genes. The SRY gene (sex-determining region Y) located on the Y chromosome encodes a protein that triggers the development of the testes and through an extended hormonal pathway causes a developing foetus to become male.

With the exception of two regions, PAR 1 and 2 (PAR = pseudoautosomal region), located at the tips of the chromosome, no recombination occurs during meiosis. The remaining 95% of theY chromosome is non-recombining, male specific, and is passed from father to son unchanged, except when mutations occur. The lack of recombination may be the reason why there are relatively few genes on the Y chromosome. If there is no chromosome crossing over, mutations within genes have little chance to be repaired or rectified and hence will be passed onto the next generation.

Y Chromosome Polymorphisms

The Y chromosome contains a large number of polymorphisms including variable number and short tandem repeats (VNTRs and STRs), insertions, deletions and *single nucleotide polymorphisms* (SNPs).

The first STR locus to be identified on the Y chromosome was DYS19. Since then hundreds of Y chromosome STR have been described. The development of Y STR typing has mirrored the development of the autosomal STRs, and multiplexes have been developed with increasing numbers of robust and highly discriminating Y STR multiplexes. The growth in interest in Y STR loci has led to numerous population studies to establish allele frequency databases. The 'Y Chromosome Haplotype Reference Database' was established to collate STR haplotypes. To ensure comparability between datasets, minimal and extended haplotypes were defined. Two commercial kits, the PowerPlex Y and the AmpF*l*STR Yfiler incorporate all of the extended haplotype loci.

Table 14.1. The Y chromosome STR loci that are commonly used in forensic analysis

Minimal haplotype	*Extended haplotype*	*PowerPlex Y*	*AmpFlSTR Yfiler*
DYS19	DYS19	DYS19	DYS19
DYS385 a/b	DYS385 a/b	DYS385 a/b	DYS385
DYS389 I	DYS389 I	DYS389 I	DYS389 I
DYS389 II	DYS389 II	DYS389 II	DYS389 II
DYS390	DYS390	DYS390	DYS390
DYS391	DYS391	DYS391	DYS391
DYS392	DYS392	DYS392	DYS392
DYS393	DYS393	DYS393	DYS393
	DYS438	DYS437	DYS437
	DYS439	DYS438	DYS438
		DYS439	DYS439
			DYS448
			DYS456
			DYS458
			DYS635
			GATA H4

Forensic Applications of Y Chromosome Polymorphisms

That theY chromosome is only found in males makes it a valuable tool, in particular for the analysis of male and female mixtures after sexual assaults when differential DNA extraction is not possible; Y STR analysis has been successful with female:male ratios of up to 2000:1. The presence of male DNA has also been detected when vaginal swabs are analysed, even when no spermatozoa have been detected – either through the assailant being azoospermic (1–2% of rape cases) or through the deterioration of the spermatozoa. The Y STRs can also be used to detect the presence of two male profiles – the interpretation of the mixtures depends on the presence of major and minor contributors.

In addition to using Y chromosome testing for the identification of evidential samples, it has also been used for paternity testing and is particularly valuable in deficient cases, where the alleged father is not available for testing. In these cases, any male relative who is paternally related to the alleged father can be used as a reference. An extreme example of where this has been used is the paternity analysis that linked the third US president, Thomas Jefferson to the child of one of his slaves, Sally Hemings. Cases involving human identification have also used theY chromosome as a tool to link remains to paternal family members, and as with deficient paternity cases the use of the Y chromosome is particularly advantageous when there are no parents or children to use as reference material; it also simplifies the sorting of the material following mass disasters. The mutation rate in Y STR loci is similar to autosomal STRs, at approximately 2.8×10^{-3}. The Y chromosome will accumulate mutations as it is passed through the patrilineal line and direct comparison between males on the same lineage may result in a false exclusion if mutations are not considered.

The non-random distribution of the Y chromosome among global populations, due largely to the widespread practice of patrilocality (where the female moves to the male's birth place/residence after marriage), makes it a useful tool for inferring the geographical origins of biological material recovered from a crime scene and human remains. In some cultures, where the male name is passed onto male children, there is also the potential of attributing surnames to Y profiles.

Interpretation and Evaluation of Y STR Profiles

When the Y chromosome profiles from a reference and an unknown sample match, the significance of the match has to be assessed. The first step is to assess the frequencies of the Y STR haplotypes in the population of interest. The simplest method is to report the frequency of the Y STR haplotype in the population, known as the counting method. The figure quoted is entirely dependent upon the size of the database and is normally based on frequency databases that are constructed for the major ethnic groups represented within individual countries, although comparisons can also be made to the combined data in the yhrd databases with over 40000 haplotypes (representing at least the minimal haplotype). So, for example, a match can be reported as 'the haplotype has been seen twice in 400 UK Caucasian individuals'.

Difficulties arise in the interpretation of theY chromosome. This is primarily caused by the patrilineal inheritance and clustering of male family members in relatively small geographic areas. This geographical clustering of male relatives coupled with the limited size of the haplotype frequency databases (many haplotypes are seen only once) makes the estimation of profile frequencies hazardous. An alternative method for assessing the significance of a match is to use a likelihood ratio and to incorporate population subdivisions with the increased potential for common co-ancestry. Regardless of the method used to calculate the matching frequency, when presenting the results of Y chromosome analysis, as with mtDNA, there is a need clearly to state how the use of Y STR typing varies from that of autosomal markers and that there will be other males in the population with the same Y STR haplotype.

15

Programmed Cell Death

Phosphatidylserine Oxidation

Membrane phospholipids are gaining increasing attention as important mediators in a variety of signal transduction processes. Oxidation and changes in membrane topography of lipids are probably important elements in the regulation of phospholipid-dependent signaling. *Phosphatidylserine* (PS), in particular, is implicated in the regulation of macrophage-dependent clearance of apoptotic cell "*corpses*" in a pathway probably mediated by selective oxidation and translocation of PS in the plasma membrane. Here we describe our highly sensitive and specific assay to measure differential lipid peroxidation in individual phospholipid classes in live cells using metabolic integration of the fluorescent oxidation-sensitive fatty acid analog *cis*-parinaric acid (*cis*-PnA) and resolution of specific phospholipids by *high-performance liquid chromatography* (HPLC). These experimental approaches can provide insight into the roles and mechanisms of PS oxidation in the identification and clearance of apoptotic cells.

Oxidative stress has been implicated as a functional component of the final common pathway of apoptosis execution, but the precise molecular events responsible for redox signaling and their functional consequences remain elusive. Membrane phospholipids are gaining increasing importance in our understanding of cell signaling phenomenon; by virtue of their content of polyunsaturated fatty acids, they are extremely sensitive to modification by low levels of oxidative stress. Thus, oxidation of various membrane phospholipids could play a role in the initiation or regulation of programmed cell death. To characterize phospholipid oxidation during apoptosis more fully, we utilized *cis-parinaric acid* (*cis*-PnA), a naturally derived highly fluorescent fatty acid to label phospholipids metabolically in live cells. The presence of an extensive conjugated double-bond system in *cis*-PnA renders it highly sensitive to oxidation, with concomitant loss of its intrinsic fluorescence. Thus, comparison of the fluorescent content of various cellular derived phospholipid classes following their resolution by *high-performance liquid chromatography* (HPLC) can be used to assess site-selective phospholipid oxidation in the presence of various apoptotic stimuli. Using 32D cells, we first described the selective oxidation of *phosphatidylserine* (PS) during paraquat-induced apoptosis. Selective oxidation occurred early in the course of apoptosis, preceded PS externalization, and was blocked by over-expression of the antiapoptotic protein BCL-2. Further studies revealed that apoptosis-related PS oxidation was insensitive to vitamin E analogs, suggesting that PS oxidation proceeds via a unique mechanism different from randomly directed chain reactions among membrane lipids. More recently, we confirmed that specific PS oxidation occurred in a multitude of cell types following a variety of stimuli, including those not directly associated with the ability to cause oxidative stress, such as Fas/FasL ligation and staurosporine. Thus, PS oxidation appears to be a nearly universal feature of apoptosis. Although its exact function remains elusive, we hypothesize that it may, in part, regulate PS translocation and/or its recognition by phagocytic macrophage. The utilization of directed oxidation of select phospholipids may represent a previously unappreciated feature of lipid-based signal transduction systems.

We describe here our highly sensitive method to measure oxidation in specific phospholipid classes based on the metabolic incorporation of *cis*-PnA. Its utility arises from the fact that it can report exceedingly low levels of oxidation in live cells, even in the presence of efficient phospholipid repair. We believe that this technique will greatly aid in studying the mechanistic connection between lipid peroxidation and translocation events during apoptosis.

Materials

Preparation of cis-PnA/hSA complex

1. cis-PnA: 9Z, 11E, 13E, 15Z-octadecatetraenoic acid.
2. Dimethyl sulfoxide (DMSO).
3. Fatty acid-free *human serum albumin* (hSA).
4. Phosphate-buffered saline (PBS).
5. 0.45-μm Filter.

Metabolic labeling of cells with cis-PnA

1. Cells of interest.
2. Incubation media (tissue culture media formulation usually used for maintenance of the cell line of interest), without phenol red and fetal bovine serum.
3. Trypan blue, 0.4% solution.
4. Hemocytometer.
5. Tabletop centrifuge.
6. 37°C, 5% CO_2-Tissue culture incubator.
7. 0.5 mg/mL hSA in medium.
8. 15- and 50-mL Polypropylene centrifuge tubes.

Lipid extraction

1. PBS.
2. Tabletop centrifuge.
3. Methanol (HPLC grade).
4. Butylated hydroxytoluene (ACS grade or higher).
5. Chloroform (HPLC grade).
6. Evaporation apparatus.
7. 0.1 M NaCl.
8. Vortex.
9. 4:3:0.16 (v/v/v) Isopropanol/hexane/water (all HPLC grade).
10. 13 × 100-mm Pyrex glass test tubes with screw-cap.

HPLC resolution of phospholipid classes

1. Shimadzu LC-600 high-performance liquid chromatograph equipped with in-line fluorescence detector and UV-VIS detector. Apparatus is interfaced to a PC computer capable of acquiring the UV and fluorescence data in digital form and running Shimadzu EZChrom software.
2. 5 μm Supelcosil LC-Si column.
3. 100-μL Glass microsyringe for HPLC sample injection.
4. Solvent A: 56:42:2 isopropanol/hexane/water.
5. Solvent B: 54:41:10 isopropanol/hexane/40 nM ammonium acetate.
6. Programmable automated gradient maker (low-pressure mixing LPH-600).
7. Spectrofluorometer.
8. Spectrophotometer.

Determination of total lipid phosphorus

1. Cell culture disposable glass tubes.
2. Evaporation apparatus.
3. $HClO_4$.
4. Heating apparatus to achieve 170–180°C.
5. 4.2% Sodium molybdate (ACS grade or higher) in 1:3 5 M HCl/ 0.2% malachite green (ACS grade or higher).
6. 1.5% Tween-20.
7. Spectrophotometer.
8. NaH_2PO_4.

Determination of inorganic phosphorus content of specific phospholipid classes

1. Obtain a set of phospholipid standards: cardiolipin (CL), phosphatidylcholine (PC), phosphatidyl-ethanoloamine (PE), phosphatidylinositol (PS), sphingomyelin, diphosphatidylglycerol, and lysophosphatidylcholine.
2. 5 × 5-cm Whatman silica G thin-layer chromatography plates.
3. Chromatography chambers.
4. 65:25:5 chloroform/methanol/28% ammonium hydroxide (HPLC grade).
5. Appropriate "*forced air blower*".
6. 50:20:10:10:5 chloroform/acetone/methanol/glacial acetic acid/water (all HPLC grade).
7. Iodine crystals.
8. 13 × 100-mm Borosilicate glass tubes.
9. 70% Perchloric acid (ACS grade).
10. Heating apparatus to achieve 170–180°C and 90–100°C.
11. 2.5% Sodium molybdate.
12. 10% Ascorbic acid.
13. Tabletop centrifuge.
14. Spectrophotometer.

Methods

Preparation of cis-PnA/hSA complex

1. Dissolve *cis*-PnA in DMSO to a final concentration of 20 mg/mL.
2. Add 1.8 μmol *cis*-PnA in 25 μL to 50 mg hSA (760 nmol) in 1 mL of PBS.

3. Incubate this reaction mixture for 30 min at room temperature, then filter (0.45 mm). Aliquot solution, and store frozen at –80°C until use.

Metabolic labeling of cells with cis-PnA

1. Obtain cells from cultures in late log phase growth, and determine cell number and viability using trypan blue exclusion and a hemacytometer.
2. Wash suspension cells twice with centrifugation (400g, 10 min) in incubation medium, and then resuspend to a density of 1 × 10^6/mL. Similarly, rinse monolayer cultures with two changes of incubation medium, and then add 10 mL (for a 75-cm^2 flask) or 3 mL incubation medium.
3. Add cis-PnA/hSA complex to a final concentration of 1–5 μg/mL, and incubate for 2 h at 37°C in a tissue culture incubator.
4. Wash labeled cells once with incubation medium containing 0.5 mg/mL fatty acid-freeh-SA, and again without hSA.
5. Resuspend cell pellets or monolayers in a medium appropriate to apply an apoptotic (or other) stimulus, and incubate for desired times prior to lipid extractions.

Lipid extraction

1. Obtain approx 1 × 10^6 cells, wash once in PBS, and resuspend or scrape in 1 mL PBS.
2. Centrifuge cell suspensions (400g, 10 min), resuspend in 3 mL methanol containing 0.1 mg butylated hydroxytoluene, mix with 3 mL chloroform, then place under nitrogen atmosphere on ice in the dark for 1 h. Add 0.1 mL of 0.1 M NaCl to each sample, and vortex vigorously.
3. Collect the bottom chloroform layer after separation by centrifugation (1500g, 5 min), and evaporate to dryness under oxygen-free N2.
4. Dissolve the resultant lipid film in 0.2 mL 4:3:0.16 (v/v/v) isopropanol/hexane/water.

HPLC resolution of phospholipid classes

1. Prepare a dilution series of *cis*-PnA solutions for generation of standard curve (1, 2, 4, 6, 8, and 10 ng/100 μL prepared in 4:3:0.16 [v/v/v] isopropanol/hexane/water).
2. Apply a 100-μL sample of lipid extract to the injector port of an HPLC apparatus equipped with a 5-μm Supelcosil LC-Si column (4.6 × 250 mm) equilibrated with 1:9 solvent A: solvent B.

3. Elute the column using a preprogrammed automated gradient maker for 3 min with a linear gradient from 10% solvent B to 37% solvent B, then 3–15 min with isocratic 37% solvent B, 15–23 min with a linear gradient to 100% solvent B, and finally 23–45 min with isocratic solvent B. Apply the mobile phase at a flow rate of 1 mL/min.

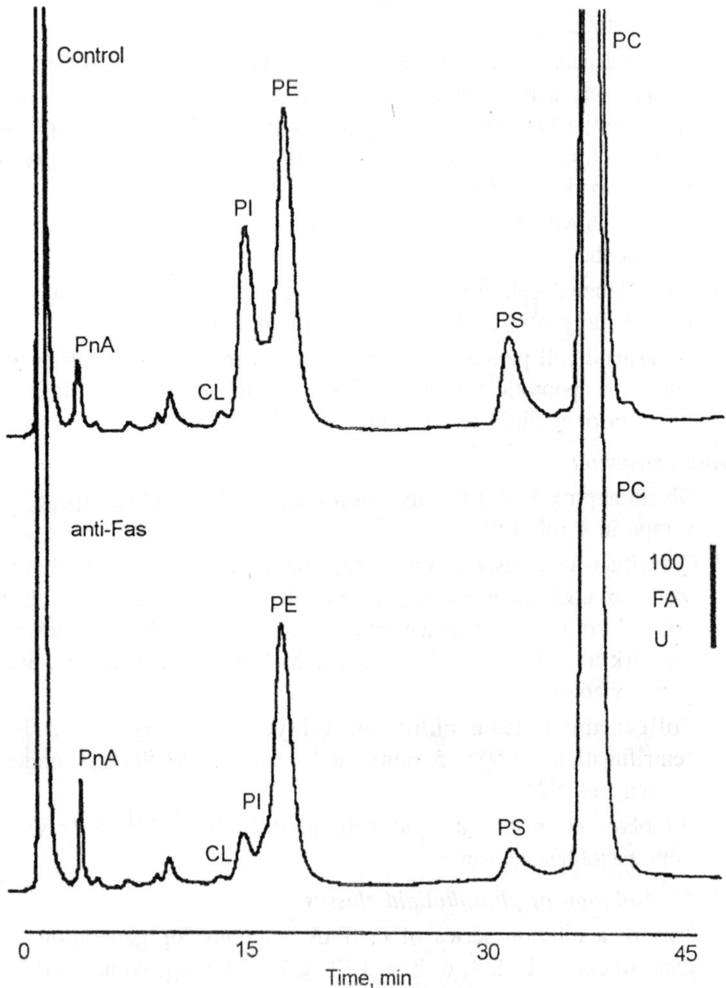

Fig. 15.1. HPLC chromatograms of cis-PnA-labeled phospholipids derived from control (top tracing) and anti-Fas-treated Jurkat cells (bottom tracing). CL, cardiolipin; PC, phosphatidylcholine; PE, phosphatidylethanoloamine; PI, inorganic phosphorus; PnA, parinaric acid; PS, phosphatidylserine.

4. Monitor the column effluent simultaneously for *cis*-PnA fluorescence at emission wavelength 420 nm after excitation at 324 nm, as well as absorbance at 205 nm for total lipids.
5. Determine the *cis*-PnA content of each phospholipid class by calculating the fluorescent peak area using EZChrom software and comparison with the standard curve constructed using various amounts *cis*-PnA alone.
6. Normalize the amount of *cis*-PnA fluorescence in each individual phospholipid class to the amount of inorganic phosphorous (Pi) contained in the total lipid extract (relative PnA oxidation), as well as the Pi content of the individual phospholipid class (specific PnA oxidation) determined from parallel *high-performance thin-layer chromatography* (HP-TLC) plates.

Determination of total and specific lipid phosphorus

1. Prepare a dilution series of NaH_2PO_4 of four to six concentrations between 1 and 10 nmol to generate a standard curve.
2. Pipet 50-μL aliquots of lipid extracts into test tubes, and evaporate the solvent to dryness under oxygen-free N2.
3. Add 50 μL of $HClO_4$ to the dried samples, and incubate for 20 min at 170–180°C.
4. Prepare a stock solution of 200 mM NaH_2PO_4 in water. To generate a standard curve, pipet 100, 60, 40, 20, and 10 μL into separate tubes in duplicate, corresponding to 10, 6, 4, 2, and 1 nmol phosphate. Add water to yield a final volume of 4 mL.
5. After allowing the samples to cool, add 0.4 mL of water to each tube followed by 2 mL sodium molybdate-malachite green reagent solution and 80 μL of 1.5% Tween-20.
6. Shake the tubes immediately to stabilize the developed color, and quantify at 660 nm in a spectrophotometer.
7. Determine Pi content by comparison with the linear standard curve. Fluorescence can be normalized to the total amount of lipid phosphorus in each sample for determination of relative content of *cis*-PnA in each phospholipid class.

Determination of Pi content of specific phospholipid classes

1. Activate HP-TLC plates by heating for 20 min at 120°C to remove all traces of H_2O.
2. Spot 20-μL aliquots of lipid extracts onto Whatman silica G TLC plates (5 × 5 cm), and allow to air-dry.

3. Spot similar preparations of phospholipid standards for comparison with experimental samples (e.g., 2.5 mg each per phospholipid).
4. Perform 2D HP-TLC by development of the spotted TLC plate(s) in the first dimension using 65:25:5 (v/v/v) chloroform/methanol/ 28% ammonium hydroxide. After removing the first solvent using a forced air blower, the TLC plate is rotated 90° and developed in the second dimension with 50:20:10:10:5 (v/v/v/v/v) chloroform/ acetone/methanol/glacial acetic acid/water.
5. Place the plate in a chromatographic tank containing approx 0.5 g iodine crystals until dark spots corresponding to resolved lipids are observed. The length of time required depends on the age and amount of iodine crystals. Identify specific phospholipid classes by comparison with migration of authentic phospholipid standards. Scrape the spots corresponding to specific phospholipid classes from the plates, and transfer them to 13 × 100-mm borosilicate disposable glass tubes.
6. Add 125 mL of 70% perchloric acid to each silica gel sample, and heat to 175–180°C.
7. After cooling, add 825 μL of H_2O to each tube, followed by 125 μL 2.5% sodium molybdate, followed by 125 μL 10% ascorbic acid. Vortex immediately, and then heat to 90–100°C.
8. After cooling, clarify samples by centrifugation at 1000g for 5–10 min, and measure the absorbance of the supernatant at 797 nm. The Pi content of the samples is derived from comparison with the standard curve constructed with known amounts of NaH_2PO_4.

Notes

1. The purity of each batch of *cis*-PnA is determined by UV spectroscopy using the molar extinction $e_{304\ nm\ (EtOH)} = 80 \times 10^3$/ mM/cm.
2. Suspension cells (7–10 × 10^5 cells per mL) or monolayer cells (70–80% confluence) can be used. The number of cells and wells/ dishes required depends on the number of desired experimental points. Cell number and viability for monolayer cultures can be obtained after trypsinization of parallel plates or wells set up identically to those for *cis*-PnA assay. Lipids derived from approx 1 × 10^6 cells provide enough material designated for a single sample subjected to HPLC and fluorescent quantification.
3. We originally utilized L1210 buffer (115 mM NaCl, 5 mM KCl, 1 mM $MgCl_2$, 5 mM NaH_2PO_4, 10 mM glucose, and 25 mM

HEPES, pH 7.4) but have found that other medium formulations such as RPMI-1640 and KGM-2 (keratinocyte growth medium) are compatible with incorporation of *cis*-PnA, provided they are utilized in the absence of fetal calf serum and phenol red.

4. It is necessary to derive the appropriate *cis*-PnA concentration empirically for each cell line to achieve maximal metabolic incorporation, while minimizing any potential toxicity of *cis*-PnA.
5. Some knowledge of the time-course and conditions for apoptosis is useful in designing the experiment. We usually restrict our incubations to no more than 2 h. The study of certain stimuli with prolonged induction of apoptosis, such as growth factor withdrawal, may be problematic given the confounding factors of basal spontaneous oxidation of *cis*-PnA and the continuing synthesis of new unlabeled phospholipids. Most stimuli that we have applied have an observable apoptotic response (changes in nuclear morphology, DNA fragmentation) in about 4–8 h and show selective PS oxidation within 2 h.
6. Media formulation may be important, as the presence of serum or other defined growth factors may be required to prevent apoptosis in the control untreated cells. For example, when using the interleukin-3 (IL-3)-dependent cell line 32D, we utilized media containing 10% media preconditioned by WeHi 3B cells as a source of IL-3.
7. Cells can be stored at –80°C at this point until lipid extraction.
8. We have also found a 5-mm (4.5 × 250-mm) Microsorb-MV column from Rainin to be suitable.
9. It is strongly recommended that each laboratory calibrate the migration of specific phospholipid classes using purified authenticated standards.

Phosphatidylserine Externalization

We present here the application of a novel assay that measures the absolute amount of *phosphatidylserine* (PS) externalized on the surface of cells. Although the assay is based on the same annexin binding principle as the fluorescent flow cytometry assay, we use paramagnetic iron as the ultimate reporter molecule, establishing a linear relationship between signal amplitude and amount of PS on the cell surface, allowing a quantitative assay of PS externalization over a wide dynamic range. The application of this technique, alone and in concert with the PS oxidation method presented previously, will greatly aid in studying the mechanistic connection between lipid peroxidation and translocation events during apoptosis.

A characteristic of nearly all normal cells is the maintenance of an asymmetric distribution of phospholipids across cell membranes. Under normal conditions, *phosphatidylcholine* (PC) and sphingomyelin (SPH) are located primarily in the outer leaflet of plasma membrane, whereas aminophospholipids—phosphatidylethanolamine (PE) and phosphatidylserine (PS)—are found almost entirely in the inner leaflet. One of the hallmarks of apoptosis, however, is the translocation and externalization of PS, where it serves as a target for recognition and engulfment by phagocytic macrophages. Because externalized PS can bind the protein annexin V with high affinity in a Ca^{2+}-dependent manner, the use of fluorescently labeled annexin V has formed the basis for a widely used assay to enumerate apoptotic cells. However, this flow cytometric approach provides little information regarding the absolute amounts of PS appearing on the cell surface and does not report any structural modifications to the PS molecule that may be coincident with its externalization.

Although it is clear that profound redistribution of membrane phospholipids accompanies apoptosis, the quantitative aspects of PS externalization have received little attention. The flow cytometric-based assay using the fluorescent-labeled cell-impermeable protein annexin V was designed to assess the number of apoptotic cells with externalized PS rather than quantify the amount of externalized PS available for annexin binding. Another approach involves chemical modification of aminophospholipids with cellimpermeable reagents for primary amines such as fluorescamine or trinitrobenzene sulfonic acid, followed by subsequent chromatographic separation of the modified PS and PE. This approach is time-consuming, lacks sensitivity, and requires ultimate lysis of the target cells. For this reason, we sought to develop a novel sensitive and specific quantitative assay for PS externalization on cell surfaces using annexin V-conjugated iron nanoparticles. These magnetic microbeads have been developed to isolate apoptotic cells physically from a mixed cell population by application of a magnetic field. We, however, exploited the paramagnetic properties of iron in order to quantify annexin V binding using *electron paramagnetic resonance* (EPR) spectroscopy. We have effectively used this approach to measure PS externalization on normal and apoptotic cells, as well as incorporation of exogenous PS into the plasma membrane. The amount of externalized PS on the surface of normal Jurkat and HL-60 cells is approx 1 pmol/10^6 cells. Treatment of Jurkat and HL-60 cells with camptothecin induces apoptosis with 240 pmol externalized PS/10^6 cells and 30 pmol PS/10^6 cells, respectively. Using naive cells with exogenously applied PS, it appears that only 20–40 pmol PS/10^6 cells is sufficient to trigger recognition and phagocytosis by macrophages.

Materials

Preparation of PS-containing liposomes

1. Phospholipids: 1-palmitoyl (C16:0)-2-arachidonyl (C20:4)-3-phosphatidylserine (PS) and phosphatidylcholine from brain.
2. Chloroform (high-performance liquid chromatography [HPLC] grade).
3. 13 × 100-mm Borosilicate glass tubes.
4. Evaporation apparatus.
5. Phosphate-buffered saline (PBS).
6. Vortex.
7. Sonicator.
8. Microcentrifuge tubes.

Incorporation of PS into plasma membrane

1. Cells of interest.
2. Incubation media: tissue culture media formulation usually used for maintenance of the cell line of interest.
3. Trypan blue.
4. Hemocytometer.
5. Appropriate centrifuge.
6. PBS.
7. N-ethylmaleimide (NEM).
8. Appropriate means of incubating cells and phospholipids at 37°C.

HP-TLC assay for evaluation of externalized PS by labeling with fluorescamine

1. Labeling buffer: 150 mM NaCl, 5 mM KCl, 1 mM $MgCl_2$, 2 mM $CaCl_2$, 5 mM $NaHCO_3$, 5 mM glucose, 20 mM HEPES, pH 8.0.
2. Fluorescamine (ACS grade or higher).
3. 40 mM Tris-HCl, pH 7.4.
4. Bio-Rad Fluor-S MultiImager or other apparatus to allow UV visualization of fluorescamine-labeled PS on high-performance thin-layer liquid chromatography (HP-TLC) plates.

Annexin V-microbead EPR assay for quantification of externalized PS

1. Annexin V-microbead apoptosis detection kit and Basic microbeads.
2. 0.1% Bovine serum albumin (BSA; fraction V, fatty acid-free).
3. Gas-permeable Teflon tubing.
4. Appropriate EPR quartz tube.
5. JEOL RE1X EPR spectrometer.

Annexin V-FITC flow cytometric assay for quantification of cells with externalized PS

1. Annexin V-microbead apoptosis detection kit and Basic microbeads.
2. Propidium iodide (PI).
3. Annexin V-fluorescein isothiocyanate (FITC).
4. Flow cytometer.

Methods

Relative PS externalization on the cell surface can be simply determined by labeling cells with annexin V-microbeads followed by analysis by EPR spectroscopy. To establish the absolute amounts of PS_{ext}, however, one needs to prepare cells with known amounts of PS_{ext} on their surface and calibrate the resultant EPR signal of annexin V-microbeads. To this end, cells are coincubated with PC/PS liposomes to incorporate various amounts of PS into the plasma membrane. To ensure that all exogenous PS remains on the cell surface, the cells are pretreated with NEM, a thiol-specific reagent shown to poison the PS-internalizing activity of aminophospholipid translocase metabolically. PS-enriched cells are then analyzed by both EPR-based annexin–iron bead assay and by HP-TLC assay of surface PS derivatized with fluorescamine to create a calibration curve of EPR signal vs amount of PS_{ext}. Finally, the traditional annexin V-FITC flow cytometry assay can be applied for discriminating and quantifying cells with high and low levels of externalized PS, so that the amount of PS_{ext} obtained by EPR-based assay can be recalculated per number of cells that externalize high levels of PS.

Preparation of PS-containing liposomes

1. Dissolve purified phospholipids (PC and PS) in chloroform (100 mM final concentration). Frozen stocks can stored at –80°C for at least 2 mo.
2. Make small unilamellar liposomes by making a 1:1 mix of the PC and PS stocks in a glass tube by adding 2.52 μmol (25.2 μL) of each phospholipid stock (2.4 μmol are required for analysis of

fluorescamine-labeled PS by HP-TLC, and 0.12 μmol are required for EPR assay).

3. Evaporate chloroform from the liposome preparations under a stream of compressed nitrogen.
4. Add 5.0 mL PBS for a final concentration of 1 mM total lipids, and then mix the lipid mixture by vortexing vigorously.
5. Sonicate liposomes five times for 30 s on ice using a microtip and 20% output.
6. Prepare aliquots of liposomes in the following concentrations: 1 mM, 750 μM, 500 μM, 250 μM, 125 μM. (Concentrations in aliquots are five-fold greater than final concentration in solution with cells.) The total volume of each aliquot should be at least 1.68 mL (1.6 mL for HP-TLC and 0.08 mL for the EPR assay).

Incorporation of PS into plasma membrane

1. Obtain cells from cultures in late log phase growth, and determine cell number and viability using trypan blue exclusion and a hemacytometer.
2. Wash suspension cells or harvested monolayer culture cells (method appropriate to cell type) twice with centrifugation (1000g) in incubation medium, and then resuspend in PBS at a density of 6.25×10^6 cells/mL The number of cells required for one series of measurements for a complete calibration curve is 252×10^6 cells (249×10^6 for HP-TLC and 12×10^6 for the EPR assay.
3. Treat cells with 10–50 μM NEM for 5 min at 37°C to inhibit aminophospholipid translocase activity.
4. To incorporate phospholipids into plasma membrane of cells, incubate cells with the indicated amounts (25, 50, 100, 150, and 200 μM) of the PS-containing liposomes (4 parts of cell solution to 1 part liposomes, prepared as described above) for 30 min at 37°C. Sample volume for each experimental point is 8.4 mL (8 mL for HP-TLC and 0.4 mL for the EPR assay).
5. Remove unincorporated liposomes by washing cells twice with 1 mL PBS and centrifugation for 1000g for 5 min.

HP-TLC assay for evaluation of externalized PS by labeling with fluorescamine

1. Resuspend 4×10^7 cells in 2 mL labeling buffer. Add 2 μL of 200 mM fluorescamine dissolved in dimethylsulfoxide (DMSO) to a final concentration of 200 μM, and agitate cells gently for 15 s. Add 3 mL of 40 mM Tris-HCl, pH 7.4.

2. Centrifuge cells (1000g for 5 min), and extract lipids.
3. Separate specific phospholipid classes using HP-TLC.
4. Localize fluorescamine-modified PS (mPS) on an HP-TLC plate by exposure to UV light using a Fluor-S MultiImager. Unmodified phospholipids can be localized by visible light after exposure of HP-TLC plates to iodine vapor. The identities of specific phospholipid species are determined by comparison with purified standards.
5. Determine the inorganic phosphorus (Pi) content of the externalized and nonexternalized PS.

Annexin V-microbead EPR assay for quantification of externalized PS

1. Obtain cells from cultures in late log phase growth, and determine cell number and viability using trypan blue exclusion and a hemacytometer.
2. Wash suspension cells or harvested monolayer culture cells (method appropriate to cell type) twice with centrifugation (1000g) in incubation medium, and then wash 2×10^6 cells twice in 1 mL 1X Binding Buffer.
3. Resuspend cells in 40 μL of Binding Buffer, and incubate with 10 μL of annexin V-microbead solution or equivalent amount of Basic beads for 5 min.
4. Wash cells twice with 1 mL Binding Buffer (1000g for 5 min) to remove unbound annexin V-microbeads, and resuspend in 50 μL of Binding Buffer for EPR assay.
5. EPR measurements can be performed in gas-permeable Teflon tubing. Fill the tube with 50 μL of sample, and place in an EPR quartz tube and then in an EPR resonator.
6. Determine the amplitude of the PS-specific EPR signal as the difference between the EPR signals from annexin V-microbeads and Basic beads.
7. Construct a calibration curve of PS-specific EPR signal amplitude vs Pi from fluorescamine-modified PS to find the relationship between EPR signal amplitude and amount of PS on cell surface.

Annexin V-FITC flow cytometric assay for quantification of cells with externalized PS

1. Centrifuge 0.5×10^6 cells at 1000g for 5 min, and resuspend in 1 mL of Binding Buffer.

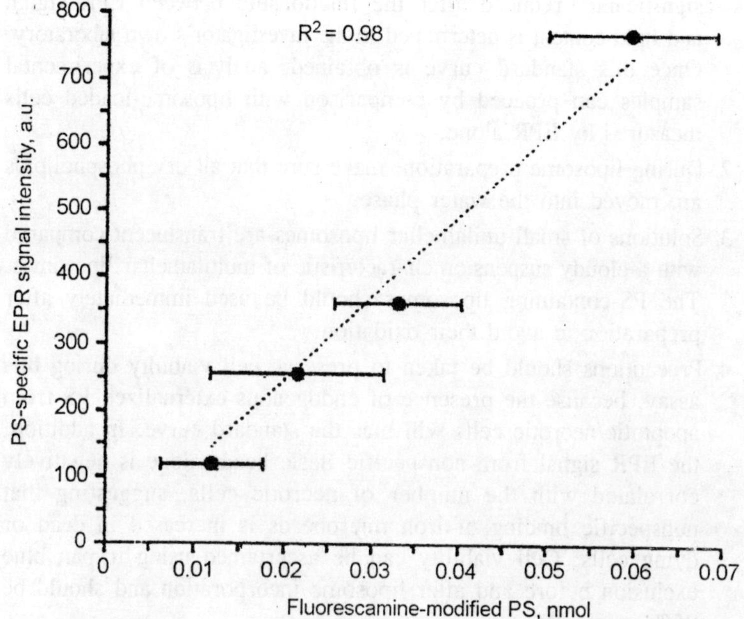

Fig. 15.2: Linear relationship between amount of external PS incorporated into plasma membrane and EPR signal measured with annexin V-magnetic microbeads in Jurkat cells.

2. Incubate the cell suspension with annexin V-FITC (1 μg/mL final concentration) and PI (5 μg/mL) in the dark for 5 min at room temperature.
3. Analyze labeled cell samples by flow cytometry. Gate out low fluorescent debris and necrotic cells prior to analysis. Collect 10,000 "events" (or "cell equivalents") per sample to analyze the annexin V-FITC–positive and PI-negative populations, which represent the apoptotic cells expressing PS on the external cell surface.
4. Recalculate the amount of externalized PS obtained by the EPR-based assay per number of annexin V-FITC–positive cells based on the cytometric analysis.

Notes

1. Volumes and amounts given for the preparation of liposomes and incorporation into cells correspond to those necessary to construct a 6-point standard curve comparing EPR signal intensity and externalized PS measured by fluorescamine. Over 90% of the required liposomes are necessary for the fluorescamine determination by HP-TLC, and hence volumes of reagents can be

significantly reduced after the relationship between EPR signal and lipid content is determined in the investigator's own laboratory. Once this standard curve is obtained, analysis of experimental samples can proceed by comparison with liposome-loaded cells measured by EPR alone.

2. During liposome preparation, make sure that all dry phospholipids are moved into the water phase.
3. Solutions of small unilamellar liposomes are translucent compared with a cloudy suspension characteristic of multilamellar liposomes. The PS-containing liposomes should be used immediately after preparation to avoid their oxidation.
4. Precautions should be taken to preserve cell viability during this assay, because the presence of endogenous externalized PS from apoptotic/necrotic cells will bias the standard curve. In addition, the EPR signal from nonspecific Basic beads alone is negatively correlated with the number of necrotic cells, suggesting that nonspecific binding of iron microbeads is increased in dead or dying cells. Cell viability can be ascertained using trypan blue exclusion before and after liposome incorporation and should be 95% or greater.
5. The optimum concentration of NEM for effective inhibition of aminophospholipid translocase should be determined empirically for each cell line using the NBD-PS internalization assay described in detail by McIntyre and Sleight.
6. Before use, the annexin V-microbeads supplied with the kit should be washed on the magnetic column with 0.1% BSA solution to remove sodium azide and unbound annexin V as follows. Place separation column in the magnet for separation. Apply 0.5 mL of BSA solution on top of the column, and let the solution run through (do not let the column dry). Then apply microbeads solution (not more than 0.5 mL) onto the column, and allow the solution to flow through. Wash column twice with BSA solution. To remove microbeads from the column, add a volume of BSA solution equal to that originally applied to column. Immediately remove column from the magnet and flush out microbeads into the collection tube using the plunger. The volume of microbead solution collected, as well as the EPR signal intensity from the solution, should be equal to that of the initial solution of microbeads.
7. Do not keep cells on ice after labeling with annexin V-microbeads. This may cause precipitation of microbeads and lead to erroneous

results. For best results, utilize annexin Vmicrobeads and Basic microbeads kits within 6 mo because nonspecific binding of annexin V-microbeads and Basic microbeads increases over time.

8. EPR spectra are recorded at room temperature under the following settings: 10 mW microwave power; 9.445 GHz microwave frequency; 300 mT center field; 150 mT sweep width; 2 mT field modulation; × 100 – × 1000 gain range; 0.3 s time constant; 1 min time scan.
9. First, use forward scattering (FSC) and side scattering (SSC) corrections to gate out cell debris, which have significantly lower FSC and SSC signals than live cells. Then set channel FL1 (530/30-nm bandpass filter) to collect annexin V-FITC fluorescence signal and channel FL3 (>650-nm long-pass filter) to collect PI fluorescence. Use untreated cells that possess nominal FL1 and FL3 signals to set threshold on channel FL1 for cells not expressing PS on the surface (annexin V-FITC–negative cells) and threshold on Fl3 for live cells (PI-negative cells). Collect 10,000 events per sample of cells of interest. Annexin V- and PI-positive cells can be arbitrarily defined as events that possess 50-fold greater signal intensity than the modal intensity of Fl1 and Fl3 channels, respectively, observed in a negative control viable nonapoptotic cell population.

Caspase Activation

Many environmental toxins cause DNA damage. Cells that have sustained significant DNA damage must attempt to repair the damage prior to replication, in which aberrant base incorporation can result in an irreversible mutation. If a cell cannot repair the damage, however, it may commit suicide through a genetically regulated *programmed cell death* (PCD) pathway. Crucial to the ultimate execution of PCD is a family of cysteine proteases called *caspases*. Activation of these enzymes occurs late in the PCD pathway, when a cell can no longer avoid cell death, but earlier than other PCD markers, such as morphological changes or DNA fragmentation. This protocol details a method for using fluorochrome-conjugated caspase inhibitors for the detection of activated caspases in intact cells using fluorescent microscopy.

Every day we are exposed to a variety of toxic environmental and occupational agents. Some are inhaled, such as particulate toxins including asbestos and diesel exhaust, which generate reactive oxygen species that can damage the body, and some are ingested in over-the-counter remedies such as toremifene or doxycycline. Most toxins that are known or suspected carcinogens are *genotoxic*, meaning they directly damage DNA, even at low doses. Normally, the cell repairs such damage prior to DNA replication, but when it cannot adequately repair the damage, the cell is genetically programmed to halt replication and commit suicide. This outcome arises through a regulated pathway(s) called *programmed cell death* (PCD).

PCD is often associated with distinct morphological changes that distinguish it from a necrotic death. Necrosis typically involves many cells and occurs in response to a severe insult to the cell, such as cytotoxicity, hypoxia, or depletion of ATP. These severe conditions result in the dramatic release of the cellular contents into the intercellular space, causing an inflammatory response. PCD, on the other hand, signals a single damaged cell to enter a series of genetically regulated steps that culminate in the removal of the cell without releasing the cytoplasmic contents, thus avoiding any inflammatory response. During this process, the chromatin condenses and is subsequently digested into fragments in an organized manner, unlike necrosis, in which the DNA is digested in an apparently random pattern. The surface of the cell then retracts, breaking cell contact with its neighbors, followed by cellular blebbing. The cellular contents, including the now fragmented genome, are sequestered into small "*apoptotic bodies*," which are then phagocytosed by neighboring cells or macrophages and finally digested.

Maintaining normal genetic regulation of PCD is crucial for an organism's fitness and survival. Any change in the rate of PCD in either direction, even subtle changes, can manifest as a life-threatening disease. Excessive PCD contributes to several human diseases, including the neurodegenerative diseases named for Parkinson and Alzheimer. Decreased rates of PCD, on the other hand, are observed in diseases such as autoimmune diabetes, local self-reactive disorder, and cancer. Although some individuals inherit a higher susceptibility to these disorders, most are theorized to arise from a lifetime of exposure to a variety of known and unknown toxins.

There are two major pathways of PCD, which are usually distinct but may have overlapping signals. One pathway is regulated through receptors on the plasma membrane known as *death receptors* and include the *tumor necrosis factor receptor* (TNFR) family, such as Fas, TNFR1, DR3/WSL and TNF-related apoptosis-inducing ligand (TRAIL)/Apo-2L. These receptors respond to ligands presented by other cells or to toxins that mimic these ligands. The absence of a ligand, in particular growth factors, can also trigger a PCD signal of this type. When a PCD signal occurs in a receptor-based PCD pathway, the death receptor forms a *death-inducing signal complex* (DISC), which in turn activates additional downstream signals. The other major PCD pathway is mediated by the mitochondria and can be triggered by the inability to repair DNA damage caused by ionizing radiation or genotoxic effects, metabolic or cell cycle perturbation, or free radicals. This pathway is partially regulated through homo- and heterodimerization of PCD inducers, such as Bax and Bid, and inhibitors, such as Bcl-2 and Bcl-xL. These proteins are sequestered to the outer mitochondrial membrane and control the intracellular regulation of cytochrome c. Homodimerization of PCD inhibitors prevents the release of cytochrome c, whereas heterodimerization of PCD inducers with PCD inhibitors allows the release of cytochrome c from the mitochondria into the cytosol, irreversibly committing the cell to the PCD pathway. Regardless of whether a receptor- or mitochondrial-based pathway is initiated, both involve the activation of a family of proteins called *caspases* that results in the morphological and physiological changes characteristic of PCD, including DNA fragmentation, surface blebbing, and the eventual formation of apoptotic bodies.

Caspases are a family of highly conserved enzymes that are expressed in organisms from worms to humans. There are currently 14 known mammalian caspases, 8 of which have been shown to be crucial in human PCD pathways. Caspases are catalytically inactive cysteine proteases that are cleaved to reveal a recognition sequence, producing a proteolytically active protein. These enzymes are functionally categorized as initiators, which include caspases-2, -8, -9, and -10, and effectors, which include caspases-3, -6, and -7. Initiators are characterized by a large prodomain (>90 residues), which is important to their function after undergoing autocleavage. Effectors, on the other hand, have small prodomains, between 20 and 30 residues, which are not required for the active protein to function. Each caspase contains a unique four-residue recognition sequence, which is used to specifically target substrates particular for the given caspase. Currently, a wide range of synthetic substrates have been developed that use thes recognition sequences to target and covalently bind to the caspase proteins, permanently inactivating them. Given the unique nature of the recognition sequences, inhibitor substrates can target individual caspases, or they may target broad groups of caspases, using a binding sequence compatible with multiple caspases.

Clearly, caspases are a critical, if not essential, feature of the PCD pathway and appear to serve as a point of convergence of the PCD signal transduction pathways necessary for the execution of death. For this reason, the activation of caspases is a very good marker for PCD induction. Caspase activation detection also has advantages over other assays for PCD induction, such as cell viability or DNA fragmentation, since it detects events earlier in the PCD pathway and does not overlap with necrosis. Detecting morphological changes associated with PCD, which, if they do occur, are typically late events during PCD, is usually labor-intensive and limited to analyzing a small number of cells. On the other hand, caspase activation analysis can detect most cells undergoing PCD and can utilize flow cytometry, fluorescent spectrophotometry, or microscopy in which large numbers of cells can be easily and accurately assayed.

Caspase activation can be detected using either cellular lysates or intact cells. Cell lysates can be used to detect pro- or cleaved-caspases or their cleaved substrates using Western blot analysis. Quantification of caspase activation can also be performed on cell lysates using caspase substrates that are conjugated to chromophores or fluorochromes and detected spectrophotometrically on a microplate reader. Although assays using cell lysates can easily process a large number of cells, their limitations include antibody nonspecificity, inability to determine the number of cells undergoing PCD, and difficulty in identifying specific activated caspases owing to overlapping substrates. Intact cells can be analyzed using immunogenic staining against active caspases, conjugated-substrate cleavage, or fluorescent inhibitors that target either specific or nonspecific (pan) caspase active sites. Although there are some disadvantages to using intact cells, such as the inability to determine the amount of caspase activation within a specific cell or the potential of nonspecificity of antibodies, the advantages far outweigh these limitations. Using these assays for intact cells, the exact number of cells undergoing PCD can be determined at a given timepoint, small to large cell numbers can be easily analyzed, and analysis can utilize either a fluorescence or laser confocal microscope or a flow cytometer. For a more complete analysis of cells undergoing PCD, the use of fluorescent-conjugated inhibitors of activated caspases (an early PCD event) can be combined with nuclear staining to detect morphological changes (apoptotic bodies, a late PCD event) and analyzed simultaneously using darkfield microscopy.

The following protocol describes how to detect simultaneously caspase activation (using a pan or specific fluorescent-conjugated caspase inhibitor) and morphological changes associated with the induction of PCD using darkfield microscopy.

Materials

Cell culturing and genotoxic exposure

1. Sterile 24-well tissue culture plates.
2. Sterile medium with supplements appropriate for cells of choice (e.g., RPMI-1640 supplemented with *fetal bovine serum* [FBS]).
3. Genotoxic agent to be tested.

Solutions

1. Caspase detection kit, which contains:
   (a) Lyophilized carboxyfluorescein-benzyloxycarbonyl-valyl-alanyl-aspartic acid-fluoromethyl ketone (FAM-VAD-FMK) pan-caspase inhibitor (light-sensitive; store in the dark).
   (b) Hoechst 33342 stain stock solution (200 μg/mL). *Caution*: possible mutagen, handle with care, using gloves and a mask.
   (c) 10X Wash buffer. *Caution*: contains sodium azide, which is harmful if absorbed through skin; handle with care, using gloves.
   (d) 10X Fixative solution. *Caution*: contains paraformaldehyde, which is toxic; handle with care, using gloves and a mask.
   (e) Store kit at 4°C.
2. Sterile dimethylsulfoxide (DMSO). *Caution*: DMSO is toxic. Handle with care, using gloves and a mask.
3. Sterile cell culture grade 1X phosphate-buffered saline (PBS): 1.06 mM KH_2PO_4, 154 mM NaCl, 2.71 mM Na_2PO_4, pH 7.4.
4. Sterile deionized water.

Cell labeling and counterstaining

1. Sterile small-bore transfer pipets.
2. Sterile serum-free tissue culture medium appropriate for cell type of interest (e.g., RPMI-1640).
3. Hoechst 33342 stain stock solution (200 μg/mL).
4. Sterile 15-mL polypropylene conical centrifuge tubes.

Cell trypsinization and fixation

1. Sterile cell culture grade 1X trypsin-EDTA: 0.05% trypsin, 0.53 mM EDTA.
2. FBS-enriched medium appropriate for cell type of interest (10–25% FBS, depending on cell type).

3. Sterile small-bore transfer pipets.
4. Lint- and dye-free tissues.
5. 10X stock fixative.

Microscopic slide preparation

1. Glass microscope slides, precleaned, untreated, 25 × 75 × 1 mm.
2. Sterile 1X PBS.
3. Mounting medium.
4. Glass cover slips, 25 × 50 × 1 mm.
5. Coplin jar.

Fluorescence microscopy analysis

1. Fluorescence microscope with suitable light source (e.g., mercury or xenon arc lamp) and 35-mm or CCD camera for documentation.
2. Filter cubes compatible with carboxyfluorescein (e.g., bandpass filter, excitation 490 nm, emission 520 nm) and Hoechst 33342 staining (e.g., UV filter, excitation 365 nm, emission 480 nm.

Methods

Cell culturing and genotoxic exposure

1. Seed an appropriate number of cells into a sterile 24-well tissue culture plate. Allow cells to adhere and grow for 24 h.
2. Expose cells to the genotoxic agent for the desired time-points according to your specific protocol.

Solutions

1. Reconstitute lyophilized FAM-VAD-FMK inhibitor in 50 μL sterile DMSO (150X stock solution). The chemical is light-sensitive, so work in the dark. Mix well by gently swirling the bottle until inhibitor is completely dissolved.
2. Prepare an appropriate amount of 30X FAM-VAD-FMK inhibitor working solution by adding 4 parts sterile 1X PBS to 1 part 150X FAM-VAD-FMK inhibitor stock solution.
3. Prepare an appropriate amount (approx 4.5 mL/well for 24-well tissue culture plates) of 1X working wash buffer by diluting 10X stock wash buffer in a 1:10 ratio with deionized water.
4. Prewarm 1X working wash buffer at 37°C until use.
5. Prepare 1X FAM-VAD-FMK inhibitor solution by mixing 10 μL 30X FAM-VAD-FMK inhibitor working solution with 300 μL serum-free medium (310 μL of 1X FAM-VAD- FMK inhibitor/ medium solution/well for 24-well tissue culture plates).

Cell labeling and counterstaining

1. Carefully remove the medium after genotoxic exposure, using a small-bore pipet so as not to collect detached cells, and discard medium.
2. Add 310 μL 1X FAM-VAD-FMK inhibitor/serum-free medium solution to each well. Incubate for 1 h at 37°C in a humidified atmosphere with 5% CO_2.
3. Add 1.5 μL Hoechst 33342 stock stain solution to each well, mix well by gently swirling plate, and incubate for 5 min at 37°C in a humidified atmosphere with 5% CO_2.
4. Carefully remove the medium from each well using a small-bore pipet, and save in a labeled sterile 15-mL conical centrifuge tube.

Cell trypsinization and fixation

1. Add 0.5 mL of 0.5X trypsin-EDTA to each well, and incubate for 5 min at 37°C in a humidified atmosphere with 5% CO_2.
2. Ensure that all cells are detached. Using a small-bore pipet, transfer cells to the 15-mL conical tube containing the previously removed medium.
3. Add 1 mL of FBS-enriched medium to each well, swirl plates gently to collect remaining cells in solution, and transfer medium to a 15-mL conical tube containing the previously removed medium and trypsin solution. Discard plates.
4. Centrifuge (100g) for 5 min at room temperature.
5. Carefully remove and discard the supernatant. Gently resuspend the cell pellet in 2 mL of 1X wash buffer.
6. Centrifuge (100g) for 5 min at room temperature.
7. Repeat steps 5 and 6.
8. Carefully remove and discard the supernatant. Briefly drain the tubes by inversion on a lint- and dye-free tissue to ensure that any remaining wash buffer has been removed, but do not allow the cells to dry out. Gently resuspend the pellet by pipeting in 100 μL of 1X wash buffer.
9. Add 10 μL of 10X stock fixative solution to each tube. Mix by gently swirling tubes and incubate for 15 min at room temperature.

Microscopic slide preparation

1. Pipet cells in the wash buffer/fixative solution (110 μL) onto microscopic slides appropriately labeled and spread evenly, avoiding creating bubbles.

2. Dry slides on a flat surface (approx 30 min to 1 h), checking periodically to ensure even solution distribution.
3. Carefully wash cells once in 50 mL 1X PBS in a Coplin jar for 5 min.
4. Drain off excess liquid, and allow slides to air-dry briefly (2–3 min).
5. Add 3 drops of mounting medium, and place on a cover slip, trying to avoid bubbles. Allow slides to dry overnight in the dark at room temperature.

Fluorescence microscopy analysis

1. Analyze the slides using a fluorescent microscope with the appropriate bandpass and UV filters to observe caspase activation (either green or red, depending on which fluorescently labeled substrate is used) and Hoechst 33342 stain (blue). Cells should be analyzed on the basis of presence of caspase signal and presence of apoptotic bodies, as apparent from counter-staining. Although the number of cells needed to be analyzed will differ, depending on individual goals, counts of at least 500 cells per condition should be used to obtain reasonable power in statistical analysis.

Notes

1. Alternative tissue culture plates (i.e., 96-well or 12-well) or microscopic chamber slides can be used. However, reaction volumes must be adjusted accordingly.
2. Although we typically use a pan-caspase peptide inhibitor, specific peptide inhibitors for caspases-1, -2, -3, -6, -8, -9, and -10 are available and compatible with this protocol. In addition, caspase-3 and pan-caspase peptides conjugated to sulforhodamine (SR) are commercially available.
3. *Caution*: sodium azide can react with lead- and copper-containing sink drains, forming explosive compounds. Use large volumes of water when disposing of excess wash buffer down the sink drain.
4. The SR-conjugated peptides require a filter cube with an excitation of 550 nm and emission of 595 nm.
5. Confluent growth may prevent exposure of some cells to the peptide inhibitor, resulting in uneven staining and inaccurate analysis. If one is using nonadherent cells, this protocol may be carried out in tubes rather than plates with a cell density of 10^6 cells/mL.
6. The FAM and SR fluorescent-conjugated peptide inhibitors and Hoechst 33342 are extremely sensitive to light. Avoid direct

exposure to light, as this will result in photobleaching. All sample processing, incubations, and microscopic analysis should be performed in the dark.

7. Any unused 150X FAM-VAD-FMK inhibitor stock solution should be aliquoted into appropriate volumes, stored in the dark, and desiccated at –20°C. Repeated freeze-thaw of the 150X FAM-VAD-FMK inhibitor stock solution will result in substrate degradation.
8. Only prepare enough 30X FAM-VAD-FMK inhibitor working solution for the number of wells to be analyzed. A 30X FAM-VAD-FMK inhibitor working solution cannot be stored, and any remaining unused 30 X FAM-VAD-FMK inhibitor working solution must be discarded.
9. A precipitate may form in the 10X stock wash buffer when it is stored at 4°C. Therefore, incubate the 10X stock wash buffer at 37°C for 30 min prior to use, or until precipitation is completely dissolved.
10. If detached cells are collected in the medium, the medium can be centrifuged (100g) and the supernatant discarded. The cell pellet can then be resuspended in the 310 μL 1X FAM-VAD-FMK inhibitor/serum-free medium solution from the appropriate wells and added back to the appropriate well. Recovering these detached cells is important, since many may be undergoing PCD.
11. Proper mixing after the addition of the Hoechst 33342 stain is critical for even fluorescence of the entire cell population.
12. Incubation in trypsin may be increased from 5 to 10 min if necessary to detach all adherent cells.
13. Tap plates gently but firmly against the palm to knock cells loose. Visual inspection is preferable, because light microscopy will cause photobleaching of the cells. However, because analysis of all cells is critical, inspection using an inverted light microscope may be necessary, although exposure to light should be minimized.
14. The use of FBS-enriched medium is necessary to stop the trypsin activity.
15. Removing any excess wash buffer is important, as failure to do so will increase the volume spread on the microscope slide. This may result in an increased drying time and increased background fluorescence.
16. An alternative to air-drying the fixed cells onto the microscope slides is to use a cytospin. After incubation with fixative, follow

the cytospin protocol for spinning cells onto slides. Be sure to determine an appropriate cell concentration prior to performing this caspase activation assay, as too high or low a concentration will make the subsequent microscopic analysis more difficult, if not impossible.

17. When spreading the solution onto the slides, it is important not to force air out of the pipet tip, as this will create bubbles. When dry, these bubbles will result in rings of high background and disrupt the even distribution of cells.
18. Slides should be dried on a completely level surface, as any incline will create pooling in one area of the slide, leading to high background and uneven cell distribution. It may be useful to check on the slides periodically as they dry and respread the solution on the slide as needed.
19. High background signal for the caspase staining may indicate insufficient washing of the cells. If counterstaining is weak, extend the incubation time with Hoechst 33342 to 10 min. If counterstaining is too strong, shorten the incubation time as needed.

16

Foot in Forensic Science

Academic physical anthropologists are well aware of the importance of the foot (as more enduringly represented by its bony skeleton) in understanding human evolution, which is literally based on the acquisition of upright posture. The relative size of ancient calcanei and other tarsals, along with the curvature of the metatarsals that create the arches of the foot, provide direct clues as to the location and timing of the appearance of the "first" humans.

"The Game is Afoot!"

Role of the Foot in Death Investigation

In our own research on the ancient Maya of Mexico and Central America, the bones of the foot yield interesting information about the activities these individuals engaged. Ubelaker associated distal articular changes in metatarsals with habitual extreme upward and backward flexion of the toes, as occurs when kneeling with the toes bent back—perhaps to grind maize or when weaving. "*Squatting facets*"— flexion facets on the anterior surface of the distal tibia that are produced by frequent extreme dorsiflexion of the foot—may indicate a habitual squatting or "*hunkering*" posture or repeated climbing up steep hills and/or ladders. Pathological findings—including healed fractures of metatarsals, sharply marked (even lipped) articular borders of tarsals, and osteoarthritic lipping of foot phalanges—reflect the difficulties inherent in moving about in rugged terrain.

Fortunately, the weight bearing involved in upright posture and locomotion has not only influenced the basic structure of the bones of the foot and ankle, but has also increased the strength and density of the trabeculae within these bones, which helps them survive the hazards of taphonomy (i.e., what happens to the body after death).

The survival of tarsals, metatarsals, and phalanges as sources of information in modern forensic cases is further enhanced by our custom of wearing shoes and boots. Footwear serves as protective "*armor*" in crashes, explosions, fires, and similar situations, then continues to serve as literal storage containers for feet that would otherwise be exposed to other taphonomic events, such as insect and animal activity and weathering. The skin of the foot may be breached by postmortem changes even when shoes are worn, but footgear helps to keep the foot bones "together" a while longer. The US Air Force took note of the identification potential of feet when they instituted a footprinting program for flying personnel during the late 1950s. It was observed as early as World War II that the heavy boots required to protect fliers against the extreme cold of high altitudes also protected the foot and its *dermatoglyphics* (friction ridges) in the event of a crash.

Role of the Anthropologist in Death Investigation

A basic contribution of the forensic anthropologist in the standard forensic setting (coroner/medical examiner office) is to help create a biographic profile based on skeletal assessment of sex, age, ancestry, stature, etc., for the otherwise unidentified (including "*unidentifiable*") individual so that appropriate antemortem dental and medical radiographs and other means of identification can be obtained from a variably sized pool of missing persons for comparison. These profiles may also include fleshed characteristics, when available. (Of note, "*unidentifiable*" usually refers to skeletonized, burned, decomposed, fragmented, or otherwise damaged remains. However, even relatively fresh and intact bodies require more accurate age estimates than can be provided by visual inspection.)

In mass fatality incidents, the situation is similar, but antemortem radiographs and other information can be immediately sought for a known relatively limited pool of presumed victims (i.e., passengers and crew on a flight manifest). The anthropologists create biographic profiles for each unit of remains, whether an intact body or a body fragment, such as a detached foot, so that when (and if) the antemortem radiographs arrive, potentially matching postmortem radiographs for each unit will be available for immediate comparison. Positive identification might then be based on an intact body or a disassociated body part, depending on availability. The biographic profile of a unit is based primarily on the anthropologist's assessment of the skeletal remains within the unit. Aside from visualization using radiography, anthropologists may use appropriate dissection and cleaning techniques to obtain the biographic information stored in the bone. In addition to profile characteristics, the anthropologist will attempt to record side and other descriptive information that may later be used in considering whether to reassociate the unit with an incomplete set of remains with a similar biographic profile that is lacking that part. This descriptive information is also noted when DNA samples are taken.

Reassociation of units of fragmented remains with matching biographic profiles may be based on a positive identification of each unit to be reassociated. DNA is useful for this purpose, but its analysis is both expensive and relatively slow; therefore, fingerprints and dental and medical radiographs have been used most often for this purpose. In addition, a reassociation may be considered positive if fracture or joint articular surfaces can be physically linked and thereby matched. Strong presumptive reassociations may be based on surface morphology and radiographic comparisons (e.g., proportions and internal structure), as well as the process of elimination, which is sometimes based on well-defined age characteristics (i.e., immaturity) or sex (the only male present).

A qualified forensic anthropologist may compare antemortem and postmortem medical (non-dental) radiographs to establish a positive identification of the victim. Forensic radiologists are rare; fortunately, forensic anthropologists are experienced in the potential variations of the human skeleton, usually including its radiology (especially growth and development). These non-dental radiographic identifications are based on human variation. Just as fingerprints (or noses or ears) of individuals are inherently different, bones are also dissimilar. Anthropologists not only look for obvious differences and similarities, such as healed trauma and surgical intervention, but also for such aspects as bone contours, density, cortical thickness, and trabecular patterns. As in dental identifications, any differences that cannot be explained by the passage of time or perimortem trauma result in a non-identification. Comparison of postmortem biographic profiles with antemortem information aids in the prevention of misidentifications.

In the examples that follow, we will demonstrate how we have used the lower extremities of victims to solve a series of forensic puzzles. In these cases, and in a variety of others (which include plane crashes, a train–truck crash, and a fireworks factory explosion), feet have provided us with information about the following:

1. The identity of otherwise unidentifiable remains
2. Commingling of remains: peri- and postmortem
3. Reassociation of severed feet with appropriate individuals (including one survivor)
4. Who was flying a small plane that crashed
5. Taphonomic processes

Fireworks factory explosion

A fireworks factory exploded in Osseo, Michigan, on December 11, 1998. The explosion destroyed all but the foundation of the building and resulted in the deaths of seven individuals. After the explosion, six "bodies" were said to have been recovered by local emergency workers and Bureau of Alcohol, Tobacco, and Firearms agents. The seventh individual, who was believed to have been inside the building, was still unaccounted for when all the remains were brought to the Lucas County Coroner's Office in Toledo, Ohio, in 12 body bags.

Blast forces produced severe fragmentation of the building's occupants. Almost all the legs were fractured and the fractures were concentrated in the lower leg, reflecting the ground shock effects produced as the wave of energy passed through the solid floor. In some instances, the force of the explosion cleanly separated right and left hipbones from the sacrum by means of disarticulation of the sacroiliac joints.

The fragmented remains were commingled in the body bags. Body bag contents ranged from three bodies lacking some portions (three bags) through torsos lacking major portions (two bags); seven bags contained only commingled body parts. The bags containing "major" body parts also contained smaller fragments.

Dental remains provided the basis for positive identification (by a local odontologist) of portions of four victims based on the comparison of antemortem dental radiographs with radiographs obtained from the dental remains.

In a similar fashion, we positively identified portions of the other three individuals, including the "missing" seventh individual, by comparing antemortem medical and postmortem radiographs selected using matching biographic profiles. In two of these cases, right feet were sufficiently preserved to provide the identification. The frequency of sprained ankles and other foot and ankle trauma during life that require radiographic examination can be an advantage when a positive identification is needed. Radiographic comparisons of portions of the vertebral column and clavicles also produced positive identifications. A third individual was positively identified using radiographic comparisons of several portions of the vertebral column. Identified separated body parts (i.e., foot/ankle) could then in some cases be reassociated with other positively identified body parts, such as a torso that had been positively identified using dental radiographs. In addition, we reassociated a number of body parts having matching biographic profiles by linking fractures through direct matching of fracture surfaces and rearticulating joint surfaces. In some instances, presumptive associations were made using mirror imaging, sexual dimorphism (there was only one male among the victims), and proportions.

As an example, we positively identified a lower torso by comparing antemortem and postmortem radiographs of the attached right foot/ ankle (the left thigh was also attached). This right foot was morphologically distinctive, with an unusually long great toe, enabling us to reassociate the lower torso and right leg with a separate left foot/ankle with a matching biographic profile and the same distinctive

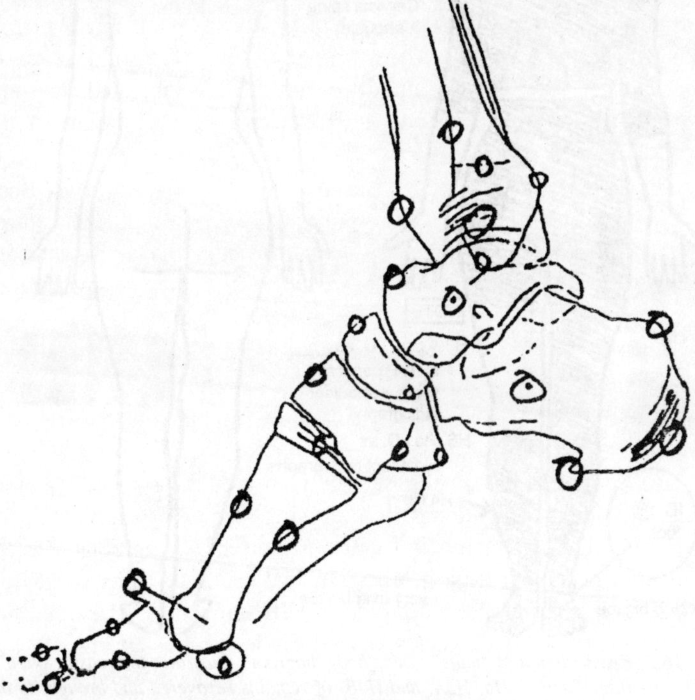

Fig. 16.1. Transparent overlay tracing of the postmortem radiograph.

configuration, including an unusually long great toe. A separate upper torso with neck was also positively identified as this same individual by comparison of antemortem and postmortem radiographs of the cervical spine and shoulder. A body diagram illustrates the reassociation of these parts from three separate body bags. Unfortunately, there

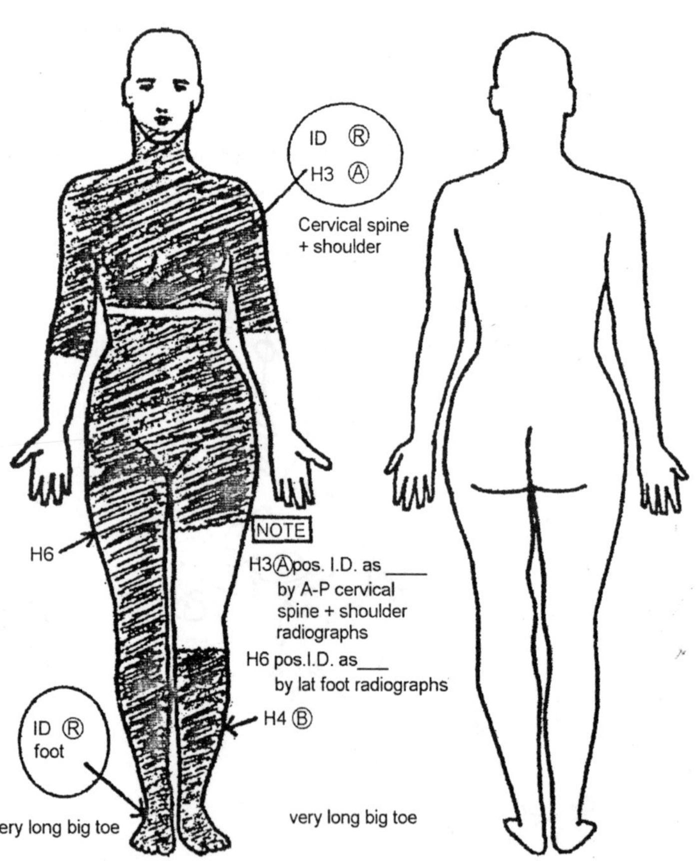

Fig. 16.2. Reassociation of "units". This "body diagram" illustrates the reassociation of three "units" (H6, H3A, and H4B) of remains recovered and brought to our morgue in separate body bags after a fireworks factory explosion.

were some portions that could not be reassociated or positively identified by the above techniques and were therefore considered "*common tissue*" and buried in a common grave.

However, these procedures did enable us to locate and reassociate body parts from 11 separate body bags, thereby "*rebuilding*" and positively identifying the initially unaccounted-for seventh victim, whose family was then able to bury their loved one. This individual was one of those who suffered disarticulation at the sacroiliac joints and was so severely fragmented and widely dispersed about the scene that we suspect that he was close to the point of explosion.

Comair commuter plane and the Korean airlines plane crashes

Fragmentation is expected in explosions such as the previously mentioned fire-works factory explosion. It is also a frequent consequence of airplane and other high-energy impact crashes. We first encountered this in the January 1997 crash of a Comair commuter flight en route from the Cincinnati, Ohio–Covington, Kentucky airport to the Detroit, Michigan airport. The aircraft had icing problems and plunged more or less straight down into frozen ground. This resulted in tremendous fragmentation of bodies, flaying of skin, and defleshing of bone. Twenty-nine identifications were obtained within less than a week, but priorities dictated that time was not available for reassociation of a number of dismembered feet and ankles that consequently became "*common tissue*" and were buried with other unidentified tissue in a common grave.

When Korean Air Lines Flight no. 801 made a "controlled-flight-into-terrain" (i.e., landed too soon and in the wrong place) on Guam, we made a special and at least partially successful effort to reassociate feet and ankles by keeping track of them from the beginning of the operation. Reassociations were made by matching biographic profiles and noting any lack of duplication plus morphological and other similarities of the contralateral part, followed by (preferably) separate positive identification via a comparison of ante- and postmortem radiographs of the part in question, direct linkage of fractures, or articulation of joints.

In one notable case involving a separate female left foot and ankle with distinctive nail polish, we all were alerted to keep watch for a right foot with similar polish (hopefully attached to a body). Eventually, a female body was spotted with the toenails of the right foot coated with what appeared to be the same nail polish. The left foot was missing. Biographic profiles of both sets of remains were examined and were consistent. There was no duplication or overlapping of parts.

Examination of both feet, side by side, showed strong similarities in size and configuration of feet, toes, and toenails. The nails were cut and polished in an apparently identical manner. Fracture surfaces of the proximal ends of the left tibia and fibula fragments of the separate foot could not be fracture-linked to the distal ends of the left tibia and fibula attached to the body, due to destruction and loss of intermediate bone.

The young woman's body had been positively identified, so it might have been possible to compare antemortem clinical radiographs of her left foot with the postmortem radiographs of the separate left foot that we hoped to reassociate. Unfortunately, there were no antemortem clinical radiographs of either right or left lower leg and foot. We then retrieved postmortem radiographs of both the right and left feet and lower legs and examined them. Bone contours, trabecular bone patterns, density, cortical bone thickness of the left and right lower legs were essentially mirror images of each other. Based on all of these striking similarities (biographic profile, matching morphology of feet, toes and nails, matching polish, and nearly identical right and left postmortem radiographs), we proposed this to be a strong presumptive match, and with the agreement of the Medical Examiner the left foot was reassociated with the body.

In another instance, we were fortunately not led astray by bright red polish on the toenails of a victim. There is a tendency to assume that polished toenails will only be found on a female. In this case, we later learned that the male victim's toenails were painted at a bachelor party that he had attended the night before.

Amtrak train–truck crash

Our most unusual reassociation occurred as a consequence of the Amtrak train–truck crash in March 1999. The "City of New Orleans," en route from Chicago, IL, to New Orleans, LA, was proceeding normally until several hours after leaving Chicago, when it encountered a steel-laden truck that had failed to stop at a marked crossing in Bourbonnais, IL. Eleven passengers of various ages and origins died in the ensuing fiery crash.

Almost all of the recovered remains had been subjected to intense heat, ranging from charring on through calcined bone. Fragmentation was present to a lesser degree than occurs in plane crashes. Interestingly enough, several feet were separated from the leg by disarticulation at the tibio–talar joint. Some of these could be reassociated through matching biographic profiles and direct re-articulation.

When we arrived at the scene the day following the crash, we were handed remains that we identified as the distal (lower) part of the tibia of a child. We later learned that several female members of a family (grandmother, mothers, daughters, cousins) were returning from a wonderful weekend in Chicago that had included a visit to the American Girl Doll Store. They were in the sleeper car that had struck and become "*draped*" over one of the locomotives on impact and subsequently burned for several hours. The adults and two of the younger girls died, but one young girl suffered a traumatic amputation of her foot, after which a dining car attendant saved her life by removing her from the burning car.

We suspected a possible relationship between this incident and the distal tibia fragment found at the scene, and requested the presurgical amputation radiographs made by the local hospital. On the last day of recovery of the remains, a child's foot in a shoe was recovered at the crash site. The previously recovered distal tibia fragment could be positively and directly articulated with this foot. The estimated age of the resulting foot and ankle was consistent with that of the young girl who "lost" her foot. Fracture linkage of the proximal end of the distal tibia fragment in hand and the distal end of the fractured tibia as seen in the presurgical radiograph provided the last link in the reassociation of the foot and lower tibia with a surviving victim.

There were concerns about how to handle this unusual situation, but we believed that this very courageous young lady, who had insisted on visiting the scene where her mother and other family members had died, might one day want to know where her foot was. It was deemed best to let her family make the final decision about disposition of the foot.

A newspaper clipping less than a year later informed us that she had made unusually rapid progress in her recovery and resumed playing soccer. A very resilient young lady, indeed.

Small plane crash

A small plane crash resulted in the death of three individuals: the owner (who was a licensed pilot), his son, and the pilot employed by the plane's owner. The remains of one individual, who was later identified as the professional pilot, were fairly intact and collected in one body bag. The mangled and fragmented remains of the other two men, later identified as the owner and his son, were put into two separate body bags. Each set of remains was quickly and positively identified by comparison of antemortem and postmortem dental radiographs and returned to the two families. The authors' anthropological services were not used, inasmuch as the identifications appeared to be straightforward and provided rapid closure for the families.

Unfortunately, some time later, as aircraft and other insurance claims were being processed, a dispute arose between multiple opposing law firms as to whether or not the non-pilot son of the owner might have been flying the aircraft at the time of the accident rather than one of the two licensed pilots aboard. We were called in at that belated point. Fortunately, the Coroner's Office involved in the case had a policy of always taking full body radiographs—in this case, full body-bag radiographs were provided.

We were asked to answer the following questions:

1. Was there commingling of remains within the body bags?
2. Could we help determine who was flying the plane (who was at the controls) at the time that the plane crashed?

We were able to exclude the hired pilot from consideration, because his remains were found relatively intact and at some distance from the other two "sets" of remains. The radiographs of the single body bag containing these remains showed no signs of commingling. This was a helpful starting point, because the pilot, aged approx 20 yr, was about the same age as the nonpilot son.

Age differences served as our main basis for sorting the remains of the father and the son. We looked for signs of age differences that might indicate commingling, inasmuch as the father (identified as being in bag A-52) was aged approx 45 yr at death and the son (identified as being in bag A-53) was aged approx 20 yr at death.

Our review indicated that the torso remains (vertebral column, shoulder area, pelvis) labeled A-52 were indeed those of an older individual, while the torso remains labeled A-53 were indeed those of a younger individual. These findings were based primarily on joint surface configuration and the radiographic presence or absence of persistent lines of density indicating recent epiphyseal union (sometimes called "*growth plate scars*"—not to be confused with "*Harris lines*," which are associated with growth arrest followed by growth augmentation).

However, we believed that commingling of lower legs and feet with torsos probably had occurred, as the articulated ankle and foot in bag A-52 (containing the torso of the father) showed recent fusion (a persistent line of epiphyseal union) in the distal tibia, suggesting that it belonged to someone in his early 20s. The disarticulated ankles and feet in bag A-53 (containing the torso of the son) showed no indications of recent immaturity, but rather were consistent with full maturity.

It is also possible that the articulated forearm and hand in bag A-52 ("the father") belonged to a younger individual (early 20s), based on the apparent presence of a persistent line of epiphyseal union in the distal radius suggestive of recent fusion, whereas the disarticulated hand and wrist in bag A-53 ("the son") showed no apparent signs of immaturity. The articulated hand and wrist in bag A-53 could not be evaluated, and the associated hand was consistent with that of a younger person (absence of joint surface changes).

Next, we considered the question of who was at the controls of the plane when it crashed. Although we felt that it was inappropriate for us to state who was or was not operating the controls, we felt that we were qualified to look for signs of trauma to hands and feet. The forensic pathologist could then interpret this information in the light of his own knowledge and experience.

In our report to the Coroner (8/07/95) we stated the following: "The important points would appear to be:

1. The foot associated with bag no. 52 ("the father") is fully articulated with the lower leg and shows minimal damage. It is inconsistent with being the father's foot because the distal tibia shows a radiographic line of density where the distal epiphysis of the tibia is located during adolescence i.e., a persistent epiphyseal surface line suggestive of recent immaturity. The foot probably belonged to a young adult (very late teens–early 20s) rather than to the father.
2. The feet associated with bag no. 53 ("the son") are both disarticulated from the lower legs (both show multiple fractures) and one foot shows fracturing. Neither the feet or the lower leg bones show any indication of immaturity, therefore they probably did not belong to the son."

In other words, the disarticulated and fractured feet were those of the older individual (the father, a licensed pilot), although they were located within the body bag containing other remains identified dentally as being the son. The damage present was consistent with that found in individuals "working" control pedals in both automobile and airplane crash situations. The foot of the younger individual (the son) showed minimal damage.

Missing, Present, and Left Behind

It is a common occurrence in our forensic practice to receive nearly intact remains that have been brought to us by law enforcement agents with varying numbers of small bones or fragments missing. The explanation for the incomplete recovery of skeletal remains by nonspecialists is often failure to recognize the small bones (or fragments) as being human, or even as being bone at all.

Moreover, cases such as the partially skeletonized body of a young girl found wrapped in a sleeping bag in a field near Monroe, Michigan, and brought to us with several tarsals, metatarsals, and all but two foot phalanges missing suggested scavenger activity as the probable cause, rather than strictly problems of recognition and recovery. Protruding and therefore accessible toes and feet are very attractive to hungry scavengers and, like hands, are easily detached and transported for consumption, dispersal, or both. Even if they remain in the vicinity, they may be overlooked during recovery, particularly if they have been modified by gnawing.

Taphonomic factors such as wind and water may sometimes play a part in "*creating*" incomplete remains. A number of years ago, a group of teenage boys retrieved several bags of human remains from the Maumee River in Toledo, Ohio. The bags contained 100 relatively fresh pieces of a female, ranging from the intact head on through squares of skin complete with underlying fatty layer, segments of bowel, and a torso with all the skin, fat, and muscle tissue neatly removed. The bags containing the pelvis and both lower legs and feet were not recovered. Her killer confessed that after dismembering her, he placed her remains into multiple plastic bags. He loaded them into her car and drove to a bridge spanning the Maumee River, which flows into Lake Erie. Throwing them into the river, he expected to see them disappear into the lake, but was undoubtedly startled to find that a strong wind from an unexpected direction brought most of them, other than the bags containing pelvis and lower legs (not found to this date), to the river shore like oddly shaped sailboats.

Incompleteness was more or less "natural" in the former case and "accidental" in the latter, but in the following case it was deliberate. In eastern Ohio, a young woman disappeared shortly after her divorce around 1974. A confession by her former brotherin-law led to the recovery in 2000 of skeletal female remains that had been deposited in Indiana in 1980. These unidentified remains, lacking feet and ankles, were brought to us shortly thereafter. Our examination resulted in a biographic profile that was consistent with that of the missing woman. In the absence of antemortem dental and medical radiographs for comparison with those of the skeletal remains, DNA analysis was used for a positive identification. The former brother-in-law had confessed to seeing her remains in a wooden box some 5 yr after her disappearance. Our examination revealed that her lower legs had been deliberately severed about 3 in. below the knees, presumably to fit her into the box. With the addition of her lower legs and feet, she would have been too tall for the box. Although her former husband—now convicted of her murder—had stuffed the box with a great deal of her clothing, the detached lower legs (including feet) were nowhere to be found. To this day they have not been recovered and her former husband/murderer has not revealed what he did with them.

The presence of even some of the small bones can yield important information. One sunny fall day, the incomplete skeletonized remains of a young man were found by a fisherman on a Maumee River flood plain. The young man had disappeared 3 yr earlier and last was seen some 30 mi upstream. Bones were scattered under the autumn leaves and tangled in weeds, and some were partially buried by repeated flooding of the area. Although several bones were never recovered, our ability to recognize and recover several small bones of the hands and feet, as well as a few finger and toe nails, demonstrated that although it had traveled many miles and over a dam, his body was intact when it reached the floodplain.

Occasionally we have seen the reverse, i.e., situations in which small bones or fragments ranging from femoral heads to carpals, tarsals, and phalanges have been recovered as isolated finds. We have experienced both situations in archaeologic and forensic contexts.

The explanation for isolated finds may be more complicated. It could involve such aspects of taphonomy as the animal activity discussed above, as well as erosion or even agricultural activity such as the tilling of fields or construction and development projects that involve the removal and dispersal of soil. These processes are a frequent source of Native American and historic remains in many parts of the country, including Ohio and Michigan. It has also been noted in relation to the superficial burial of massacred Guatemalan peasants in recent times, whose remains were presumed to have been damaged by the agricultural process.

A variation of the nonrecognition of small elements during recovery that actually serves the cause of justice involves attempts by the perpetrators to cover up individual and mass clandestine deaths by returning to the original deposition site some time afterwards. These remains "disappear" when they are moved elsewhere to avoid discovery or confound identification. During such a procedure, the easily seen and recognized bones are more likely to be collected, while less easily located and recognized small bones, fragments, and individual teeth may be left behind. In some cases, this "collection" seems to have been followed by the disposal of the collected remains in several widely separated locations. Fortunately, these small, initially unrecognized bones and fragments that are often left behind bear witness to the original crime. Such instances of exhumation, reburial, and dispersal of victims of genocide have been documented in several countries, including Bosnia–Herzegovina. Advances in DNA analysis have allowed these small bones and fragments to speak for the victims.

Academic physical anthropology has long recognized the importance of recovering and analyzing ancient foot bones in order to understand human evolution in relation to the acquisition of upright posture. In contrast, "traditional" forensic anthropology has focused on the informational potential of other portions of the skeleton, such as the skull and pelvis. The former yields information about such things as sex, ancestry, age, and trauma, and the latter is the most dependable guide to the sex of the individual while also yielding information such as age and parity. Information derived from teeth, long bones, ribs, and vertebrae has also been highlighted. Dentition is durable, assists in estimating age, and may provide clues to ancestry; it can also support positive identifications by the forensic odontologist. Long bones provide the basis for stature estimates. Ribs and vertebrae are examined for trauma as well as age information. Hand bones are examined for defense wounds. However, the usefulness of examinations of foot bones is underemphasized.

A recovery bias may be involved. Skulls, mandibles, and larger bones are more likely to be recognized by the public and brought to the attention of law enforcement. Searchers (both law enforcement and volunteer) are also more likely to recognize and recover such distinctive bones while ignoring small bones that appear to be stones and twigs.

Hopefully the cases presented in this section will remind the forensic community that foot and ankle remains are surprisingly durable and also have great forensic potential, particularly in regard to biographic profiles, identification, and activity in life.

FEET AND FOOTWEAR

This section will serve as a practical treatise for evaluating pedal evidence (footwear and footprints) in forensic contexts. Extensive research is necessary to help validate identification markers between the foot and footwear.

The distinguished British anatomist, Frederick Wood Jones, ably described the human being's distinguishing characteristic: "Man's foot is all his own. It is unlike any other foot. It is the most distinctly human part of his whole anatomical makeup. It is a human specialization and, whether he is proud of it or not, it is his hallmark and so long as Man has been Man and so long as he remains Man it is by his feet that he will be known from all other members of the animal kingdom".

Moreover, Sir Arthur Conan Doyle's Sherlock Holmes classic, A Study in Scarlet, Holmes recounts to Watson just how he solved the crime. Holmes states, "There is no branch of detective science which is so important and so much neglected as the art of tracing footsteps."

This text was first published in Beeton's Christmas Annual, London, in 1887. Furthermore, in his book on footwear identification, Cassidy says, "a podiatrist or orthopedic surgeon is a specialist who has the training to properly interpret the mark inside the shoe and present this form of evidence in court".

With an increased awareness of foot or foot-related evidence, most recently brought to the forefront with the O. J. Simpson case, the field of forensic podiatry has evolved. Forensic podiatry may be defined as the application of podiatric medical expertise to the legal system. Vernon and McCourt further define forensic podiatry as the "application of sound and researched podiatric knowledge in the context of forensic and mass disaster investigations. This may be for the purposes of person identification, to show the association of an individual with the scene of a crime, or to answer any other legal question concerning the foot or footwear that requires knowledge of the functioning foot".

Role of Forensic Podiatry

Footprint and footwear evidence is commonly present at a crime scene and must be discovered, recorded, and collected for further examination. When footprint analysis is required, the forensic podiatrist may act as an adjunct or a primary participant in the case. The foot is a complicated structure, and it requires years of experience to be able to distinguish all the intricacies—including *soft tissue* and *skeletal pathologies*—involved in its makeup and consequent evaluation. The use of unknowledgeable or simplistic approaches may have significant ramifications that can affect a person's freedom or even life itself.

History

There are numerous references in the literature to footwear evidence relative to footwear identification, the earliest recorded case dating back to 1876 in Scotland. However, a search of the literature on pedal cases is not replete with references relative to podiatry alone. The reader is encouraged to review the further reading section for historical references.

In the 1920s, Gerard published information and his thoughts about the foot and fingerprints, but apparently his ideas were either ahead of his time or unpopular because there is no further mention of his work. In 1935, Muir composed an article titled "Chiropody and Crime Detection," in which he offered his thoughts on a footprint case utilizing a forensic approach; however, Muir did not appear to be involved specifically in the case. One of the most infamous cases at the time was the Ruxton case, which occurred in Scotland in 1935. This forensic case involved placing dismembered feet from two profoundly mutilated individuals into the footwear of two missing persons: Mrs. Isabella Ruxton and her nursemaid. Mrs. Ruxton's chiropodist was employed for this purpose.

In 1957, Sir Sidney Smith—although not a podiatrist but a police surgeon—wrote a well-known book called "Mostly Murder." Throughout his career, he investigated several crimes involving footwear. One of his best-known cases occurred in Falkirk, Scotland, in 1937. He gave the police a description of the perpetrator's locomotor system after reviewing the evidence and scrutinizing the footwear. The accuracy of his conclusions was uncanny, because he had not seen the perpetrator's feet before his evaluation and he demonstrated a thorough knowledge of podiatric medicine.

Lucock, a British chiropodist, published an article in 1980 in the *Chiropodist* titled "Identification from Footwear." It was the first article that included a discussion of the foot and observed wear patterns on shoes relative to pathologic and biomechanical imbalances in the feet. In 1982, Dr. Norman Gunn, a podiatrist, took plaster casts of foot impressions in sand at a murder scene in Canada, and the techniques used to match the impression to the suspect's foot convinced the suspect to change his plea to guilty.

Norman Gunn is a pioneer in the field and is well known for his extensive forensic involvement worldwide. Beginning in the late 1980s and early 1990s, several other podiatrists became active and have worked criminal cases and testified in court. In Canada, Keith Bettles has worked on several pedal cases and was featured on a forensic television production. Other podiatrists who have worked abroad in this field include Vernon and McCourt in England, Jones and Bennett in Australia, and Greg Coyle in New Zealand. In the United States, Christopher Smith testified at a trial and refuted the testimony of Louise Robbins on several issues. Ronald Valmassy, Gerson Perry, Ivar Roth, Mario Campanelli, Robert Rinaldi, Henry Asin, and the author have all worked as forensic podiatrists in the United States.

Current forensic podiatry

Given the increased number and variety of applications of forensic podiatry, the field needed to be developed in an academically and scientifically robust manner similar to other disciplines, such as forensic anthropology and forensic odontology. Presently, podiatrists are active members of the American Academy of Forensic Sciences and Distinguished and Associate members of the International Association for Identification. They are also members of their forensic state societies and act as consultants to their local police departments. Podiatrists are also members of the Canadian Identification Society, British Association of Human Identification, Forensic Science Services, and the Centre for International Forensic Assistance.

The newly formed American Society of Forensic Podiatry promotes forensic sciences through continuing education for its members by means of educational seminars, research, publications, and through liaisons with other organized disciplines. An emphasis on statistically rigorous research in the forensic sciences is strongly encouraged. By virtue of training, podiatrists have a basic knowledge of footwear and significant experience with foot morphology, pathologic states, and biomechanical imbalances.

The forensic podiatrist will attend and regularly participate in academic meetings and training seminars in the scientific community. This will give the podiatrist a sound indoctrination in other subjects related to law enforcement, criminal justice, and laboratory techniques. Working in the crime laboratory and with police departments is highly recommended. The podiatric medical educational system in the United States is in the process of developing forensic programs for podiatric medical students and postgraduate courses for practicing podiatrists. In 2000, Wesley Vernon became the first podiatrist to complete a PhD program in Forensic Podiatry in the United Kingdom.

Crime Scene

Physical evidence can be defined as articles and materials found during an investigation that may establish the identity of suspects and the circumstances under which the crime was committed. Footprints are known as physical evidence, as are fingerprints. It is evidence that speaks for itself and requires no explanation, only identification.

Fingerprints are often discovered at the crime scene—but not always, because it is possible that nothing was touched or precautionary measures were taken (i.e., gloves may have been worn to preclude identification). However, it is unlikely that an individual can enter and leave the crime scene without using his or her feet. Discovering pedal evidence can be difficult, however, and a conscious effort must be made to do so. The initial officer(s) must recognize the importance of footprint evidence and try to preserve the integrity of the scene. This task can be quite difficult when medical personnel or other persons inadvertently destroy potential evidence.

Foot impression evidence is most commonly discovered on ground surfaces, such as dirt, tile, concrete, and carpeting, but at times on counter-tops or other less common locations. Prints that are transient in nature, such as in snow, must be addressed and processed immediately. A print that is latent or invisible means it can be overlooked. The importance of this evidence to crime scene personnel needs to be stressed. If one footprint is discovered, then logically there may be more. For example, if there is a homicide scene with copious amounts of blood, then the expert should anticipate a good number of prints; if not, one would need to determine why not. Perhaps the scenario was manufactured or was altered or cleaned to conceal the presence of pedal evidence.

General protocols regarding crime scenes are fairly universal. The main purpose is to discover evidence and recover it for scrutiny in the laboratory.

Secure the scene

The first step is to secure the scene. This may seem basic, but at times it is difficult to enforce because there are often extraneous individuals who try to enter. Because our interest is in pedal evidence, foot traffic should be limited.

Record the scene

The most common methods of recording the scene are photography, sketching, and note taking. The use of video taping with commentary can be helpful and may negate the need for more time-consuming methods. The scene should be recorded as promptly as possible while it is in a relatively untouched state, especially when footprint evidence is being considered.

Search the scene (discover)

A systematic approach is necessary when footprint evidence is suspected. Depending on the type of crime, certain approaches and paths through the scene may vary. For example, where was the point of entry? Is there blood or a substrate that might be efficacious in exhibiting footprints or foot impressions? Is there a major crime area or several different sites? Where is the point of exit? An examination of the immediate exterior may yield many impressions in dirt or foot/shoe prints on a concrete walkway.

Collect (record) and package evidence

If footprints are visible, they must be photographed. This process includes proper positioning of the camera using a tripod, with the film parallel to the plane of the print or impression and directly over it, i.e., perpendicular to the impression. A scale should always be included so the photograph can be enlarged to reveal the natural size of the evidence, more commonly called 1:1, wherein 1 mm on the scale equals 1 mm. It is usually a good idea to take a similar photograph without a scale. As many photographs should be taken as possible, especially macro-views that will be used later for comparisons. It cannot be stressed enough how important accurate photographs are for a proper evaluation. Pedal impression evidence is often latent or poorly visible; therefore, various types of enhancement techniques must be used. Oblique lighting techniques using a strong white light are implemented to highlight or detect footprints that may not be clearly visible to the naked eye. If there is a suspicion that there might be bloody footprints but they are not visible, then Luminol or some other method can be used. Luminol causes the heme portion of the erythrocyte to luminesce; the technique must be performed in complete darkness. The luminescent effect is usually very short lived; therefore, a chemical agent such as amido black is used to enhance and stabilize the erythrocyte in a blue-black color and the footprints can then be photographed.

An alternate light source, also known as a forensic light source, is an instrument that emits specific bands or wavelengths of light that are useful in detecting physical evidence. Depending on the device, the range can start at 365 nm (which is in the ultraviolet [UV] range) and extend through the visible spectrum to infrared capabilities in the

700-nm range and higher. This instrument can supply bright white light for the oblique technique and has capabilities for footprints often in the UV range. It is usually used to detect biological fluids, hairs, and fibers. Three-dimensional impressions of footprints are often discovered in dirt, mud, or some other impressible substrate and should be photographed first, then casts made, if possible. One recommended material for casting is dental stone, because it is more rigid and durable than plaster of Paris. It is not uncommon for plaster of Paris casts to break when in transit or while being examined by different individuals. A broken cast is not an adequate exhibit. Lifting techniques can be used for certain types of footprint evidence, using adhesive and gelatin lifters as are used for fingerprints. If dust impressions are suspected, an electrostatic dust-lifting device can be used. It uses an electric charge to actually lift the dust print onto a foil surface that can be photographed and used for later evaluation.

General protocol is used for packaging the evidence; most importantly, items must be kept separate to prevent cross-contamination. Shoes should be individually wrapped in separate paper bags, as should plaster or dental stone casts.

Submit evidence to the laboratory

The modern laboratory is equipped to handle most types of evidence. It is advantageous to acquire as much evidence as possible from the scene for transport to the laboratory for processing. This may involve removing a door, flooring, or plasterboard if it has foot or shoe prints. Evidence can be enhanced both photographically and chemically. For instance, the sock liner of a shoe may be viewed with an alternate light source, using laser or bright white light, to give the most accurate depiction of the foot image. In this instance, the sock liner was treated in a fuming chamber of cyanoacrylate ester (superglue) for 30 min at 80% humidity. Basic yellow-40 solution was applied with a soft brush; the liner was then rinsed with water for 2 min and dried. Excitation was accomplished using a Crimescope-16 (SPEX Industries) at 455-nm. The camera used was a Crimescope VRM (SPEX Industries) with an orange long-pass filter or a 550-nm band-pass filter. In many cases, it takes experimentation to determine the best wavelength to get the best image because of the variability of the color of the sock-liner covering, which can be black, green, blue, white, or any of several other assorted colors.

Many departments are using digital photography, which has certainly made the task much simpler and less time-consuming for obvious reasons. Footwear evidence that is recovered should be photographed and then, at a minimum, examined for trace evidence. Blood on footwear may be collected for DNA analysis. A general overview of the crime scene and some techniques focusing on pedal evidence were presented.

Review of Foot Anatomy

The foot has 26 bones, plus at least two sesamoid bones located under the first metatarsal head. Thus, both feet contain a total of 28% of the 206 bones in the human body. What makes the human foot unique is that it is the only foot in nature with a heel bone that touches the ground, a straight-ahead (instead of a thumb-like) great toe (hallux), and an arch. The bones are grouped into three different areas: the rearfoot (heel), midfoot (arch), and forefoot (ball and toes). The rearfoot is composed of the talus and calcaneus. The talus ("*ankle bone*") articulates with the lower end of the tibia and fibula and is responsible for dorsiflexion and plantar flexion of the foot. The calcaneus is known as the *heel bone*. The midfoot is composed of the three tarsal or cuneiform bones, the navicular bone, and the cuboid bone.

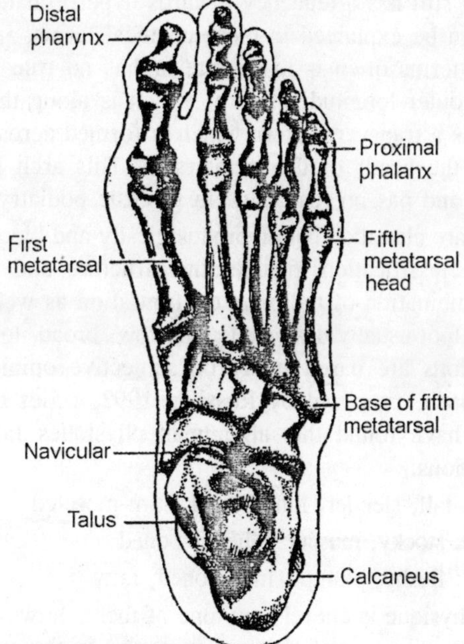

Fig. 16.3. Dorsal view of the 28 foot bones, showing some anatomic regions that may have forensic implications.

The forefoot is composed of the five metatarsal bones and the phalanges. The second to fifth toes have three separate phalangeal bones and the great toe (hallux) has two phalangeal bones. The great toe is considered the first digit or toe number one; the fifth toe is also called the "little" toe.

The bony structure is held together by soft tissue elements known as the ligaments, of which there are 107. Muscles and tendons, 19 in number, comprise the other soft tissue elements that are responsible for locomotion. The foot has 38 articulations (joints); these are sites where two bones meet and various amounts of motion occur. A complex network of blood vessels and nerves supplies the foot. The human foot presents an arch—the long arch along the inner border that is known as the inner or medial longitudinal arch. This is the most important arch in forensic applications, and it is commonly classified as either low, normal, or high. The arch is often depicted by a wide footprint for a low arch, a narrow footprint for a high arch, and a medium-width print for a normal arch. Moreover, it is possible to have what appears to be a "normal" arch (i.e., without a varus or valgus orientation) that still has a tendency towards hyperpronation (flat foot type), which can be explained in biomechanical terms, i.e., the arch height in these terms often is inaccurate or has no true meaning. In addition to the outer longitudinal arch, which is along the outside of the foot, there is a transverse arch, which is formed across the ball of the foot under the heads of the metatarsals. This arch flattens with weight bearing and has no real value in forensic podiatry.

Foot types are classified both morphologically and biomechanically. Morphological classification includes the structure and form of the foot. It is a combination of the bony configuration as well as the soft tissue, with the foot usually described as narrow, broad, long, or short. These designations are based solely on subjective opinion. A more scientific approach, proposed by Rossi in 1992, relies on anthropometrics. They have found that all human physiques fall into three main classifications:

1. *Ectomorph*: tall, slender, long-boned, slim-muscled
2. *Mesomorph*: stocky, muscular, heavy-boned
3. *Endomorph*: fleshy, plump, small-boned, fatty

No body physique is entirely any one of these; however, although it is usually a combination of all three, one type in the combination is dominant. Significantly, the foot type will be in the same category as the body type. Thus, a dominantly mesomorphic physique will invariably have a *mesomorphic* (stocky, muscular, heavy-boned) foot. Also important, each foot type will have its own functional character. For example, the mesomorphic foot tends to have a lower arch and requires a wider shoe.

This categorization may be helpful in forensic cases. If it can be determined that the footprint in question was made by a mesomorphic individual, then certain other physical characteristics can be determined that may be useful in suspect identification. It must be remembered that the bare footprint is a representation of the bony structure pressing on the soft tissue underlying it. Noncontact areas are not shown, and that is why it is important to use the foot outline whenever possible to give the total morphological picture. It is possible to look at a bare footprint that appears to have a long second toe, when in actuality the first toe may be longer due to larger soft tissue expansion in that digit.

Another anatomical region of significance in forensic contexts is the skin of the plantar aspect (sole) of the foot. The skin is composed of a superficial layer, the epidermis, and the deeper dermis layer. The epidermis varies in thickness from 0.07 to 0.12 mm throughout most of the body. On the palms of the hands and the soles of the feet it measures 0.8 to 1.4 mm thick. The sole, being 10 times thicker than the palmar aspect (palm) of the hand, presents a more durable integument capable of deforming a given surface. The plantar aspect of the foot contains eccrine glands, which secrete primarily water and some salts and traces of urea. A single foot has approx 60,000 sweat glands, which can account for the average adult foot perspiring approx 4 oz of water daily. Perspiration can vary with the ambient temperature, humidity, and activity level. The secretion of such quantities of water inside closed footwear can be of value in the forensic evaluation.

Dynamic Foot

Foot dynamics or biomechanics deals with the foot in motion. As such, it is a complex phenomenon that has to propel the body and in effect prevent it from falling forward. The foot must adapt to the surface and compensate with change to allow the human being to walk in a straight line. There are variations in foot dynamics during the gait, and many activities that form a complex series of motions, when abnormal, lead to a pathologic change. No two feet are exactly the same in terms of anatomy and morphology. Neither are the rules of biomechanics the same for all feet, thus adding another means of forensic evaluation. The dynamic foot, in addition to providing a base of support during a walking cycle, must be able to adapt to uneven terrain during initial contact with the ground and then change to a more rigid lever for push off. The gait cycle is a complex activity involving two phases. The stance phase accounts for 62% of the cycle and occurs when the foot is in contact with the ground; this includes heel contact, mid-stance, and propulsion. The swing phase accounts for 38% and occurs when the foot is swinging through to recontact the ground.

We may classify the foot according to its morphologic appearance, as previously discussed. But how do we classify the functioning foot in biomechanical terms? Foot biomechanics is the application of mechanical laws to living structures, specifically the locomotor system of the human body. It pertains to the alignment of the rearfoot with the forefoot. This classification is based on the relationship between the standing calcaneal position and the nonweight forefoot-to-rearfoot position. It is logical in its approach and aims to be as objective as possible. The foot is characterized in four levels of cavus, a rectus foot (which is neutral), and four levels of planus. This classification system begins with type 1, with an inverted calcaneus and an everted forefoot (valgus). This is the most severe cavus deformity and is often considered the classic Pes Cavo-Varus deformity or claw foot. Types two, three, and four represent diminishing degrees of severity of varus. Type 5 is the neutral foot, with the calcaneus perpendicular to the weight-bearing surface and the forefoot perpendicular to the rear foot; it is considered the "normal" foot. The subtalar joint is the position from which maximal function can occur. Types 6, 7, and 8 are increasing in degree of valgus, with type 9 being the classic Pes-Planus deformity or severe flatfoot.

Pathologic change that is seen with different biomechanical foot types is well known, and although there can be deviations from the norm, for the most part assumptions can be made with a good degree of accuracy. The patient with a planus foot often presents in clinical practice with a complaint of arch pain, heel pain, hallux abductovalgus with bunion deformity, and hammer toe deformity. Other complaints may involve joints above the ankle level including the knee and hip joints. The patient with a cavus foot often presents with complaints of chronic lateral ankle instability, digital contracture, and metatarso-phalangeal joint contracture, with increased declination of the metatarsal heads. Significant metatarsalgia with intractable plantar keratosis (deep, nucleated callus) formation may be a complaint in addition to medical concerns above the ankle. This biomechanical classification system with its inherent abnormalities in fact may lead to a better understanding of foot pathologies and how the complex system of dynamics influences pathologic entities. Entities known as subtalar or rearfoot varus or valgus deformity, forefoot varus or valgus deformity, and equinus deformity all may exist in a compensated or uncompensated form to some degree. Some of these entities are more common than others, but all may lead to an expected change in the footwear, gait pattern, or footprint. Therefore, without a keen knowledge of this subject matter, would be difficult to use in forensic contexts.

Pathology

In the physician's office, the clinical presentation of foot pain in many cases will be secondary to structural or biomechanical imbalances manifested by pathologic change. The deformities are often exacerbated by footwear, and pathologic change may be secondary to injury or disease. The foot undergoes many stresses during one's lifetime. The structure of the foot may be influenced by extrinsic factors, such as footwear, occupational stresses, and injury. Intrinsic factors may be genetically based or associated with biomechanical influences and may cause soft tissue and osseous pathology that may assist in identification efforts. Furthermore, juvenile foot problems, which are not uncommon, can lead to anatomical changes that can be translated into associated wear visible in their footwear.

A bunion deformity is an enlargement of the first metatarsal head, the presence of a bursa (fluid-filled sac), or both. If there is also an arthritic component, the joint may be affected, with restriction of motion that may have some effect on foot dynamics as well. The bunion deformity may exist by itself or may include a lateral deviation of the hallux, which is called *hallux abductovalgus*. Juvenile hallux abductovalgus deformity, which is more common in females, can begin as early as 10 or 11 yr and may be fully matured by the mid-teens. The bunion is also a common deformity in adults that can be severe and is more common in females.

Often associated with this problem is the hammer toe deformity, which most commonly affects the second toe. This deformity at the proximal interphalangeal joint may have a contractural component at the metatarsophalangeal joint, which can apply a downward force on the metatarsal head. The increased downward force leads to increased pressure in that area, with or without callus formation under the

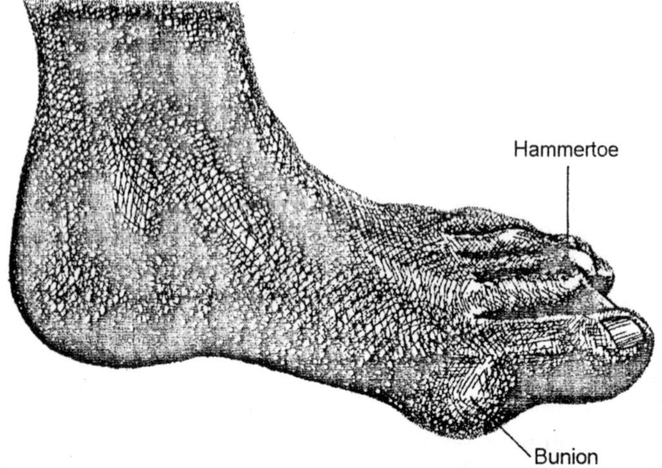

Fig. 16.4. Common foot deformities that will often leave their mark in footwear as wear on the inner liner and/or protrusion or bulge in the shoe upper.

metatarsal head. The second toe is longer than the first toe in 25 to 35% of the population and may be a component of the hammer toe deformity or not, but still has forensic implications either way. Hammer toes can affect the third and fourth toes, but more commonly the fifth toe is affected, though in a slightly different configuration. The fifth toe will, in many cases, be forced into or under the fourth toe, a condition that is specifically exacerbated by certain types of footwear. The toe is often rotated more laterally than medially and the boney prominence at the head of the proximal phalanx may develop the heloma durum ("corn") which is not uncommon.

A deformity that may be seen in younger individuals is a bunion deformity on the lateral aspect of the foot affecting the fifth metatarsal head, also known as *tailor's bunion*. The metatarsal head may be enlarged, with an inward deviation of the little toe. There may also be an outward bowing of the metatarsal shaft leading to more significant prominence laterally. Haglund's deformity affects the posterior aspect of the calcaneus by appearing as an enlargement in the back of the heel that tends to rub against the inner lining of the shoe counter, often creating an inflammation in that part of the foot. Prominence in the medial arch at the navicular bone is usually associated with hyperpronation and is seen in younger individuals. Pain is present at that site and usually occurs secondary to footwear. Dorsal hypertrophy in the area of the base of the first metatarsal bone and medial cuneiform bone often leads to a large bump on the dorsum of the foot and is painful secondary to footwear. This is most frequently found in older individuals and is chronic in nature. Deformity may also exist as a result of injury. Congenital diseases, such as poliomyelitis, may also lead to foot deformity, and possibly at an early age.

For example, a pathologic change in one foot (e.g., a bunion) does not necessarily imply that the same problem exists to the same degree in the other foot. A deformity can also be present above the level of the foot, including problems with the knees, hips, or back. Limb-length discrepancy may be implicated in some of the pathologic changes noted. In most cases, the longer side will show more deformity, both structurally and biomechanically, and often in the flatter foot.

The wide array of pathologies in the feet can only be considered beneficial in forensic contexts. The pathologic change may be translated into the footprints and into footwear. The bunion prominence may deform that part of the shoe and may cause wear on the inside upper in that location. The same scenario applies to the hammer toe. Of note is the lack of statistical analyses regarding foot pathology. Some have been presented in the literature, but none by the podiatric or orthopedic communities specifically addressing forensic needs. Further research is warranted for addressing the commonality or lack thereof of foot pathologies and their use in forensic contexts.

Footwear

A chapter on pedal evidence would not be complete without a discussion of what houses the foot most of the time. The reader may gain a greater appreciation of the characteristics of footwear and how foot pathology may lead to identification. Footwear can often be found at or near the crime scene, recovered from a residence or vehicle, or taken from a suspect when taken into custody.

Footwear is considered by many to be important as a fashion statement, but little regard is given to its negative effect on the foot. Many individuals actually wear shoes that are too small for them. This occurs in some cases because of vanity but in many cases because of improper fitting. Currently, individuals order more merchandise, including footwear, through catalogs and the electronic media, which usually precludes measuring the feet properly. It is not uncommon for the foot to increase one-half (one-sixth of an inch) to one full size (two-sixths of an inch) as one ages. This increase can be attributed to arch breakdown, with elongation of the foot, and can be influenced by joints above the ankle including the knee, hip, and spinal column. The feet should always be measured each time shoes are purchased, and that includes both feet since they are often not exactly the same size. Because shoes may be purchased by the stated size, it is fairly common for shoes not to fit properly. Many shoes that are manufactured in foreign countries are usually shorter than the stated size. It is usually advised to purchase a shoe one-half to one full size larger than the measured foot size. As a general rule, there should be one-half to five-eighths of an inch between the end of the longest toe and the end of the shoe for a proper fit.

The size of feet in general has also changed over recent years. Men's feet appear to have remained stable, with perhaps a small percentage increase in larger sizes. The most common sizes for men's shoe range from 9 to 11. Size 11 usage has increased by approx 9% over the past 10 yr, and size 8 usage has decreased approx 3 to 4% for a similar period. Women's feet generally have increased in size, which has been noted in clinical practice over the past 10 to 15 yr. It appears women are wearing larger shoe sizes. The most common sizes are 7, 8, and 9 in approximately equal numbers. However, size 9 is approx 5% more common now than it was 10 yr ago. The number of women wearing a size 10 has also increased by approx 6% over the past 10 yr.

These shoe-size changes have forensic implications regarding footwear prints. It has also become more common for women to wear men's shoes, which are generally wider than women's footwear and give more room if they have a large foot. If they have a large foot, it is often difficult to find a good assortment of shoes in women's sizes that fit properly. A woman who wears a size 10 shoe can wear a men's size 8.0 to 8.5. The fact that it is also possible to wear a shoe two sizes smaller than one's normal size (but only for a short period of time) is of importance in some forensic contexts. When a footwear print is identified as a size 7 or 8 and it appears to be a men's shoe, we should also consider the possibility that a woman was wearing those shoes. Only a small percentage of men wear sizes 7 and 8, approx 6 and 9%, respectively. The investigator may need to determine whether the foot impression/shoe print was produced by a man or woman and at times that may not be possible to absolute certainty. In the context of forensic evaluations, however, all of these factors—including improper shoe fit, biomechanical imbalances, and the subsequent pathologic changes in the foot—will make themselves known in the examination of the footwear.

While there are thousands of new shoe styles introduced to Americans each year, they are only variations of eight basic shoe types: the boot, pump, sandal, mule, clog, monk strap, moccasin, and oxford. Moreover, the latest of these styles—the oxford—is almost 300 yr old. The basic shoe components have remained the same over the years, with changes in some components due to newer, more durable, and lighter-weight materials.

Shoe components are as follows:

1. *The shoe upper*. This is the visible part that covers the foot. The makeup will vary depending on the shoe style. Athletic type shoes may use cloth, nylon, or semi-synthetic materials. Dress/fashion/style-oriented shoes may be made in a large array of materials.
2. *Insole board*. This is the surface upon which the foot directly rests. It is necessary in shoes that are constructed using cement-lasted or Goodyear welt techniques, because it is the attachment for upper and lower components.
3. *Sock liner*. Athletic footwear will often have a sock liner, a piece of material placed over the top of the insole board. It may be glued in position or it may be removable. In slip-lasted shoes, however, there is no insole board, and the sock liner lies directly on the midsole. The sock liner decreases friction between the insole board and the plantar surface of the foot, assists in shock attenuation, and absorbs perspiration. The ability to absorb perspiration and thereby leave an image of the foot is greatly aided by the large number of sweat glands on the plantar aspect of the foot as well as the forces applied with daily activity, shoe confinement, and body weight. Many materials are used for the sock liner component. In the past, they were most often sponge rubber, vinyl, and latex materials covered with a very thin layer of terry cloth or nylon. More commonly in dress casual, running shoes, and many sports type shoes, where the materials are generally of a higher quality, the sock liner is removable from the shoe. The most common materials now used include closed-cell rubbers, open-cell polyurethane foam, and closed-cell polyethylene foam; ethylene vinyl acetate is also used. A potential advantage of these newer materials is that they are more durable, wear longer, and show a better foot image in both two and three dimensions. Other materials may wear faster and must be replaced on a regular basis, but can still show a definable foot image. The foot image may be two-dimensional, three-dimensional, or a combination of the two. Some of the more impressible materials will show a depth impression of the foot, especially in the forefoot area (ball and digits). The foot image may be visualized, within a

relatively short period, in some cases days, to the point that it may be of evidentiary value. This shoe component, the sock liner, in fact may be the most important part of the shoe forensically. If two individuals were supposed to have worn the same shoe, it may be possible to see a second image on the sock liner, but this depends greatly on how long the shoe was worn by the second individual and under what conditions.

4. *Midsole.* The midsole, which is a component of an athletic type shoe, is often made of polyurethane or ethylene vinyl acetate and may show some three-dimensional wear if the shoe is cut apart for examination.
5. *Outsole.* The outsole material varies according to shoe type. Athletic shoes commonly use carbon rubber or blown rubber, which are both durable and usually will not show appreciable wear for a long period except under extreme circumstances. Leather outsoles usually show the best wear patterns, and at times a clear image of the foot including the digits and ball area may be evident on the outsole. Other materials are available; for example, work shoes and dress casual shoes often use Vibram, which is a popular soling material. This material may show wear fairly well, which may assist in forensic analysis.

As stated earlier, footwear is an important part of pedal evidence. There is a close association between the foot and shoe, in that they almost function as a single unit. The shoe is in a way an extension of the foot and functions in harmony with the foot during ambulation. The shoe is often a mirror image of the foot that it housed and much can be learned about the individual who wore it. In many cases, when perpetrators wear their shoes for a long period of time it generally leads to a good amount of wear both inside and outside, in fact, sometimes too much. There are times when the shoe is so worn it is of no value to the forensic evaluation.

Examination of Pedal Evidence

Types of pedal evidence

Pedal evidence comprises physical evidence relating to the human foot, with or without footwear. It may present in impression and print form. Impression evidence, being three-dimensional in nature, may be discovered in different materials and on varying surfaces. The substrate must be impressible to allow for depth, as well as length and width. Mud, sand, wet soil, and carpet, for example, may exhibit an impression. We expect to find barefoot impressions, sock-foot impressions, or shoe outsole impressions, but as we know, it takes a good investigator to discover them.

A three-dimensional impression may be evident on the sock liner of the shoe. Two-dimensional footprints or shoe prints are more prevalent on a hard surface, such as a tile floor or concrete walkway. A bloody trail can be most important and may present as a bare footprint, sock footprint, or footwear outsolc print. The shoe may also be evaluated secondary to foot contact within, leading to wear on inner surfaces as well as very important wear on the sock liner or footbed component of the shoe. A bloody bare footprint with adequate friction ridge skin can be as identifiable as a fingerprint; unfortunately, such a find is a rare occurrence.

Forensic team

The forensic team may include a police officer or detective, a crime scene specialist or criminalist, a footwear examiner, and an attorney. A professional tracker may be of value in certain situations. If the team is working for the defense, it may include a private investigator, a criminalist from a private laboratory, other forensic specialists, and the attorney. The footwear examiner specializes in footwear evidence and is trained to make an identification that involves class characteristics or individual (random or accidental) characteristics on the outsole. This individual must have expert knowledge of manufacturing techniques for different shoes, which can often be an important part of the evaluation. Certification in the field is now available for those specializing in footwear evidence. The footwear examiner should be responsible for footwear-related evidence when the outsole evaluation is required and seeking appropriate podiatric medical consultation, if it is foot related.

Basis of the Forensic Examination

A forensic evaluation leads to a determination of a common origin between two specimens and may establish positive identification. A questioned specimen is used in a comparative analysis with a known specimen. To establish an identification, the morphology of the foot must be distinct from that of other individuals. The foot is genetically manufactured; therefore, even the anatomical, morphological, and biomechanical configuration of identical twins is different.

Class and individual characteristics

The forensic examination begins with an agreement of class characteristics. A class characteristic is something that is common to all specimens in a given group—in this instance, the group consists of feet. All feet have a size and shape, a heel or rearfoot region, an arch or midfoot area, and a forefoot area. The forefoot is composed the metatarsophalangeal joint area (ball), including the five digits. An individual characteristic is typically something that is unique to one object and not present in other objects in a similar group, thereby leading to individualization and identification. In pedal evidence, the presence of a sixth toe or absence of a toe are extremely rare and would be considered individual characteristics because of their uncommonness.

In footwear, class characteristics include the tread pattern, logo, size, and shape of the outsole. Individual characteristics include things that are not normally part of the outsole, such as a pebble embedded in the outsole, a cut mark from a piece of glass, or a wear pattern suggestive of a foot problem. Some of these are considered accidental because of the way they are formed. Manufacturing characteristics that are present in a production run of shoes may also show randomness to help in the identification process. Similarly, a scar on the plantar aspect of the foot secondary to a laceration from a piece of glass or a puncture wound could be considered an accidental characteristic, but is still unique. The presence of unique characteristics in the foot is limited. What is known as an intermediate class characteristic falls between class and individual characteristics. Intermediate class characteristics relative to the foot include, for example, digital positioning secondary to pathologic abnormality, such as a hammer toe deformity. One foot may have a significant number of variations. Considering the digital positioning, size, and shape of just one toe, there is a significant number of possible differences. The aggregate number of intermediate class characteristics adds to the level of certainty of pedal evidence.

ACE-V

The acronym "ACE-V" (analysis, comparison, evaluation, and verification of evidence) denotes the scientific methodology used to arrive at a determination for identification purposes. ACE-V has weathered court scrutiny in fingerprint identification and can be applied to all disciplines where comparison techniques are used to make an identification. Common practice in most crime laboratories dictates that when a positive identification is made on a fingerprint, verification is required. This is also becoming a requirement in other forensic disciplines.

Analysis of the questioned item

The analysis involves the "dissection" of an item into its component parts, properties, and characteristics that can be directly observed and measured. The analysis of the questioned item is always performed before any examination on the known item. In pedal evidence, one is evaluating a bloody footprint or sock liner image to determine the quantity and quality of the image and whether it is sufficient for comparison purposes. A good number of marks or images may be present, but is there sufficient clarity to use them all? Every aspect must be evaluated and then recorded using photographs and casts of impressions, where applicable, as needed for comparison. Measurements can be taken to estimate, for example, possible height of the perpetrator, foot and/or shoe size. Once the findings are noted, they are compared with known standards to make a final determination.

Pedal evidence and forensic considerations

The crime scene often involves serologic evidence, such as blood. A gait pattern may be visible in the blood, showing either a bare or socked foot. Many variations may present themselves at one crime scene: a full print of one or both feet or a partial print of, for instance, the forefoot area of one foot and the heel of the other. Some factors to be considered (again, depending on their presentation and the abilities of the evaluator) include step length, stride length, and foot plant. If there is a sufficient number of successive steps, it may be possible to determine, among other things, whether the suspect was walking or running.

Asymmetry in step length may be an indication of disability, limb-length discrepancy, or injury. We can determine the direction of travel, number of suspects, and whether the individual was walking backwards or back and forth. Out-toeing or intoeing beyond the normal amount and other factors, which may not in themselves be conclusive, will add to the weight given to the ultimate identification. If a high-quality total-contact footprint is visible and the length can be measured, then height can be estimated, although not calculated exactly. Studies performed by Giles and Vallandigham and Gordon and Buikstra both include referencing the shoe size to height. Estimation of weight is more difficult to ascertain and has not proven very reliable.

Most footprints have to be considered as being made in a dynamic state or at least with body weight applied. In the weight-bearing foot, soft tissue expansion occurs. The amount of soft tissue between the underlying bone and the epidermis is quite uniform in most individuals and is relatively the same in both sexes. It is possible to estimate the shape of the foot and proper length of the digits from a bare bloody footprint, but there are always exceptions to the rule.

The foot image on the sock liner of the shoe is formed in both the static and dynamic state. Because the average individual takes approx 8000 steps daily, the image is more of a dynamic representation of the foot. Also distinguishable in a footprint are digital length, digital position, and the shape of the toes. Increased areas of pressure due to the presence of a plantar lesion—e.g., an intractable plantar keratosis, callus, or verruca plantaris (wart)—may leave an indentation in the sock liner. The quality of the print or impression is important, especially the clarity and sharpness of the identification lines such as the arch line, heel line, web ridge-line, and the web space outline (primarily visible on the sock liner). The web ridge-line is very individual and,

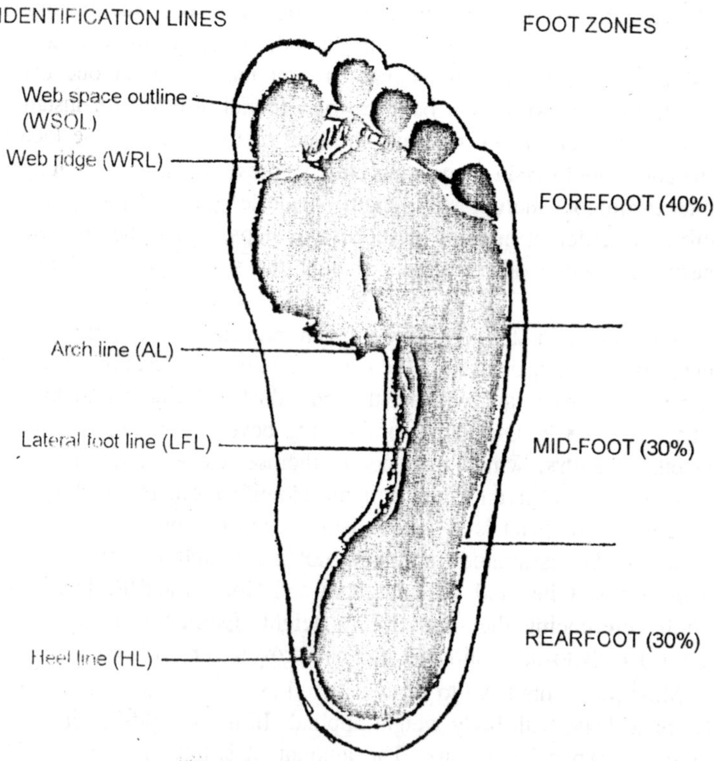

Fig. 16.5. Bare inked footprint, with foot outline.

depending on its quality, can be quite important. Whether it can be determined from the footprint if it was produced by a male or female is most commonly based on the size of the impression. Men's feet are generally longer and wider than women's feet. As previously stated, however, women's feet have generally increased in average size over the past few years, so at times a woman's footprint or shoe print is indistinguishable from a man's and, therefore, this parameter can only be used to infer the subject's gender.

If an item of footwear is involved, then the sock liner is analyzed in a similar manner to a bare footprint. The size of the shoe the individual is wearing can be correlated with height—again, within certain parameters. The upper of the shoe is evaluated for distinctive wear secondary to any pathologic change in the foot, such as a bunion deformity or hammer toe deformity, which will also show, in many cases, coincidental wear on the inside upper or actual bulging or deformity of the shoe in that area. Haglund's deformity, which is a bony enlargement on the posterior aspect of the calcaneus, commonly will result in wear in the center to lateral portion of the inside counter of the shoe. This deformity is also related to a biomechanical problem, specifically a compensated rearfoot varus deformity, which may be discovered in the suspect after biomechanical evaluation. The outsole is subject to both extrinsic and intrinsic influences. Wear can be influenced by occupation or certain activities that may put excessive weight on one part of the shoe or the other. For example, skate boarding may cause excessive posterior heel wear on one side or the other if the shoe is used for braking.

Environmental factors and poorly manufactured footwear may lead to altered or accelerated wear. Intrinsic wear is secondary to biomechanical influences and pathologic change. The outsole needs to be evaluated for a certain amount of normal wear first. Typically, wear is noted in the ball area of most shoes inferior to the second, third, and fourth metatarsal heads. Anticipated wear secondary to a moderate to severe cavus or valgus foot is not unusual. Asymmetric wear in most cases is caused by a limb-length discrepancy, disability, or injury. Different wear patterns are anticipated in a valgus type foot when there is abduction present vs no abduction. The composition of the outsole will also lead to a clear picture of different wear patterns and pathologic entities. The carbon rubber outsole on many running shoes may not show appreciable wear for many miles of use and then wear may be minimal, especially if worn for general use. Typically, wear on a leather outsole is easier to visualize, and often the entire image of the foot is present.

Fabrication of known standards

An unknown fingerprint must be compared with the fingerprint of a known individual to make an identification. The same applies to pedal evidence. Any individual who is a suspect, in many cases already in police custody, or who left evidence of his or her presence at the scene or some other related location, may need to be evaluated and required to give standards against which the unknown can be compared. If possible, the forensic podiatrist should be involved in this process. Although laboratory personnel are competent to perform many tasks, there are times when a specific technique and specialized medical expertise is required.

Photographs of the pedal evidence are taken of different positions, including the plantar aspect. Inked bare footprints, standing weight, or one step are taken with the soft tissue outlined with a thin lead pencil held perpendicular to the weight-bearing surface. This procedure is very important and needs to be performed accurately. Casting foam is used to create a weight-bearing impression, which may be taken in a step-down manner or after taking one step. These negative impressions will be filled with dental stone to create positive casts of the feet.

Radiographs, as discussed in detail in this text, represent an important tool for identification and may be taken at this time, if the circumstances warrant. An inked gait pattern is also important, especially if there is a walking pattern or some steps at the scene. However, it should always be made because it gives the most accurate representation of the dynamic foot that can be used in the comparison process. The gait pattern must be meticulously recorded. The gait pattern should be recorded at least three separate times, as should any other static or dynamic impression or print. This repetition will show the reliability of the technique and the reproducibility of the standards. The best technique is to apply black ink with a roller to the entire plantar aspect of the foot. White butcher-style paper or brown wrapping paper approximately 20 ft long and 3 ft wide is satisfactory. Most subjects will take eight to ten steps; usually the mid-pattern steps taken offer the best representation of the gait. The subject needs to be observed to ensure that there is no selfcreated change in foot plant, and step length. It is a good idea to ask questions such as, what is your date of birth, while the subject is performing this task for the purpose of taking their mind off what they are doing in case they are not cooperating or attempting to walk differently. Videotaping the entire process is also valuable, in case there are any discrepancies that need clarification later. A force-plate system yields more technical information, if needed. Specific areas of increased weight leading can be recorded and compared possibly to an area in the sock liner. In addition, the foot contact area can be compared with a bloody footprint, for example, to indicate how accurate our unknown is regarding the percentage of foot plant. Gait analysis can be further enhanced by using one of the portable in-shoe sensor systems. If bloody footprints are from a socked foot, then all standards are recorded with the subject wearing a sock or other type of hosiery.

Foot measurements can be taken with an appropriate measuring device. During these procedures, the podiatrist observes the individual, giving special attention to the weight-bearing attitude of the feet and anything that might be important in substantiating findings in the questioned evidence. During some of these procedures, the foot may be biomechanically evaluated, at a minimum to classify it in one of the biomechanical and morphological foot types.

If footwear is involved, then a representative sample of the subject's shoes must be obtained. It is best to recover shoes similar to those associated with the crime scene shoes. It is never appropriate for anyone to try on the unknown shoe for testing purposes. Photographs, foam outsole impressions that can be cast with dental stone to create a positive model of the outsole, and inked outsole prints may be required and often will be best used by the footwear examiner. The sock liner, if exhibiting a three-dimensional impression, may be cast with a thin layer of dental stone to reproduce the indentations quite accurately. The sock liner needs to be photographed and enhanced by the laboratory. An examination quality photograph is then produced.

It may be necessary to create some test impressions using one's own feet to account for certain discrepancies or other things that might be evident in the crime scene prints in order to logically explain a certain activity that took place at the scene. The importance of recording accurate measurements cannot be overstressed.

Comparison and evaluation

The comparison analysis is designed to determine whether the questioned specimen and known specimen were made by the same individual. Protocol calls for the known specimen to be compared with the questioned specimen. The overlay technique is commonly used to make a direct comparison of pedal evidence. A transparency of the known sock liner or inked footprint is compared with the questioned sock liner itself or a photograph of it. An examination-quality photograph, for example, of bloody footprints is compared with a transparency of the known standard.

Footprint and foot impression evidence presents in both two-dimensional and three-dimensional form, and it is best to compare known with unknowns of the same number of dimensions. If one recovers a foot impression in dirt that was cast with dental stone, then it is best to compare it to the known positive cast of the foot. A transparency overlay can be used to create a direct tracing of both specimens and to make a comparison. There are instances when a two-dimensional print may also be compared with a three-dimensional foot mold, but only with knowledge of tissue expansion and other factors can a valid comparison be made. The sock-liner impression can be threedimensional; however, depending on its composition or duration of wear, the depth impression may be negligible. Other methods of comparison include measurement techniques. Direct measurements can be made using a ruler, but it's usually better to use a grid system. Random subjects' standards are also used. If, for example, we have an estimated size 10 male footprint, then a number of size 10 inked standards are used to show the many differences inherent in footprints taken from a data bank of exemplars. Standards taken from others, who perhaps lived with the victim or might have been at the scene for some reason, are compared with the questioned print and can be used to eliminate those individuals.

Medical or police personnel at a crime scene occasionally need to submit exemplars for exclusion purposes. We have performed the comparison and evaluation, and we must now make a determination or answer the question posed initially. For example, did this individual make the bloody bare footprint at the crime scene? Obviously, if there is a significant discrepancy that cannot be explained, we have an exclusion or a nonidentification. The forensic field is replete with differing opinions on how best to define the eventual determination or conclusion. For example, "possible," "very possible," "likely," "highly likely," "with reasonable medical certainty," and other terms are commonly used. Answering in the affirmative indicates an identification to some degree, but with an increasing number of intermediate class characteristics, one can transcend to greater levels of certainty. If the opinion is in the negative, then it is a nonidentification. An inconclusive determination can still be used. It is neither positive nor negative and might be applicable in a situation where a bloody footprint, for example, can neither be excluded nor identified satisfactorily.

Levels of certainty

Level 1: Is it a footprint? If the answer is in the affirmative, subsequent questions may be as follows: Is it a partial or full, static or dynamic print or impression? Is there sufficient quantity or quality to continue? If the answer is still in the affirmative, then we proceed to the next level. If there is not an agreement in the response, it could lead to an inconclusive identification or nonidentification.

Level 2: General Agreement. Is there a general agreement in the size, shape, and position of the digits and foot zones?. If the answer is in the affirmative, then we proceed to the next level.

Level 3: Identification Lines. Is there sufficient agreement of the web ridge line, arch line, lateral foot line, heel line, and web space outline? If the answer is in the affirmative, then we proceed to the next level.

Level 4: Intermediate characteristics. This is where the medical practitioner's clinical expertise and knowledge of pathological, morphological, and biomechanical imbalances or deviations are used. If the aggregate of findings are sufficient and can be verified, then we proceed to level 5.

Level 5: Individual characteristics are noted or level 4 with verification.

Case Presentation

Type of crime: Homicide, 19-yr-old female

Date of Occurrence: November 1996, Phoenix, Arizona

Case history: Four female friends took an early morning drive in Phoenix, Arizona. After a failed attempt at strangling the victim, someone crushed her skull with a large rock, and the body was placed in a pond. Two different footwear impressions were discovered in soft dirt and photographed at the scene. The remaining three females, aged 15 to 18 yr, were arrested driving the victim's vehicle on November 20, 1996, and the shoes they were wearing were obtained by law enforcement for evaluation.

On November 21, 1996, four pairs of shoes were recovered from the victim's apartment.

On November 22, 1996, two pairs of shoes were recovered from the trunk of the victim's vehicle, along with other clothing items. The outsoles on these shoes gave impressions similar to those discovered at the scene, but could not be positively identified. Subsequently, two pairs of the victim's shoes were given to the police by her parents to be used for the evaluation.

Objective

Can the following be determined from the evidence presented: (1) whether the suspects most likely wore the questioned shoes, and (2) who was the predominant wearer of each?

Methodology

Initial contact was in June 1998 by the case detective, at which time an evaluation of the questioned shoes was performed. There appeared to be sufficient quality and quantity of the footwear for podiatric medical evaluation to continue. The suspects were taken into custody and standards were collected including photographs, inked bare footprints with foot outlines, impressible foam foot impressions that were cast with dental stone to create positive molds of the feet, and foot measurements. Biomechanical and structural problems were observed at this time. The laboratory personnel produced examination quality photographs as requested, including photographically enhanced images of the sock liners of the questioned footwear. Eleven pairs of shoes were examined. The questioned shoes were a brand name canvas off-court casual sneaker size 5.5, and a designer athletic type shoe with a thick outsole, the left shoe measuring 5.0 and the right shoe measuring 5.5. Other shoes included two pairs known to belong to the victim, as well as several possibly belonging to the victim, and also some possibly belonging to one of the suspects, who had lived for a short period of time with the victim. Analysis of the questioned items was performed initially. A sock liner image was visible in each shoe, as well as some inner liner wear in the toe box area of one shoe.

The inked footprints and the foot molds were compared with the foot images present on the sock liners of the questioned shoes. The pair of shoes recovered from the trunk of the vehicle appeared to be the shoes that left the impressions at the crime scene. The suspects denied that these were their shoes. These shoes, in fact, were comparable to the foot size of the suspects. (The third suspect was not involved in the actual murder but was standing by at the car. She happened to be wearing a walking cast after sustaining a sprained ankle several days before the crime was committed and was wearing a shoe on her other foot. Her shoes were approximately two sizes larger than the questioned shoes.) Using comparisons of the known exemplars to the questioned sock liners and other footwear components, in addition to the biomechanical findings, foot measurements, and pathologic changes noted, a conclusion in the affirmative was made.

This case was particularly challenging because of the morphologic similarities of the suspects' feet. However, one suspect had a bunion developing and a long second toe that already had a fairly well-formed hammer toe. It was determined that the footwear recovered from the trunk of the victim's vehicle at the time of the arrest belonged to the two main suspects, each suspect being the predominant wearer of an individual pair of the questioned shoes. Moreover, one of the suspects was actually wearing a pair of the victim's shoes at the time of their arrest. Placing the suspects in their shoes, which were considered to be the shoes that left the impressions at the crime scene, was one piece of the circumstantial evidence that ultimately led to a conviction in this homicide.

Barefoot Impression

Ongoing research in barefoot impression evidence will be discussed briefly. Further research is necessary to shed light on what constitutes a "*unique*" (individualizing) feature between barefoot and footwear evidence and to determine if these features are merely consistent with any individual or if they truly constitute an identification. Such research is critical because this evidence might not be accepted in some jurisdictions or may be at risk of not meeting the Daubert criteria in the United States and the Mohan standard in Canada.

In 1989, convicted murderer Alan Legere escaped from the Atlantic Institution in Renous, New Brunswick, Canada while being escorted to the hospital for an ear infection. During the next 6 months, he killed four people, spreading fear throughout the Miramichi region of New Brunswick. One of his victims, Father Smith, was found murdered in the rectory of a Catholic church in Chatham Head, New Brunswick. At the crime scene, bloody impressions from a pair of boots showed enough detail that they could be identified as the boots worn by the killer—if they could be found.

About a week after the murder, a pair of work boots that had been discarded was found behind a motel approx 60 mi from the murder scene and was subsequently matched to the crime scene by way of accidental characteristics on the outsole of the boots. The boots were cut apart in a search for any evidence that might link the owner of the boots to the scene. Barefoot weight-bearing impressions were evident on the insole of the boots, and it appeared that the impressions were of suitable quality for comparison with a suspect barefoot impression.

Upon further examination of the inside of the boot, a nail was found protruding through the heel area that appeared significant enough to cause damage to the foot.

When Legere was arrested in 1989, inked barefoot and molded impressions were taken of his feet. It appeared that a scar on the heel of Legere's foot was the same shape and in the same area as the nail protruding through the heel area of the boot. The inked weight-bearing areas of Legere's bare foot were consistent with the weight-bearing barefoot impressions on the insole of the boot; this linked Legere to the boot and hence to the crime scene.

To get this barefoot morphology evidence introduced into a court of law, a detailed research project was undertaken by the Royal Canadian Mounted Police (RCMP) to prove that the inked weight-bearing areas of a human foot were unique to that person. A total of 1000 volunteers gave their inked barefoot impressions and all the relevant information was entered into a database. Each impression was searched through the database against all the others in the collection. No matches other than to that of the owner of the impression were found. The evidence was presented in court and Legere was found guilty.

Overview

Anyone committing a crime must walk around the crime scene, leaving footwear impressions and, at times, barefoot impressions, making the recovery of this type of evidence important. The human foot contains ridge detail similar to that found in a fingerprint. Forensic barefoot morphology involves the comparison of the weight-bearing areas of the bottom of a barefoot without such ridge detail, as in a fingerprint, to establish a link between the barefoot of an individual and an impression found in mud, blood, or some other medium at the crime scene or on the insole of a shoe that may have been linked to a crime scene. The elimination of an individual whose feet leave an impression that is not consistent with the crime scene impression is important to the judicial system.

History

The use of barefoot impression morphology in its current form by the RCMP had its origins in the Alan Legere case in 1989. Although extensive research into the individuality ("uniqueness") of barefoot impressions was not performed until last decade, barefoot comparisons were presented in court for many years.

Historical cases

In 1948, two brothers—Donald and William Kett—were charged with a series of breaking-and-enterings in Canada. After Donald was convicted, William claimed he was innocent and that the shoes that were matched back to the crime scenes belonged to his brother. The shoes were cut open and the marks inside compared with the feet of the two brothers; it was determined that William, not Donald, had worn the shoes, and he was also convicted.

In 1953, New Scotland Yard had a case in which a burglar left a pair of shoes behind at the scene of the crime. The main suspect denied ownership of the shoes and volunteered an old pair of his own boots for comparison. The outsole of the boots and the shoes exhibited the same unusual wear patterns. To compare the impressions on the inside, a casting material was poured into the shoes and boots, the casts were shown to be very similar, and the suspect was convicted.

In 1962 in The Netherlands, a safecracker discarded the clothes he had worn while committing his crime by throwing them into a canal. The clothes, including a pair of shoes, were recovered and a prosecution expert compared the recovered shoes with the shoes from the suspect and concluded that they were worn by the same person. The defendant hired his own specialist, but was dismayed when his witness agreed with the first expert. The defendant, who until this time had not agreed to have his feet photographed or printed, asked a third expert to examine his feet. Again to his dismay, this witness also agreed with the other two. The defendant was subsequently convicted.

In a case in New Jersey in 1981, a bloody socked footprint found at the scene of a homicide was compared with the foot impressions of two suspects. One suspect had left a bloody fingerprint at the crime scene but was eliminated as the person leaving the bloody footprint. The second suspect's foot impression was compared and was found to be very similar to the print at the crime scene, leaving the expert to declare that there was a high probability that the second suspect left the impression at the murder scene. Both were convicted.

Ongoing Barefoot Research

The purpose of the research described here is to study the outlines of footprints of persons walking and to determine whether one can prove that different people make verifiably distinct footprints. To support this hypothesis, a database of footprint outlines was compiled to provide a statistical basis for deciding whether the outlines of walking footprints of various people are distinguishable.

Potential of barefeet to present individualizing features

In early casework, the individuality of human footprints was often assumed, i.e., no two prints, even from the same individual, would be identical. RCMP research has shown that barefoot impressions from the same individual may remain unchanged over several years. Impressions from the insole of several pairs of footwear worn over a 25-year period were examined and showed little change in the weight-bearing areas of the foot. Impressions taken from individuals walking a distance of 20 feet show little or no change in the weight-bearing areas imprinted on paper. Barefoot impressions taken from several identical twins show that their barefoot impressions are distinct one from the other.

A great deal of early research and casework in barefoot impressions was performed in India, probably because there people are more often barefoot or in sandals. For example, in 1965, Puri described his work of classifying and measuring barefoot impressions for comparison purposes. In 1980, Qamra published the results of a preliminary study involving the measurement of the footprints of 725 individuals.

Footprint measurements

At its inception, footprint research involved an examination of anatomic characteristics such as stature. For example, Topinard estimated that on average a person's footprint length was equal to 15% of a person's height. Gordon and Buikstra analyzed the statures and foot lengths and widths of 867 soldiers in a combat boot-fitting study. Barker and Scheuer investigated the Topinard estimate by collecting data from 105 seated and walking subjects.

Baba studied 826 males and 1018 females to prove that there were significant differences in the ratios of breadth (i.e., ball width) to foot length and of ball girth to foot length between French and Japanese populations. The length of the foot was determined to be the distance from the most posteriorly projecting point on the heel to the anterior tip of whichever toe gave the longest measurement. Hawes studied ethnic differences between 513 Asian and 708 North American males. Their method of measurement was to have each subject place all of his weight on the right foot while the left foot was on a platform raised 25 cm higher than the one on the right. Calipers were used to measure the distance from the pternion to the tip of each toe, recording foot length as the maximum such measure. Breadth was measured between the first and fifth metatarsals in a plane perpendicular to the long axis of the foot. The reliability of foot measurements of 1197

Canadian subjects was studied, as well. Kouchi and Mochimaru undertook a thorough study of 5000 Japanese footprints and proved that there was a significant distinctive out-flaring of the Japanese foot, with a mean flexion angle of 8.4°.

The Federal Bureau of Investigation, specifically Special Agent William Bodziak, has presented evidence on barefoot morphology and has conducted research to help establish the potential individuality of barefoot impressions. Bodziak's collection of impressions from 500 volunteers provided a starting point for studies of this nature. The RCMP has performed research regarding the individuality of barefoot impressions since 1989 and has extended this research considerably with the collection of samples from more than 12,000 volunteers who have given their barefoot impressions.

When the RCMP research began in 1989, impressions were traced by hand and measured with a ruler to obtain the 19 measurements needed. These measurements were entered into the database for each foot (e.g., overall length of foot from heel to longest toe, width of ball of foot, distance of toe pads from edge of heel). The system was capable of accepting these data and searching them against data already in the system to determine whether any other foot matched this set of data. With 5000 impressions in this database, no false matches were found. Each time, only the person being entered was found if his or her impression was already in the database. In 1994, this manual system was changed to an automated system in which the foot was scanned and automatically traced and measured by the computer. The number of areas measured went from 19 to approx 120 per foot.

Initial research indicates that bare feet have characteristics that may form the basis for identification and that these characteristics can be compared to eliminate or link a suspect to the scene of a crime. This research is statistical in nature and based on anatomic measurements; however, the actual forensic examination involves a comparison of the contours, shapes, and placements of parts of the foot, and the bare feet from different people may show a degree of individuality. In a study based on the population from which our samples come, barefoot impressions show a high degree of individuality. The probability of a chance match was estimated to be less than 1 in 108. A subsequent analysis based on a larger sample size yielded a chance-match probability of 1 in 1011. Of note, the mathematical database is used strictly for research purposes to establish the individuality of barefoot impressions.

The footprint impressions are collected from volunteers using a commercially available inkless pad and chemically treated paper. The pad is placed on the floor about one stride from the volunteer and the paper is placed approximately one stride ahead of the pad. The footprint impressions are taken in a one-step method not in a dynamic mode (i.e., walking mode). The volunteer walks toward the pad, steps on the inkless pad with one of his or her feet, and continues walking until that foot walks on the paper, creating a darkened impression. The process is repeated with the other foot so that we have a left and a right barefoot impression on each sheet of paper. The impressions are scanned and entered into a computer database. The computer program is capable of adding data to the system and, as entry of new data takes place, it is searched against all the data presently in the system to determine whether a match exists. The system is capable of extracting data in any order for analysis by mathematicians and statisticians.

Damage or injury to the foot should be considered during the comparison process; it may explain a difference in impressions or produce an individualizing impression. Flexion creases on the foot can also be used to aid in the comparison and in sufficient number can be used to "*individualize*" the barefoot. While partial impressions may not contain sufficient information to individualize a barefoot, they may still be useful evidence in a court of law and for the possible elimination of a suspect.

Case Studies

Case study 1

The investigation of a murder in Ontario, Canada, is an example of the comparison of a barefoot crime scene impression with a barefoot impression from a suspect. The police received a report that a woman accidentally shot her husband as he tried to kill her. She contended that he went to the gun locker in the basement and returned to the bedroom carrying a rifle, with the intention of shooting her. She claimed that a struggle ensued and the rifle went off, killing him. The police found a set of barefoot impressions in dust on the concrete floor that led to the gun cabinet and then away. Barefoot impressions of the victim, his wife, and her sister were received and examined. It was determined that the barefoot impressions were too small to be the victim's and did not match the sister's, but did match the wife's barefoot impressions. These findings, along with other evidence gathered during the investigation, was presented in court, and she was subsequently found guilty of the murder.

Case study 2

A successful link between footwear from a crime scene and the accused was established in 1993, when an inmate in a prison in Quebec was found dead in his cell as a result of knife wounds in his neck and chest. Eighteen inmates lived in this section of the prison, providing a limited pool of suspects. Of the seventeen remaining prisoners, two brothers stood out as the prime suspects. The younger brother had only a short time left to serve, while the older brother, who then admitted to the killing, was serving a life sentence for murder.

A pair of blood-spattered running shoes, a pair of bloodstained jogging pants, and a nametag were found in the trash. The blood stains were eventually matched to the victim. Footwear and barefoot impressions were taken from both brothers and submitted, along with the running shoes found in the trash, to the Forensic Identification Research Services Section at RCMP Headquarters. The shoes were cut apart, and the impressions on the insoles were examined and compared with the barefoot impressions of the two suspects. The older brother's impressions did not match those found in the running shoes, but the impressions of the younger brother were a good match. The case went to court, and the younger brother was found guilty and is presently serving a life sentence.

Barefoot morphology has been used successfully in jurisdictions to exclude or include a suspect as having been at the scene of a crime. This evidence is based on an evaluation of the shapes and placement of various weight-bearing parts of the foot. Although statistical research has been performed to establish the potential individuality of barefoot impressions to meet the stringent jurisprudence standards in the United States, Canada and elsewhere, further studies may be necessary to help validate identification markers between the barefoot and shoe wear.

INDEX